Write To Success

A Handbook and Rhetoric with Readings for First-year Writing

English Program

Indiana University Kokomo

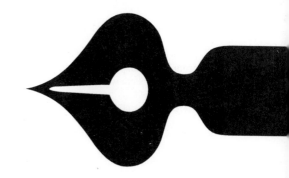

FOUNTAINHEAD
PRESS

Our "green" initiatives include:

Electronic Products
We deliver products in nonpaper form whenever possible. This includes PDF down-loadables, flash drives, and CDs.

Electronic Samples
We use a new electronic sampling system, called Xample. Instructor samples are sent via a personalized Web page that links to PDF downloads.

FSC

® **FSC Certified Printers**
All of our printers are certified by the Forest Service Council which promotes environmentally and socially responsible management of the world's forests. This program allows consumer groups, individual consumers, and businesses to work together to promote responsible use of the world's forests as a renewable and sustainable resource.

Recycled Paper
Most of our products are printed on a minimum of 30% post consumer waste recycled paper.

Support of Green Causes
When we do print, we donate a portion of our revenue to Green causes. Listed below are a few of the organizations that have received donations from Fountainhead Press. We welcome your feedback and suggestions for contributions, as we are always searching for worthy initiatives.
Rainforest 2 Reef
Environmental Working Group

Cover photo: IU Kokomo Office of Media and Marketing
Book Layout: OffCenter Concept House

For information, please call or write:

1-800-586-0330

Fountainhead Press
Southlake, TX 76092

Web site: www.fountainheadpress.com
E-mail: customerservice@fountainheadpress.com

ISBN: 978-1-59871-850-8

Printed in the United States of America

Contents

1
The IU Kokomo
English Program

Welcome to the English Program at Indiana University Kokomo

The English program at IU Kokomo offers three BA degree options from which students can choose. First, there's the Language and Literature concentration, which helps students develop reading and writing expertise and a solid grounding in literature, critical analysis, and the larger terrain of English studies. Second, students in the Writing, Editing, and Media concentration develop expertise in writing, editing, and publishing in a variety of print and digital media. Third, our Pre-Law concentration provides students planning to enter law school with ample opportunities to practice the research, communication, and critical thinking skills recommended by the American Bar Association.

Indiana University
Kokomo
logo credit Jacob Lee Cook

So, beyond these three tracks, what is "English," exactly?

That's a great question. In its relatively short, 100-year (or so) history, the academic study of English has undergone some big changes. English today, in a nutshell, is the study of how humans produce, consume, interpret, and think about *texts*, which includes everything from "capital-L" works of Literature (*Moby Dick* and Shakespeare, for example) to emerging genres like micro-fiction and web writing and pretty much everything in between.

English majors take exciting courses in fields as diverse as film studies, rhetoric, creative nonfiction, children's literature, American and British Literatures, critical theory, and Irish studies.

English also comprises the study of how people communicate—orally, in writing, and through the use of images and sounds—and how we use these various "symbol systems" to persuade, entertain, and inform one another about important social, cultural, political, and even technological issues.

This textbook, which is used by all students enrolled in ENG-W 131 and ENG-W 132 at IU Kokomo, will introduce you to readings and ideas that may seem new or even controversial to you at first glance. And, in a way, that's precisely the point: to give you a "way in" to the complex social and political issues of our day, and to help you develop your voice as a burgeoning student-scholar and engaged citizen.

English Course Offerings at Indiana University Kokomo

ENG-W 131	READING, WRITING, & INQUIRY I
ENG-W 132	READING, WRITING, & INQUIRY II
ENG-A 202	LITERARY INTERPRETATION-ADVANCED COLLEGE PROJECT
ENG-A 303	TOPICS IN AFRICAN AMERICAN STUDIES:HARLEM RENNAISSANCE
ENG-E 301	LITERATURES IN ENGLISH TO 1600
ENG-E 302	LITERATURES IN ENGLISH 1600-1800
ENG-E 303	LITERATURES IN ENGLISH 1800-1900
ENG-E 304	LITERATURES IN ENGLISH 1900-PRESENT
ENG-L 101	WESTERN WORLD MASTERPIECES I
ENG-L 102	WESTERN WORLD MASTERPIECES II
ENG-L 202	LITERARY INTERPRETATION
ENG-L 203	INTRODUCTION TO DRAMA
ENG-L 204	INTRODUCTION TO FICTION
ENG-L 205	INTRODUCTION TO POETRY
ENG-L 207	WOMEN AND LITERATURE
ENG-L 209	TPCS IN AMERICAN LIT & CULTURE
ENG-L 220	INTRODUCTION TO SHAKESPEARE
ENG-L 225	INTRO TO WORLD MASTERPIECES
ENG-L 230	INTRO TO SCIENCE FICTION
ENG-L 240	LITERATURE AND PUBLIC LIFE
ENG-L 295	AMERICAN FILM CULTURE
ENG-L 305	CHAUCER
ENG-L 306	MIDDLE ENGLISH LITERATURE
ENG-L 308	ELIZABETHAN & 17TH CENT DRAMA
ENG-L 313	EARLY PLAYS OF SHAKESPEARE
ENG-L 314	LATE PLAYS OF SHAKESPEARE
ENG-L 315	MAJOR PLAYS OF SHAKESPEARE
ENG-L 317	ENG POETRY OF EARLY 17TH CENT
ENG-L 318	MILTON
ENG-L 320	RESTORATION & EARLY 18TH-CEN LIT
ENG-L 326	MAJOR AUTHORS OF THE 18TH CENT
ENG-L 327	LATER 18TH-CENTURY LITERATURE
ENG-L 331	ST IN 19TH-CENTURY BRITISH LIT
ENG-L 332	ROMANTIC LITERATURE
ENG-L 335	VICTORIAN LITERATURE
ENG-L 345	20TH CENTURY BRITISH POETRY
ENG-L 346	20TH CENTURY BRITISH FICTION
ENG-L 347	BRITISH FICTION TO 1800
ENG-L 348	19TH CENTURY BRITISH FICTION
ENG-L 350	EARLY AMER WRTNG & CUL TO 1800

ENG-L 351	AMERICAN LITERATURE 1800-1865
ENG-L 352	AMERICAN LITERATURE 1865-1914
ENG-L 354	AMERICAN LITERATURE SINCE 1914
ENG-L 355	AMERICAN FICTION TO 1900
ENG-L 357	20TH CENTURY AMERICAN POETRY
ENG-L 358	AMERICAN LITERATURE, 1914-1960
ENG-L 364	NATIVE AMERICAN LITERATURE
ENG-L 365	MODERN DRAMA CONTINENTAL
ENG-L 366	MODERN ENGLISH DRAMA—POST COLONIAL
ENG-L 369	STUDIES IN BRITISH AND AMERICAN AUTHORS
ENG-L 371	CRITICAL PRACTICES
ENG-L 378	STUDIES IN WOMEN & LIT
ENG-L 379	AMERICAN ETHNIC & MINORITY LIT
ENG-L 381	RECENT WRITING
ENG-L 383	STDS IN BRIT OR COMM WLTH CUL
ENG-L 388	STUDIES IN IRISH LIT & CULTURE
ENG-L 390	CHILDREN'S LITERATURE
ENG-L 391	LITERATURE FOR YOUNG ADULTS
ENG-L 395	BRITISH & AMERICAN FILM STDS
ENG-L 399	JUNIOR SEMINAR
ENG-L 406	TOPICS IN AFRICAN-AMERICAN LIT
ENG-L 431	TOPICS IN LITERARY STUDY
ENG-L 433	CONVERSATIONS WITH SHAKESPEARE
ENG-L 450	SEMINAR: BRITISH & AM AUTHORS
ENG-L 460	SEMINAR: LIT FORM MODE & THEME
ENG-L 495	INDIVIDUAL READING IN ENGLISH
ENG-L 498	INTERNSHIP IN ENGLISH
ENG-L 499	SR INDPT STUDY FOR HONORS
ENG-W 103	INTRODUCTORY CREATIVE WRITING
ENG-W 202	ENGLISH GRAMMAR REVIEW
ENG-W 203	CREATIVE WRITING
ENG-W 210	LITERACY AND PUBLIC LIFE
ENG-W 231	PROFESSIONAL WRITING SKILLS
ENG-W 232	INTRO TO BUSINESS WRITING
ENG-W 233	INTERMEDIATE EXPOSITORY WRITING
ENG-W 250	WRITING IN CONTEXT
ENG-W 301	WRITING FICTION
ENG-W 303	WRITING POETRY
ENG-W 311	WRITING CREATIVE NONFICTION
ENG-W 315	WRITING FOR THE WEB
ENG-W 321	ADVANCED TECHNICAL WRITING
ENG-W 331	BUS & ADMINISTRATIVE WRITING
ENG-W 350	ADVANCED EXPOSITORY WRITING
ENG-W 365	THEOR & PRACTICES OF EDITING
ENG-W 368	RESEARCH METHODS AND RESOURCES
ENG-W 395	INDIVIDUAL STUDY OF WRITING (INDIV STUDY OF WRITING)
ENG-W 398	INTERNSHIP IN WRITING
ENG-W 400	ISSUES IN TEACHING WRITING
ENG-W 403	ADVANCED POETRY WRITING

Bethann Duly
photo credit IU Kokomo Office
of Media and Marketing

I graduated in 2014 as an English major with a minor in Spanish, and I had some absolutely incredible experiences at IU Kokomo. Far more than just going to classes and studying, these opportunities have been about making connections and learning about who I am.

I attended the lifetime achievement ceremony for Pulitzer Prize-winning author Toni Morrison at Virginia Tech, met Japanese veterans of World War II in Hawaii and traveled to Colombia. These experiences, along with classes in English and Spanish, have helped me to develop the goal of teaching English as a Second Language (ESL).

Before college I had never put my feet in and taken those kinds of risks. Then Karla Stouse, a Senior Lecturer in English, told me I needed to apply for the Innovation Symposium, and the next thing I knew, I was on my way to England. After that I wanted to go everywhere. It was Karla's push, and giving me those experiences, and telling me I would benefit from going, that made the difference.

Additionally, I have developed my Spanish language fluency in classes and through my travels with J.R. Pico, Senior Lecturer in Spanish, and I credit him for teaching me that language is more than memorizing vocabulary. When you learn a language, it's not just the words; it's learning about the culture of the people. You can't learn a language without diving into the culture, and trying to live how they live. Language is a window into someone else's perspective.

I graduated with experiences that are priceless. We have teachers here who really love what they do, and they want you to leave here a better person. That's what I love about this campus.

Teaching ESL will give me the platform I have always wanted in the Latin community. It gives me a way to go wherever I want and is a springboard into humanitarian work. That's what I want to do. I want to affect a lot of people in my life.

Cameron Huffman
photo credit Cameron
Huffman

I graduated in 2011 as a double major in English, with university honors, and New Media Communication. While a student at IU Kokomo, I participated in some incredible experiences. I was chief editor of *From the Well House* and participated in the Innovation Symposium. The time spent as an editor as well as my travel to England undoubtedly helped my confidence as well as prepared me academically for my next challenges.

In 2014, I received my Juris Doctor from the IU McKinney School of Law. Pending my successful admission to the Indiana State Bar, I hope to serve as a Deputy Prosecuting Attorney with the Marion County Prosecutor's Office, where I have been an intern for the past two years.

Without a doubt, my IU Kokomo degree left me well prepared for the study of law. While a student there, I took as many classes focusing on literary theory or composition as I could. Theory classes taught me the skills to parse writings and consider them from multiple points of view. Composition classes trained me to write clearly and effectively, a crucial skill when it comes to adversarial legal proceedings. The program's curriculum as a whole taught me to combine those skills and form the foundation upon which my legal education was built. I am truly thankful for the education I received both within and outside the classroom at IU Kokomo.

Emily Ross

photo credit IU Kokomo Office of Media and Marketing

I recently graduated from IU Kokomo in May 2014 with a degree in English, and I even received recognition as the Outstanding Student in English. I was chosen through a competitive application process to edit the *Journal of Teaching Writing* published by the Indiana Teachers of Writing and sponsored by IUPUI. It includes articles for teachers of all levels of writing from preschool through university. This responsibility will be undertaken as I complete a Master of Arts in English at IUPUI, which I will begin Fall 2014. As an added bonus, I have earned a prestigious assistantship, one that will pay for me to earn my graduate degree.

I'm excited to be out in the real world, working on my future by gaining publishing experience, which gives me even more career options. I know this opportunity would not have been possible without the positions I held at IU Kokomo. I was the editor-in-chief of *From the Well House*, our literary and arts publication, and also edited our student newspaper *The Correspondent*.

In addition to editing, I completed a writing internship at IU Kokomo that was designed specifically for me. I was able to observe freshman composition classes and even present a lesson and review student papers. This was an invaluable experience as I want to teach first-year college-level writing classes after earning my master's degree—it helped me learn there's a lot "behind the scenes" that goes into teaching.

Learning to write well is vital to every part of a successful college experience. There are fun, creative ways to teach people to be good writers, and they need those skills, no matter what major they choose.

English is more a degree on *how* to think, rather than *what* to think and is a springboard for a lot of careers. English covered all of the bases as far as what I was interested in and what I wanted to do.

English Award

Each year the English Program honors a student with the Outstanding Student in English award. To be considered for the award, the English majors with the top four highest grade point averages are identified for the faculty who then vote for the winner. The 2014 recipient, Emily Ross, is featured in this chapter's student profiles.

Undergraduate Scholarships

Kokomo Woman's Department Club Scholarship

Each recipient shall be a legal resident of Howard County, be a junior or senior student enrolled in a minimum of 9 credit hours per semester or a graduating senior who wishes to pursue a graduate degree in his or her undergraduate major field at Indiana University Kokomo, have a declared interest in the field of study relating to art, music, nursing, humanities, history or education and have a record of academic excellence as demonstrated by a GPA of 2.5 on a 4.0 point scale. In selecting recipients, preference shall be given to a student who demonstrates financial need. The amount and recipient of the scholarship will be determined by the Scholarship Committee of Indiana University Kokomo. The Scholarship Committee may divide the award between two students or award the entire amount to one student, at its discretion.

Bob Williams Memorial Scholarship

Each recipient of this scholarship should be an undergraduate student, enrolled full time in the School of Humanities and Social Sciences, with a concentration in English Literature and/or performing arts. The recipient must have a minimum GPA of 2.5 on a 4.0 scale. The scholarship may be renewable as long as the student continues to meet criteria. The number, amount, and recipient(s) of the scholarship will be selected by the Scholarship Committee at Indiana University Kokomo.

Giesecke Family Scholarship

Each recipient of this scholarship should be an undergraduate student majoring in a field of study in Humanities, Social Sciences and/or Sciences. This scholarship may be awarded to an incoming freshman or a continuing student. The student must have demonstrated financial need and a minimum GPA of 2.5 on a 4.0 scale. The number, amount, and recipient(s) of the scholarship will be determined by the Scholarship Committee in consultation with the donors.

Note: Please see the Office of Scholarships and Financial Aid for numerous other scholarship opportunities across disciplines.

2
Engaging in Campus Life and Succeeding in Academics

Living Campus Life

"When writing the story of your life, don't let anyone else hold the pen"
– author unknown

Earning one's degree is just as much about the journey as it is about the diploma, and one way to begin that journey is for students to educate themselves about all that IU Kokomo has to offer. There are many ways to get involved on campus, and there are several reasons to do so. Students who take the time and make the effort to seek out opportunities feel more connected to campus life and are often more successful academically. In the process of becoming an active part of campus life, students learn more about themselves, realize their potential, and explore their strengths. In addition, future employers will be impressed by a résumé that demonstrates an applicant's ability to work well with others, take initiative, and juggle responsibilities. This chapter focuses on just a handful of these opportunities. Visit http://www.iuk.edu/campus-life/ for more ways to get involved. Remember, engaging in campus life includes *more* than attending classes.

Arts and Literary Publication

From the Well House is an arts and literary publication that is exclusively run by students and faculty from our campus. It is both a student organization on Indiana University Kokomo's campus and an international arts magazine that publishes all types of creative works either in print or online. *From the Well House* was started by faculty member Dr. Eva White and student Matt Russell in 2007 and was designed to give talented individuals an outlet for publishing their art. Works submitted to *From* the Well House undergo a double-blind, extensive peer review before being selected, which ensures that the works in this publication are top notch. In short, *From the Well House* in an awesome outlet for local and international talent and really puts Indiana University Kokomo on the map globally.

There are a couple different ways to get involved with *From the Well House*. The first is for all poets, writers, musicians, photographers, painters, sculptors, builders, videographers, researchers, and other creative minds out there to submit their work for publication. We accept submissions for both the print and online issues year-round. In the fall, our review boards select works for our Online Issue, which goes live on our website (fromthewellhouse.org) at the end of November. For this issue, we particularly encourage submissions of music, video, and scholarly papers, which cannot be featured in our print issue. During the spring semester, we focus primarily on writing and art submissions for our print issue. To find out more information on submissions and to actually submit creative works, please visit our website at www. fromthewellhouse.org. There visitors can contribute to our Story of the Month feature and check out our past online and print issues.

The second way to get involved is to become part of the *From the Well House* staff. Being a part of an international college publication is something that will significantly enhance any college student's resume or C.V. Students do not have to be artists or writers to contribute their talents to our organization. Everyone, not English majors alone, can benefit from this publication. We have staff positions in graphic design, public relations, writing, media, marketing, web development, and more available to all IU Kokomo students. These are examples of volunteer options for students to acquire real world, hands-on experience, but we also have internships for academic credit available. Those interested in participating in *From the Well House* as a student staff member or who would just simply like some more information, should email us at fromthewellhouse@gmail.com, visit and like our Facebook page, or request a meeting to discuss this opportunity further.

Fabio Sassi, *Screaming Wall*   Satyabrata Adhikary, *Deepest of Truths*

The Innovation Symposium

This course was created to give IU Kokomo's best and brightest thinkers an opportunity to analyze important innovations and create new approaches to address global and local issues. The world needs thinkers with the courage to innovate, to try new approaches, and to take the risks necessary to make positive changes.

By examining writings on philanthropic, environmental, and technological innovations and by observing the innovations of others, students can begin to appreciate the processes, effects, and opportunities involved. As they study historical and current innovators and innovations, they practice thinking outside the box, and examine new ways to solve problems. After studying in England for three weeks, students incorporate the insights of others with their own innovative thinking and actions to begin implementing positive change by developing their own projects on a local level. Read on for how this experience inspired one student. . .

photo courtesy of IU Kokomo Office of Media and Marketing

Automotive industry leftovers fueled Korey West's dreams of educating third-world children. He envisioned recycling tires, seat belts, and carpet from cars, making shoes from these scraps, and giving them to children in places like South America and Africa, where they walk miles to school and risk injury to their bare feet. Korey presented his vision for "Junkyard Shoes" as his final project for the Innovation Symposium. West, Class of 2013, who completed his degree in communication arts with the symposium, came up with his idea based on mission trips he's taken, and then studied the TOMS shoe company, which offers customers a chance to send a pair of shoes to someone else for each pair they purchase for themselves.

In England, West and his fellow students discussed social entrepreneurship at celebrity chef Jamie Oliver's foundation, which offers unemployed young people the chance to train for careers in the restaurant industry. They toured Covent Garden, with homeless people as their tour guides. They also visited the London Science Museum, Isaac Newton's home, the laboratory of penicillin discoverer Alexander Fleming, the Bodlein Library, the British Library, the British Museum, and Westminster Abbey. For the environmental part of the program, students went to the Isles of Mull and Iona in Scotland. They spent two weeks at Harlaxton Manor, meeting for class twice daily and working on their final projects.

Innovation Symposium participants are nominated by faculty and chosen through an essay application and interview process.

Theater Arts
photo courtesy IU Kokomo Office of Media and Marketing

Theater Arts

There a number of opportunities to be involved in performing arts on campus, either as a performer or as an audience member. For students who have a general interest in all aspects of theater, they might consider joining the Drama Club. The club is active in performances here on campus, participating in campus and community activities, attending live performances as a group and having the occasional film night. Recently, the drama club sponsored Visiting Artists, Rob and Jen Johansen, professional actors from Indianapolis.

University Theater presents student productions in the fall and spring semesters. Recent productions have included *Crimes of the Heart* and *Pride and Prejudice*. Auditions are open to all currently enrolled IUKokomo students. There are opportunities to be involved in set, costumes and makeup as well as publicity and promotion.

Another student group is the Improvisational team, SumAntics. This group has a public performance each semester and performs for various campus and community events throughout the year. Auditions for new members are held each semester.

Additionally, students may have the opportunity to take a field trip to a number of live performances in the Central Indiana area. Classes have attended performances at Indianapolis Repertory Theater, Ball State University Theater, Purdue University, and IU in Bloomington. There is also a minor in Creative Arts, which allows students to select a concentration in Theater, Music or Fine Arts.

For more information on Theater Arts on the IU Kokomo campus, see the Facebook page IUK Theater Arts

Student Newspaper

The Correspondent is "the Student Voice of Indiana University Kokomo and Purdue College of Technology at Kokomo." It is a student-run newspaper, released approximately every two weeks. The staff strives to inform the campus of current news, issues, and activities. Opportunities exist for those interested in writing, editing, photography, and advertising. To apply for a position please complete an application and return it to the Office of Student Activities, KC210.

Honors Program

The Indiana University Kokomo Honors Program provides unique educational and cultural opportunities to allow highly-motived students a way to challenge themselves and further their educational goals. Students in the Honors Program are able to take a series of specially-designed courses and participate in activities that enhance their understanding of humanity, culture, society and our world. By participating in the Honors Program, students have opportunities to develop critical thinking skills, innovative thinking and problem solving, and appreciation of the connections among different academic disciplines. Students in the Honors Program are eligible for early registration, can apply for Honors Program scholarships, and if they complete the program will have their Honors status noted on their transcripts and diploma.

To complete the Honors Program students take two HON-H399 colloquium courses, three H-option course and present at a conference.

HON-H399 courses are unique courses on different topics each fall and spring semester. These are a wonderful opportunity for Honors students to explore current issues that impact our world while working closely with a faculty member in a class of no more than twelve students. In the H-Option course, students choose classes that they would already be taking and work with their professor to modify the course into an Honors course.

Current IU Kokomo students who have completed at least twelve credit hours can join if they have at least a 3.3 GPA. New students are eligible to join the Honors Program if they have a combined SAT score of 1100, or ACT score of 24 and a high school GPA of 3.3 or higher and ranked in the top 20% of their high school class. Transfer students must complete at least twelve credit hours at IU Kokomo and have a at least a 3.3 GPA in order to join the program.

For more information visit iuk.edu/academics/majors/honors/index.shtml

Freshman Learning Communities: Project Engage

Indiana University Kokomo provides a unique experience for entering freshmen designed to help them become acclimated to a new college environment. These learning communities known collectively as Project Engage help students become part of the campus community while providing them with valuable content in subject areas taught, in many cases, by faculty members who are world-class scholars and award-winning teachers.

Course structures from one community to another vary, yet what remains consistent across all formats are faculty members and campus staff who are committed to student success. Advisors play a key role in these communities by providing important notices regarding registration and campus services. Other characteristics of the communities are increased opportunities for engagement outside of the classroom on field trips and campus events.

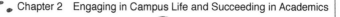

Examples of course titles unique to Project Engage are Monsters, a seminar exploring the repulsion yet fascination with these dark, monstrous manifestations; The Mockingjay and Other Symbols of Power, a course that explores the human yearning that seeks power for the powerless or right over wrong; Images, Text, and Reality, which focuses on the production of visual and written text to understand and portray reality. Some communities are tied to majors such as education, business, allied health and nursing, to name just a few.

Participation in these unique course offerings allows students to meet new people, to belong to a community of learners and instructors, and to pursue a topic of mutual interest. Consult your advisor for a schedule of Project Engage course offerings.

Student Success Center (SSC)

Note: All of the services below can be accessed by calling the SSC at 765-455-9425.

Writing Center w/Spanish Tutoring

The Writing Center, located on the first floor of the campus Learning Commons, provides a variety of *free* services to all IU Kokomo students. Students may receive assistance on writing related activities for all courses—from help with brainstorming topic ideas, to feedback on drafts, to clarification on citing sources. Numerous handouts, office supplies, style guides, computer stations, and even a relaxed atmosphere in which to work are available to students. The Writing Center is open for student use even when the tutors are not on duty.

IU Kokomo Library and home of the Student Success Center
credit IU Kokomo Office of Media and Marketing

Writing Tutors are often graduate students and English or English education majors. They have excelled in W131 and W132 and have a sincere interest in helping their fellow students with writing. Unfortunately, many new students view tutoring as something only the weaker writer needs; in reality sharing one's writing with an "audience" is a necessary part of the writing process on which accomplished writers have learned to rely . As former Writing Center Director and Professor Emeritus of English Dr. Nadene Keene observed, "Using the Writing Center as a resource is often the distinguishing characteristic between a successful student and one who fails." In the 2012-13 academic year, there were over 2,500 visits to the Center, although some students may hesitate to take advantage of these services because the concept of a Writing Center is new to them. The Writing Center staff offers this advice to all students who are faced with a writing assignment: Come early and come often.

English as a Second Language (ESL)

As part of the Student Success Center, an ESL tutor is available for international students who need help in English proficiency. Working one-on-one with an ESL tutor, students learn and practice the writing, reading, and proofreading strategies necessary for critical, college-level writing.

ESL Services are customized to address the students' knowledge levels as well as language and cultural learning style differences. Efforts are directed toward helping students acclimate to American educational and societal customs as they learn to interact with American professors and students.

Academic Coaching

Academic advisors are available to assist students with study skills. If organization, test anxiety, note taking, motivation, and or personal issues are interfering with academic performance, there are advisors and mentors trained to work with individuals to alleviate these burdens and assist in the student's first steps toward achieving success. Individual appointments can be made with an Academic Advisor or a peer advisor.

IT Training

The mission of the IT Training Center is "Removing technology roadblocks to enable student success!" Students can receive one-on-one assistance on technology issues by appointment or by simply walk-in service. All technology support is available at no charge to students.

The IT Training Center staff is Microsoft Certified and provides focused technology training and tutoring on projects that students experience at IU Kokomo, including various citation and bibliography tools for research papers, PowerPoint projects with embedded multimedia, podcast creation with Audacity, and large format posters for class projects and symposiums. Assistance is available for individual students or student work groups.

The IT Training Center is focused on providing student support for the entire IU technology toolset including the Canvas and Oncourse course management systems, Onestart and One.iu.edu student portal, IUware and IUanyWare for all student software needs, IU Box for cloud storage solutions, IU Mobile apps, and Lynda.com for comprehensive multimedia tutorials.

Additional Clubs and Organizations

The opportunities for engaging in campus life described in this chapter are simply the "tip of the iceberg," as they say. Please visit Clubs and Organization on the campus website for over thirty-five more ways to get involved and a detailed guide for those interested in creating a club or organization.

3
First-Year
Writing Program

First-Year Writing:
ENG-W131 and ENG-W132

The first year on any campus is an important one for students; consequently, the first-year writing courses at IU Kokomo are designed to help students understand the unique demands of writing in an academic setting. The characteristics of such demands will be discussed in depth later in this text. On the following pages are detailed descriptions of the two one hundred level writing courses that are part of the general education requirement along with learning outcomes for these courses.

The Grading Criteria used in the IU Kokomo writing courses is also included in this chapter and illustrates a good comparison among the various levels of achievement, but perhaps a better way to view the distinctions is to imagine a continuum where the lower grades indicate not the work of a "poor" writer but the work of a writer who turned in the paper before adequately revising and editing.

The Editing Policy is an important document for any student who plans to seek out a reader, formally or informally, to review his or her writing. The policy clarifies how writers and their readers should work together responsibly.

Finally, this chapter contains two sample papers from IU Kokomo students who have successfully completed W131 and W132. These assigments illustrate the distinction between two essential skills in these courses: summarizing and analyzing. Bekah's is a summary of Meghan McCarthy's article, and Alex's is a critical analysis of Gish Jen's short story. These students are successful writers because they have learned to consider the expectations of the assignment as well as the audience. Writing well is hard work, yet these student-writers have come to appreciate that with the sense of relief one feels when a paper's final draft is finished comes a tremendous sense of accomplishment.

ENG-W131: Reading, Writing & Inquiry I

Course Description:

W131 teaches skills of critical reading, thinking, and writing designed to help students meaningfully engage artifacts, events, and issues in our world. The course develops students' abilities to read written and cultural texts critically; to analyze those texts in ways that engage both students' own experiences and the perspectives of others; and to write about those texts for a range of audiences and purposes as a means of participating in broader conversations about issues. Assignments emphasize the analysis and synthesis of sources in making and developing claims.

Learning Outcomes:

- Demonstrate an understanding of the writing process
- Exhibit control over one's audience and purpose given the nature of the assignment
- Demonstrate responsible use of borrowing while avoiding plagiarism
- Demonstrate an understanding of the expectations for the following types of writing: summary, analysis, and argument
- Demonstrate an understanding of the unique expectations for impromptu essays
- Employ the techniques of critical reading and rhetorical analysis
- Demonstrate satisfactory knowledge of writing conventions
- Demonstrate an ability to utilize IUCAT and Academic Search Premier for the purpose of identifying and locating sources

ENG-W132: Reading, Writing, & Inquiry II

Note: In 2014, W132 went through a revised course title and description. You may still see the former title (Elementary Composition II) on some documents.

Course Description:

W132 builds upon the skills of critical reading and analysis introduced in W131 with an added focus on researched arguments. The course develops students' abilities to plan, draft, and revise research projects; assess and choose appropriate information sources; and tailor their projects for specific audiences and purposes. Students should expect to develop a sustained research project, treating research and writing as a dynamic process of inquiry. Assignments emphasize the location, analysis, and application of research sources in sustaining and supporting claims. Students will also learn and apply a variety of appropriate documentation styles.

Learning Outcomes:

- Demonstrate composing/research skills appropriate for an academic audience
- Demonstrate skills in using the IU Kokomo library for locating a wide variety of sources, including discipline specific databases
- Demonstrate an understanding of the characteristics of scholarly sources

- Integrate research smoothly and appropriately into a paper
- Demonstrate clear understanding of the conventions of both MLA and APA documentation styles
- Create a thesis/research question that is supported in a way that demonstrates control of the sources
- Demonstrate an understanding of the distinction between primary and secondary sources

IU Kokomo W131 and W132 Grading Criteria

Superior—The A paper exhibits these strengths:

1. Has a controlling sense of purpose (to persuade, to inform, or to express).
2. Exhibits a mature level of thought (that is, exhibits the ability to draw inferences and analogies that show insight into the topic).
3. Is tailored for a given audience.
4. Achieves clarity throughout.
5. Has unified organization with an apt introduction, graceful transitions, and a vigorous conclusion.
6. Has a clear thesis developed thoroughly with abundant, fresh support (such as concrete details, examples, and reasoning).
7. Uses variety of sentence structure, precise word choice, emphasis, and figures of speech.
8. Is free from any serious errors in Standard English and from common weaknesses in writing (ineffective use of passive voice, inappropriate word choice, inappropriate shifts, wordiness).

Good—The B paper exhibits most of these strengths:

1. Has a controlling sense of purpose (to persuade, to inform, or to express).
2. Exhibits a mature level of thought.
3. Is tailored for a given audience.
4. Achieves clarity throughout.
5. Has unified organization with an apt introduction, clear transitions, and a good conclusion.
6. Has a clear thesis, reasonably developed with effective support (concrete details and examples).
7. Uses a variety of sentence structure and accurate word choice.
8. Has a few errors in Standard English and few stylistic weaknesses (ineffective use of passive voice, inappropriate word choice, in appropriate shifts, wordiness). NOTE: Mere absence of errors will not be awarded with a B.

Satisfactory—The C paper exhibits these characteristics:

1. Has a controlling sense of purpose (to persuade, to inform, or to express).
2. Is logical but rarely thought-provoking.
3. Displays a sense of audience and usually addresses this audience.
4. Is clear throughout.
5. Is organized well enough to be easily readable, with a beginning, middle, and end.
6. Has a clear thesis, reasonably developed with some concrete details and examples.
7. Has adequate but undistinguished word choice and sentence structure.
8. Contains almost no serious errors in sentence boundaries, grammar, punctuation, and spelling.

Deficient—The D paper exhibits some but not all of the following weaknesses:

1. Fails to rise above the obvious in content, substitutes repetition for development, or relies too heavily on a secondary source.
2. Lacks sense of appropriate audience.
3. Has lapses in clarity.
4. Has lapses in organization, shows weakness in introduction, transition, and/or conclusion.
5. Has a single subject but no controlling idea.
6. Lacks variety in sentence structure and/or accuracy of word choice.
7. Has some errors in Standard English.
    a. mixed constructions (confused sentences)
    b. sentence boundary errors: such as run-on (or fused) sentences, unjustifiable sentence fragments, comma splices
    c. agreement errors (subject/verb or pronoun/antecedent)
    d. inappropriate shifts in tense, voice, mood, or person
    e. confusion of its/it's, there/their/there, to/too/two, no/know, your/you're, and so forth
    f. punctuation errors
    g. excessive misspellings

NOTE: Originality of style or thought will not excuse the deficiencies listed for D or F papers.

Failing—The F paper exhibits some of the following weaknesses:

1. Lacks content.
2. Lacks any sense of audience.
3. Consistently lacks clarity.
4. Lacks unified organization: lacks adequate introduction, transition and/or conclusion.

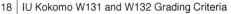

5. Lacks both a single subject and a controlling idea.
6. Has frequent errors in Standard English. (See list for D paper, item 7.)

NOTE: Failure to fulfill the assignment will result in a grade of F.

Editing Policy for Student Writers

Purpose: Even though seeking an audience to one's work is an integral part of the writing process, the writer is ultimately responsible for ensuring that the end product is a fair representation of his or her ability. This is true whether the student-writer is seeking help from a family member, a classmate, or a Writing Center tutor; in fact, the Editing Policy is posted in the Writing Center and is incorporated in the professional development for tutors.

The following are guidelines for writers and readers when reviewing student work:

1. Readers should not "correct" a paper by proofreading for errors in spelling, sentence structure or usage.
2. Readers might suggest that a general problem exists: "I noticed quite a few comma splices in that first section." They may explain the nature of the problem using an example from the paper. The student would be responsible for reviewing the paper for other similar instances. Alternatively, readers might place check marks in the margins by lines with errors in order to alert the student to problems.
3. The student should *always* be present at the editing session.
4. The readers should use questions to help clarify their ideas but should not suggest or add original content.

Bekah Hochstedler
Kristen Snoddy
English W-131
3 October 2012

Cell-Phone Safety Ignored in Washington
By Meghan McCarthy

The lack of government concern on cell-phone safety is addressed in Meghan McCarthy's essay titled "Cell-Phone Safety Ignored in Washington." McCarthy first explains how potential risks from cell-phone use have not been tested for over a decade, and because of this McCarthy suggests that many safety organizations are worried the public does not have adequate knowledge of the potential harm associated with cell phone use. She points out that many government agencies do not think it is necessary to produce more research because they believe there is not enough evidence of the possible dangers. She says that the only "harm" that has been discovered is that a person's body tissue warms up during cell phone use, but the government doesn't believe this warrants further research. McCarthy does stress that a select few government agencies are attempting to put together research to find potential harms, but she states that these agencies do not have enough aid to support their desire for research. To show evidence of the lack of finances being provided to these organizations, she lists many safety organizations that have conducted research in the last twenty years but today have no aid to continue it. Lastly, McCarthy goes into brief detail about cell-phone companies' warning labels. She views it as the responsibility of cell-phone companies to warn their consumers of the potential harmful effects. She says that most cell-phone companies do inform customers of these potential dangers, but McCarthy argues that the little information they do give is presented in too few details.

Original article: approximately 817 words
My summary: 254 words
McCarthy, Meghan. "Cell-Phone Safety Ignored in Washington." *National Journal* 9 Apr. 2011: 20. *Expanded Academic Search Premier.* Web. 27 Sept. 2012.

Alexandra Glenn
Kristen Snoddy
W132
28 April 2014

Gish Jen's "In the American Society": A Portrayal
of Collectivism Versus Individualism

According to founder Alison Granucci's website *Blue Flower Arts*, which includes biographies of various prominent writers, author Gish Jen is a Harvard University graduate who has received much recognition for her writing ("Gish"). Her short story "In the American Society" highlights the cultural differences between Eastern and Western society and the transitions that new immigrants to the U.S. must face. The Westernized U.S. represents a society of individualism, while the Chang family's Eastern home, China, represents a collectivist society. Individualism, as explained by Stephen Franzoi in his book *Social Psychology*, emphasizes a mentality in which uniqueness and autonomy are highly valued for personal identity and where people prefer more freedom and distance in their social relationships (19). In Franzoi's same book, collectivism is defined as "a philosophy of life stressing the priority of group needs over individual needs, a preference for tightly knit social relationships, and a willingness to submit to the influence of one's group" (20). In her story "In the American Society," author Gish Jen contrasts Ralph Chang's Eastern expectations with his experiences in Western culture to emphasize the difference in values between a collectivistic Eastern culture and an individualistic Western culture.

"In the American Society" is divided into two sections, titled "His Own Society" and "In the American Society." "His Own Society" portrays Ralph Chang's (the father of the main character) struggle to entrepreneur a business which can support his family. Ralph has difficulty keeping help at his pancake restaurant because of his over-demanding attitude toward employees. Eventually, desperate for workers, he hires two illegal Chinese immigrants named Booker and Cedric. Ralph acts as a father figure toward them, and in return they are willing to do chores that other employees refused. In the end, Booker and Cedric are caught by immigration and taken to jail. Dismayed, Ralph attempts to help them, but they end up fleeing from the immigration officers, leaving only a note and some money for their bail behind. In the second section, "In the American Society," the family attempts to blend in with families from the local country club at a party. Mrs. Lardner, who is a member of the club, hosts a party for another member named Jeremy Brothers. Ralph goes out of his way to buy an expensive suit for the occasion yet does not remove the tags, perhaps hoping to later return the suit. When they get there, Ralph is harassed by a drunken Jeremy and is embarrassed when Jeremy discovers the intact tags on his suit. Fed up with being mocked, Ralph angrily retaliates by throwing his suit jacket in the pool and storming out with the rest of his family, having given up on fitting in with such an unpalatable crowd.

Ralph Chang's attitude toward his employees in the first section of Gish Jen's story, titled "His Own Society," depicts his unwillingness to let go of the collectivist ideals of Eastern society. He often makes supererogatory demands of his employees because he expects a degree of loyalty from his workers that would only exist in a collectivist society. The narrator, one of Ralph's daughters, describes how the employees react: "The cooks and busboys complained that he asked them to fix radiators and trim hedges, not only at the restaurant, but at our house; the waitresses that he sent them on errands and made them chauffeur him around" (384, 385). Eventually, the employees start to quit, such as the head waitress: "'It's not just the blacks don't believe in slavery,' she said when she quit" (385). When Ralph eventually hires Booker and Cedric, who also come from a collectivist background, he finally gets the committed workers he desires. Ralph forms a close bond with them and is willing to go out of his way to help them in return when they are caught by the immigration officers: "The next day my father posted bail for 'his boys' and waited apprehensively for something to happen" (390). He is even willing to talk to a judge (and possibly offer a bribe) in order to defend Booker and Cedric, but his wife criticizes him for taking so much risk for a couple employees. In response to her criticism, Ralph explains his collectivist values: "'In the war my father sent our cook to the soldiers to use. He always said it-the province comes before the town, the town comes before the family'" (390). Ralph's actions and ideals in this section represent collectivism very well. His restaurant can be viewed as a community, with Ralph as the head of the community. He always puts the greater good of the community first by supporting his employees when they need help, and in return he expects them to do the same by doing extra work when needed; this idea of valuing group needs over individual needs is the epitome of collectivism.

The second section of Gish Jen's story, titled "In the American Society," reveals the individualistic nature of society in the Westernized U.S. The protagonist and her family are invited to a party hosted by members of the local country club, and they are forced to endure the antics of two self-centered characters, Jeremy and Mrs. Lardner. Mrs. Lardner, who is clearly more concerned with her image as a good hostess than with the comfort of her guests, asks the protagonist (a mere child) to hand out hors d'oeuvres: "Mrs. Lardner came by to bewail her shortage of servers. Her caterers were criminals, I agreed; and the next thing I knew I was handing out bits of marine life, making the rounds as amicably as I could" (393). Had Mrs. Lardner possessed collectivist values, she would have valued the comfort of her guests more than her own comfort, and she would have been the one handing out food.

Meanwhile, Jeremy, in a drunken state, accosts Ralph: "Jeremy began to roar. 'This is my party, *my party*, and I've never seen you before in my life...*Who are you? WHO ARE YOU?*" (394). Jeremy then proceeds to forcefully remove Ralph's suit jacket, revealing the still-attached price tag underneath, much to the embarrassment of Ralph. Jeremy's belligerently drunken state represents a level of self-centeredness and anti-social behavior that would not be approved of in a collectivist society. In response, even Ralph Chang loosens his collectivist morals enough to go against the social norm by storming out of the party: "My father hurled the coat into the pool too. 'We're leaving,' he said grimly. 'Leaving!'" (396). By standing up to Jeremy and leaving the party, Ralph and his family display individualism by rebelling against the societal norms of the country club and by putting the family's needs above the needs of the country club society.

Gish Jen has received a fellowship to the American Academy of Arts and Sciences in 2009, grants from prestigious institutions—Guggenheim Foundation, the Radcliffe Institute, and the National Endowment for the Arts—and the Lannan Literary Award for Fiction ("Gish"). She is valued for her ability to accurately and subtly portray the experience of adjustment that immigrants to America face in their new homes. The well-intended struggles of Ralph Chang and his family to find their place in an individualistic American society highlight the striking difference in the way of life between collectivist Eastern societies, such as China, and individualist Western societies, such as the U.S. Ralph, with his collectivist upbringing, treats his employees as a part of his family; he offers them extra financial support, and in return he expects them to perform above and beyond the regular expectations of cooks and waitresses by completing whatever chores he demands of them. In contrast, the family's individualistic employees and country club friends value their autonomy and self-expression most highly, and they demonstrate this preference through their resistance to Ralph's ways. Through her casual and subtle narrative style, author Gish Jen cleverly portrays the tension caused by conflicting interests between collectivism and individualism, which any immigrant family from an Eastern society will face when trying to find their place in a new Western society.

Works Cited

Franzoi, Stephen. *Social Psychology*. Redding: BVT Publishing, 2012. Print.

"Gish Jen." *Blue Flower Arts*. Blue Flower Arts, LLC, n.d. Web. 28 Apr. 2014.

Jen, Gish. "In the American Society." *Fiction: A Pocket Anthology*. Ed. R. S. Gwynn.

Boston: Longman, 2012. 383-396. Print.

4
Practicing Rhetoric

Praxis in Action: Why Rhetoric Is Important in My Writing
by Elizabeth Jimenez

Elizabeth Jimenez writes that understanding rhetoric gives her the power to persuade an audience.

Rhetoric is an intangible power that has the ability to motivate and manipulate. If I master rhetoric, I know I possess the ability to move my audience toward my goal.

I communicate effectively when I gain the confidence of the audience. Influencing my class and professor is my number one goal and is done so by my ethos. My use of rhetoric is validated by my credibility in the subject I disseminate. I must possess credibility if I am to be a reputable source of information.

Once I have gained the attention of the audience, I obtain logos when I clearly and logically disseminate my thoughts. I accomplish my purpose when I prove my statements. This is done by substantiating my thoughts with supporting evidence. Many contributing factors that come into play have an influence on my argument, such as bias. If my argument is biased, this can strongly detract from my goal.

Persuasive rhetoric is not necessarily accomplished when I use too much emotion. I find if I overuse pathos, the general idea gets lost. If I want my idea to be well received, it is important for me to communicate with levelheadedness.

These elements help me to establish effective rhetoric, which is crucial as I write for different audiences in college. Rhetoric will open doors throughout my college career as I discover new ways of conveying information and opinions.

Through Praxis, Theory Becomes Action

The word **praxis** can be translated as "process" or "practice." Aristotle, the great Greek rhetorician, employed the term in a special way to mean practical reasoning, for which the goal was action. To be practical in the Aristotelian sense is a little different from what being practical means today. It indicates the ability to apply abstract theory to concrete situations and thus, to move from theory to action. Moreover, praxis embodies a creative element that raises it above the mundane or merely pragmatic. Therefore, "practicing rhetoric" is not practice in the sense of rehearsal. Rather, it is performing, or applying, or acting out rhetoric—taking theory and turning it into action.

So, if we understand praxis or the "practicing" part of "practicing rhetoric," what does the "rhetoric" part of the chapter title mean? In common usage, the word *argument* has a narrow definition that emphasizes heated or angry exchanges of clashing and often irreconcilable viewpoints. Moreover, sides in such arguments are limited to black and white opposites and include no shades of gray. If one person is right, then the other must be wrong.

In academia, in contrast, we argue because it causes us to examine critically our own as well as others' ideas. Argument compels us to consider conflicting claims, to evaluate evidence, and to clarify our thoughts. We know that even wise, well-intentioned people don't always agree, so we consider others' ideas respectfully. After one person presents an argument, either orally or in writing, others respond with arguments that support, modify, or contradict the original one. Then, in turn, more individuals counter with their own versions, and thus, the interchange becomes a conversation.

Academic arguments can be divided into several different categories, depending upon the extent of the writer's desire to persuade and the scope of the conversational exchange.

1. One type of argument simply makes a point about the topic. For example, later in this chapter you will read an article titled, "San Ysidro Shooting Survivor Lives His Dream of Being a Cop." In the article, the author describes the wounds inflicted on a young man during the McDonald's Massacre in San Ysidro in 1984 and then explains how and why this young man later became a cop. No one is likely to disagree with the writer's line of reasoning, at least not if the author offers sufficient evidence to back up the original statement that, for this man, being a cop is his dream. This article is a profile, a type of argument more often seen in magazines and newspapers than in journals.

2. A second type of argument involves a controversial issue, and the writer's aim is to persuade the audience to change its stance on the matter. The ideal result, for the writer, would be that members of the audience alter their positions to coincide with the writer's viewpoint. In this second type of argument, it is essential that the writer offer the complete structure of thesis, evidence, possible opposition viewpoints which are discussed and countered, and a conclusion. "The Sleepover Question," another reading in this chapter, presents this kind of argument. The author, who has conducted research in both America and Holland, argues the controversial position that if American parents would adopt more liberal attitudes toward their children's sexuality, like the parents in Holland, "the transition into adulthood need not be so painful for parents or children." A reading in Chapter 3, "Why Executions Should Be Televised," offers a more extreme

version of this type of argument. Either executions are televised or they aren't, and the writer advocates that they should be.

3. A third type of argument emphasizes multiple perspectives and viewpoints and tries to find common ground that participants can agree upon. In Chapter 4, several readings are collected in a casebook called "The $300 House." The *Harvard Business Review* initiated a design competition intended to spark inclusive argument with the aim of gathering ideas about how to build inexpensive but adequate homes for the poor in the world's slums. "Hands Off Our Houses," one response to the competition that appears in the casebook, argues, for example, that bringing $300 houses into the slums of Mumbai is not the answer to the housing problem. In contrast, other responses posted on a website associated with the competition suggest ways the idea of the $300 house might work, while admitting enormous difficulties.

These three types of arguments represent points in a spectrum, and all persuasive texts may not neatly fit into one of the three categories. A crucial thing to remember, though, is that all arguments involve the presentation of a line of reasoning about a topic or an issue—a thesis, hypothesis, or claim—and the support of that reasoning with evidence.

Become Part of the Academic Conversation

As a student, you are expected to join academic conversations that are already in progress. How do you do that? How do you know what kind of response is appropriate? Have you ever entered a party where everyone is talking excitedly? Most likely, you paused near the doorway to get a sense of who was there and what they were discussing before you decided who to talk to and what to say. Or, have you become part of a Facebook group or a listserv discussion group? If so, you know it is a good idea to "lurk" for a while before asking questions or contributing a remark. Writing an academic paper involves a similar process. You read about a subject until you have a good grasp of the points authorities are debating. Then you find a way to integrate your own ideas about that subject with the ideas of others and create an informed contribution to the conversation.

For example, the following students' introductions to movie reviews demonstrate they not only understand the films and have interesting things to say about them; their writing also displays knowledge of what others have written about the films, whether the students agree with those evaluations or not.

- Roger Ebert claims that audience members who haven't seen the first two *Lord of the Rings* films (Peter Jackson, 2001, 2002) will likely "be adrift during the early passages of [the third] film's 200 minutes." But then again, Ebert continues, "to be adrift occasionally during this nine-hour saga comes with the territory" (par. 3). Ebert, though, misses one crucial fact regarding *Lord of the Rings: The Return of the King* (2003). This third installment opens with a flashback intended to familiarize new spectators about what happened in the previous two films. Within these five minutes, the audience discovers how Gollum (Andy Serkis) came to be corrupt through the destructive power of the Ring. The viewer, therefore, will not necessarily be "adrift," as Ebert claims, since the lighting, setting, and sound in the opening of *The Return of the King* show the lighter, more peaceful

world before Gollum finds the ring, compared to the darker, more sinister world thereafter.

- "It's hard to resist a satire, even when it wobbles, that insists the most unbelievable parts are the most true" (*Rolling Stone* par. 1). This is Peter Travers's overarching view of Grant Heslov's satire, *The Men Who Stare at Goats* (2009). Travers is correct here; after all, Goats's opening title card, which reads, "More of this is real than you would believe," humorously teases the viewer that some of the film's most "unbelievable parts" will, in fact, offer the most truth. We experience this via Bill Wilson's (Ewan McGregor) interview of an ex "psy-ops" soldier, when Wilson's life spirals out of control, and all the other farfetched actions presenting "reality." But again, it is the film's opening—specifically, its setting, camera movements and angles, dialogue, effects, and ambient noise— that sets the foundation for an unbelievably realistic satire."[1]

In both of these introductions, the students quote reviews by professional film critics and respond to the critics' opinions. Moreover, the students continue their arguments by using the critics' ideas as springboards for their own arguments. These two short examples indicate these students have learned how to counter positions advocated by authorities without losing their own voices. If the rest of their essays continue as they have begun, the students will have written essays to which others can reply, thus continuing the conversation. Later in this textbook, you will have your own chance to enter the conversation of film reviews by reviewing a favorite movie of your own.

Collaborative Groups Help Students Enter the Academic Conversation

Likely, your writing class will include collaborative group work as part of the mix of activities, along with lecture, class discussion, and in-class writing. You may wonder why there is so much talk in a writing class, which is a good question. Use of collaborative groups is based on extensive research, which shows that students who work in small groups as part of their courses tend to learn more and retain the knowledge longer than students who are not asked to work in groups. Also, research shows students who participate in collaborative group work generally are more satisfied with the course. Groups give students a chance to apply knowledge they have learned and provide a change of pace from lectures or other class activities. There are several types of groups, and your class may include one or all of them:

- Informal, one-time pairs or groups. After presenting some material, your instructor may ask you to turn to the person next to you and discuss the topic or answer a question.

- Ongoing small classroom groups. Usually, these groups work together for a significant part of the semester, and your instructor may assign roles to members of the group such as recorder, facilitator, editor, and spokesperson. Often, the roles will rotate, so that everyone has a chance to try out each job. Your instructor may give you a job description for each role or train the class in the tasks for each role.

1* Kelli Marshall. "Entering a Conversation, Teaching the Academic Essay," *Unmuzzled Thoughts about Teaching and Pop Culture*, October 23, 2010, http://kellimarshall.net/unmuzzledthoughts/teaching/academic-essay/. Accessed August 30, 2011.

- Task groups. These groups are formed to write a report, complete a project, or do some other task together. These groups meet several times, often outside of class. The products of these groups are usually graded, and your instructor will often require members to rate each other on their performance.

- Peer editing groups. When you have completed a draft of an essay or other text, your instructor may ask you to exchange papers in pairs or within small groups. You will be asked to read your classmate's paper carefully and make comments, either on a peer editing form or on the paper itself. Likewise, your classmate will read and make comments on your paper. Then, when you receive your paper back, you can make revisions based on your classmate's comments.

An added benefit to the use of collaborative groups in writing classes is that students can help each other figure out what the ongoing conversation is for a particular topic or issue before writing about it. Also, groups provide a forum where students can practice making comments that are part of that conversation.

Rhetoric and Argument

The structure of an argument—introduction (including a thesis), supporting evidence, counterarguments, and conclusion—will be familiar to you from previous English classes. What you may not realize is that ancient Greeks developed this argumentative structure out of necessity. Their democratic system of government required that citizens be able to speak persuasively in public, as there were no attorneys or professional politicians. Ancient Greeks called their persuasive strategies rhetoric, and rhetoric became the primary means of education of the elite youth in Athens.

Rhetoric, like argument, is a word that has both a popular meaning and an academic meaning. You have probably heard someone say of a politician's speech, "Oh, that's just rhetoric," meaning the politician's words are empty verbiage or hot air. The politician is attempting to sound impressive while saying nothing that has real meaning. Or perhaps the politician is making promises that listeners believe he or she has no intention of keeping. Politicians who engage in verbal deception often succeed only in acquiring the reputation of dishonesty.

In the field of rhetoric and composition today, rhetoric has a much different meaning. Though definitions vary somewhat from one practitioner to another, rhetoric generally means the study and use of persuasive communication (or argument), a meaning that traces its roots back to the original use of the term by ancient Greeks. Rhetoric, in the form of oratory, was essential to the Greeks, as they used it to resolve disputes in the law courts and to promote political action in the Assembly.

♀ Are We All Greeks? As Americans, we owe an immense debt to ancient Greek civilization. Our laws, our democratic form of government, our literature, and our art have their roots in ancient Athens. Earlier generations of Americans and Western Europeans, who often studied Latin and Greek, may have had a clearer understanding of the direct connections of our culture to Athens of the 4th and 5th centuries BCE. Indeed, the English poet Percy Bysshe Shelley famously said, "We are all Greeks" because of the essential influence of ancient Greek culture upon Western civilization. However, even translated into 21st century American English, the linkage is still there.

Something quite amazing happened in Athens, around 500 BCE. Instead of being invaded by a foreign country who appointed a puppet ruler or experiencing a coup in which a strong man seized power, the people peaceably chose to put in place a direct democracy. Attica was not the only city-state to have a democracy, but it was the most successful. During the golden age of Greece, from roughly 500 BCE to 300 BCE, art, architecture, and literature thrived.

Direct or radical democracy meant all male citizens of Attica over the age of 20 could vote in the Assembly, the policy-making body of the city-state. They did not elect senators or representatives as we do today. Each of these men *voted directly*. Moreover, they could settle differences with fellow citizens by suing in the law courts. Out of 250,000 to 300,000 residents in Attica, some 30,000 were citizens. Amazingly, it was not unusual for 10,000 of these eligible men to vote in the Assembly. The law courts had juries of 500 or more. Imagine trying to speak to an audience of 10,000 people without modern loudspeakers. Even with the wonderful acoustics in Greek theatres, it would have been a challenge.

Ordinary citizens were required to speak in the Assembly or the courts to promote laws or defend themselves from lawsuits, as there were no attorneys or professional politicians. Certainly, speaking before such large audiences necessitated special skills acquired only through extensive training and practice. Many sought out teachers to help them learn how to speak persuasively, and, indeed, training in rhetoric became the primary method of education for the elite young men of Athens. A few women were also educated in rhetoric, but they were in the minority.

The earliest teachers of verbal persuasive skills we now call rhetoric were Sophists who migrated from Sicily and other Greek states. Some of their viewpoints were curiously modern—for example, that knowledge is relative and that pure truth does not exist. However, they became known for teaching their pupils to persuade an audience to think whatever they wanted them to believe. Sophists such as Gorgias themselves often presented entertainment speeches during which they would argue, on the spur of the moment, on any topic raised by the audience, just to show they were able to construct effective arguments on any subject.

The term rhetoric comes from the Greek word *rhetorike*, which Plato coined as a criticism of the Sophists, claiming the Sophists' rhetoric could be employed to manipulate the masses for good or ill, and that rhetoricians used it irresponsibly. Ironically, Plato demonstrates excellent rhetorical techniques himself when he condemns rhetoric and argues that only the elite who are educated in philosophy are suited to rule, not the rhetoricians. Aristotle, Plato's student, took a more moderate viewpoint toward rhetoric. Indeed, he was the first philosopher to classify rhetoric as a tool for practical debate with general audiences. His book *On Rhetoric* (though it was probably lecture notes possibly combined with student responses, rather than a manuscript intended for publication) is the single most important text that establishes rhetoric as a system of persuasive communication.

Athens, even in its glory days, seethed with controversy and bickering over the many inefficiencies of democracy. Men trained in rhetoric executed two coups, the Tyranny of the Four Hundred in 411 BCE and the Tyranny of the Thirty in 404 BCE, neither of which was an improvement; after each coup, democracy returned. Moreover, Athenians fought wars with Persia (the Battle of Marathon in 490 BCE and the Battle of Thermopylae in 480 BCE) and Sparta (the Peloponnesian War in 431–404 BCE and the Corinthian War of 395–387 BCE). Finally, the armies of Philip II of Macedonia defeated Athens at the

Battle of Chaeronea in 338 BCE, ending Athenian independence. Despite coups and wars, democracy remained in place in Athens for nearly 200 years.

If Americans might be called Greeks because our country is based on Greek traditions, this is not to say that rhetoric appears in all cultures. True, one might say that all civilizations have some sort of persuasive negotiation process; but profound differences exist between cultures in terms of what verbal strategies are persuasive. Indeed, disparity in expectations and the actions of individuals and groups from different traditions can be a cause of strife.

Rhetoric and Power

Aristotle defined rhetoric as "the faculty of discovering, in a given instance, the available means of persuasion," which we might paraphrase as the power to see the means of persuasion available in any given situation. Each part of this definition is important. Rhetoric is power; the person who is able to speak eloquently, choosing the most suitable arguments about a topic for a specific audience in a particular situation, is the person most likely to persuade. In both Greece and Rome, the primary use of rhetoric was oratory—persuasion through public speaking. However, the texts of many famous speeches were recorded and studied as models by students, and prominent rhetoricians wrote treatises and handbooks for teaching rhetoric. To Greeks and Romans, a person who could use rhetoric effectively was a person of influence and power because he could persuade his audience to action. The effective orator could win court cases; the effective orator could influence the passage or failure of laws; the effective orator could send a nation to war or negotiate peace.

Skill with rhetoric has conveyed power through the ages, though in our contemporary world, rhetoric is often displayed in written text such as a book, newspaper or magazine article, or scientific report, rather than presented as a speech. Persuasive communication also can be expressed visually, as an illustration that accompanies a text or a cartoon that conveys its own message. Indeed, in our highly visual society, with television, movies, video games, and the Internet, images can often persuade more powerfully than words alone.

Using rhetoric effectively means being able to interpret the rhetoric we are presented with in our everyday lives. Knowledge of persuasive communication or rhetoric empowers us to present our views and persuade others to modify their ideas. Through changes in ideas, rhetoric leads to action. Through changes in actions, rhetoric affects society.

Selected Definitions of Rhetoric

Aristotle, 350 BCE—*Rhetoric is "the faculty of discovering, in a given instance, the available means of persuasion."*

Cicero, 90 BCE—*Rhetoric is "speech designed to persuade" and "eloquence based on the rules of art."*

Quintilian, 95 CE—*Rhetoric is "the science of speaking well."*

Augustine of Hippo, ca. 426 CE—*Rhetoric is "the art of persuading people to accept something, whether it is true or false."*

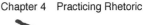

Anonymous, ca. 1490–1495—*Rhetoric is "the science which refreshes the hungry, renders the mute articulate, makes the blind see, and teaches one to avoid every lingual ineptitude."*

Heinrich Cornelius Agrippa, 1531—*"To confess the truth, it is generally granted that the entire discipline of rhetoric from start to finish is nothing other than an art of flattery, adulation, and, as some say more audaciously, lying, in that, if it cannot persuade others through the truth of the case, it does so by means of deceitful speech."*

Hoyt Hudson, 1923—*"In this sense, plainly, the man who speaks most persuasively uses the most, or certainly the best, rhetoric; and the man whom we censure for inflation of style and strained effects is suffering not from too much rhetoric, but from a lack of it."*

I. A. Richards, 1936—*"Rhetoric, I shall urge, should be a study of misunderstanding and its remedies."*

Sister Miriam Joseph, 1937—*Rhetoric is "the art of communicating thought from one mind to another, the adaptation of language to circumstance."*

Kenneth Burke, 1950—*"[T]he basic function of rhetoric [is] the use of words by human agents to form attitudes or to induce actions in other human agents."*

Gerard A. Hauser, 2002—*"Rhetoric, as an area of study, is concerned with how humans use symbols, especially language, to reach agreement that permits coordinated effort of some sort."*

Activity 4.1 **Explore:** Historical Usage of the Word "Rhetoric"

Read through the list of historical definitions of the word "rhetoric" on the previous page, and choose one that you find interesting. In a discussion, compare your chosen definition with those of your classmates.

Activity 4.2 **Collaborate:** Contemporary Usage of the Word "Rhetoric"

Find at least two recent but different examples involving use of the word "rhetoric." For example, search your local newspaper for an example of how the word "rhetoric" is being used. A search of the *Dallas Morning News* for the word "rhetoric" led to a story about citizen efforts to clean up a neglected area of town: "He now hopes for help to finally fill the gap between rhetoric and reality." Or ask a friend, fellow employee, or a family member to tell you what the word "rhetoric" means and write down what they say. Discuss your examples in your small group and present the best ones to the class.

Visual Map of Meanings for the Word "Rhetoric"

The word map for the word "rhetoric" shown in figure 4.1 has branches for different meanings of the word, with some branches splitting again to display subtle subsets of connotation. It was created by a website, Visual Thesaurus (www.visualthesaurus. com), which computes visual word maps for any word inputted in its search box. The idea is that words lead to branches that lead to more words, inspiring users to think of language in new ways.

At the Visual Thesaurus site, if you place your cursor over one of the circles connecting the branches, a small box will pop up that defines that connection. One of these connection boxes is visible. Notice it says, "using language effectively to please or persuade." This is the branch of the visual map that is closest to the meaning of "rhetoric" as used in this book. The other branches illustrate other contemporary uses of the word.

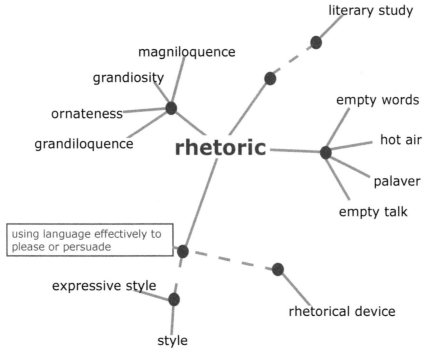

Figure 4.1

Activity 4.3 Explore: the Visual Map of the Word "Rhetoric"

In your small group, choose one of the five branches of words in the visual map of the word "rhetoric." Go to one or more good dictionaries and explore the meanings of the words in that branch. A good place to start would be the *Oxford English Dictionary*, which your college library may offer online. The *OED* offers intricate analyses of the histories of word meanings. Report to the class what you find out about the words on your particular branch.

Rhetorical Argument

Often, in our culture, the word "argument" is taken to mean a disagreement or even a fight, with raised voices, rash words, and hurt feelings. We have the perception of an argument as something that has victory and defeat, winners and losers. Argument, in the sense of a **rhetorical argument**, however, means the carefully crafted presentation of a viewpoint or position on a topic and the giving of thoughts, ideas, and opinions along with reasons for their support. The persuasive strength of an argument rests upon the rhetorical skills of the rhetor (the speaker or the writer) in utilizing the tools of language to persuade a particular audience.

Aristotle identified three appeals (see figure 4.2) or three ways to persuade an audience, and we are still using these today, though often without using the Greek terms to identify the means of persuasion:

- **Ethos**—The rhetor convinces an audience by means of his character or credibility. In oratory, the speaker projects an air of confidence and authority. In writing, ethos is conveyed by the qualifications of the writer or the authorities that are cited and also by the quality of the writing.

- **Pathos**—The rhetor persuades by playing upon the listener's (or reader's) emotions. He or she may refer to children, death, disaster, injustice, or other topics that arouse pity, fear, or other emotions.

- **Logos**—The rhetor persuades by the use of reasoning and evidence. Arguments based on logos employ deductive or inductive reasoning.

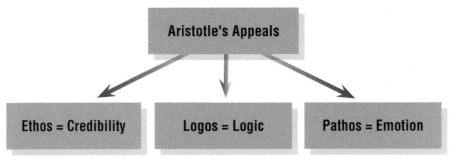

Figure 4.2

Although a good argument will contain at least traces of all three appeals, skilled rhetors analyze their audiences to determine which of the three would be most persuasive to that particular audience. Then, they construct arguments that emphasize that particular appeal.

In addition, a knowledgeable rhetor considers the time, place, audience, topic, and other aspects of the occasion for writing or speaking to determine the **kairos**, or opportune moment of the composition (see figure 4.3). This factor or critical moment both provides and limits opportunities for appeals suitable to that moment. For example, someone giving a commencement address has certain opportunities and constraints. Likewise, an attorney writing a last-minute appeal for someone on death row has a very different set of options.

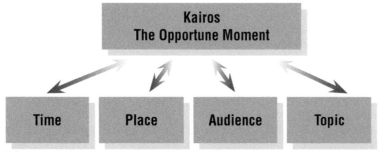

Figure 4.3

The editorial below addresses the shooting attack on Arizona Congresswoman Gabrielle Giffords that killed six and left Giffords and others seriously wounded. The text, published on Time magazine's website shortly after the attack, addresses the kairos of the situation—a United States Congresswoman has been shot, certainly an exceptional moment in many ways. The editorial demonstrates several important things to remember in understanding rhetoric and its use in American society.   The author, Nathan Thornburgh, addresses the controversy about whether "overheated rhetoric" (exaggerated pathos) had inspired the shooting, an important question considering the often-inflammatory language of political rhetoric in the United States. However, his text is not filled with rash or harsh words that could further inflame the controversy. Though the text is an opinion piece, taking a position regarding this controversy and offering evidence to support his opinion, it is not itself "overheated rhetoric." As you read the text, think about whether he emphasizes ethos, pathos, or logos. You may or may not agree with his position. Rhetorical language is never neutral; its purpose is to persuade an audience to share the author's opinion. Good arguments, though, do not use "overheated rhetoric," false evidence, or logical fallacies to win over an audience.

Reading 4.1

Violent Rhetoric and Arizona Politics by Nathan Thornburgh. This editorial by Nathan Thornburgh was originally printed in Time shortly after the shooting of Arizona Congresswoman Gabrielle Giffords.

Sometimes, rumors of violence beget actual violence. Saturday's mass shooting at a Safeway on North Oracle Road in Tucson, which killed six and left Democratic Congresswoman Gabrielle Giffords and others gravely wounded, may well be one of those occasions.

It's impossible to know this early what the motivations for the attack were. Was the alleged shooter—who has been identified as 22-year-old Tucsonan Jared Loughner—angry about immigration? Or perhaps another hot-button issue? YouTube videos ascribed to him bore the mark of mental illness—they were conspiratorial, unintelligible, espousing no particular cause—but no matter his mental state, his crime took place in an overheated political environment. Last March, at the height of the health care reform battle, Giffords's office was vandalized. She mentioned in an MSNBC interview that a Sarah Palin graphic had depicted her district in the crosshairs of a gun sight. "They've got to realize there are consequences to that," she said. "The rhetoric is incredibly heated." The corner next to her office had also become, she said, a popular spot for Tea Party protests.

As Pima County Sheriff Clarence Dupnik put it in an extraordinary and melancholic press conference after the shooting, "we have become the Mecca for prejudice and bigotry." He added that he's "not aware of any public officials who are not receiving threats."

Another shooting victim, a federal judge named John Roll, had been placed under 24-hour security in 2009 after ruling in favor of illegal immigrants in a high-profile case. It's unclear why he was at the supermarket event. But for almost a year now, Arizona's leaders have been grappling with anti-immigration sentiments, inflamed by reports of crossborder violence. National media attention, with its attendant voices of hysteria, only added to the churn. Pundits spoke gravely about a wave of violence, born in Mexico and now flooding Arizona. Arizona's two most famous politicians fueled the fury. Republican Senator John McCain, facing an unexpected reelection challenge from the right, ran a campaign obsessed with crossborder crime. And GOP Governor Jan Brewer, who invited the national spotlight by championing strict anti-illegal immigrant legislation, talked of beheadings in the desert.

The only problem with all this talk about a massive crossborder crime wave is that it wasn't true. Phoenix had not become one of the world's kidnapping capitals. Crime rates in Arizona had been steady or even fallen in some areas. There had been no beheadings in the desert. There were plenty of deaths there, but they were pathetic and meek tragedies: impoverished border-crossers, abandoned by their heartless guides, dying of exposure and dehydration.

But the idea of a state under siege took hold. When I was on the border last year reporting on the murder of rancher Rob Krentz, I talked to many who sincerely believed that they were under attack. Krentz's murder was a terrible event, but it was an isolated event. The relatively small number of home invasions, holdups and other crimes deeply disturbed border communities, but only because they had been living in such calm for so long. Their crime rates still don't match most cities in the states.

The supermarket meet-and-greet where Giffords was shot was actually a testimony to just how safe southern Arizona is. As a press release from her office last week put it, "'Congress on Your Corner' allows residents of Arizona's 8th Congressional District to meet their congresswoman one-on-one and discuss with her any issue, concern or problem involving the federal government." Not exactly the kind of event a politician would hold in a war zone.

It's true that Giffords was not a fan of the state's anti-immigration bill SB1070, but there were higher-profile opponents, such as her fellow Congressional Representative in Tucson, Raul Grijalva. Yet the idea that Arizona is under attack has been pushed hard enough that it's very possible that the coward who shot her (in the head, according to a Tucson paper) believed that the 40-year-old Democrat, who had been tarred by some as soft on immigration because she didn't support SB1070, was contributing to larger-scale violence against Arizonans.

If that is the case, it would only add to the tragedy. The fact is, that among all the overwrought promises and all the panic I heard last summer in Arizona, I found that Giffords was one of the few politicians offering concrete law enforcement steps that would actually work against the drug cartels and other smugglers. It's not just that she fought for more money and police for border protection, although she did that. She co-sponsored legislation last year with a California Republican that aimed to give law enforcement important new tools in cracking down on the cash cards that were a favored method of money-laundering. It was one of the many sensible, pragmatic ideas she had for cracking down on crime.

Whatever dark fantasies drove someone to try to take her life, Giffords is a sensible politician who was likely shot because she dealt with Arizona's reality, not its rumors.

Activity 4.4 **Compose:** Write a Summary of "Violent Rhetoric and Arizona Politics"

Summarizing is an excellent technique to use when preparing for an exam or doing research for an essay. It allows you to discern the main points of a text and how they fit together. With a classmate, review the editorial by Thornburgh. Read the article together carefully, and list the main points individually. After you've listed the main points, put them into paragraph form.

Caution: Beware of the temptation to add your own analysis of what the text is saying. For example, if you are summarizing a scientist's article on global warming, you need to be careful not to reveal your personal opinion about whether or not global warming is occurring or whether or not human actions are to blame. In this assignment, you summarize only. You do not argue or analyze.

When you're finished, compare your summary with that of your partner.

Activity 4.5 **Explore:** Analyzing "Violent Rhetoric and Arizona Politics"

1. What does Nathan Thornburgh mean when he uses the term "overheated rhetoric"?
2. What is the argument that Thornburgh is making about the cause of the attack on Representative Giffords?
3. What evidence does Thornburgh offer to support his argument?
4. Does Thornburgh make his case? Is he convincing? Why or why not?

Reading 4.2

The Sleepover Question by Amy Schalet. This text by Amy Schalet was first published in *The New York Times.* "The Sleepover Question" hazards an argument that many Americans—or at least American parents—may find controversial. Backed by her credentials as a professor of sociology, she cites research from 130 interviews, both in the United States and the Netherlands, and tackles the issue of whether or not American parents should allow their adolescent children to have sex in the family home. Pay particular attention, for she shows how to argue a subject that is not only controversial but often ignored.

NOT under my roof. That's the attitude most American parents have toward teenagers and their sex lives. Squeamishness and concern describe most parents' approach to their offspring's carnality. We don't want them doing it—whatever "it" is!—in our homes. Not surprisingly, teenage sex is a source of conflict in many American families.

Would Americans increase peace in family life and strengthen family bonds if they adopted more accepting attitudes about sex and what's allowable under the family roof? I've interviewed 130 people, all white, middle class and not particularly religious, as part of a study of teenage sex and family life here and in the Netherlands. My look into cultural differences suggests family life might be much improved, for all, if Americans had more open ideas about teenage sex. The question of who sleeps where when a teenager brings a boyfriend or girlfriend home for the night fits within the larger world of culturally divergent ideas about teenage sex, lust and capacity for love.

Kimberly and Natalie dramatize the cultural differences in the way young women experience their sexuality. (I have changed their names to protect confidentiality.) Kimberly, a 16-year-old American, never received sex education at home. "God, no! No, no! That's not going to happen," she told me. She'd like to tell her parents that she and her boyfriend are having sex, but she believes it is easier for her parents not to know because the truth would "shatter" their image of her as their "little princess."

Natalie, who is also 16 but Dutch, didn't tell her parents immediately when she first had intercourse with her boyfriend of three months. But, soon after, she says, she was so happy, she wanted to share the good news. Initially her father was upset and worried about his daughter and his honor. "Talk to him," his wife advised Natalie; after she did, her father made peace with the change. Essentially Natalie and her family negotiated a life change together and figured out, as a family, how to adjust to changed circumstance.

Respecting what she understood as her family's "don't ask, don't tell" policy, Kimberly only slept with her boyfriend at his house, when no one was home. She enjoyed being close to her boyfriend but did not like having to keep an important part of her life secret from her parents. In contrast, Natalie and her boyfriend enjoyed time and a new closeness with her family; the fact that her parents knew and approved of her boyfriend seemed a source of pleasure.

The difference in their experiences stems from divergent cultural ideas about sex and what responsible parents ought to do about it. Here, we see teenagers as helpless victims beset by raging hormones and believe parents should protect them from urges they cannot control. Matters aren't helped by the stereotype that all boys want the same thing, and all girls want love and cuddling. This compounds the burden on parents to steer teenage children away from relationships that will do more harm than good.

The Dutch parents I interviewed regard teenagers, girls and boys, as capable of falling in love, and of reasonably assessing their own readiness for sex. Dutch parents like Natalie's talk to their children about sex and its unintended consequences and urge them to use contraceptives and practice safe sex.

Cultural differences about teenage sex are more complicated than clichéd images of puritanical Americans and permissive Europeans. Normalizing ideas about teenage sex in fact allows the Dutch to exert more control over their children. Most of the parents I interviewed actively discouraged promiscuous behavior. And Dutch teenagers often reinforced what we see as 1950s-style mores: eager to win approval, they bring up their partners in conversation, introduce them to their parents and help them make favorable impressions.

Some Dutch teenagers went so far as to express their ideas about sex and love in self-consciously traditional terms; one Dutch boy said the advantage of spending the night with a partner was that it was "Like Mom and Dad, like when you're married, you also wake up next to the person you love."

Normalizing teenage sex under the family roof opens the way for more responsible sex education. In a national survey, 7 of 10 Dutch girls reported that by the time they were 16, their parents had talked to them about pregnancy and contraception. It seems these conversations helped teenagers prepare, responsibly, for active sex lives: 6 of 10 Dutch girls said they were on the pill when they first had intercourse. Widespread use of oral contraceptives contributes to low teenage pregnancy rates — more than 4 times lower in the Netherlands than in the United States.

Obviously sleepovers aren't a direct route to family happiness. But even the most traditional parents can appreciate the virtue of having their children be comfortable bringing a girlfriend or boyfriend home, rather than have them sneak around.

Unlike the American teenagers I interviewed, who said they felt they had to split their burgeoning sexual selves from their family roles, the Dutch teens had a chance to integrate different parts of themselves into their family life. When children feel safe enough to tell parents what they are doing and feeling, presumably it's that much easier for them to ask for help. This allows parents to have more influence, to control through connection.

Sexual maturation is awkward and difficult. The Dutch experience suggests that it is possible for families to stay connected when teenagers start having sex, and that if they do, the transition into adulthood need not be so painful for parents or children.

Activity 4.6 **Analyze** "The Sleepover Question"

1. What do you think about the "not under my roof" approach to a parent controlling a teen's sexuality versus the Dutch approach of allowing a teen's partner to sleep over? Discuss in your small group.
2. How do stereotypes play against the argument for a more open approach to teen sex in America? How much of parents' discomfort with their teen potentially having sex is guided by how their parents treated the subject when they were teens?
3. "The Sleepover Question" emphasizes logos. Can you paraphrase the logic of the argument? How does emotion (pathos) play a role in resistance to this argument?
4. In the article, the writer discusses the link between the use of oral contraceptives and lower teen pregnancy rates but does not mention the risk of STDs or condom use. Is it irresponsible of the author not to discuss the risk of STDs and sex, especially when she is willing to discuss teen pregnancy? Does it feel like an incomplete argument without discussing STDs?
5. If you were going to write a letter to the editor about this article, what would you say?

Why Study Rhetoric?

Rhetoric, or persuasive communication, happens all around us every day, in conversation at the grocery store, in blogs, on television, and in the classroom. We Americans constantly air our opinions about almost everything. Sometimes it is to convince others to share our opinions, sometimes the reason is to engage in a dialogue that will help us understand the world around us, and sometimes it is to persuade others to action.

Argument is essential to human interaction and to society, for it is through the interplay of ideas in argument that we discover answers to problems, try out new ideas, shape scientific experiments, communicate with family members, recruit others to join a team, and work out any of the multitude of human interactions essential for society to function. When issues are complex, arguments do not result in immediate persuasion of the audience; rather, argument is part of an ongoing conversation between concerned parties who seek resolution, rather than speedy answers.

Rhetoric provides a useful framework for looking at the world, as well as for evaluating and initiating communications. In the modern world, writing and communicating persuasively is a necessary skill. Those who can present effective arguments in writing are, in the business world, often the ones who are promoted. In addition, those who are able to evaluate the arguments presented to them, whether by politicians, advertisers, or even family members, are less likely to be swayed by logical fallacies or ill-supported research.

Also, writing rhetorically is a tool with sometimes surprising uses. Research shows that, as students, we are more likely to remember material we have written about rather than simply memorized. Also, through the process of writing, writers often find that they initiate ideas and connections between ideas that they might not otherwise have found. Thus, writing may lead to new discoveries.

Rhetoric is a part of our everyday lives. When we're in a conversation with someone, we use rhetoric on a conscious or subconscious level. If you go to class wearing the T-shirt of your favorite musician or band, you're ultimately sending a rhetorical message identifying you as a fan of that artist or group.

If you've ever written a profile on a dating site, you've used rhetorical principles to convince an audience of potential partners to contact you or to write you back if you have chosen to make the first contact. You build ethos by talking about yourself in order to build credibility among potential partners, and you establish pathos when you talk about an interest that is shared by a potential mate.

Being able to use the tools of rhetoric effectively gives you the power to control your communication—both incoming and outgoing—and to affect your environment in a positive way.

Reading 3

San Ysidro Shooting Survivor Lives His Dream of Being a Cop by Janine Zuniga. In this feature story from the San Diego Union-Tribune, Janine Zuniga describes vividly how Alberto Leos, then a 17-year-old cook and high school football star, was shot and left for dead during James Oliver Huberty's rampage at a San Ysidro McDonald's in 1984. The 21 dead and 19 wounded made the massacre the worst one-day shooting by a single individual in United States history at the time. But Leos's story did not end there. The young man underwent surgeries and completed rehabilitation, going on to become a policeman. Notice how the author makes use of both ethos and pathos in writing this profile.

The shots fired at point-blank range pierced both arms, his right leg, stomach and chest, and Alberto Leos crumpled to the kitchen floor next to three co-workers at a San Ysidro McDonald's. Even with his injuries, the 17-year-old cook, three weeks into his first job, knew the others were dead. He could tell by the lifeless positions of their bodies.

San Diego police sergeant, Alberto Leos, preparing to go out on patrol recently, overcame five surgeries and two years of painful therapy after the McDonald's Massacre to fulfill his childhood dream of becoming a police officer. Photo by Howard Lipin / Union-Tribune

During a harrowing 77 minutes 20 years ago today, Leos, a high school football star, watched in helpless horror as a heavily armed James Oliver Huberty "executed, killed families, babies, my manager."

In all, 21 people were killed and 19 wounded in what was, up to that time, the worst one-day massacre by a single gunman in U.S. history. "All I remember is saying a prayer," Leos said. "I prayed to see my family one more time . . . before I died."

The McDonald's Massacre, as it came to be called, has faded for many San Diegans during the past two decades, but for those such as Leos who survived, it became the defining moment of their lives.

Leos's recovery included three months in the hospital, where he underwent five surgeries to remove the bullets and repair damage. He spent two years in therapy, for both physical and emotional injuries.

Despite painful rehabilitation, scars and memories, Leos became even more determined to fulfill his childhood dream of becoming a police officer. He has been a cop for 17 years.

After stints with the National City and Chula Vista police departments, Leos is now a San Diego police sergeant working the Southern Division, which includes routine patrols of San Ysidro.

"I was born to do this work," said Leos, who is married and lives in Chula Vista. "I was born to be in this profession. That's how I feel."

Leos said that while growing up in Cudahy, a city southeast of Los Angeles, the only time he saw deputies was when they were taking someone to jail. But that image changed one day when an L.A. County sheriff's deputy visited his third-grade classroom.

"To see him in the school setting, I was in awe—his uniform, his nice, shiny badge," Leos said. "He told us they were there to help people, to help those who can't help themselves. I told myself that when I was older, I wanted to do that."

But Leos's parents quickly and, for a decade, successfully discouraged him from pursuing the dream, saying it was too dangerous a career for their only son. Their opposition vanished on the day he almost lost his life.

"When I was shot and my friends and co-workers were killed, my parents were very, very supportive of me doing whatever I wanted," Leos said. "I guess they felt I had a second chance."

The short sleeves of Leos's dark-blue uniform can't hide the scars on his arms, but he doesn't often share the details of that day. The 5-foot-8, clean-shaven officer is soft-spoken and somewhat formal.

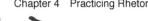

"Even as a young, young man, I could tell he was a serious kind of person, not in a sober sense, but in that he had a job and wanted to help his folks, that he was a good kid," said Andrea Skorepa, who as an employee of the local social-services agency Casa Familiar helped administer a $1.4 million fund for survivors and those injured in the McDonald's Massacre.

Skorepa, who has remained friends with the officer, said some who lived through it, such as Leos, have accomplished their goals, while others have succumbed to the tragedy.

"For the people who survived, that day was the beginning of a new life for them," Skorepa said. "What they have done with their lives becomes the important story. He doesn't live as a victim. He's not gone that way."

He tries to get assigned to San Ysidro when he can, because he wants to give back to the community and to Casa Familiar. The agency not only helped with the fund but helped get his family through a very tough time.

"That's when I learned about community service and how much it's needed," Leos said.

Said Skorepa, now executive director of Casa Familiar, "I think it gives you a different perspective, if you've come that close to losing your life and are somehow spared, on how to live your life."

In all his years in law enforcement, Leos has never fired his weapon at anyone. He's sure he will if he has to, but his instincts, which he has learned to trust, help guide him more calmly through tense situations.

Now, if a situation doesn't feel right, he will take a few steps back and think it through. Back on that unforgettable day, Leos said something told him not to go to work, but he didn't listen to his gut.

"I woke up with this feeling that I shouldn't go in," said Leos, who will turn 38 next month. "My friends were going to the beach and invited me to go. But it was the first job I ever had, and I talked myself out of it."

Activity 4.7 Collaborate: Consider a Profile

6. In your small group, decide what argument Janine Zuniga is making in this profile of the San Ysidro massacre survivor.
7. Describe what you think are the best specific details the writer includes, either of the shooting or of Leos's subsequent recovery and career as a policeman. How do these details contribute to the story?
8. A profile generally emphasizes the ethos of the subject. In this profile, how does the author do that? How does the author also make use of pathos?
9. As the readers, what conclusion are you left with after you read the article? Is this the impression that the writer wanted you to have, do you think?

Reading 4.7

Memories of McDonald's Rhetorical Actions 20 Years Later. Shortly after the shooting that injured Alberto Leos, wounded 18 others, and killed 21 people (see the reading on page 22), a committee in San Ysidro, California, collected 1,400 signatures asking that the McDonald's be razed and a memorial park built. Although McDonald's was in no way responsible for the attack, it responded to the committee's rhetorical appeal. Bob Kaiser, director of media relations for McDonald's, said, "The concern is for the people, not simply business" and reported that the company's decision whether to reopen the restaurant was being held in abeyance. Later, the company tore down the restaurant and donated the land to the city. After debating what to do with the land, the city used it to build a community college.

In 2004, twenty years after the massacre, a memorial service was held at the site, and the media ran stories about the anniversary. Many people contributed to a blog associated with the anniversary story in the local newspaper:

Jennifer wrote: "I live in La Jolla, exactly twenty five miles north of the former McDonald's where this tragedy took place some twenty plus years ago. The site is now the home of Southwestern College, but I have seen the memorial and am always filled with sadness when I go there. They have done a wonderful job on the memorial which is just in front of the former McDonald's building which you can tell was once the eatery, but has been painted grey, though the general shape of the building is still there. I am especially touched by the comments in this story and it is great that the memory of what happened not so long ago in our city is kept alive. ALL those that survived or not on that very sad day, were heroes, but their memories will never be in vain and we, as the citizens of this beautiful city will always be proud of their bravery and courage."

Leonor wrote: "I was seven at the time and I lived half a block from McDonald's. I saw bullets flying in the air and I remember police officers not letting us go to our house. They told us to get down in our car and not move. It was scary because we did not know what was going on. We were going to eat at McDonald's but my grandma invited us to her house. I still live in San Ysidro and I graduated from Southwestern College and I see the area everyday. It's not easy to forget what I do remember."

Armida wrote: "I remember that day. I was there. I had just turned 17. This was my first job. I lost my cousin and two friends because they threw a coffee pot at him to save this guy who became a cop. I saved a co-worker. I never told anybody or wrote about this day till now."

Sergio wrote: "I still remember this event. I'm now 33 years old and I was 9 years old. I still remember the gun shots, many of them. I grew up about 3 blocks away. I remember the countless police officers blocking the streets of Sunset Lane, which was my street. Two of my friends were murdered. I could have been there. My best friend died that day. This has been a funeral I will always remember. I just like to share a tiny bit on that day in the summer of July."

Joe Bloggs wrote: "I remember this happening. I was only about 12 years old at the time and living in Australia, but it is something I never forget about. Why America is so obsessed with guns I will never understand. Nobody except the police and army should have access to firearms. The private ownership of guns should be illegal and there should be gun amnesty days where guns can be handed in to be crushed. This is going to happen time and time again, people, unless you stand up and say no to gun ownership."

The blog entries show the impact of the event, even 20 years later. Notice that there are no negative comments about the McDonald's, nor about what the community decided to do with the land. Nothing McDonald's could have done would have erased the pain of the event, but its rhetorical actions, in both word and deed, did not add to the trauma of the event. McDonald's response to the citizens' request to tear down the building and donate the land to the city continues to be praised 20 years later.

Activity 4.8 **Collaborate:** Blogging and Responding to Blogging

In your group, discuss the blog entries above about the San Ysidro shooting. Which blog entry attracts your attention the most? What do you think was the author's rhetorical purpose?

Write your own blog entry in response to the McDonald's story. What would you say to the citizens who remember the event? What would you say to the people at McDonald's who made the decision to tear down the building and donate the land to the city?

Do you blog? Why? Do you check your blog frequently? How do you feel if there are responses to your comments? How do you feel if there are no responses to your comments? Does it matter if the response is positive or negative?

Activity 4.9 **Compose:** Write about Everyday Arguments

Read your local newspaper or magazines such as *Time* or *Fortune* or search the Internet and bring to class a copy of a recent text or visual image that makes an argument about an issue. You might find, for example, an editorial in your local newspaper about recycling efforts in your community or a blog entry about parenting practices. Be sure, however, that the text or image takes a position on the issue. Write a paragraph of approximately 100 to 150 words describing the argument to your classmates and your reaction to it.

Encountering Visual Rhetoric

Why is a visual so powerful? Colors, shapes, and symbols impact viewers in ways text alone cannot. Many images present arguments and, because they are visual, they communicate more quickly and, sometimes, more powerfully than words.

The images on the next page are covers from *GQ* magazine. On the left, Sacha Baron Cohen, in the Bruno character, graces the humor edition of the magazine in a pose echoing that of Jennifer Aniston, on the right, which was printed on a cover a few months previously. What do you think when you see a man positioned in a way that is typical for a scantily dressed (or nude) female? Is it funny? Many think so, but not everyone. A posting on a blog called thesocietypages.org says of Cohen, "The contrast between the meaning of the pose (sexy and feminine) with the fact that he's male draws attention to how powerfully gendered the pose is… women look sexy when they pose like this, men look stupid when they do."

A photo's ability to persuade can be significant, whether it is a news photo or an advertisement. However, not everyone interprets images the same way, especially when they evoke stereotypes of gender, race, or religion.

Compare these two cover photos from *GQ* magazine. Though the poses are similar, because the figure on the left is a man and the one on the right is a woman, they evoke very different responses from readers. Some see the photo on the left as paying humorous tribute to the one on the right. Others interpret both images as exploiting feminine gender stereotypes.

Activity 4.10 **Compose:** Write a Caption for a Photo or a Pair of Photos

Choose a news photo or advertisement from a newspaper, magazine, or the Internet that presents an argument. Alternatively, compare two news photos or advertisements. Copy or paste the photo or photos on a piece of paper and write a caption that expresses the argument(s) you see in the photo.

Rhetorical Arguments Stand the Test of Time

Abraham Lincoln's Gettysburg Address is the short speech that the president delivered at the site of the battle of Gettysburg where, four months previously, the Union Army defeated Confederate forces. His was not the only talk that day at the dedication of the Soldiers' National Cemetery, but it is the only one remembered. In just over two minutes, he was able to reframe the Civil War not just as a victory for the North but as a "new birth of freedom" for all Americans. Now, during the 150th anniversary of the Civil War, is a good time to remember Lincoln's rhetoric—in terms of both the content and the style of his speech.

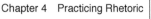

Reading 4.5

Four score and seven years ago our fathers brought forth on this continent, a new nation, conceived in Liberty, and dedicated to the proposition that all men are created equal.

Now we are engaged in a great civil war, testing whether that nation, or any nation so conceived and so dedicated, can long endure. We are met on a great battlefield of that war. We have come to dedicate a portion of that field, as a final resting place for those who here gave their lives that that nation might live. It is altogether fitting and proper that we should do this.

But, in a larger sense, we cannot dedicate—we cannot consecrate—we cannot hallow—this ground. The brave men, living and dead, who struggled here, have consecrated it, far above our poor power to add or detract. The world will little note, nor long remember what we say here, but it can never forget what they did here. It is for us the living, rather, to be dedicated here to the unfinished work which they who fought here have thus far so nobly advanced. It is rather for us to be here dedicated to the great task remaining before us—that from these honored dead we take increased devotion to that cause for which they gave the last full measure of devotion—that we here highly resolve that these dead shall not have died in vain—that this nation, under God, shall have a new birth of freedom—and that government of the people, by the people, for the people, shall not perish from the earth.

Though no actual recording exists of Lincoln giving the speech, you can listen to it if you search on the Internet for "recording of Gettysburg Address." Listen to the speech, noting the phrase "Four score and seven years ago," which is so famous that Americans know instantly, when it is quoted by orators or writers, that it is a reference to Lincoln. Consider what arguments the president makes in his speech. Think about their relevance today.

Activity 4.11 **Compose:** Paraphrase the Gettysburg Address

Rephrase each sentence of the Gettysburg Address, one by one, in your own words, putting it in 21st century wording rather than Lincoln's ceremonial, 19th century phrasing. In a paraphrase, the text does not become shorter; it is recreated in different words. This is a useful technique in helping you understand a text. It is also helpful when you are writing an analysis of a text because you can use your paraphrase rather than long, block quotes. Remember, though, when you are writing an essay, you must cite a paraphrase in the text and also include it in your list of references.

Activity 4.12 **Compose:** Keep a Commonplace Book

Ancient rhetoricians performed speeches with little warning, often to advertise their services as teachers of rhetoric. Thus, they frequently memorized arguments about specific topics that could be adapted to the audience and situation on a moment's notice. They called these memorized arguments "commonplaces." Commonplace books are an outgrowth of the Greek concept of commonplaces, but they are a little different. They became popular in the Middle Ages as notebooks in which individuals would write down quotes or ideas about a particular topic. These notations might later be used to generate an idea for a composition. In more modern times, people have created commonplace books in the form of scrapbooks in which they collect quotes as well as drawings and clippings. Thus, they become a record of a person's intellectual life and can be saved for later reference.

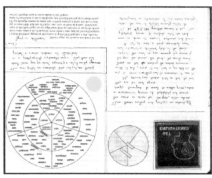

For this class, take a notebook, perhaps one with a colorful or interesting cover, and keep notes, quotes, vocabulary words, and clippings related to the topics discussed in class. As your instructor directs, this commonplace book may be graded as evidence of class participation or it may be a private journal. Take a look at the commonplace books shown here for ideas. Be creative and enjoy adapting this ancient journal form to record ideas that interest you.

For thousands of years, people have been keeping commonplace books, a kind of journal or diary in which the author includes quotes, drawings, and images.

Activity 4.13 **Compose:** Create Your Own Blog

Create a home page for a professional blog using a site like Blogger, WordPress, or Live Journal. Blogger is the easiest to use, but the others have more flexible options. Read the help screens for instructions on how to create your blog. Your design choices should reflect your personality. Keep in mind, though, that you are building an "academic self," so all the topics you write about should be of an academic nature and in an academic tone. Some students decide to have two blogs, one for their friends and one for professional networking, so you may want to do this, especially if you already have a blog.

During this class, you'll use the blog to explore different aspects of each chapter in the textbook (and other topics that your instructor directs). You can also blog about other topics related to your writing this semester, and you can link to other blogs that you think your readers would find of interest.

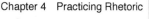

After you have created the look of your blog, write a first entry that introduces you to your readers. You might include your major, your college, and something interesting that might attract readers to your blog.

Home   About Me   My Videos   My CMC Degree

End of the Year... My Favorite Memory
May 15, 2011

Exactly one week ago, I was at my graduation ceremony receiving my college degree. Normally, graduating would be the last thing a student would do before summer vacation however I am still at CMC working away. You see, me and my RA crew had to stay in the residence halls for a few days after graduation to close down the building. Although they left 2 days ago, I am still here working on a special project. Sitting in an empty 250 bedroom mansion has given me a lot of time to think about my year. With all this reminiscing, I tried to think of my favorite memory of 2nd semester. It was difficult to choose but my 2nd semester Sky Club trip was my favorite memory of all.

For our 2nd semester Sky Club trip, we went to the McDonald Observatory in Fort David Texas. This was the 2nd trip we took and it was my favorite. We embarked out on April Fools Day (no joke) and headed south towards Texas. It was nice because we took two 11 man vans and only had 14 people on the trip so the drive was very comfortable.

We stopped in several spots throughout the day and finally 15 hours later we arrived in the famous town of Fort Davis! We were all shocked to actually be in Texas because our amusement for the entire ski season in Steamboat was making fun of Texan tourists. Since we were now tourists in Texas, we began acting like tourists. Immediately we busted out cameras and took pictures of anything and everything we could see.

5
Responding
Rhetorically

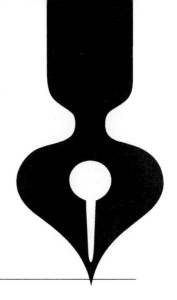

Praxis in Action: Why I Annotate Readings by Lauren Connolly

Annotating a reading gives me the ability to participate in a conversation with the author of the text in order to develop my ideas for writing and understanding the information presented. My annotation style uses two methods: one is with a pencil and the other is with a highlighter.

    As with a conversation, my side comments may be to protest the author's ideas or to make connections with other things in my life, other readings for the class, or my other classes. By making notes, I am actively participating in the conversation, opposed to passively taking in the information presented, and it gives me an opportunity to create something meaningful from the text. Using the highlighter sparingly, I only mark a word or phrase, in order to point out specific ideas or words that I want to reference, understand, or quote in my writing at a later point in time. The meaningful interaction is when, using a pencil, I write comments in the margins in response to these highlights. These comments are frequently a part of my prewriting stage, as I use my marginal comments directly in my early written drafts. Annotating allows me to respond, clarify, and develop my ideas about what I have learned, enabling me to use the ideas later in both my writing and research.

Lauren Connolly likes to annotate readings because it allows her to have a conversation with the writer.

Thinking Critically, Reading Rhetorically

In contemporary times we study texts to encourage students to develop critical thinking, a skill which is essential for understanding the scientific method and for making effective judgments in the workplace and in civil life. This student-centered emphasis would have seemed strange to ancient Greek and Roman rhetoricians and their students. They believed that a rhetor's skill was best developed by honoring the skills of those who excelled in the past. Therefore, a large part of the educational process involved having students study the texts of well-regarded speeches, memorize and recite them, and model new compositions based on their approaches to topics and language style. As Isocrates explained:

> Since language is of such a nature that it is possible to discourse on the same subject matter in many different ways—to represent the great as lowly or invest the little with grandeur, to recount the things of old in a new manner or set forth events of recent date in an old fashion—it follows that one must not shun the subjects upon which others have composed before, but must try to compose better than they . . . (Panegyricus).

Thus, students in ancient Greece or Rome would have been presented with a text, often read aloud by a teacher, and they would be asked to transcribe or copy it down with the idea that they would internalize the skills of the master rhetor who had originally given the speech. Then, they would be asked to write about the same subject in a way that built upon what they had learned from the master text but incorporated their own personal attitudes or perspectives.

Today, rather than being asked to model new compositions based upon the techniques of classic texts, students are asked to read texts carefully and then to engage in critical thinking and discussion about those texts.

Critical thinking involves considering issues thoughtfully and independently. Critical thinkers do not believe facts or opinions just because they are published—whether it is in newspapers, textbooks, on television, or on the Internet. Nor do they focus upon just understanding or memorizing information, as in facts and figures. Critical thinkers examine the reasoning of the information in front of them, looking for premises and considering the inferences drawn from those premises. They are able to think for themselves, making logical connections between ideas, seeing cause and effect relationships, and using information to solve problems.

Reading rhetorically makes use of critical thinking skills, but it also involves looking at texts as arguments and evaluating them for validity, adequacy of evidence, and presence of bias. Moreover, reading rhetorically involves having a knowledge of rhetoric and specialized Greek terms such as logos, pathos, ethos, and kairos—words that were defined briefly in Chapter 1 and will be discussed more extensively in Chapter 3. Practice reading rhetorically as you read the following article on the Strauss-Kahn sexual assault case.

Reading 5.1

In Sex-Crime Cases, Credibility a Thorny Issue by Paul Duggan. In 2011, Dominique Strauss-Kahn, the head of the International Monetary Fund (IMF), was accused of sexual assault by a housekeeper at the Sofitel New York hotel. He pled not guilty. During the case, the victim's credibility was called into question, as she had reportedly lied to the police in her first statement about the case. The following article, by Paul Duggan, published in The Washington Post, talks about the credibility of alleged victims in sex-crime cases, and how, in the Strauss-Kahn case, it could affect the outcome. To begin a critical reading of an article, you want to read the entire piece first for content. Then, reread the introduction. How does the author attempt to capture the audience's attention? How does the author use the Lanigan case as a frame of reference?

A wealthy public figure accused of sexual misconduct in a swanky hotel says that the charge is trumped up, that his alleged victim lacks credibility.

In their eagerness to bag a famous name, the defendant says, investigators have rushed to judgment. He says they have failed to carefully consider whether the woman who reported being accosted had a motive to lie.

That's what Dominque Strauss-Kahn says, through his attorneys.

And that's what lawyer A. Scott Bolden says. He represents Washington Redskins lineman Albert Haynesworth, awaiting trial on a misdemeanor charge that he indecently groped a waitress at the posh W Hotel in Washington.

"Let me tell you something about sex-crimes prosecutors," said Bolden, a former sex-crimes prosecutor. "They tend to be true believers. I mean, they've never met a victim they don't want to save or who they don't believe. . . . And when credibility issues arise, they tend to just want to explain them away."

As authorities Friday acknowledged doubts about the credibility of Strauss-Kahn's accuser in New York, and the rape case against the former head of the International Monetary Fund seemed in jeopardy, Bolden and other lawyers said the news highlights one of the thorniest issues in sex-crimes prosecutions:

Will jurors believe the alleged victim?

Sometimes the believability issue has nothing to do with the allegation itself. The witness may have a troubled past that could cast doubt on her testimony.

Harry O'Reilly, a retired New York City police detective who helped create the department's Special Victims Unit in the early 1970s—the unit that handled the Strauss-Kahn case—said investigators often deal with accusers who have less-than-savory backgrounds and who offer changing accounts of alleged assaults.

"It's quite common for there to be credibility issues," he said. He said detectives initially should focus only on whether the alleged crime occurred, and not be deterred by the woman's personal history, even if it involves dishonesty.

"If someone makes an allegation, we listen," he said. "And then we look for chinks in the story. And if the story begins to dissipate, then we go from there. But at the onset, we're not looking at things in her past that aren't relevant to the allegation."

Attorney Peter Greenspun, who defended Fairfax County teacher Sean Lanigan, acquitted this year of sexually molesting a 12-year-old female student, said authorities have to proceed in such cases with caution.

"These are the kinds of cases where the most care has to be exercised before anyone is charged, because of what allegations like this do to people," Greenspun said.

Jurors in the Fairfax trial later voiced outrage at the dearth of evidence against Lanigan, a married father of three whose life was shattered by the allegations.

"These are devastating charges," Greenspun said. "There's an assumption of guilt by the public, and reputations and life trajectories are destroyed."

In New York, prosecutors acknowledged that the hotel maid who accused Strauss-Kahn of raping her in his luxury suite May 14 later lied to investigators about her personal history and gave them inconsistent accounts of the moments after the alleged assault.

Strauss-Kahn, 62, who was arrested hours after the allegation and resigned from the IMF, was ordered released from home confinement in Manhattan on Friday. But the district attorney's office has not moved to dismiss the rape case.

"She said it happened, and he's sort of a pompous guy with a reputation . . . for grabbing women, so they thought, well, of course, it must have happened," Greenspun

said. He said police generally spend too little time investigating such cases before making arrests, especially when the suspects are prominent men.

Even if Strauss-Kahn's attorneys have information about his accuser that they could use in court to cast doubt on her veracity, prosecutors have a "moral obligation" to proceed with the case if they believe that the woman is being truthful, said lawyer Mai Fernandez, director of the National Center for Victims of Crime.

"You could have Attila the Hun come to you and say he's a victim, and the truth of the matter is, in this particular case, he may be," Fernandez said.

"You have to look first at the evidence that's directly related to the case at hand," she added. "The victim? Well, everybody has a past. None of us is without sin. There's always something that a defense lawyer can use to tarnish your reputation."

Kristina Korobov, a former prosecutor, agreed with Fernandez, but only to an extent.

"It's true that you can't just say to a victim, 'Well, you have a credibility problem, so too bad,' and then, based on that, you don't proceed with the case," Korobov said. "Because that just rewards offenders who choose victims with credibility problems."

In a case like Strauss-Kahn's, she said, prosecutors are probably weighing whether the woman's credibility is so badly damaged that a conviction would be highly unlikely.

"There were a number of victims in my lifetime who I legitimately believed had been victimized, but I didn't file a charge," said Korobov, now a senior attorney with the National Center for the Prosecution of Violence Against Women. "You've got to be very selective about what cases you bring, based on what you think you can prove."

Activity 5.1 **Explore:** Analyze a Text

In your small group, discuss the following questions and then report your group's opinion(s) to the class.
1. What is the problem that the author is concerned about in regard to prosecuting sex crimes?
2. What court cases does he mention? How was the victim's ethos involved?
3. How does the writer appeal to logos? To pathos?
4. If your group were writing a letter to the editor of the *Washington Post* commenting about this article, what might you say about the controversy the writer presents?

Rhetoric's Visual Heritage and Impact

The first televised presidential debate in September 1960 is a famous example of the power of visual rhetoric and a vivid illustration of the fact that visual elements must be considered when "reading" rhetorical situations. Radio listeners who could hear but not see the debate rated Vice President Richard Nixon as the winner over Senator John F. Kennedy—Nixon's arguments sounded more logical and were more clearly expressed. However, the television audience experienced a new element in the history of presidential debates: They could see the performances of the handsome and tan Senator Kennedy and the pasty-white and ill-looking Vice President Nixon, and they clearly preferred Kennedy. He *looked and acted presidential*, which overcame the drawbacks that had troubled his campaign previously—that he was relatively unknown, young, and Catholic. It overcame any advantage that Nixon may have had in presenting logical arguments and also by being an incumbent vice president. And unfortunately for Nixon, by 1960, 88 percent of Americans had televisions. "It's one of those unusual points on the timeline of history where you can say things changed very dramatically—in this case, in a single night," says Alan Schroeder, a media historian who authored the book, *Presidential Debates: Forty Years of High-Risk TV.*[1] Indeed, after the unexpected impact of the Kennedy-Nixon debates, presidential candidates were so apprehensive about competing on television that it was 16 years before candidates (President Gerald R. Ford and former Governor Jimmy Carter) were again willing to risk presenting themselves side by side on television.

Why did the experience of seeing the two candidates, rather than hearing them or reading their speeches, make such a difference? The ancient Greeks and Romans who developed rhetoric would have understood the reason: It was what they called ethos, which can be translated only imperfectly as credibility. A person's ethos is determined partially by his or her reputation, but as Richard Nixon learned the hard way, it is conveyed even more powerfully by appearance, gestures, tone, and cadence of speech. It is important to remember that the standards and perceptions of Americans are heavily influenced by rhetoric as it was defined and implemented by the Greeks and Romans—first in oral presentations.   Many of the attributes of rhetoric translate to written texts, but not all. Thus, when considering a text that was originally presented as a speech, reading rhetorically means thinking about visual rhetoric—the impact the speech would have had on an audience that was *watching and listening to the presentation*.

The first presidential debate between Vice President Richard Nixon and Senator John F. Kennedy illustrated the power of visual rhetoric.

1* Kayla Webley, "How the Nixon-Kennedy Debate Changed the World" *Breaking News, Analysis, Politics, Blogs, News Photos, Video, Tech Reviews,* September 23, 2010. http://www.time.com/time/nation/article/0,8599,2021078,00.html. Accessed July 30, 2011.

Moreover, the impact of visual rhetoric involves more than speeches: It concerns television shows, films, photographs, paintings, advertisements, and even the typesetting layout of a text that has no illustrations. We will consider these types of visual rhetoric in more detail later in this chapter.

On the next page, we reprint President Barack Obama's speech announcing the death of Osama bin Laden. This speech is available widely on the Internet at such sites as AmericanRhetoric.com, NYTimes.com, and YouTube.com. If possible, watch the speech before you read the text, and as you do so think about the impact of the speech, including the president's verbal presentation and the setting at the White House, as well as the content of the speech. Think about the various audiences President Obama was speaking to—Americans and people around the world who might be watching at that moment, as well as a historic audience of people such as yourself who would be viewing the speech months or years later.

The Rhetorical Triangle

When reading a text or listening to a speech, keep in mind the three parts of the rhetorical triangle—writer, audience, and subject (see figure 5.1). Each of these can be framed as a question:

- Who is the writer? What is the impression the writer wants to make on the audience? What does the writer do to establish credibility (ethos)? How does the writer create common ground with the audience?
- Who is the intended audience? How would a logical appeal influence the audience? An ethical appeal? An emotional appeal? What does the audience anticipate in terms of organization and format of the presentation or paper? What is the extent of their knowledge about the subject, and do they have prejudices or preferences?
- What is the purpose of the communication? In the case of an argument, the purpose would be to persuade. Is that the case with this reading? Is it clear what the writer wants to persuade the audience to believe or to do? Is the request phrased in a logical manner?

Figure 5.1

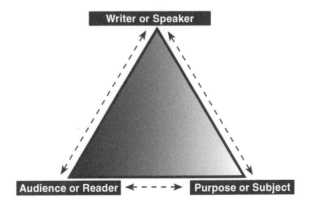

Activity 5.2 **Explore:** Apply the Rhetorical Triangle

For each of the readings presented thus far in the textbook, identify the speaker, the audience, and the purpose. Then analyze how each of those elements affects the content of the reading.

1. "Violent Rhetoric and Arizona Politics" (Chapter 4, p. 35)
2. "The Sleepover Question" (Chapter 4, p. 37)
3. "San Ysidro Shooting Survivor Lives His Dream of Being a Cop" (Chapter 4, p. 40)
4. "In Sex-Crime Cases, Credibility a Thorny Issue" (Chapter 5, p. 35)

Reading 5.2

President Barack Obama on the Death of Osama bin Laden

Good evening. Tonight, I can report to the American people and to the world that the United States has conducted an operation that killed Osama bin Laden, the leader of al Qaeda, and a terrorist who's responsible for the murder of thousands of innocent men, women, and children.

President Barack Obama announced the death of Osama bin Laden.

It was nearly 10 years ago that a bright September day was darkened by the worst attack on the American people in our history. The images of 9/11 are seared into our national memory— hijacked planes cutting through a cloudless September sky; the Twin Towers collapsing to the ground; black smoke billowing up from the Pentagon; the wreckage of Flight 93 in Shanksville, Pennsylvania, where the actions of heroic citizens saved even more heartbreak and destruction.

And yet we know that the worst images are those that were unseen to the world. The empty seat at the dinner table. Children who were forced to grow up without their mother or their father. Parents who would never know the feeling of their child's embrace. Nearly 3,000 citizens taken from us, leaving a gaping hole in our hearts.

On September 11, 2001, in our time of grief, the American people came together. We offered our neighbors a hand, and we offered the wounded our blood. We reaffirmed our ties to each other, and our love of community and country. On that day, no matter where we came from, what God we prayed to, or what race or ethnicity we were, we were united as one American family.

We were also united in our resolve to protect our nation and to bring those who committed this vicious attack to justice. We quickly learned that the 9/11 attacks were carried out by al Qaeda—an organization headed by Osama bin Laden, which had openly declared war on the United States and was committed to killing innocents in our country and around the globe. And so we went to war against al Qaeda to protect our citizens, our friends, and our allies.

Over the last 10 years, thanks to the tireless and heroic work of our military and our counterterrorism professionals, we've made great strides in that effort. We've disrupted terrorist attacks and strengthened our homeland defense. In Afghanistan,

we removed the Taliban government, which had given Bin Laden and al Qaeda safe haven and support. And around the globe, we worked with our friends and allies to capture or kill scores of al Qaeda terrorists, including several who were a part of the 9/11 plot.

Yet Osama bin Laden avoided capture and escaped across the Afghan border into Pakistan. Meanwhile, al Qaeda continued to operate from along that border and operate through its affiliates across the world. And so shortly after taking office, I directed Leon Panetta, the director of the CIA, to make the killing or capture of Bin Laden the top priority of our war against al Qaeda, even as we continued our broader efforts to disrupt, dismantle, and defeat his network.

Then, last August, after years of painstaking work by our intelligence community, I was briefed on a possible lead to Bin Laden. It was far from certain, and it took many months to run this thread to ground. I met repeatedly with my national security team as we developed more information about the possibility that we had located Bin Laden hiding within a compound deep inside of Pakistan. And finally, last week, I determined that we had enough intelligence to take action, and authorized an operation to get Osama bin Laden and bring him to justice.

Today, at my direction, the United States launched a targeted operation against that compound in Abbottabad, Pakistan. A small team of Americans carried out the operation with extraordinary courage and capability. No Americans were harmed. They took care to avoid civilian casualties. After a firefight, they killed Osama bin Laden and took custody of his body.

For over two decades, Bin Laden has been al Qaeda's leader and symbol, and has continued to plot attacks against our country and our friends and allies. The death of Bin Laden marks the most significant achievement to date in our nation's effort to defeat al Qaeda.

Yet his death does not mark the end of our effort. There's no doubt that al Qaeda will continue to pursue attacks against us. We must—and we will— remain vigilant at home and abroad.

As we do, we must also reaffirm that the United States is not—and never will be—at war with Islam. I've made clear, just as President Bush did shortly after 9/11, that our war is not against Islam. Bin Laden was not a Muslim leader; he was a mass murderer of Muslims. Indeed, al Qaeda has slaughtered scores of Muslims in many countries, including our own. So his demise should be welcomed by all who believe in peace and human dignity.

Over the years, I've repeatedly made clear that we would take action within Pakistan if we knew where Bin Laden was. That is what we've done. But it's important to note that our counterterrorism cooperation with Pakistan helped lead us to Bin Laden and the compound where he was hiding. Indeed, Bin Laden had declared war against Pakistan as well, and ordered attacks against the Pakistani people.

Tonight, I called President Zardari, and my team has also spoken with their Pakistani counterparts. They agree that this is a good and historic day for both of our nations. And going forward, it is essential that Pakistan continue to join us in the fight against al Qaeda and its affiliates.

The American people did not choose this fight. It came to our shores, and started with the senseless slaughter of our citizens. After nearly 10 years of service, struggle, and sacrifice, we know well the costs of war. These efforts weigh on me every time I, as Commander-in-Chief, have to sign a letter to a family that has lost a loved one, or look into the eyes of a service member who's been gravely wounded.

So Americans understand the costs of war. Yet as a country, we will never tolerate our security being threatened, nor stand idly by when our people have been killed. We will be relentless in defense of our citizens and our friends and allies. We will be true to the values that make us who we are. And on nights like this one, we can say to those families who have lost loved ones to al Qaeda's terror: Justice has been done.

Tonight, we give thanks to the countless intelligence and counterterrorism professionals who've worked tirelessly to achieve this outcome. The American people do not see their work, nor know their names. But tonight, they feel the satisfaction of their work and the result of their pursuit of justice.

We give thanks for the men who carried out this operation, for they exemplify the professionalism, patriotism, and unparalleled courage of those who serve our country. And they are part of a generation that has borne the heaviest share of the burden since that September day.

Finally, let me say to the families who lost loved ones on 9/11 that we have never forgotten your loss, nor wavered in our commitment to see that we do whatever it takes to prevent another attack on our shores.

And tonight, let us think back to the sense of unity that prevailed on 9/11. I know that it has, at times, frayed. Yet today's achievement is a testament to the greatness of our country and the determination of the American people.

The cause of securing our country is not complete. But tonight, we are once again reminded that America can do whatever we set our mind to. That is the story of our history, whether it's the pursuit of prosperity for our people, or the struggle for equality for all our citizens; our commitment to stand up for our values abroad, and our sacrifices to make the world a safer place.

Let us remember that we can do these things not just because of wealth or power, but because of who we are: one nation, under God, indivisible, with liberty and justice for all.

Thank you.

May God bless you.

And may God bless the United States of America.

Activity 5.3 **Collaborate:** Evaluate the President's Speech

After you have both watched President Obama's speech on the Internet and read the text, discuss these questions in your small group and then present the consensus of your group's answers to the class.

1. Discuss the president's presentation of the speech. Do you think the speech had a different impact on those who watched it on television versus those who heard it on the radio? What about those who neither saw nor heard it but rather read the speech?

2. How would you describe the president's tone, appearance, and mannerisms (all part of his ethos)? What about the location he chose for the speech and the timing just after news agencies had announced Bin Laden's death (the kairos)?

3. Summarize what the president says about the government's reasons for seeking Osama bin Laden and killing him. Does the president make a good argument for the necessity and importance of this act?
4. Notice that the president uses visual imagery in his speech. For example, in paragraph two, immediately after he announces his news, he refers to 9/11—"a bright September day was darkened by the worst attack on the American people in our history." What is the purpose of the visual descriptions in his speech?
5. Do you agree or disagree with what the president has to say? How so?

Activity 5.4 **Explore:** Research Reactions to President Obama's Speech

Using Google or another search engine, research the reactions to the president's speech announcing the death of Bin Laden.
1. In the days after the speech, what did the media report about the attack on Bin Laden's compound?
2. What were some American reactions to the speech and to the killing of Bin Laden?
3. What was the reaction around the world, both in Muslim and non-Muslim countries?
4. Did you learn anything during your research that surprised you? How so?

As your instructor directs, either discuss these questions in class or turn in written answers to the questions.

Reading 5.3

The Lexicon by Charles McGrath. A lexicon is a synonym for dictionary, thesaurus, and wordlist. Charles McGrath, in his New York Times essay, "The Lexicon," examines the changes that 9/11 wrought in the English language. The attack on the World Trade Center, unlike other world-changing violent events, hasn't yet created many new words, he decides. Rather, it has brought already-existing words to our everyday vocabulary—such as jihad, T.S.A. shoe bomber, and sleeper cell. These not-so-pretty words are the lexicon of 9/11.

Ground zero, sleeper cells, progressive vertical collapse: The most resonant phrases of 9/11 are imbued with what might be called antipoetry, a resistance to prettification.

Unlike some other momentous events in our history—World War II, say, or the Vietnam War—the attacks that took place on Sept. 11, 2001, have not particularly changed or enriched our vocabulary. Sometimes these things take a while. It wasn't until the 1960s, for example, that the term "holocaust," which used to mean any large-scale massacre, took on the specific connotations it has today. For now, though, you could argue that the events of 9/11 still seem so unfathomable that they have actually impoverished the language a little, leaving us with a vacuous phrase like **war on terror**, which manages to empty both "war" and "terror" of much their meaning, or the creepy, Nazi-sounding **homeland**, which seems a far less pleasant place to live than just plain America.

We do know a lot of words now that we probably should have known before, like **jihad, Taliban, mujahedeen** and **Al Qaeda**. And some that we'd just as soon forget, like **T.S.A., security checkpoint, shoe bomber** and **progressive vertical collapse**.

A term like **sleeper cell** probably sticks in our heads because it contains a tiny hint of embedded poetry, and for the same reason it's hard to forget those **72 black-eyed virgins** whom the terrorists believed they were on their way to meet. The "black-eyed" bit is a brilliant touch, even if it's probably a mistranslation.

But the most resonant phrases that have taken residence in our consciousness since that September morning are ones imbued with what might be called antipoetry, a resistance to metaphor or to prettification. **Ground zero**, for example—a term that originated with the Manhattan Project and was originally used in connection with nuclear explosions—seems particularly apt in this new context, with its sense of absolute finality, of a point that is both an end and a beginning and to which everything else refers.

And even **9/11** itself has a kind of rightness. No one says "September 11th" anymore as shorthand for that awful day. (To do so, a friend once joked, would be "so September 10th.") There's a pleasing, no-nonsense simplicity and precision to the expression—the same effect created by "24/7," only starker, and with none of the exaggeration. These four syllables are right at the end of language, where words turn into abstraction. Individually, they're just random, empty numbers, but yoked by that fateful slash they contain volumes. 9/11—everyone knows what that means, and to say any more would be pointless. Sometimes words fail.

Activity 5.5 **Compose:** Develop a Lexicon

Choose one of the following activities and create a lexicon as a group or individually:

1. Reread President Obama's speech about the death of Osama bin Laden. What words have become a more frequent part of the nation's vocabulary as a result of Bin Laden's actions? Al Qaeda and Taliban are two. Can you find others? Do an Internet search for Osama bin Laden, until you have five to seven words. Then write a 250 to 300 word essay, similar to McGrath's, in which you consider how Bin Laden's life and death have affected our country's vocabulary.

2. Do a search on the Internet for "new words." You will find lists of words and phrases that have been added to new editions of dictionaries. Examples may include such words as "aquascape," "soul patch," and "sandwich generation." Choose five to seven new words that are related to each other in some way. Create a lexicon of your own with a paragraph about each word that emphasizes the invention or recent history of the word. Give examples of each word's usage in blogs or other publications.

Ways of Reading Rhetorically

Reading theorist Louise Rosenblatt suggests a technique for analyzing written texts—particularly those with few visual cues other than words on paper or a computer screen. She says that we take the pattern of verbal signs left by the author and use them to recreate the text, not in the exact way the author perceived the text, but guided by it.

So, as we read, there is a constant stream of response to the text. However, Rosenblatt says that even as the reader is recreating the text, he or she is also reacting to it. Thus, there are two interacting streams of response involved as the person moves through the text. The reader, rather than being a passive receptor for the author's text, actually participates in the creative process during reading.

However, we read differently depending on the text and the occasion. For example, if you take a paperback novel on an airplane trip, you probably read simply for entertainment and to pass the time in the air. If you read *King Lear* for a literature class, you read for the plot, characterization, and other elements that you know will be discussed in class. If you read a chapter in your chemistry textbook before an exam, you are focusing on remembering concepts and details that might be on the test. Reading as a writer is another type of reading. You examine the text with an eye for the choices the writer made when crafting the text, such as whether the writer begins with a narrative introduction, a quote from a noted authority, or a startling statement. You notice, for example, what people are mentioned in the text, either as authorities or participants in activities.

Rosenblatt also makes a useful distinction between two main kinds of reading—aesthetic reading and efferent reading. In **aesthetic reading**, the reader is most interested in what happens "during the reading event, as he fixes his attention on the actual experience he is living through," according to Rosenblatt. Readers focus upon the ideas, images, and story of the text that evoke an aesthetic experience in the moment of reading. **Efferent readers**, in contrast, read to learn from the text, and, thus, according to Rosenblatt, "concentrate on the information, the concepts, the guides to action, that will be left with him when the reading is over."

Reading rhetorically is efferent reading, focusing not on the experience of reading but on the information the text conveys and upon the way an argument is established and supported in a text. Some arguments are written in an engaging style that is a pleasure to read, while others are written in a highly emotional tone that arouses a visceral response in the reader. A text that inspires aesthetic reading must sometimes be read several times in order for the reader to focus on the structure of the argument beneath the creative language.

Some theorists say that critical thinking is "thinking about thinking" or "reasoning about reasoning," and that is exactly what reading rhetorically involves—reasoning about whether or not a text presents a reasoned argument. A good way to begin reading rhetorically is to be aware of the essential elements of an argument and identify these elements in the text you are evaluating. See the Checklist of Essential Elements in an Argument presented below.

Checklist of Essential Elements in an Argument

√ *A debatable issue.* By definition, for a text to be an argument, there must be at least two sides that can be asserted and supported.

√ *A clearly stated position, claim statement, or thesis.* Arguments assert different kinds of claims, such as taking a position on an issue of fact, asserting a cause and effect relationship, declaring the value of some entity, or advocating a solution to a problem; but, in each case, after you read the argument, you should be able to restate or summarize the position, claim, or thesis in one or two sentences.

√ *An audience.* To evaluate an argument, you need to know the original intended audience or place of publication, so that you can decide if the argument takes into account the audience's attitudes, background, and other factors. Ask yourself, for example, if the writer is assuming too much or too little background knowledge on the part of the audience or if the writer is using language that assumes the reader's agreement on the issue when that assumption is not warranted.

√ *Evidence from reliable sources.* Quotes, statistics, and other evidence should be credited to reputable sources, even if your text is not a document that offers academic-style citations. The evidence should be sufficient to support the author's position or thesis.

√ *Acknowledgment of the opposing argument.* A good rhetorician does not ignore any potential weaknesses in the argument. It is better to acknowledge points in favor of the opposing argument and then, if possible, refute the opposition's strong points than it is to allow an audience to poke holes in an argument.

√ *A conclusion and/or call to action.* An argument can be concluded in a variety of effective ways, but it is important to note that it does, indeed, conclude. The conclusion can be a call to action on the part of the audience, but it should not be the beginning of an additional argument that is not supported by the evidence presented.

Reading 5.4

The Web Means the End of Forgetting by Jeffrey Rosen Several years ago, Stacy Snyder was a fairly typical 25-year-old college student training to be a teacher. That all changed forever when she did something that she probably thought was harmless fun—she posted a photo of herself on a social network site. In this article published in The New York Times, Jeffrey Rosen uses Snyder's case to illustrate how notions of privacy are changing because of the ever-growing presence and popularity of social networking sites. What is even more alarming, according to Rosen, is that photos and information, once posted on the web, are there forever. The web does not forget, and this lack of forgetting is changing society's ability to forgive and forget.
You may enjoy posting status updates about your life on a MySpace, Facebook, or Twitter account; however, with employers increasingly conducting background checks on such sites, it's very important to be careful about what you choose to post. This includes status updates, photographs, and videos. If you read the following article carefully, you may never look at social networking sites quite the same again.

Four years ago, Stacy Snyder, then a 25-year-old teacher in training at Conestoga Valley High School in Lancaster, Pa., posted a photo on her MySpace page that showed her at a party wearing a pirate hat and drinking from a plastic cup, with the caption "Drunken Pirate." After discovering the page, her supervisor at the high school told her the photo was "unprofessional," and the dean of Millersville University School of Education, where Snyder was enrolled, said she was promoting drinking in virtual view of her underage students. As a result, days before Snyder's scheduled graduation, the university denied her a teaching degree. Snyder sued, arguing that the university had violated her First Amendment rights by penalizing her for her (perfectly legal) after-hours behavior. But in 2008, a federal district judge rejected the claim, saying that because Snyder was a public employee whose photo didn't relate to matters of public concern, her "Drunken Pirate" post was not protected speech.

When historians of the future look back on the perils of the early digital age, Stacy Snyder may well be an icon. The problem she faced is only one example of a challenge that, in big and small ways, is confronting millions of people around the globe: how best to live our lives in a world where the Internet records everything and forgets nothing—where every online photo, status update, Twitter post and blog entry by and about us can be stored forever. With websites like LOL Facebook Moments, which collects and shares embarrassing personal revelations from Facebook users, ill-advised photos and online chatter are coming back to haunt people months or years after the fact.

Examples are proliferating daily: there was the 16-year-old British girl who was fired from her office job for complaining on Facebook, "I'm so totally bored!!"; there was the 66-year-old Canadian psychotherapist who tried to enter the United States but was turned away at the border—and barred permanently from visiting the country—after a border guard's Internet search found that the therapist had written an article in a philosophy journal describing his experiments 30 years ago with LSD. According to a recent survey by Microsoft, 75 percent of U.S. recruiters and human-resource professionals report that their companies require them to do online research about candidates, and many use a range of sites when scrutinizing applicants—including search engines, social networking sites, photo- and video-sharing sites, personal websites and blogs, Twitter and online gaming sites. Seventy percent of U.S. recruiters report that they have rejected candidates because of information found online, like photos and discussion-board conversations and membership in controversial groups.

Technological advances, of course, have often presented new threats to privacy. In 1890, in perhaps the most famous article on privacy ever written, Samuel Warren and Louis Brandeis complained that because of new technology—like the Kodak camera and the tabloid press—"gossip is no longer the resource of the idle and of the vicious but has become a trade." But the mild society gossip of the Gilded Age pales before the volume of revelations contained in the photos, video and chatter on social media sites and elsewhere across the Internet. Facebook, which surpassed MySpace in 2008 as the largest social-networking site, now has nearly 500 million members, or 22 percent of all Internet users, who spend more than 500 billion minutes a month on the site. Facebook users share more than 25 billion pieces of content each month (including news stories, blog posts and photos), and the average user creates 70 pieces of content a month. There are more than 100 million registered Twitter users, and the Library of Congress recently announced that it will be acquiring—and permanently storing—the entire archive of public Twitter posts since 2006.

In Brandeis's day—and until recently, in ours—you had to be a celebrity to be gossiped about in public: today all of us are learning to expect the scrutiny that used to be reserved for the famous and the infamous. A 26-year-old Manhattan woman told The New York Times that she was afraid of being tagged in online photos because it might reveal that she wears only two outfits when out on the town—a Lynyrd Skynyrd T-shirt or a basic black dress. "You have movie-star issues," she said, "and you're just a person."

We've known for years that the web allows for unprecedented voyeurism, exhibitionism and inadvertent indiscretion, but we are only beginning to understand the costs of an age in which so much of what we say, and of what others say about us, goes into our permanent—and public—digital files. The fact that the Internet never seems to forget is threatening, at an almost existential level, our ability to control our identities; to preserve the option of reinventing ourselves and starting anew; to overcome our checkered pasts.

In a recent book, "Delete: The Virtue of Forgetting in the Digital Age," the cyberscholar Viktor Mayer-Schönberger cites Stacy Snyder's case as a reminder of the importance of "societal forgetting." By "erasing external memories," he says in the book, "our society accepts that human beings evolve over time, that we have the capacity to learn from past experiences and adjust our behavior." In traditional societies, where missteps are observed but not necessarily recorded, the limits of human memory ensure that people's sins are eventually forgotten. By contrast, Mayer-Schönberger notes, a society in which everything is recorded "will forever tether us to all our past actions, making it impossible, in practice, to escape them." He concludes that "without some form of forgetting, forgiving becomes a difficult undertaking."

It's often said that we live in a permissive era, one with infinite second chances. But the truth is that for a great many people, the permanent memory bank of the web increasingly means there are no second chances—no opportunities to escape a scarlet letter in your digital past. Now the worst thing you've done is often the first thing everyone knows about you.

The Crisis—and the Solution?

Concern about these developments has intensified this year, as Facebook took steps to make the digital profiles of its users generally more public than private. Last December, the company announced that parts of user profiles that had previously been private—including every user's friends, relationship status and family relations—would become public and accessible to other users. Then in April, Facebook introduced an interactive system called Open Graph that can share your profile information and friends with the Facebook partner sites you visit.

What followed was an avalanche of criticism from users, privacy regulators and advocates around the world. Four Democratic senators—Charles Schumer of New York, Michael Bennet of Colorado, Mark Begich of Alaska and Al Franken of Minnesota—wrote to the chief executive of Facebook, Mark Zuckerberg, expressing concern about the "instant personalization" feature and the new privacy settings. In May, Facebook responded to all the criticism by introducing a new set of privacy controls that the company said would make it easier for users to understand what kind of information they were sharing in various contexts.

Facebook's partial retreat has not quieted the desire to do something about an urgent problem. All around the world, political leaders, scholars and citizens are searching for responses to the challenge of preserving control of our identities in a digital world that never forgets. Are the most promising solutions going to be technological? Legislative? Judicial? Ethical? A result of shifting social norms and cultural expectations? Or some mix of the above? Alex Türk, the French data protection commissioner, has called for a "constitutional right to oblivion" that would allow citizens to maintain a greater degree of anonymity online and in public places. In Argentina, the writers Alejandro Tortolini and Enrique Quagliano have started a campaign to "reinvent forgetting on the Internet," exploring a range of political and technological ways of making data disappear. In February, the European Union helped finance a campaign called "Think B4 U post!" that urges young people to consider the "potential consequences" of publishing photos of themselves or their friends without "thinking carefully" and asking permission. And in the United States, a group of technologists, legal scholars and cyberthinkers are exploring ways of recreating the possibility of digital forgetting. These approaches share the common goal of reconstructing a form of control over our identities: the ability to reinvent ourselves, to escape our pasts and to improve the selves that we present to the world. [. . .]

[. . .] In the near future, Internet searches for images are likely to be combined with social-network aggregator search engines, like today's Spokeo and Pipl, which combine data from online sources—including political contributions, blog posts, YouTube videos, web comments, real estate listings and photo albums. Increasingly these aggregator sites will rank people's public and private reputations, like the new website Unvarnished, a reputation marketplace where people can write anonymous reviews about anyone. In the Web 3.0 world, Michael Fertik, a Harvard Law School graduate, predicts people will be rated, assessed and scored based not on their creditworthiness but on their trustworthiness as good parents, good dates, good employees, good baby sitters or good insurance risks.

One legal option for responding to online setbacks to your reputation is to sue under current law. There's already a sharp rise in lawsuits known as Twittergation— that is, suits to force websites to remove slanderous or false posts. Last year, Courtney Love was sued for libel by the fashion designer Boudoir Queen for supposedly slanderous comments posted on Twitter, on Love's MySpace page and on the designer's online marketplace-feedback page. But even if you win a U.S. libel lawsuit, the website doesn't have to take the offending material down any more than a newspaper that has lost a libel suit has to remove the offending content from its archive.

Some scholars, therefore, have proposed creating new legal rights to force websites to remove false or slanderous statements. Cass Sunstein, the Obama administration's regulatory czar, suggests in his new book, "On Rumors," that there might be "a general right to demand retraction after a clear demonstration that a statement is both false and damaging." (If a newspaper or blogger refuses to post a retraction, they might be liable for damages.) Sunstein adds that websites might be required to take down false postings after receiving notice that they are false—an approach modeled on the Digital Millennium Copyright Act, which requires websites to remove content that supposedly infringes intellectual property rights after receiving a complaint.

As Stacy Snyder's "Drunken Pirate" photo suggests, however, many people aren't worried about false information posted by others—they're worried about true information they've posted about themselves when it is taken out of context or given undue weight. And defamation law doesn't apply to true information or statements of opinion. Some legal scholars want to expand the ability to sue over true but embarrassing violations of privacy—although it appears to be a quixotic goal.

Daniel Solove, a George Washington University law professor and author of the book, *The Future of Reputation*, says that laws forbidding people to breach confidences could be expanded to allow you to sue your Facebook friends if they share your embarrassing photos or posts in violation of your privacy settings. Expanding legal rights in this way, however, would run up against the First Amendment rights of others. Invoking the right to free speech, the U.S. Supreme Court has already held that the media can't be prohibited from publishing the name of a rape victim that they obtained from public records. Generally, American judges hold that if you disclose something to a few people, you can't stop them from sharing the information with the rest of the world.

That's one reason that the most promising solutions to the problem of embarrassing but true information online may be not legal but technological ones. Instead of suing after the damage is done (or hiring a firm to clean up our messes), we need to explore ways of preemptively making the offending words or pictures disappear.

Zuckerberg said in January to the founder of the publication TechCrunch that Facebook had an obligation to reflect "current social norms" that favored exposure over privacy. "People have really gotten comfortable not only sharing more information and different kinds but more openly and with more people, and that social norm is just something that has evolved over time," he said.

However, norms are already developing to recreate off-the-record spaces in public, with no photos, Twitter posts or blogging allowed. Milk and Honey, an exclusive bar on Manhattan's Lower East Side, requires potential members to sign an agreement promising not to blog about the bar's goings on or to post photos on social-networking sites, and other bars and nightclubs are adopting similar policies. I've been at dinners recently where someone has requested, in all seriousness, "Please don't tweet this"—a custom that is likely to spread.

But what happens when people transgress those norms, using Twitter or tagging photos in ways that cause us serious embarrassment? Can we imagine a world in which new norms develop that make it easier for people to forgive and forget one another's digital sins? [. . .]

[. . .] Perhaps society will become more forgiving of drunken Facebook pictures in the way Samuel Gosling, the University of Texas, Austin, psychology professor says he expects it might. And some may welcome the end of the segmented self, on the grounds that it will discourage bad behavior and hypocrisy: it's harder to have clandestine affairs when you're broadcasting your every move on Facebook, Twitter and Foursquare. But a humane society values privacy, because it allows people to cultivate different aspects of their personalities in different contexts; and at the moment, the enforced merging of identities that used to be separate is leaving many casualties in its wake. Stacy Snyder couldn't reconcile her "aspiring-teacher self" with her "having-a-few-drinks self": even the impression, correct or not, that she had a drink in a pirate hat at an off-campus party was enough to derail her teaching career.

That doesn't mean, however, that it had to derail her life. After taking down her MySpace profile, Snyder is understandably trying to maintain her privacy: her lawyer told me in a recent interview that she is now working in human resources; she did not respond to a request for comment. But her success as a human being who can change and evolve, learning from her mistakes and growing in wisdom, has nothing to do with the digital file she can never entirely escape. Our character, ultimately, can't be judged by strangers on the basis of our Facebook or Google profiles; it can be judged by only those who know us and have time to evaluate our strengths and weaknesses, face to face and in context, with insight and understanding. In the meantime, as all of us stumble over the challenges of living in a world without forgetting, we need to learn new forms of empathy, new ways of defining ourselves without reference to what others say about us and new ways of forgiving one another for the digital trails that will follow us forever.

Activity 5.6 **Explore** Discuss "The Web Means the End of Forgetting"

1. What is the significance of the title, "The Web Means the End of Forgetting"?
2. What does Jeffrey Rosen mean when he suggests that in the future Stacy Snyder may be an icon?
3. What is the main point in Jeffrey Rosen's main essay? What is he arguing?

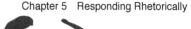

4. Does Rosen offer sufficient evidence to make you take his argument seriously? Why or why not?
5. Are you a member of any social networking sites? What can you do in order to protect your reputation?
6. A woman interviewed in the article said, in regard to being tagged in online photos, "you have movie-star issues—and you're just a person." If you are a member of any social networking sites, do you tag friends in photos? Is it important to be careful about this? Why or why not?

Activity 5.7 **Explore:** What Is the Current State of Identity Protection in Social Networking Sites?

In your group, explore news, watchdog, and government sites to see if any new laws or other protections have been implemented to safeguard individuals posting personal information on the web. Report what you learn to the class.

Close Reading of a Text

Rhetorical reading involves careful and patient attention to the text, even reading the text several times. Following are several strategies for reading critically. You do not need to use all of the reading strategies suggested for each essay you read, but as you begin to read critically, you should try all of the strategies at least once to see which ones supplement your natural reading and learning style.

1. **Learn about the author.** Knowing whether an author is a biologist, a professional writer, or a politician can guide your expectations of the essay. If you are reading in a magazine or journal, you can often discover information in the contributor's notes at the beginning or end of the essay or at the beginning or end of the magazine. Many books have a dust jacket or a page giving a short biography of the author. As you learn about the author, jot down any impressions you may have about the author's purpose in writing the essay. Does the author have an obvious agenda in promoting a certain viewpoint on the topic?

2. **Skim the text.** Once you've gotten to know the author a little, it is helpful to read the essay quickly and superficially by reading the introduction, the first sentence in every paragraph, and the conclusion. Read quickly. When you skim a text, you are not trying to understand it. You are preparing for the more careful read that will follow. If the essay tells a story, skimming will give you a good sense of the chronology of the story. When is the story taking place? How much time seems to pass? If the essay is argumentative, skimming will provide knowledge of the basic structure of the argument and will introduce you to the main points of support. If the essay is primarily informative, you will learn some of the important distinctions and classifications the author uses to organize the information.

    It may be interesting to note whether you can get the gist of the reading by skimming. Has the writer provided topic sentences for paragraphs or sections? If so, the writer is trying to make his or her message easily accessible.

3. **Explore your own knowledge and beliefs on the subject.** Make a list of what you already know about the topic of the text. Then make a list of what you believe

about this topic. Finally, make a note beside each entry that marks where that information or belief came from.

4. **Reflect on the topic.** The final step before reading is reflecting on what you expect from the essay before you begin a careful reading. What does the title lead you to expect from the essay? Does your quick glance at the essay seem to support the title? How do you feel about the essay so far? Does it anger you, interest you, bore you? Do you think you have any experience that relates to the essay? Will your experience and the author's experience lead you to the same conclusions? One effective way to reflect is to freewrite on the topic of the essay. Exploring what you know before you embark on a careful reading of the essay can deepen your responses.

5. **Annotate.** Read the essay slowly, thinking about what meaning the author is trying to convey. It is a good idea to annotate as you read, particularly points that seem important and/or raise questions in your mind. If you don't want to write in your text, try photocopying assigned essays so you can annotate them. You'll probably develop your own system of annotation as you begin to use this technique more often, but here are some basic guidelines to help you begin your annotations:

   • Underline sentences, phrases, and words that seem important to the essay.

   • Circle words you don't know but think you understand from the context. Then you can look them up later to see if the dictionary definition matches the definition you assumed from the context.

   • Write questions in the margins. If the margins aren't large enough to write a complete question, a couple of words to remind you of what you were thinking and a question mark will do. You can also write brief comments in the margins, again just a few words to remind you of your thoughts.

   • Number or put check marks in the margin by major points. Careful annotation of each point in the margin will help you later if you choose to outline.

   • Use arrows, lines, and symbols in the margins to connect ideas in the essay that seem related or depend on each other.

   • Note transitions, sentence structures, examples, topic sentences, and other rhetorical moves that seem particularly effective in the essay by writing a brief comment or an exclamation mark in the margin next to the underlined text.

   See figure 5.2 on page 60 for an example of an annotated article.

6. **Outline.** An excellent way to distill the meaning of a text is to create an informal outline of the argument. If, as part of annotating the essay, you jot down the main subject of each paragraph in the margin, this will allow you to see the organization of the essay and outline it easily. An outline should list the focus of the essay and track how that focus unfolds paragraph by paragraph. If you are outlining a narrative essay, the outline will probably follow the chronology of the events. Outlining an informative essay, you might find that the outline tracks the steps of a process or reveals divisions and classifications. Outlining an argumentative essay, you'll probably find your outline works to prove a thesis by making statements which support that thesis, raising objections and refuting them, or, perhaps, proposing solutions to solve a problem.

7. **Freewrite about the text.** Another way to distill the meaning of a text after you have read it carefully is to lay the essay aside and freewrite for a few minutes about the content and purpose of the essay. If you have not tried freewriting

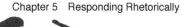

before, it is easy. You simply put your pen to the paper, focus the topic in your mind, and write whatever comes to mind about the topic for a set period of time, perhaps five minutes. If you cannot think of anything to write, you write, "I can't think of anything to write," and then you continue writing what is in your mind. You may find it helpful to begin your freewriting by writing, "This essay is about . . ." and continue writing, explaining to yourself what you think the essay is about.

8. **Summarize the text.** Write a summary of what you consider to be the primary meaning of the text. Your summary should answer these questions about claims, support, purpose, and audience:

- What is the author of the essay trying to show or prove (claim)?

- What does the writer use to convince me that he or she is well informed or right (support)?

- Why did the writer choose to write this essay (purpose)?

- Who is the author addressing or writing for (audience)?

To write a clear summary, you have to understand the essay. You might test your understanding by reading the essay again and deciding whether your summary is accurate. Writing summaries helps you understand your assignments and prepares you for the numerous summaries you will complete.

Responding to Oral and Visual Media

Increasingly, young "politically minded viewers" are plugging into YouTube, Facebook, and comedy shows like "The Daily Show" and other alternative media instead of traditional news outlets. According to a *New York Times* article, surveys and interviews during the 2008 presidential election indicate that "younger voters tend to be not just consumers of news and current events but conduits as well—sending out e-mailed links and videos to friends and their social networks. And in turn, they rely on friends and online connections for news to come to them." **Word of mouth** (via e-mail) is replacing traditional media as the major news filter, at least for young viewers. In this new process, moreover, "viewers" or "writers of e-mail" move seamlessly back and forth between e-mail, text-messaging, television viewing, and Internet surfing, appreciating and sharing the choicest rhetorical pieces with others. "We're talking about a generation that doesn't just like seeing the video in addition to the story—they expect it," said Danny Shea, 23, the associate media editor for *The Huffington Post* (huffingtonpost.com). "And they'll find it elsewhere if you don't give it to them, and then that's the link that's going to be passed around over e-mail and instant message." This multistream, cross-platform method of communication among younger viewers/readers is a fertile forum for rhetorical analysis.

Actually, the lines between oral, written, and visual "texts" have always been somewhat blurred. Speeches delivered orally in person or on television have a visual component, as the audience sees the speaker present the text. A written text is also, in a sense, visual because the audience's mind must process the little squiggles of ink on paper or on the computer screen into words. A visual text such as an advertisement or cartoon often includes written text, and, even if it does not, the image will inspire thoughts that are often distilled into language for expression. Reasonably, many of the same techniques used to analyze written and oral texts also can be applied to visual media (cartoons, advertisements, television, etc.).

Good evening. Tonight, I can report to the American people and to the world that the United States has conducted an operation that killed Osama bin Laden, the leader of al Qaeda, and a terrorist who's responsible for the murder of thousands of innocent men, women, and children.

It was nearly 10 years ago that a bright September day was darkened by the worst attack on the American people in our history. The images of 9/11 are seared into our national memory— hijacked planes cutting through a cloudless September sky; the Twin Towers collapsing to the ground; black smoke billowing up from the Pentagon; the wreckage of Flight 93 in Shanksville, Pennsylvania, where the actions of heroic citizens saved even more heartbreak and destruction.

President Barack Obama announced the death of Osama bin Laden.

And yet we know that the worst images are those that were unseen to the world. The empty seat at the dinner table. Children who were forced to grow up without their mother or their father. Parents who would never know the

---

Reading 5.5

Let's Roll by Neil Young Music lyrics are performance texts, just as are speeches. They are written to be heard, not written to be read. However, you can analyze the argument in song lyrics, such as "Let's Roll," reprinted here, which was written by Neil Young. The song was inspired by the last words of a passenger named Todd Beamer, who died in the hijacking of Flight 93 on September 11, 2001. To analyze the song's lyrics rhetorically, you can consider whether the lyrics have a debatable issue, a clear thesis or claim, evidence to support that claim, a particular audience, and a conclusion. With a song, moreover, you can also consider the impact of the lyrics as they are presented by a vocalist accompanied by musical instruments. How does the musical presentation of the lyrics affect their impact as an argument?

I know I said I love you,

I know you know it's true,
I've got to put the phone down,
and do what we got to do.

One's standing in the aisleway,
Two more at the door,
We've got to get inside there,
Before they kill some more.

Time is runnin' out,
Let's roll.
Time is runnin' out,
Let's roll.

No time for indecision,
We've got to make a move,
I hope that we're forgiven,
For what we got to do

How this all got started,
I'll never understand,
I hope someone can fly this thing,
And get us back to land.

Time is runnin' out,
Let's roll.
Time is runnin' out,
Let's roll.

No one has the answer,
But one thing is true,
You've got to turn on evil,
When it's coming after you,
You've gotta face it down,
And when it tries to hide,
You've gotta go in after it,
And never be denied,

Time is runnin' out,
Let's roll.

Let's roll for freedom,
Let's roll for love,
We're going after Satan,
On the wings of a dove,
Let's roll for justice,
Let's roll for truth,
Let's not let our children,
Grow up fearful in their youth.

Time is runnin' out,
Let's roll.
Time is runnin' out,
Let's roll.
Time is runnin' out,
Let's roll.

Activity 5.8 **Explore:** Respond to Song Lyrics

1. Reflect on what you know about the September 11 attacks. At the end of the first stanza, Young writes, "I've got to put the phone down, and do what we got to do." What is the call to action he is making here? What rhetorical significance does it have in this historical context?
2. Who is Young referring to when he says, "We're going after Satan"? What action is he advocating?

Activity 5.9 **Collaborate:** Consider a Song as an Argument

In your small group, explore the Internet for a song that seems to make an argument, and answer the following questions. Share your findings with the class.

1. What message is the artist/group trying to transmit with the song?
2. What are some lyrics that help to support this message?
3. How would you describe the musical style of the song? In what ways does the style of singing and instrumentation help the rhetorical message?

Responding to Visual Rhetoric

Methods of analyzing visual rhetoric draw upon several theoretical traditions. In art criticism, viewers may look for symbolism in an image or consider what meaning the artist was trying to convey. Semiotics views images as having intertextuality, as similar images come to have similar meanings, and those meanings may create similar emotions in the viewer. Rhetoricians, as you might expect, consider the argument that an image may present to a viewer. They think about how the subject of the image is presented in relation to other elements in the visual, how the image is cropped, and what types of lighting and colors are present. Rhetoricians also pay particular attention to the interplay between the visual image and any text that may appear with the image and how the two together construct an argument.

In the BMW advertisement shown above, for example, a beautiful blonde-haired young woman is presented without

Courtesy BMW premium advertising.

clothes and lying down with her hair artfully arranged in waves. *Salon* magazine reprinted a copy of the BMW advertisement, pointing out that, "in small print scrawled across her bare shoulder, it reads: 'You know you're not the first.' As your eyes drift to the bottom of the advertisement—and the top of her chest—you learn that it's an advertisement for BMW's premium selection of used cars."

Of course, sexual appeal has been used for decades to sell a whole range of products. However, what do you think is BMW's argument here? *Salon* thinks the ad is implying, "Used cars, used women" and that the ad gives a "whole new meaning" to BMW's slogan, printed in the ad: "Sheer Driving Pleasure."

The image that appears below, surprisingly, isn't advertising a car. No, it is selling a community college, West Hills College, capitalizing on the idea that with all the money you would save by going to a community college, you could buy a nice car.

"YOU'D BE AMAZED WHAT YOU CAN LEARN ᵥIN TWO YEARS."
and save

Two years at West Hills College: $600

vs.

Two years at a UC school: $28,000*

Why not spend $27,400 on something else?

ONCE YOU GO HERE, YOU CAN GO ANYWHERE.

1-800-266-1114 or www.westhillscollege.com

WEST HILLS COMMUNITY COLLEGE DISTRICT

COALINGA   LEMOORE   FIREBAUGH

Courtesy West Hills College

Activity 5.10 **Explore:** Interpret Advertisements

1. What is the symbolism of the beautiful young woman (presumably naked) posed as she is in the BMW advertisement?
2. What meaning do you think the tag line, "You know you're not the first," adds to the image? Then, when you realize that the image is an ad for BMW used cars, does your interpretation of this tag line's meaning change?
3. What are the creators of the West Hills College advertisement trying to say by showing the image of the student sitting on the car?
4. The use of fonts is another important element in transmitting a message in an advertisement. In the West Hills College ad, why are the words "and save" written in a different font and inserted with the caret?
5. As a college student, would you be convinced by the West Hills advertisement? Why or why not? What elements exist in the ad that would or would not convince you to attend the college mentioned?
6. Do you find the BMW advertisement amusing, objectionable, or appealing? Does it make you want to buy a used BMW?

Activity 5.11 **Collaborate:** Find Advertisements with Effective Arguments

Bring to class an advertisement that you think makes an effective argument. It can be torn from a magazine or downloaded from the Internet. In your small group, evaluate each advertisement for its effectiveness in selling something, and choose the one with the most effective argument. Present your choice to the class along with an explanation of why you think it is effective.

Interaction between Texts and Images

Many of the texts we encounter in everyday life—in newspapers, magazines, and on the Internet—are not texts in isolation but texts combined with images. Indeed, when readers first glance at one of these media, likely their attention is caught first by photos, then by headlines. Only after being engaged by these attention-getting visual elements (for headlines are visual elements as well as written) are readers likely to focus on the written text. Student writers today, like professionals, have access to the use of visual elements in their compositions, and adding photos can not only catch the reader's attention but also emphasize particular points of an argument or create an overall mood.

All-Star Rockers Salute Buddy Holly

McCartney, Cee Lo, the Black Keys, Kid Rock and more cut killer covers disc

When Buddy Holly died in a plane crash in 1959, he was just 22 years old and had been writing and recording songs for only about two years. But that music—including immortal hits like "Not Fade Away" and "Peggy Sue"—has had an incalculable impact on rock history. "He was a major influence on the Beatles," Paul McCartney told Rolling Stone recently. "John and I spent hours trying to work out how to play the opening riff to "That'll Be the Day," and we were truly blessed by the heavens the day we figured it out. It was the first song John, George and I ever recorded."

A half-century later, McCartney has returned to Holly's catalog, cutting a smoking rendition of "It's So Easy." It's one of 19 newly recorded Holly covers—by an all-star lineup including the Black Keys, My Morning Jacket, Kid Rock Fiona Apple, Patti Smith, and Lou Reed—for the tribute

NOT FADE AWAY
Holly in 1958. McCartney and Cee Lo recorded new covers commemorating Holly's 75th birthday.

disc *Rave on Buddy Holly*, spearheaded by Randall Poster, music supervisor of movies such as *The Royal Tenenbaums* and *I'm Not There*. "We wanted to commemorate Buddy's 75th birthday," Poster says. "I've used a lot of his songs in movies, and they're so powerful and so ripe for interpretation."

Florence and the Machine cut a New Orleans-flavored version of "Not Fade Away" while on tour in the Big Easy last year. "My grandmother took me to the musical *Buddy: The Buddy Holly Story* when I was a kid, and it changed my life," says singer Florence Welch. "When we were in New Orleans, we decided it would be good to use the environment around us, so we brought in local Cajun musicians." Cee Lo Green tackled the relatively obscure "You're So Square (Baby, I Don't Care)." "We wanted to keep the rockabilly intact," he says. "But we broadened it and gave it a bit of something unique to me. There's something Americana about it, something country and something African." Smith selected "Words of Love." "During the song she talks in Spanish and is sort of channeling [Holly's widow] Maria Elena Holly," says Poster. "It's so romantic and so novel. More times than not, we were just overwhelmed by the power of the renditions that we received." Despite Holly's extremely brief career, Poster thinks the set could have been even longer: "There's probably a half-dozen more songs we could have done. If I had more time and more of a budget, I would have kept on going."   ANDY GREENE

Activity 5.12 **Explore:** Analyze Interaction between Texts and Images

Read the article, "All-Star Rockers Salute Buddy Holly," by Andy Greene, published in **Rolling Stone** magazine. Look at how the images and layout work together and answer the questions:

1. What rhetorical purpose do the photos of these musicians achieve in relation to the article? Hint: think about the ethos (credibility, reputation, power) of these particular musicians, especially when they appear together on the page.
2. Consider the way the text is wrapped around the pictures. In particular, notice how this layout suggests a close relationship between Buddy Holly, Paul McCartney, and Cee Lo Green. What does this layout signify?

Activity 5.13 **Compose:** Write a Summary

Summarizing is an excellent technique to use when preparing for an exam or researching for an essay. It allows you to discern the main points of a text to see what is beneficial for you to know for the exam or paper. With a classmate, search for an article from a newspaper or magazine that presents a strong argument. Read the article, and list the main points individually. After you've listed the main points, put them into paragraph form. Caution: Beware of the temptation to add your own analysis of what the text is saying. For example, if you are summarizing a scientist's article on global warming, you need to be careful not to reveal your personal opinion about whether or not global warming is occurring or whether or not human actions are to blame. In this assignment, you summarize only. You do not argue or analyze.

When you're finished, compare your summary with that of your partner.

Reading 5.7

How to Make a Kindle Cover from a Hollowed Out Hardback Book by Justin Meyers The author of the following article explains why you would want to make a Kindle cover out of an old book instead of buying a new Kindle cover. What does the article say are the drawbacks of the Kindle? Think about it. These instructions are an argument, saying in text and photos that as wonderful as the Kindle is, it does not satisfy the needs of a reader to touch and smell a book. The author attempts to rectify the Kindle's shortcomings through these instructions for making a cover out of a book.

Notice also how the author uses photos to illustrate his text. If you had just the text and no photos, following the instructions would be much more difficult.

Kindle users love reading. But let's face it—nothing compares to the feel of a book is in your hands.

Sure, Amazon's Kindle makes it possible to read more books, clears up a lot of shelf space, fits snugly in anyone's baggage and can actually be cheaper in the long run. But each reading feels the same. The only difference is the words you read and your reaction to them. You begin to miss that sometimes rough feel of a hardback book, along with the slick, almost slippery design of a paperback. Each book seems to have a smell of its own, something unique. And getting your hands dirty with ink from the finely written words was half the journey.

The Kindle erases that part of your reading experience. It feels the same, smells the same and even looks the same. Instead of turning pages, which is different sizes, thicknesses and colors from book to book, you're pressing the same button over and over again. In some ways, reading a classic on your Kindle actually devalues its adventure. But the eBook reader is convenient, practically weightless and serves up immediate literature consumption.

So where's the compromise?

Well, you can have the best of both worlds—sort of . . .

ebonical has crafted the perfect Kindle case—out of a hardcover book. Kindle cases can be expensive, so making a homemade Kindle cover is the perfect weekend project. And chances are you already have the perfect book for your Kindle collecting dust on your bookshelf. If not, you'll need to shop the local bookstores.

"I decided to carve out the pages of a printed book and thus complete the poetic circle of digital book readers destroying the printed word.

"Getting the right book turned out to be harder than I thought as most hardcover books are designed to be a particular size and variance is slight. Too small and the edges would be brittle. Too large and it would just become a hassle and ruin the point of having the small digital reader in the first place. With some time spent scouring thrift shops and second hand book stalls I managed, with some luck, to find what seemed to be the right book."

So, then how do you actually make the Kindle book cover?

STEP 1 Gather the Materials

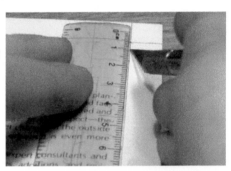

- Your perfectly-sized hardcover book
- Hobby PVA glue (polyvinyl acetate) or Elmer's white glue
- Paintbrush
- Scalpel, box cutter or other sharp utility knife
- Ruler
- Pencil
- More books (for use as weights)

STEP 2 Crafting Your Kindle Case

Getting your book ready for your Kindle is an easy process, though a lengthy one.

You begin by choosing where you want your hole to start. Once you have your spot picked, you use the paintbrush to spread the glue onto the edges of the pages where the hole will be cut. Use your extra books to weigh it down during the drying process.

When dry, open the book back up to your chosen starting point. Use the ruler and pencil to mark your hole the size of the Kindle. Once all marked, use your utility knife to start cutting on the outline. It's probably best to use your ruler as a straight edge to help guide the blade along, for a better, straighter cut. This is the longest step, because you have a lot to cut through. The time will vary depending on how deep your book is. I wouldn't recommend *War and Peace*.

Once you've gotten all the way to the back cover, the rest is easy. Just clean up the edges of your cuts as best you can, then use your paintbrush again to spread some glue along the cut edges.

TIP: When choosing your first page to cut, it's good to actually save it for later. Don't cut with the rest of them. When you have your hole fully cut open and have applied the glue, apply another thin line on the top border of your actual first page cut (essentially, the second page). Then close the book and add the weights to the top and let dry. Saving the first page helps reduce the chance of you accidentally gluing unwanted pages to cut ones, causing you to have to cut the pages you didn't want to cut to open the hole back up. Saving your first page makes it premeditated.

After fully dried, open it up and cut the final page (first page) to open the hole up. Then, you'll need to let it dry again, with the book open. After dried, that's it. You're done!

Activity 5.14 **Compose:** Write and Illustrate Instructions

Write and illustrate your own set of instructions for an activity that includes an argument. For example, during a lawn party at the White House, First Lady Michelle Obama served Carrot Lemonade to children who gave the drink rave reviews. Such a recipe could include an introduction explaining that creating healthy adaptations of popular foods and drinks for children only works if they taste good. Or, you might write instructions for how to remove geotags from photos before posting them on Facebook or other social networking sites. In your instructions you could explain that this process prevents people that you don't know from learning where you took the picture—and possibly learning where you live if you took it at home. Your argument would be that it is important to protect your privacy when you post photos on the Internet.

Try out your instructions on a friend, so you are sure you have included all the necessary steps and illustrated them adequately. Don't forget to include a brief statement of your argument, as does the writer of the Kindle cover article.

Activity 5.15 **Compose:** Create Your Own Blog

Read an article on the Internet related to a topic in which you're interested. Make sure the article has a substantial amount of text, as well as related images. In your blog, discuss how the text and the images both contribute to the article's rhetorical message. Include the title of the article, the author, the name of the publication or web page, and a link to the article.

Activity 5.16 **Compose:** Write in Your Commonplace Book

What do you read for fun? Magazines, blogs, books? Do you engage in what Louise Rosenblatt calls "aesthetic reading"? (See the section titled, "Ways of Reading Rhetorically") Write down a quote in your commonplace book from something that you have read for fun. First, reflect about what the quote means to you. Then, comment about why it is important to read things for fun and how that experience is different than reading to learn.

6
Analyzing Rhetorically

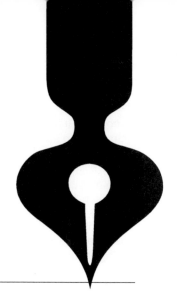

Praxis in Action: Analyzing Arguments Improves My Writing by Eurydice Saucedo

Reading enables my creative mind to soar to undreamed-of worlds, to visit the deepest of memories, and to laugh as words describe a child's joy. Yes, reading enables me to be a bigger dreamer, but it also opens my eyes to better understand this world we live in.

Eurydice Saucedo writes, "Every text, just like everything else in life, needs to be taken with a grain of salt, slowly simmered, and thought about before the final evaluation can be made."

Reading essays teaches me definitions and meanings, and, with practice, allows me to discern the validity and reliability of arguments. I can distinguish between fair representation of an issue, embellishment of truth, and bitter sarcasm. Every sentence has more than just simple grammar and punctuation. Every text, just like everything else in life, needs to be taken with a grain of salt, slowly simmered, and thought about before the final evaluation can be made. If I know rhetorical concepts, I can recognize when a text is trying to persuade me of something, and I can decide if the writer presents a good argument and sufficient evidence to merit serious consideration.

Reading and analyzing texts helps me learn how to structure my own argument. I may find a flaw in an argument, for example, a lack of acknowledgement of a counterargument that causes me to distrust a text. This causes me to be more careful to include the counterargument in my own text. And when I read and reread a classic argument such as Martin Luther King's "I Have a Dream" speech, I may make note of a strategy that I can use later. For example, Dr. King's adapting of President Lincoln's memorable language, saying, "five score years ago" instead of Lincoln's "four score and seven years ago" is highly effective. Perhaps I will try adapting a highly memorable quote when it fits in my argument.

One of the best ways to become a better writer is to read good writing.

Discover the Kairos–The Opening for Argument

Kairos is a Greek word often translated as the right or opportune moment to do something, though it has no exact English translation. The first recorded use of the word kairos is in Homer's *Iliad*, where it appears as an adjective referring to an arrow striking the "deadliest spot" on the human body. When the word appears again later in Greek writing as a noun—a kairos— it retains this essential meaning as an opening or aperture. Twelve bronze axes with ring openings for wooden shanks are positioned in a line, so archers can practice by aiming at the kairos or ring opening, with the arrow passing down the line, through each ax. Clearly, launching an arrow through the kairos of twelve axes placed a yard apart required strength, training, practice, and a precise visual and muscle awareness of place. When people today say, "I saw my opening, and I took it, " they are conveying this meaning of kairos as an opening, combined with the idea of kairos as an opportunity.[1]

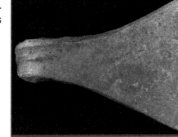

Ancient Greek archer

Ancient bronze ax with a ring hole for a wooden shank

Each time a rhetor (a speaker or writer) constructs an argument, he or she is working within a context of a certain moment, a particular time and place, that come together in a unique opportunity or opening for action—a kairos. A kairos both constrains and enables what a rhetor can say or write effectively in a particular situation. So, to compose the most effective text, a rhetor must do more than develop a thesis or statement of the main idea that takes a position about the subject—he or she must discover the kairos of the argument and its ramifications. What opportunities does the kairos present for making a persuasive argument, and what restrictions may be wise in consideration of the audience or occasion?

Use Kairos to Make Your Own Argument

Consider the following suggestions for determining the kairotic moment for your argument—the opening of sensitivity where you can shoot your metaphoric arrow:

- *Consider timeliness.* What is going on right now with the issue and how can you emphasize that in an argument? For example, if you are writing about the death penalty, choose to write about the current cases on death row or the most recent person to be executed. Or, if your topic is about the unemployed exhausting their government benefits and you have, yourself, recently become unemployed, you can use your own experience as an illustration of the problem.

- *Know your audience.* What are the characteristics of the audience? Do they agree with your position on the issue or not? What is their educational level and the extent of their knowledge about the subject? For example, if you are writing about immigration policy reform, does your audience believe there is a need for

---

[1] Thomas Rickert, "Invention in the Wild: On Locating Kairos in Space-Time," in *The Locations of Composition.* eds. Christopher J. Keller and Christian R. Weisser (Albany: SUNY Press, 2007) pp. 72–76.

reform? Do they have personal experience with illegal or legal immigrants? You can judge the amount of background information you need to provide based upon the characteristics of your audience. Also, the most important members of the audience, so far as an argument is concerned, are not those who already agree with you but those who are neutral or even slightly opposed to your position but willing to listen. Be careful not to phrase your argument in ways that are insulting to people who do not agree with you, for if you do so, they will stop listening to you.

- *Find a place to stand.* In the reading that follows, Martin Luther King, Jr., stood in front of the Lincoln Memorial as he gave his famous speech, "I Have a Dream." This location greatly impacts the speech and increases King's ethos, which we discuss in more detail below. You can make a similar rhetorical move, for example, if you live in a border community because you stand, metaphorically and physically, at an important juncture for issues such as immigration, free trade, and national security.

When Martin Luther King, Jr., gave his "I Have a Dream" speech, his words were carefully crafted to take into consideration the setting in front of the Lincoln Memorial. He said, "Five score years ago, a great American, in whose symbolic shadow we stand today, signed the Emancipation Proclamation." The words "five score" recall the "four score and seven years ago" of Lincoln's words in the Gettysburg Address. And King also pointed out that he and his audience that day stood in the "symbolic shadow" of the president who signed the Emancipation Proclamation. In these ways, he made use of Lincoln's shadow to legitimize what he was saying about civil rights.

In other ways, however, the kairos of the moment limited what he could say. His audience included both the thousands of people in front of him who were dedicated to the cause of racial equality and also the audience of those millions watching on television who may or may not have agreed with his message. Thus, the tone of his message needed to be subtly measured not to antagonize those among his audience, particularly the television audience, who may have opposed aspects of the civil rights movement such as school integration. However, he spoke to let both his supporters and his opponents know, "The whirlwinds of revolt will continue to shake the foundations of our nation until the bright day of justice emerges." Yes, King advocated nonviolent demonstrations, but they were demonstrations nonetheless; he was putting opponents on notice that the disruptions caused by demonstrations would continue "until justice emerges." King consistently took the high road, while maintaining the power of the kairotic moment when he spoke. This is one reason why his words continue to be studied decades after his death.

Reading 6.1

I Have a Dream by Martin Luther King, Jr. Martin Luther King, Jr., delivered this speech on August 28, 1963, at the Lincoln Memorial in Washington, D.C., as part of the March on Washington for Jobs and Freedom. A Baptist minister, King received the Nobel Peace Prize in 1964 for his efforts to end racial discrimination through nonviolent means. He was assassinated in 1968.

I am happy to join with you today in what will go down in history as the greatest demonstration for freedom in the history of our nation.

Five score years ago, a great American, in whose symbolic shadow we stand today, signed the Emancipation Proclamation. This momentous decree came as a

great beacon light of hope to millions of Negro slaves who had been seared in the flames of withering injustice. It came as a joyous daybreak to end the long night of their captivity.

But one hundred years later, the Negro still is not free. One hundred years later, the life of the Negro is still sadly crippled by the manacles of segregation and the chains of discrimination. One hundred years later, the Negro lives on a lonely island of poverty in the midst of a vast ocean of material prosperity. One hundred years later, the Negro is still languished in the corners of American society and finds himself an exile in his own land. And so we've come here today to dramatize a shameful condition.

In a sense we've come to our nation's capital to cash a check. When the architects of our republic wrote the magnificent words of the Constitution and the Declaration of Independence, they were signing a promissory note to which every American was to fall heir. This note was a promise that all men, yes, black men as well as white men, would be guaranteed the "unalienable Rights" of "Life, Liberty and the pursuit of Happiness." It is obvious today that America has defaulted on this promissory note, insofar as her citizens of color are concerned. Instead of honoring this sacred obligation, America has given the Negro people a bad check, a check which has come back marked "insufficient funds."

But we refuse to believe that the bank of justice is bankrupt. We refuse to believe that there are insufficient funds in the great vaults of opportunity of this nation. And so, we've come to cash this check, a check that will give us upon demand the riches of freedom and the security of justice.

We have also come to this hallowed spot to remind America of the fierce urgency of Now. This is no time to engage in the luxury of cooling off or to take the tranquilizing drug of gradualism. Now is the time to make real the promises of democracy. Now is the time to rise from the dark and desolate valley of segregation to the sunlit path of racial justice. Now is the time to lift our nation from the quicksands of racial injustice to the solid rock of brotherhood. Now is the time to make justice a reality for all of God's children.

It would be fatal for the nation to overlook the urgency of the moment. This sweltering summer of the Negro's legitimate discontent will not pass until there is an invigorating autumn of freedom and equality. Nineteen sixty-three is not an end, but a beginning. And those who hope that the Negro needed to blow off steam and will now be content will have a rude awakening if the nation returns to business as usual. And there will be neither rest nor tranquility in America until the Negro is granted his citizenship rights. The whirlwinds of revolt will continue to shake the foundations of our nation until the bright day of justice emerges.

But there is something that I must say to my people, who stand on the warm threshold which leads into the palace of justice: In the process of gaining our rightful place, we must not be guilty of wrongful deeds. Let us not seek to satisfy our thirst for freedom by drinking from the cup of bitterness and hatred. We must forever conduct our struggle on the high plane of dignity and discipline. We must not allow our creative protest to degenerate into physical violence. Again and again, we must rise to the majestic heights of meeting physical force with soul force.

The marvelous new militancy which has engulfed the Negro community must not lead us to a distrust of all white people, for many of our white brothers, as evidenced by their presence here today, have come to realize that their destiny is tied up with our destiny. And they have come to realize that their freedom is inextricably bound to our freedom.

We cannot walk alone.

And as we walk, we must make the pledge that we shall always march ahead. We cannot turn back.

There are those who are asking the devotees of civil rights, "When will you be satisfied?" We can never be satisfied as long as the Negro is the victim of the unspeakable horrors of police brutality. We can never be satisfied as long as our bodies, heavy with the fatigue of travel, cannot gain lodging in the motels of the highways and the hotels of the cities. We cannot be satisfied as long as the negro's basic mobility is from a smaller ghetto to a larger one. We can never be satisfied as long as our children are stripped of their selfhood and robbed of their dignity by a sign stating: "For Whites Only." We cannot be satisfied as long as a Negro in Mississippi cannot vote and a Negro in New York believes he has nothing for which to vote. No, no, we are not satisfied, and we will not be satisfied until "justice rolls down like waters, and righteousness like a mighty stream."[2]

I am not unmindful that some of you have come here out of great trials and tribulations. Some of you have come fresh from narrow jail cells. And some of you have come from areas where your quest—quest for freedom left you battered by the storms of persecution and staggered by the winds of police brutality. You have been the veterans of creative suffering. Continue to work with the faith that unearned suffering is redemptive. Go back to Mississippi, go back to Alabama, go back to South Carolina, go back to Georgia, go back to Louisiana, go back to the slums and ghettos of our northern cities, knowing that somehow this situation can and will be changed.

Let us not wallow in the valley of despair, I say to you today, my friends.

And so even though we face the difficulties of today and tomorrow, I still have a dream. It is a dream deeply rooted in the American dream.

I have a dream that one day this nation will rise up and live out the true meaning of its creed: "We hold these truths to be self-evident, that all men are created equal."

I have a dream that one day on the red hills of Georgia, the sons of former slaves and the sons of former slave owners will be able to sit down together at the table of brotherhood.

I have a dream that one day even the state of Mississippi, a state sweltering with the heat of injustice, sweltering with the heat of oppression, will be transformed into an oasis of freedom and justice.

I have a dream that my four little children will one day live in a nation where they will not be judged by the color of their skin but by the content of their character.

I have a dream today!

I have a dream that one day, down in Alabama, with its vicious racists, with its governor having his lips dripping with the words of "interposition" and "nullification"—one day right there in Alabama little black boys and black girls will be able to join hands with little white boys and white girls as sisters and brothers.

I have a dream today!

I have a dream that one day every valley shall be exalted, and every hill and mountain shall be made low, the rough places will be made plain, and the crooked places will be made straight; "and the glory of the Lord shall be revealed and all flesh shall see it together."[3]

This is our hope, and this is the faith that I go back to the South with.

---

2 Amos 5:24 (rendered precisely in The American Standard Version of the Holy Bible)
3 Isaiah 40:4–5 (King James Version of the Holy Bible). Quotation marks are excluded from part of this moment in the text because King's rendering of Isaiah 40:4 does not precisely follow the KJV version from which he quotes (e.g., "hill" and "mountain" are reversed in the KJV). King's rendering of Isaiah 40:5, however, is precisely quoted from the KJV.

With this faith, we will be able to hew out of the mountain of despair a stone of hope. With this faith, we will be able to transform the jangling discords of our nation into a beautiful symphony of brotherhood. With this faith, we will be able to work together, to pray together, to struggle together, to go to jail together, to stand up for freedom together, knowing that we will be free one day.

And this will be the day—this will be the day when all of God's children will be able to sing with new meaning:

> My country 'tis of thee, sweet land of liberty, of thee I sing.
> Land where my fathers died, land of the Pilgrim's pride,
> From every mountainside, let freedom ring!
> And if America is to be a great nation, this must become true.
> And so let freedom ring from the prodigious hilltops of New Hampshire.
> Let freedom ring from the mighty mountains of New York.
> Let freedom ring from the heightening Alleghenies of Pennsylvania.
> Let freedom ring from the snow-capped Rockies of Colorado.
> Let freedom ring from the curvaceous slopes of California.
> But not only that:
> Let freedom ring from Stone Mountain of Georgia.
> Let freedom ring from Lookout Mountain of Tennessee.
> Let freedom ring from every hill and molehill of Mississippi.
> From every mountainside, let freedom ring.

And when this happens, when we allow freedom to ring, when we let it ring from every village and every hamlet, from every state and every city, we will be able to speed up that day when all of God's children, black men and white men, Jews and Gentiles, Protestants and Catholics, will be able to join hands and sing in the words of the old Negro spiritual:

Free at last! Free at last!
Thank God Almighty, we are free at last![4]

---

4 "Free at Last" from *American Negro Songs* by J. W. Work.

Activity 6.1 **Compose:** Use Microsoft's Comment Feature to Annotate a Text

If you download Dr. Martin Luther King's speech from AmericanRhetoric.com, you can make use of Microsoft's Comment feature to annotate the speech with your comments, as is done in the example below. In Microsoft Word, highlight the text you want to annotate, go to the "Insert" pull-down menu, and select "Comment." A box will appear where you can enter your comment.

I am happy to join with you today in what will go down in history as the greatest demonstration for freedom in the history of our nation.

Five score years ago, a great American, in whose symbolic shadow we stand today, signed the Emancipation Proclamation. This momentous decree came as a great beacon light of hope to millions of Negro slaves who had been seared in the flames of withering injustice. It came as a joyous daybreak to end the long night of their captivity.

> **2/7/09 12:38 AM**
> **Comment:** Reference to Lincoln's Gettysburg Address

But one hundred years later, the Negro still is not free. One hundred years later, the life of the Negro is still sadly crippled by the manacles of segregation and the chains of discrimination. One hundred years later, the Negro lives on a lonely island of poverty in the midst of a vast ocean of material prosperity. One hundred years later, the Negro is

---

Activity 6.2 **Collaborate:** Discuss "I Have a Dream"

Read the "I Have a Dream" speech by Rev. Martin Luther King, Jr., and, if possible, watch the speech. It is archived at http://www.americanrhetoric.com, where it is listed as the most requested speech and #1 in its list of the top 100 American speeches.
1. Discuss the kairos of Dr. King's speech. What was the occasion? Who was his audience, both present and absent? What were the issues he spoke about?
2. How did Dr. King take advantage of the kairos of the situation in the wording of his speech?
3. Why do you think the speech continues to be so popular and influential?

Activity 6.3 **Collaborate:** Identify the Kairos

Identifying the kairos in Martin Luther King's speech in front of the Lincoln Memorial is easy. In some speeches, however, identifying the kairos is more difficult. Every speech and every text has a kairos, but some rhetors are better at identifying it and utilizing it than others. Identify the kairos in the following readings that have appeared thus far in the text. Then discuss in your group how the writer or speaker does or does not utilize kairos to maximum effect.
1. "Violent Rhetoric and Arizona Politics" (Chapter 4, p. 35)
2. "The Sleepover Question" (Chapter 4, p. 37)

3. "San Ysidro Shooting Survivor Lives His Dream of Being a Cop" (Chapter 4, p. 40)
4. "President Barack Obama on the Death of Osama bin Laden" (Chapter 5, p. 55)
5. "The Web Means the End of Forgetting" (Chapter 5, p. 61)

Activity 6.4 **Compose:** Analyze an Audience

Select a group that you do not belong to and analyze it as a potential audience. As one method, you might locate a blog on the Internet that advocates a point of view different from your own. For example, if you believe in global warming, read a blog frequented by those who do not share that belief. If you are a Democrat, look for a Tea Party or Republican blog. Find a yoga blog if you are a football fan. Read blog entries for a week and write a one-page analysis. Answer these questions:

1. What are the two or three issues of primary interest to the group? What is the general position on each issue?
2. Who are these people? Where do they live? What is their educational level?
3. What is the extent of their knowledge about the issues of primary interest? Are they familiar with the evidence, or do they just repeat opinions?
4. What types of appeals would make a difference to the readers of this blog: ethos, pathos, or logos? How so?

Aristotle's Persuasive Appeals

Some theorists associate the rhetorical triangle directly with Aristotle's **appeals** (or proofs): ethos, pathos, and logos. **Ethos** refers to the writer's (or speaker's) credibility; **pathos** refers to emotion used to sway the audience; and, finally, **logos** refers to the writer's purpose (or subject), for an effective argument will include evidence and other supporting details to back up the author's claims.

Aristotle wrote:

> Of those proofs that are furnished through the speech there are three kinds. Some reside in the character [*ethos*] of the speaker, some in a certain disposition [*pathos*] of the audience and some in the speech itself, through its demonstrating or seeming to demonstrate [*logos*].

Contemporary theorist Wayne C. Booth said something similar:

> The common ingredient that I find in all writing that I admire—excluding for now novels, plays, and poems—is something that I shall reluctantly call the rhetorical stance, a stance which depends upon discovering and maintaining in any writing situation a proper balance among the three elements that are at work in any communicative effort: the available arguments about the subject itself [*logos*], the interests and peculiarities of the audience [*pathos*], and the voice, the implied character of the speaker [*ethos*].

Arguments from Logos

Logos or reason was Aristotle's favorite of the three persuasive appeals, and he bemoaned the fact that humans could not be persuaded through reason alone, indeed that they sometimes chose emotion over reason. Aristotle also used the term *logos* to mean rational discourse. To appeal to logos means to organize an argument with a clear claim or thesis, supported by logical reasons that are presented in a well-organized manner that is internally consistent. It can also mean the use of facts and statistics as evidence. However, logos without elements of pathos and ethos can be dry, hard to understand, and boring.

Consider the following logical argument that advocates the televising of executions.

Reading 6.2

Executions Should Be Televised by Zachary B. Shemtob and David Lat In this opinion piece published in The New York Times, Zachary B. Shemtob and David Lat argue what they know is going to be an unpopular position in the United States—that executions should be televised. Shemtob is an assistant professor of criminal justice at Connecticut State University and Lat is a former federal prosecutor who also founded a legal blog, Above the Law. They reason, "democracy demands maximum accountability and transparency." Knowing that their position contradicts present policy, they carefully address possible objections to their position, such as the idea that executions are too gruesome to put on television.

Earlier this month, Georgia conducted its third execution this year. This would have passed relatively unnoticed if not for a controversy surrounding its videotaping. Lawyers for the condemned inmate, Andrew Grant DeYoung, had persuaded a judge to allow the recording of his last moments as part of an effort to obtain evidence on whether lethal injection caused unnecessary suffering.

Though he argued for videotaping, one of Mr. DeYoung's defense lawyers, Brian Kammer, spoke out against releasing the footage to the public. "It's a horrible thing that Andrew DeYoung had to go through," Mr. Kammer said, "and it's not for the public to see that."

We respectfully disagree. Executions in the United States ought to be made public.

Right now, executions are generally open only to the press and a few select witnesses. For the rest of us, the vague contours are provided in the morning paper. Yet a functioning democracy demands maximum accountability and transparency. As long as executions remain behind closed doors, those are impossible. The people should have the right to see what is being done in their name and with their tax dollars.

This is particularly relevant given the current debate on whether specific methods of lethal injection constitute cruel and unusual punishment and therefore violate the Constitution.

There is a dramatic difference between reading or hearing of such an event and observing it through image and sound. (This is obvious to those who saw the footage of Saddam Hussein's hanging in 2006 or the death of Neda Agha-Soltan during the protests in Iran in 2009.) We are not calling for opening executions completely to the

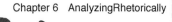

public—conducting them before a live crowd—but rather for broadcasting them live or recording them for future release, on the Web or TV.

When another Georgia inmate, Roy Blankenship, was executed in June, the prisoner jerked his head, grimaced, gasped and lurched, according to a medical expert's affidavit. The *Atlanta Journal-Constitution* reported that Mr. DeYoung, executed in the same manner, "showed no violent signs in death." Voters should not have to rely on media accounts to understand what takes place when a man is put to death.

Cameras record legislative sessions and presidential debates, and courtrooms are allowing greater television access. When he was an Illinois state senator, President Obama successfully pressed for the videotaping of homicide interrogations and confessions. The most serious penalty of all surely demands equal if not greater scrutiny.

Opponents of our proposal offer many objections. State lawyers argued that making Mr. DeYoung's execution public raised safety concerns. While rioting and pickpocketing occasionally marred executions in the public square in the 18th and 19th centuries, modern security and technology obviate this concern. Little would change in the death chamber; the faces of witnesses and executioners could be edited out, for privacy reasons, before a video was released.

Of greater concern is the possibility that broadcasting executions could have a numbing effect. Douglas A. Berman, a law professor, fears that people might come to equate human executions with putting pets to sleep. Yet this seems overstated. While public indifference might result over time, the initial broadcasts would undoubtedly get attention and stir debate.

Still others say that broadcasting an execution would offer an unbalanced picture—making the condemned seem helpless and sympathetic, while keeping the victims of the crime out of the picture. But this is beside the point: the defendant is being executed precisely because a jury found that his crimes were so heinous that he deserved to die.

Ultimately the main opposition to our idea seems to flow from an unthinking disgust—a sense that public executions are archaic, noxious, even barbarous. Albert Camus related in his essay "Reflections on the Guillotine" that viewing executions turned him against capital punishment. The legal scholar John D. Bessler suggests that public executions might have the same effect on the public today; Sister Helen Prejean, the death penalty abolitionist, has urged just such a strategy.

That is not our view. We leave open the possibility that making executions public could strengthen support for them; undecided viewers might find them less disturbing than anticipated.

Like many of our fellow citizens, we are deeply conflicted about the death penalty and how it has been administered. Our focus is on accountability and openness. As Justice John Paul Stevens wrote in *Baze v. Rees*, a 2008 case involving a challenge to lethal injection, capital punishment is too often "the product of habit and inattention rather than an acceptable deliberative process that weighs the costs and risks of administering that penalty against its identifiable benefits."

A democracy demands a citizenry as informed as possible about the costs and benefits of society's ultimate punishment.

Activity 6.5 **Collaborate:** Analyze an Argument from Logos

1. In your small group, go over the Checklist of Essential Elements in an Argument (Chapter 2), and decide if the authors of this article fulfill each one. Be prepared to defend your decisions to the class.
2. Shemtob and Lat present a logical argument about why executions should be televised. Ignoring your own reaction to their editorial, outline the main points.
3. How do the authors handle their audience's possible emotional objections to their argument? Give an example.
4. What is your reaction to the argument that executions should be televised? Did reading and evaluating the article cause you to see the issue differently? If so, in what way?

Deductive Reasoning

Aristotle was the first person in Western culture to write systematically about logic, and he is credited with developing and promoting syllogistic or **deductive reasoning** in which statements are combined to draw a **conclusion**. He wrote that "a statement is persuasive and credible either because it is directly self-evident or because it appears to be proved from other statements that are so." This logical structure is called a **syllogism**, in which premises lead to a conclusion. The following is perhaps the most famous syllogism:

Major premise:	All humans are mortal.
Minor premise:	Socrates is human.
Conclusion:	Socrates is mortal.

The **major premise** is a general statement accepted by everyone that makes an observation about all people. The second statement of the syllogism is the **minor premise**, which makes a statement about a particular case within the class of all people. Comparison of the two premises, the general class of "all humans" and the particular case of "Socrates" within the class of "all humans" leads to the conclusion that Socrates also fits in the class "mortal," and thus his death is unavoidable. Thus, the logic moves from the general to the particular.

Similarly, if you try the pumpkin bread at one Starbucks and like it, you may infer that you will like the pumpkin bread at another Starbucks. The argument would look like this:

Major premise:	Food products at Starbucks are standardized from one Starbucks to another.
Minor premise:	You like the pumpkin bread at one Starbucks.
Conclusion:	You will like the pumpkin bread at another Starbucks.

However, if your major premise is wrong, and the owner of one Starbucks substitutes an inferior stock of pumpkin bread, then your conclusion is wrong. Deductive reasoning is dependent upon the validity of each premise; otherwise the syllogism does not hold true. If the major premise that food products are standardized at all Starbucks franchises does not hold true, then the argument is not valid. A good deductive argument is known as a valid argument and is such that if all its premises are true, then its conclusion must be true. Indeed, for a deductive argument to be valid, it must be absolutely impossible for both its premises to be true and its conclusion to be false.

Inductive Reasoning

Aristotle identified another way to move logically between premises, which he called "the progress from particulars to universals." Later logicians labeled this type of logic as **inductive reasoning**. Inductive arguments are based on probability. Even if an inductive argument's premises are true, that doesn't establish with 100 percent certainty that its conclusions are true. Even the best inductive argument falls short of deductive validity.

Consider the following examples of inductive reasoning:

Particular statement:	Milk does not spoil as quickly if kept cold.
General statement:	All perishable foods do not spoil as quickly if kept cold.
Particular statement:	Microwaves cook popcorn more quickly than conventional heat.
General statement:	All foods cook more quickly in a microwave.

In the first example, inductive reasoning works well because cold tends to prolong the useable life of most perishable foods. The second example is more problematic. While it is true that popcorn cooks more quickly in a microwave oven, the peculiarities of microwave interaction with food molecules does not produce a uniform effect on all food stuffs. Rice, for example, does not cook much, if any, faster in a microwave than it does on a stovetop. Also, whole eggs may explode if cooked in their shells.

A good inductive argument is known as a strong (or "cogent") inductive argument. It is such that if the premises are true, the conclusion is likely to be true.

Activity 6.6 **Collaborate:** Identify Deductive and Inductive Reasoning

In your small group, identify an example of a deductive argument and list the premises and conclusion. Then identify an inductive argument and identify the particular statement and the general statement. Report to the class.

Logical Fallacies

Generally speaking, a **logical fallacy** is an error in reasoning, as opposed to a factual error, which is simply being wrong about the facts. A **deductive fallacy** (sometimes called a *formal fallacy*) is a deductive argument that has premises that are all true, but they lead to a false conclusion, making it an invalid argument. An **inductive fallacy** (sometimes called an *informal fallacy*) appears to be an inductive argument, but the premises do not provide enough support for the conclusion to be probable. Some logical fallacies are more common than others and, thus, have been labeled and defined. Following are a few of the most well-known types:

Ad hominem (to the man) are arguments that attempt to discredit a point of view through personal attacks upon the person who has that point of view. These arguments are not relevant to the actual issue because the character of the person that holds a view says nothing about the truth of that viewpoint.

Example: Noam Chomsky is a liberal activist who opposes American intervention in other countries. Noam Chomsky's theory of transformational grammar, which suggests that humans have an innate ability to learn language, is ridiculous.

Non sequitur (Latin for "it does not follow") arguments have conclusions that do not follow from the premises. Usually, the author has left out a step in the logic, expecting the reader to make the leap over the gap.

> Example: "Well, look at the size of this administration building; it is obvious this university does not need more funding."

Either/or or **false dichotomy** arguments force an either/or choice when, in reality, more options are available. Issues are presented as being either black or white.

> Example: With all the budget cuts, "we either raise tuition or massively increase class size."

Red herring arguments avoid the issue and attempt to distract with a side issue.

> Example: "Why do you question my private life issues, when we have social problems with which to deal?"

Ad populum (Latin for "appeal to the people") arguments appeal to popularity. If a lot of people believe it, it must be true.

> Example: "Why shouldn't I cheat on this exam? Everyone else cheats."

Ad verecundium (Latin for "argument from that which is improper") arguments appeal to an irrelevant authority.

> Example: "If the President of Harvard says it is a good idea, then we should follow suit." Or, "That is how we have always done it."

Begging the question arguments simply assume that a point of view is true because the truth of the premise is assumed. Simply assuming a premise is true does not amount to evidence that it *is* true.

> Example: A woman's place is in the home; therefore, women should not work.

Confusing cause and effect is a common problem with scientific studies in which the fact that two events are correlated implies that one causes the other.

> Example: Obese people drink a lot of diet soda; therefore, diet soda causes obesity.

Post hoc (from the Latin phrase "Post hoc, ergo proper hoc," or after this, therefore because of this) is a fallacy that concludes that one event caused another just because one occurred before the other.

> Example: The Great Depression caused World War II.

In a **straw man** fallacy, a position of an opponent is exaggerated or weakened, so that it is easier for the opponent to argue against it.

> Example: Pro-choice advocates believe in murdering unborn children.

A **slippery slope** argument asserts that one event will inevitably lead to another event.

Example: the Dilbert cartoon below:

DILBERT: © Scott Adams/Dist. by United Feature Syndicate, Inc.

These logical fallacies are summarized in table 6.1.

Table 6.1

Fallacy	The Error in Reasoning	Example
Ad populum	When we attempt to persuade people by arguing our position is reasonable because so many other people are doing it or agree with it.	"Why shouldn't I cheat on this exam? Everyone else cheats."
Ad verecundium	An appeal to persuasion based on higher authority or tradition.	"If the president of Harvard says it is a good idea, then we should follow suit." Or, "That is how we have always done it."
Begging the question	When a speaker presumes certain things are facts when they have not yet been proven to be truthful.	"Oh, everyone knows that we are all Christians."
Confusing cause and effect	A common problem with scientific studies in which the fact that two events are correlated implies that one causes the other.	"Obese people drink a lot of diet soda; therefore, diet soda causes obesity."
Either/or	Presents two options and declares that one of them must be correct while the other must be incorrect.	"We either raise tuition or massively increase class size."
Non sequitur	When you make an unwarranted move from one idea to the next.	"Well, look at the size of this administration building; it is obvious this university does not need more funding."

Fallacy	The Error in Reasoning	Example
Post hoc	Assumes that because one event happened after another, then the preceding event caused the event that followed.	"Every time Sheila goes to a game with us, our team loses. She is bad luck."
Red herring	When a speaker introduces an irrelevant issue or piece of evidence to divert attention from the subject of the speech.	"Why do you question my private life issues, when we have social problems with which to deal?"
Slippery slope	Assumes that once an action begins it will follow, undeterred, to an eventual and inevitable conclusion.	"If we let the government dictate where we can pray, soon the government will tell us we cannot pray."

Activity 6.7 **Explore:** Identify Logical Fallacies

Match the following types of logical fallacies with the examples below:

Types:

Ad hominem

Begging the question

Confusing cause and effect

Post hoc

Straw man

Slippery slope

Examples:
1. Legalization of medical marijuana will lead to increased marijuana use by the general population.
2. Twenty-one is the best age limit for drinking because people do not mature until they are 21.
3. If you teach birth control methods, more teenage girls will get pregnant.
4. The culture wars of the 1960s were a result of parents being unable to control their children after the post–World War II baby boom.
5. Al Gore claims that global warming is a dangerous trend. Al Gore is a liberal. Therefore, there is no global warming.
6. Immigration reform advocates want to separate families and children.

Activity 6.8 **Collaborate:** Create Examples of Logical Fallacies

In your small group, work through the chart of logical fallacies above and create a new example for each type of fallacy. Then report to the class, one fallacy at a time, with the instructor making a list of each group's examples on the chalk board. Discuss any examples that are not clear cases of a particular fallacy.

Arguments from Pathos

Pathos makes use of emotion to persuade an audience.
Aristotle wrote:

> Proofs from the disposition of the audience are produced whenever they are
> induced by the speech into an emotional state. We do not give judgment in the
> same way when aggrieved and when pleased, in sympathy and in revulsion.

Effective rhetors know their audiences, particularly what emotions they hold that
are relevant to the issue under consideration. What motivates them? What are their
fears, their hopes, their desires, and their doubts? If the audience has the same
emotions as you do, fine. However, if they do not already hold those emotions, you
need to bring them to share the hurt, the anger, or the joy that will persuade them
to share your viewpoint—through the stories you tell, the statistics you cite, and the
reasoning you offer.

For example, when Martin Luther King, Jr., in his "I Have a Dream" speech
(reprinted earlier in this chapter) referred to the "hallowed spot" of the Lincoln
Memorial, he was appealing to his audience's feelings of patriotism and reverence
for the accomplishments of President Lincoln. Subtly, he was also garnering this
emotion toward Lincoln in contemporary support of civil rights. Lincoln had issued the
Emancipation Proclamation that declared all slaves to be free, yet, according to King,
America had not lived up to Lincoln's promise.

Reading 6.3

People for Sale by E. Benjamin Skinner E. Benjamin Skinner has written on a wide range of
topics. His articles have appeared in *Newsweek International, Travel and Leisure,* and other
magazines. This essay was adapted from *A Crime So Monstrous: Face-to-Face with Modern-Day
Slavery* and appeared in *Foreign Policy.*

Most people imagine that slavery died in the 19th century. Since 1810, more than a
dozen international conventions banning the slave trade have been signed. Yet today
there are more slaves than at any time in human history.

And if you're going to buy one in five hours, you'd better get a move on. First, hail
a taxi to JFK International Airport and hop on a direct flight to Port-au-Prince, Haiti.
The flight takes three hours. After landing, take a tap-tap, a flatbed pickup retrofitted
with benches and a canopy, three-quarters of the way up Route de Delmas, the
capital's main street. There, on a side street, you will find a group of men standing in
front of Le Réseau (the Network) barbershop. As you approach, a man steps forward:
"Are you looking to get a person?"

Meet Benavil Lebhom. He smiles easily. He has a trim mustache and wears
a multicolored striped golf shirt, a gold chain, and Doc Martens knockoffs. Benavil
is a courtier, or broker. He holds an official real estate license and calls himself an
employment agent. Two-thirds of the employees he places are child slaves. The total
number of Haitian children in bondage in their own country stands at 300,000. They
are restavèks, the "stay-withs," as they are euphemistically known in Creole. Forced,
unpaid, they work in captivity from before dawn until night. Benavil and thousands of
other formal and informal traffickers lure these children from desperately impoverished
rural parents with promises of free schooling and a better life.

The negotiation to buy a child slave might sound a bit like this:

"How quickly do you think it would be possible to bring a child in? Somebody who could clean and cook?" you ask. "I don't have a very big place; I have a small apartment. But I'm wondering how much that would cost? And how quickly?"

"Three days," Benavil responds.

"And you could bring the child here?" you inquire. "Or are there children here already?"

"I don't have any here in Port-au-Prince right now," says Benavil, his eyes widening at the thought of a foreign client. "I would go out to the countryside."

You ask about additional expenses. "Would I have to pay for transportation?"

"Bon," says Benavil. "A hundred U.S."

Smelling a rip-off, you press him, "And that's just for transportation?"

"Transportation would be about 100 Haitian," says Benavil, "because you'd have to get out there. Plus, [hotel and] food on the trip. Five hundred gourdes"—around $13.

"OK, 500 Haitian," you say.

Now you ask the big question: "And what would your fee be?" Benavil's eyes narrow as he determines how much he can take you for.

"A hundred. American."

"That seems like a lot," you say, with a smile so as not to kill the deal. "Could you bring down your fee to 50 U.S.?"

Benavil pauses. But only for effect. He knows he's still got you for much more than a Haitian would pay. "Oui," he says with a smile.

But the deal isn't done. Benavil leans in close. "This is a rather delicate question. Is this someone you want as just a worker? Or also someone who will be a 'partner'? You understand what I mean?"

You don't blink at being asked if you want the child for sex. "Is it possible to have someone who could be both?"

"Oui!" Benavil responds enthusiastically.

If you're interested in taking your purchase back to the United States, Benavil tells you that he can "arrange" the proper papers to make it look as though you've adopted the child.

He offers you a 13-year-old girl.

"That's a little bit old," you say.

"I know of another girl who's 12. Then ones that are 10, 11," he responds.

The negotiation is finished, and you tell Benavil not to make any moves without further word from you. You have successfully arranged to buy a human being for 50 bucks.

It would be nice if that conversation were fictional. It is not. I recorded it in October 2005 as part of four years of research into slavery on five continents. In the popular consciousness, "slavery" has come to be little more than just a metaphor for undue hardship. Investment bankers routinely refer to themselves as "high-paid wage slaves." Human rights activists may call $1-an-hour sweatshop laborers slaves, regardless of the fact that they are paid and can often walk away from the job.

The reality of slavery is far different. Slavery exists today on an unprecedented scale. In Africa, tens of thousands are chattel slaves, seized in war or tucked away for generations. Across Europe, Asia, and the Americas, traffickers have forced as many as 2 million into prostitution or labor. In South Asia, which has the highest concentration of slaves on the planet, nearly 10 million languish in bondage, unable to leave their captors until they pay off "debts," legal fictions that in many cases are generations old.

Few in the developed world have a grasp of the enormity of modern-day slavery. Fewer still are doing anything to combat it. . . . Between 2000 and 2006, the U.S. Justice Department increased human trafficking prosecutions from 3 to 32, and convictions from 10 to 98. By the end of 2006, 27 states had passed anti-trafficking laws. Yet, during the same period, the United States liberated only about 2 percent of its own modern-day slaves. As many as 17,500 new slaves continue to enter bondage in the United States every year . . . Many feel that sex slavery is particularly revolting—and it is. I saw it firsthand. In a Bucharest brothel, I was offered a mentally handicapped suicidal girl in exchange for a used car. But for every woman or child enslaved in commercial sex, there are some 15 men, women, and children enslaved in other fields, such as domestic work or agricultural labor.

Save for the fact that he is male, Gonoo Lal Kol typifies the average slave of our modern age. (At his request, I have changed his name.) Like a majority of the world's slaves, Gonoo is in debt bondage in South Asia. In his case, in an Indian quarry. Like most slaves, Gonoo is illiterate and unaware of the Indian laws that ban his bondage and provide for sanctions against his master. His story, told to me near his four-foot-high stone and grass hutch, represents the other side of the "Indian Miracle."

Gonoo lives in Lohagara Dhal, a forgotten corner of Uttar Pradesh, a north Indian state that contains 8 percent of the world's poor. I met him one evening in December 2005 as he walked with two dozen other laborers in tattered and filthy clothes. Behind them was the quarry. In that pit, Gonoo, a member of the historically outcast Kol tribe, worked with his family 14 hours a day. His tools were a hammer and a pike. His hands were covered in calluses, his fingertips worn away.

Gonoo's master is a tall, stout, surly contractor named Ramesh Garg. He makes his money by enslaving entire families forced to work for no pay beyond alcohol, grain, and subsistence expenses. Slavery scholar Kevin Bales estimates that a slave in the 19th-century American South had to work 20 years to recoup his or her purchase price. Gonoo and the other slaves earn a profit for Garg in two years.

Every single man, woman, and child in Lohagara Dhal is a slave. But, in theory at least, Garg neither bought nor owns them. The seed of Gonoo's slavery, for instance, was a loan of 62 cents. In 1958 his grandfather borrowed that amount from the owner of a farm where he worked. Three generations and three slave masters later, Gonoo's family remains in bondage.

Recently, many bold, underfunded groups have taken up the challenge of tearing out the roots of slavery. Some gained fame through dramatic slave rescues. Most learned that freeing slaves is impossible unless the slaves themselves choose to be free. Among the Kol of Uttar Pradesh, for instance, an organization called Pragati Gramodyog Sansthan (PGS)—the Progressive Institute for Village Enterprises—has helped hundreds of families break the grip of the quarry contractors.

The psychological, social, and economic bonds of slavery run deep, and for governments to be truly effective in eradicating slavery, they must partner with groups that can offer slaves a way to pull themselves up from bondage. One way to do that is to replicate the work of grassroots organizations such as the India-based MSEMVS (Society for Human Development and Women's Empowerment). In 1996 the group launched free transitional schools where children who had been enslaved learned skills and acquired enough literacy to move on to formal schooling. The group also targeted mothers, providing them with training and start-up materials for microenterprises. . . . In recent years, the United States has shown an increasing willingness to help fund these kinds of organizations, one encouraging sign that the message may be getting through.

For four years, I encountered dozens of enslaved people, several of whom traffickers like Benavil actually offered to sell to me. I did not pay for a human life anywhere. And, with one exception, I always withheld action to save any one person, in the hope that my research would later help to save many more. At times, that still feels like an excuse for cowardice. But the hard work of real emancipation can't be the burden of a select few. For thousands of slaves, grassroots groups like PGS and MSEMVS can help bring freedom. Until governments define slavery in appropriately concise terms, prosecute the crime aggressively in all its forms, and encourage groups that empower slaves to free themselves, however, millions more will remain in bondage. And our collective promise of abolition will continue to mean nothing at all.

Activity 6.9 **Explore:** Analyze an Argument from Pathos

After reading Skinner's essay on slavery, reread the passage in which he negotiated to buy a child slave. Then freewrite for five minutes about how that negotiation made you feel.

Most people feel emotional when they read about a child in distress, and Skinner further highlights that emotional effect by putting this particular episode in dialogue, always a point of emphasis in an essay. Do you think Skinner deliberately appealed to pathos in this part of his essay?   Discuss in your group.

List other areas where the essay evokes an emotional response. Consider why, and freewrite on the feelings and beliefs that are brought into play. How did the author know that you would probably react this way?

Although much of Skinner's argument relies on pathos, he also provides statistics and references to authorities to bolster his argument. Identify the paragraphs which provide statistics or other evidence that would qualify as logos.

Arguments from Ethos

No exact translation exists in English for the word *ethos*, but it can be loosely translated as the credibility of the speaker. This credibility generates good will which colors all the arguments, examples, and quotes the rhetor utilizes in his text. Rhetors can enhance their credibility by evidence of intelligence, virtue, and goodwill and diminish it by seeming petty, dishonest, and mean-spirited. In addition, a speaker or writer can enhance his or her own credibility by references to quotes or the actions of authorities or leaders.

Aristotle wrote:

> Proofs from character [ethos] are produced, whenever the speech is given in such a way as to render the speaker worthy of credence—we more readily and sooner believe reasonable men on all matters in general and absolutely on questions where precision is impossible and two views can be maintained.

For example, Martin Luther King, Jr., pointed out in his "I Have a Dream" speech, that, according to the framers of the Constitution and the Declaration of Independence, "unalienable Rights" of "Life, Liberty and the pursuit of Happiness" apply equally to black men and white men. He was, in effect, borrowing the ethos of Thomas Jefferson and the framers of the Constitution in support of the unalienable rights of blacks.

Consider the following article and how the author's credibility or ethos enhances the appeal of his arguments.

Reading 6.4

Alien Life Coming Slowly into View by Ray Jayawardhana Ray Jayawardhana, the author of "Alien Life Coming Slowly into View," which was originally published in *The New York Times,* is a professor of astronomy and astrophysics at the University of Toronto. He is also the author of *Strange New Worlds: The Search for Alien Planets and Life Beyond Our Solar System.*

I remember the first time the concept of another world entered my mind. It was during a walk with my father in our garden in Sri Lanka. He pointed to the Moon and told me that people had walked on it. I was astonished: Suddenly that bright light became a place that one could visit.

Schoolchildren may feel a similar sense of wonder when they see pictures of a Martian landscape or Saturn's rings. And soon their views of alien worlds may not be confined to the planets in our own solar system.

After millenniums of musings and a century of failed attempts, astronomers first detected an exoplanet, a planet orbiting a normal star other than the Sun, in 1995. Now they are finding hundreds of such worlds each year. Last month, NASA announced that 1,235 new possible planets had been observed by Kepler, a telescope on a space satellite. Six of the planets that Kepler found circle one star, and the orbits of five of them would fit within that of Mercury, the closest planet to our Sun.

By timing the passages of these five planets across their sun's visage—which provides confirmation of their planetary nature—we can witness their graceful dance with one another, choreographed by gravity. These discoveries remind us that nature is often richer and more wondrous than our imagination. The diversity of alien worlds has surprised us and challenged our preconceptions many times over.

It is quite a change from merely 20 years ago, when we knew for sure of just one planetary system: ours. The pace of discovery, supported by new instruments and missions and innovative strategies by planet seekers, has been astounding.

What's more, from measurements of their masses and sizes, we can infer what some of these worlds are made of: gases, ice or rocks. Astronomers have been able to take the temperature of planets around other stars, first with telescopes in space but more recently with ground-based instruments, as my collaborators and I have done.

Two and a half years ago, we even managed to capture the first direct pictures of alien worlds. There is something about a photo of an alien planet—even if it only appears as a faint dot next to a bright, overexposed star—that makes it "real." Given that stars shine like floodlights next to the planetary embers huddled around them, success required painstaking efforts and clever innovations. One essential tool is adaptive optics technology, which, in effect, takes the twinkle out of the stars, thus providing sharper images from telescopes on the ground than would otherwise be possible.

At the crux of this grand pursuit is one basic question: Is our warm, wet, rocky world, teeming with life, the exception or the norm? It is an important question for every one of us, not just for scientists. It seems absurd, if not arrogant, to think that ours is the only life-bearing world in the galaxy, given hundreds of billions of other suns, the apparent ubiquity of planets, and the cosmic abundance of life's ingredients. It may be that life is fairly common, but that "intelligent" life is rare.

Of course, the vast majority of the extra-solar worlds discovered to date are quite unlike our own: many are gas giants, and some are boiling hot while others endure everlasting chills. Just a handful are close in size to our planet, and only a few of those may be rocky like the Earth, rather than gaseous like Jupiter or icy like Neptune.

But within the next few years, astronomers expect to find dozens of alien earths that are roughly the size of our planet. Some of them will likely be in the so-called habitable zone, where the temperatures are just right for liquid water. The discovery of "Earth twins," with conditions similar to what we find here, will inevitably bring questions about alien life to the forefront.

Detecting signs of life elsewhere will not be easy, but it may well occur in my lifetime, if not during the next decade. Given the daunting distances between the stars, the real-life version will almost certainly be a lot less sensational than the movies depicting alien invasions or crash-landing spaceships.

The evidence may be circumstantial at first—say, spectral bar codes of interesting molecules like oxygen, ozone, methane and water—and leave room for alternative interpretations. It may take years of additional data-gathering, and perhaps the construction of new telescopes, to satisfy our doubts. Besides, we won't know whether such "biosignatures" are an indication of slime or civilization. Most people will likely move on to other, more immediate concerns of life here on Earth while scientists get down to work.

If, on the other hand, an alien radio signal were to be detected, that would constitute a more clear-cut and exciting moment. Even if the contents of the message remained elusive for decades, we would know that there was someone "intelligent" at the other end. The search for extraterrestrial intelligence with radio telescopes has come of age recently, 50 years after the first feeble attempt. The construction of the Allen Telescope Array on an arid plateau in northern California greatly expands the number of star systems from which astronomers could detect signals.

However it arrives, the first definitive evidence of life elsewhere will mark a turning point in our intellectual history, perhaps only rivaled by Copernicus's heliocentric theory or Darwin's theory of evolution. If life can spring up on two planets independently, why not on a thousand or even a billion others? The ramifications of finding out for sure that ours isn't the only inhabited world are likely to be felt, over time, in many areas of human thought and endeavor—from biology and philosophy to religion and art.

Some people worry that discovering life elsewhere, especially if it turns out to be in possession of incredible technology, will make us feel small and insignificant. They seem concerned that it will constitute a horrific blow to our collective ego.

I happen to be an optimist. It may take decades after the initial indications of alien life for scientists to gather enough evidence to be certain or to decipher a signal of artificial origin. The full ramifications of the discovery may not be felt for generations, giving us plenty of time to get used to the presence of our galactic neighbors. Besides, knowing that we are not alone just might be the kick in the pants we need to grow up as a species.

Activity 6.10 **Explore:** Analyzing an Argument from Ethos

1. In the above article, Ray Jayawardhana draws upon the ethos of his position as a professor of astronomy and astrophysics to formulate a convincing argument for the strong possibility of the existence of alien life. In your group, discuss how Jayawardhana's profession increases the credibility of his argument.
2. How do you think this essay would compare to essays by people of more credentials who argue that no alien life exists? What kinds of other evidence could Jayawardhana have offered that would strengthen his argument?
3. Is Jayawardhana appealing to pathos with his opening narrative? What effect does he want to have on his audience by describing this childhood memory?

Combining Ethos, Pathos, and Logos

The ethos, pathos, and logos appeals are equally important and merit equal attention in the writing process. No text is purely based on one of the three appeals, though more of the argument in a particular text may be based on one appeal rather than another. In each writing situation, however, an effective rhetor will think about how each plays into the structure of the argument.

In today's world, for example, a public speaker's effectiveness is affected by the ability to use a teleprompter, or, if one is not available, to memorize a speech well enough so he or she can speak without frequently referring to notes. If a speaker's eyes flit from left to right across the text of a teleprompter, it shows on television. This reduces the credibility, or ethos, of the speaker, no matter how well the other appeals are executed in the speech. The equivalent of presentation for a written text would be to produce a document that is essentially free from grammatical errors, spell-checked, and printed on good paper stock with the correct margins and type size. If the document does not look professional, it will lose credibility or ethos no matter what it says.

To give another example, E. Benjamin Skinner's essay, "People for Sale," relies on the highly emotional image of a child being sold into slavery for its major appeal. However, if you read back through the essay, you will see that it has a clear thesis, which could be stated as the following: Slavery exists in the present time, even in the United States, and it is not even that difficult to buy a slave. The essay is well organized and offers a variety of evidence, including statistics and first-person observation. Logos may not stand out as the primary appeal in Skinner's essay, but it is nevertheless strong in its appeal to logos.

If you want to develop your writing skills, it is essential that you pay attention to each of Aristotle's appeals—ethos, pathos, and logos.

Activity 6.11 **Compose:** Writing about Ethos, Pathos, and Logos

Choose one of the texts in Chapters 1, 2, or 3 and write an essay that identifies the ethos, pathos, and logos of the particular text. Then discuss how the three appeals together are used by the author to produce an effective essay. Alternatively, discuss which of the appeals is weak in the particular essay and how that affects the effectiveness of the essay.

Photos Heighten Ethos or Pathos

When Steve Jobs was in the process of turning over the reins of Apple to Tim Cook, the two appeared in a series of photos in a variety of publications. For example, see the photo below (from wired.com). Notice the "twinning effect," as both Jobs and Cook wear blue jeans and black pullover sweaters. In a not-so-subtle way, Apple was using ethos to visually state that since Jobs and Cook look alike, they must be alike. Thus, Cook would be successful in running Apple.

Photos can be equally effective in presenting pathos, though logos is more problematic.

Meet Tim Cook: The Man in Charge of Apple

For millions of Apple fans, Steve Jobs is irreplaceable. But if there's one man Jobs himself trusts to stand in his shoes it is his second in command Apple Chief Operating Officer Tim Cook.

Activity 6.12 **Compose:** Logos Activity: Write a Letter to the Editor

In the following letter, originally published on the blog, *The Frisky* (www. thefrisky.com), the author uses both humor and logic to argue that *The New Yorker* reviews shouldn't give away the ending of movies.

An Open Letter To The New Yorker
via The Frisky on 4/25/11

Dear *New Yorker*,

Obviously, you are an awesome magazine. However, I have one small, teensy weensy beef. Could you please—possibly—stop ruining the ending of movies for me? Last night, on a 10-hour flight from Buenos Aires to New York, I sat down determined to catch up on your last three issues. In one, I read a review of Jake Gyllenhaal's newish movie, "Source Code." I had been planning to see it. Emphasis on the *had*. While you didn't go into details, you told me how it unfolds in the end. Which sort of takes the wind out of a movie's sail, doesn't it? But even worse, in a fantastic article about Anna Faris and her specific brand of girl humor, you let me know the surprise twist ending of her upcoming click, "What's Your Number?" Which. Doesn't. Even. Come. Out. Until. SEPTEMBER. Reading this reminded me of the collective sigh of 100 students in my Intro to Film Studies class in college when our professor told us the secret to "Chinatown" before we watched.

Choose one of your favorite magazines and write a letter to the editor. You can protest something the magazine has done recently that bothered you, or you can praise something that it has done well. Your letter does not need to be long, but you need to make your argument clear and support it with specific examples. If appropriate for your target publication, use humor as does the author of the letter to the editor of *The New Yorker*.

After you have written your letter to the editor, write a paragraph describing your target publication, what you have written in your letter, and why your letter is an illustration of logos.

Activity 6.13 **Compose:** Pathos Activity: Portray an Emotion in a Collage

Think of an emotion that you've been feeling lately and that you are willing to explore. Create a collage to express that emotion. Use these criteria.
* You can create your collage with cut and paste paper or you can create it through a computer program.
* Have little white space. Use colors with emotional connotations (blue for calm, for example).

- Have at least three images. You can find these on the Internet or in magazines, or take your own photos.
- Before you begin your collage, write down the emotion you are trying to explore and describe how you plan to represent it. In other words, make a plan, even though you will likely deviate from it.
- When you finish, write a paragraph describing the experience of creating the collage. Turn your paragraph in with your collage.

Activity 6.14 **Compose:** Ethos Activity: Create a Professional Facebook Page

Facebook is not just used to tell your friends about what you did over the weekend. Corporations use it as a networking tool. As you learned in the reading in Chapter 2, "The Web Means the End of Forgetting," it is a good idea to be cautious about what you post about yourself on Facebook because information and photos may be seen by unintended audiences, including future employers. Some individuals choose to have two Facebook pages, one for their personal friends and one for networking.

For this assignment, create a professional Facebook page similar to the one shown here. Consider in your small group what information and photos you want to post on a page you will use for networking. In effect, you are creating an ethos for yourself by these choices.

After you have completed your Facebook page, write a paragraph that explains the ethos you wanted to project in your page and how your content choices project that ethos.

Activity 6.15 **Compose:** Write a Rhetorical Analysis

In this essay you will make use of rhetorical vocabulary to analyze a text or combined text and images. The sample student essay in Chapter 7 (see page 190) analyzes a speech archived on the American Rhetoric website (http://www.americanrhetoric.com), which features many presidential and other prominent speeches. Alternatively, you can write a rhetorical analysis of a Facebook page, a newspaper or magazine article, or website.

In your analysis, apply several of the rhetorical concepts you have studied this semester:

- Speaker or writer—Does the speaker's identity affect the text?
- Purpose—What was the speaker or writer trying to achieve?
- Audience—Who was the speech/text directed to? Are there multiple audiences?
- Rhetorical appeals—How does the speaker or writer use ethos, pathos, and logos?
- Kairos—What is special about the rhetorical moment of the text/speech in terms of place and time?

Activity 6.16 **Compose:** Write on Your Blog

In your blog, do a freewrite exercise in which you argue for some type of policy change related to a topic you are interested in writing about. What is the kairos of your topic? Where can you use the three rhetorical appeals (pathos, ethos, and logos)?

Activity 6.17 **Compose:** Write in Your Commonplace Book

Do a search on the Internet for kairos, ethos, pathos, and logos. Print out and paste a short section about each from the Internet. Then comment briefly about each section.

7

Inventing Rhetorically

Praxis in Action: How I Do Invention by Adam Webb

Before I start a research and writing project, I like to explore as many perspectives, arguments, or interpretations of a topic as possible. After I have chosen my topic, I write down everything I know about it. Next, I read broadly about my topic. I call this early stage of the research process "reading around," similar to information gathering.

Lauren Connolly likes to annotate readings because it allows her to have a conversation with the writer.

Then, I usually ask myself a series of questions, such as: (1) Why is this topic important to me? (2) What has been said or written on this topic? (3) Who has already written on this topic? (4) How do these perspectives or arguments relate to my own perspective on this topic? and (5) How has media, such as television or the Internet, portrayed this topic? If I don't know the answers, either from my personal knowledge or my "reading around," I ask individuals who are knowledgeable about my topic. By answering these questions, I usually develop a larger contextual framework in which I can better understand and situate myself within the various perspectives on my topic. This is all before I start to integrate specific material from research sources.

Next, I start locating any recurring terms, themes, symbols, connections, or references as well as listing other ideas, beliefs, or values that might be relevant to my topic. In order to keep track of my ideas and information, I like to use Dragon Dictation, a note-taking and voice recording program application on my smartphone. I sometimes use this application to start writing an outline of my ideas.

By this time, I know what I want to argue and the general framework of my project. Then I can begin adding in specific paraphrases and quotes from my research.

Aristotle's Classification of Rhetoric

Aristotle, in *The Art of Rhetoric* (or *On Rhetoric*), laid the groundwork for today's persuasive writing by being the first to write systemically about how to teach rhetoric. His teacher Plato, in contrast, had distrusted rhetoric. Plato deplored the way rhetoricians (or politicians) of his era skillfully manipulated the people of Athens, particularly the masses of up to 10,000 voters in the Assembly or 500 in the juries of the law courts. Aristotle, on the other hand, perceived great potential in rhetoric, when taught properly. Rhetoric, as he envisioned it, could be both persuasive and ethical, and in *The Art of Rhetoric* he laid out an organization and classification of rhetoric as he believed it should be taught.

Aristotle divided the process of writing and delivering a composition into five parts. The first of these was **invention**, during which the writer or speaker expanded a topic into ideas that were later arranged into a text or speech. According to the ancient Greeks, the rhetor *invented* these ideas, though they may have mirrored or adapted thoughts presented by previous rhetors. Today, we call this the **prewriting stage** of the writing process, an adaptation of Aristotle's invention stage.

In the previous chapter, we discussed the three appeals or means that a rhetor can use to persuade an audience: ethos, pathos, and logos. In *The Art of Rhetoric*, Aristotle divides these appeals or means of persuasion into two types of proofs: artistic and inartistic. Today, these proofs are still part of the writing process though we call them by different names.

Artistic Proofs

Artistic proofs are logical arguments constructed by rhetors from ideas plucked from their minds. An individual then develops these thoughts into a line of reasoning and, in the process, explores and narrows the topic, creates a thesis, and determines the ideas that need to be conveyed to the audience. These proofs are the ones that Aristotle and other ancient rhetoricians believed were critically important, for they are the ones developed from the *rhetor's own mind* and, thus, *invented*. These ideas can be shaped into two types of arguments—deductive and inductive—which we will discuss in the next few pages.

Inartistic Proofs

Inartistic proofs are direct evidence that the speaker might use to support the argument, such as testimony, documents, and anything else that rhetors do not invent through their own thinking. Today, we would call these proofs research. They, also, are essential to writing, but they should *support* the writer's ideas, rather than lead them.

For Aristotle's students, the use of artistic and inartistic proofs might not have been a two-step process—first one and then the other, though the proofs are arranged that way in *The Art of Rhetoric*, as they are in this book. Rather, similar to the process used by Adam Webb (see the *Praxis in Action* at the beginning of this chapter), they might have developed both proofs in an alternating or recursive process. After developing basic ideas for a composition through invention, these students would then collect information from authorities (testimony), what Webb refers to as "reading around." Then they would return to inventing artistic proofs about the project, followed by more references to inartistic proofs. Today, we have more resources for research than did the ancient Greeks, but this does not make artistic proofs any less important. The differences between artistic and inartistic proofs are summarized in table 7.1 below.

Table 7.1

Aristotle's Artistic and Inartistic Proofs	
Artistic Ideas from the rhetor's own mind, thus invented	Inartistic Information gained from external sources
Personal knowledge	Authorities
Observation	Testimony
Patterns of reasoning	Documents

The Five Canons of Rhetoric

Greek and Roman teachers of rhetoric divided rhetoric into five parts or canons. These canons corresponded to the order of activities in creating a speech, as they perceived the process: Invention, arrangement, style, memory, and delivery. These five parts are described in many handbooks of rhetorical instruction, including the *Rhetorica ad Herennium*, which was composed by an unknown author between 86 and 82 CE:

> The speaker . . . should possess the faculties of Invention, Arrangement, Style, Memory, and Delivery. Invention is the devising of matter, true or plausible, that would make the case convincing. Arrangement is the ordering and distribution of the matter, making clear the place to which each thing is to be assigned. Style is the adaptation of suitable words and sentences to the matter devised. Memory is the firm retention in the mind of the matter, words, and arrangement. Delivery is the graceful regulation of voice, countenance, and gesture.

Today, classes in composition or writing studies still emphasize the necessity of **invention**, now interpreted as prewriting activities that enable writers to develop the logic and words needed for effective arguments. **Arrangement** involves organizing an argument into a logical format that leads the reader easily from the thesis to the conclusion. **Style** has to do with the author's voice and tone and the structure of sentences and paragraphs. **Memory** is used somewhat differently today, as students are no longer required to memorize compositions for oral presentation. Instead, memory is utilized in ways such as remembering how and where to retrieve information from the Internet, books, and other reference materials. Finally, **delivery**, which once involved gestures and tone of voice in an oral presentation, today has to do with document design, so that the final product is presented in a professional manner according to Modern Language Association (MLA) or American Psychological Association (APA) style. Delivery also involves grammatical accuracy because surface errors detract from the effective impact of a document. See table 7.2 below for a summary of the five parts of rhetoric.

Table 7.2

The Five Parts (or Canons) of Rhetoric		
English	**Greek**	**Latin**
invention	heuresis	inventio
arrangement	taxis	dispositio
style	lesis	elocutio
memory	mneme	memoria
delivery	hypocrisis	actin

The Modern Writing Process Overview

Prewriting (Inventing)

Writing is not only about putting the pen to paper. As did rhetors in ancient Greece and Rome, you have to think deeply and critically about a subject before you begin a composition. The "invention" step of the writer's process is designed to help you find a worthwhile topic and develop your ideas about that topic before you start to write a draft. It includes writing, discussion, and research, as well as informal writing to help you explore your thoughts and feelings about a subject. Whatever method you choose, keep a record of your thoughts and discoveries as you spend this time in close examination of your subject.

Drafting

It may seem odd that writing a draft should come in the middle of the writer's process. However, research has shown that students and professionals alike write more effective essays when they don't reach for the pen too quickly. If you have spent enough time in the invention stage, the actual drafting stage may go more quickly. After writing the first draft, in succeeding drafts you can add details, observations, illustrations, examples, expert testimony, and other support to help your essay entertain, illuminate, or convince your audience.

Revising

Today, we talk more about the revision stage of writing than did ancient rhetoricians. If you are a student who tends to write assigned essays at the last minute, you may have missed this step entirely, yet many writers claim this is the longest and most rewarding step in the writing process. To revise, you must, in a sense, learn to let go of your writing. Some students think their first drafts should stay exactly the way they are written because they are true to their feelings and experience. Many writers find, however, that first drafts assume too much about the reader's knowledge and reactions. Sometimes readers, reading a first draft essay, are left scratching their heads and wondering what it is the writer is trying to convey. Writers who revise try to read their writing as readers would, taking note of gaps in logic, the absence of clear examples, the need for reordering information, and so on. Then they can revise their content with the reader in mind.

Editing and Polishing

Once writers have clarified their messages and the methods by which they will present those messages, one more step must be taken. Particularly because their compositions are written, rather than presented orally, they must go over their work again to check for correct spelling, grammar, and punctuation, as well as the use of Standard Written English. Some students finish with an essay, print it, and turn it in without ever examining the final copy. This is a critical mistake, because misspelled words and typographical and formatting errors can make an otherwise well-written essay lose its credibility. The five canons of rhetoric and the modern writing process are summarized in table 7.3 below.

Table 7.3

The Five Canons of Rhetoric and the Modern Writing Process	
Five Canons of Rhetoric	**Modern Writing Process**
Invention—Devising the arguments that will make the case convincing, often basing them on models of famous speeches.	Prewriting—Determining the thesis, points of argument, counterargument, and rebuttal. Researching evidence to support the argument.
Arrangement—Ordering the argument into a logical format. Style—Finding suitable words and figures of speech. [Note: This may have been a recursive process, but the ancients did not consider that aspect important.]	Drafting, revising, and editing—Putting ideas and prewriting into a useable form through a recursive process of drafting, revising, and editing.
Memory—Retaining the argument in the mind, including its content and arrangement.	Remembering how and where to retrieve information from the Internet, books, and other reference materials.
Delivery—Effective use of voice and gestures to present argument.	Publication—Putting text, images, and other elements in a suitable format and releasing the document to an audience.

Activity 7.1   **Collaborate:** Compare the Five Canons of Rhetoric and the Modern Writing Process

In your group, reread the discussions in this chapter on the five canons of rhetoric and the modern writing process and review the table above. What parts of the five canons correspond to the modern writing process? What step in the five canons is not included in the contemporary writing process? If the similarities and differences are not clear to you, consult the Internet. If you search for either "Five Canons of Rhetoric" or "Writing Process" you will find resources. What explanations can you offer for the differences? The similarities?

Stasis Theory Identifies Critical Point in Controversy

Stasis theory presents a series of four questions that were developed by Greek and Roman rhetoricians, primarily Aristotle, Quintilian, and Hermagoras. Answering these questions for an issue enabled rhetors to determine the critical (or stasis) point in a disagreement. This was a technique the ancients developed for the law courts to enable advocates to focus their arguments on the crux of the case. Quintilian, the great Roman teacher of rhetoric, explained in regard to a defendant:

> By far the strongest mode of defense is if the charge which is made can be denied; the next, if an act of the kind charged against the accused can be said not to have been done; the third, and most honorable, if what is done is proved to have been justly done. If we cannot command these methods, the last and only mode of defense is that of eluding an accusation, which can neither be denied nor combated, by the aid of some point of law, so as to make it appear that the action has not been brought in due legal form.

In other words, Quintilian is saying that in law cases, advocates have four choices in developing a focus for their arguments. You have probably watched a courtroom drama on television or film and can recall various defenses made on behalf of defendants. The strongest and most obvious defense is that the defendant is not guilty, that is, he or she did not do the deed in question. The same was true in Quintilian's day. However, sometimes an argument of innocence is not possible, perhaps because it seems obvious that the defendant did perform the deed in question. Thus, the advocate must develop a different strategy. For example, in defense of one accused of murder, the attorney may argue self-defense or mitigating circumstances (such as that the killing was an act of war). In rare cases, other defenses are offered; for example, if the supposed victim's body has not been found, the advocate can argue that the victim may still be alive. An attorney can discover these possible defenses by using stasis theory to analyze the situation.

Another great advantage of stasis theory is that, if pursued diligently, it prevents the rhetor from making the mistake of organizing an argument by simply forwarding reasons why he or she is correct and the opposition is wrong. That approach may please people who agree with the rhetor, but it will not likely gain any support from the opposition. Answering the stasis questions carefully forces the writer to consider aspects of the issue that may have been overlooked but are crucial to an effective argument.

The wording of the four questions has varied somewhat over time, but essentially they are questions of fact, definition, quality, and policy. The same questions can be applied to any issue, not only issues of law. The four stasis questions are as follows:

1. What are the facts? (conjecture)
2. What is the meaning or nature of the issue? (definition)
3. What is the seriousness of the issue? (quality)
4. What is the best plan of action or procedure? (policy)

Many writers prefer stasis theory to other prewriting techniques because answering the questions determines whether or not the different sides of an argument are at stasis. Being at **stasis** means that the opponents are in agreement about their disagreement—the stasis point—which can be identified by one of the four stasis questions. If the sides are at stasis, they have common ground to build upon, for they are arguing the same issue. There is, thus, a greater chance the sides can reach a workable consensus or compromise. If opponents are not at stasis, there is much more work to be done to reach consensus.

> The point where the opposing sides agree upon their disagreement is the stasis point.

For example, in the argument about the teaching of evolution and/or intelligent design in schools, the two sides are not in agreement about how to discuss the issue. Those in favor of teaching evolution claim intelligent design should not be called science, which is an issue of definition. Those who propose teaching intelligent design along with (or instead of) evolution tend to focus on "proving" evidence, an issue of fact. Until the two sides can agree upon what is the stasis point, or crux of the issue, they cannot debate effectively. They are not presenting arguments about the same question.

The four stasis questions can be broken into the subquestions listed in table 7.4. If you want to find the stasis point, work through the list for your issue, answering all of the subquestions. However, for each question, you must identify not only how *you* would answer the question but also how the opposing side or sides would answer. For example, if you are considering the issue of global warming, people with different positions will not agree on the facts. Thus, you must identify the basic facts of global warming represented by your side, and then identify the facts that might be presented by the opposing side.

Table 7.4

Stasis Questions
Fact
• Did something happen?   • What are the facts?   • Is there a problem/issue?   • How did it begin and what are its causes?   • What changed to create the problem/issue?   • Can it be changed?   It also may be useful to ask the following critical questions of your own research and conclusions: • Where did I obtain my data and are these sources reliable?   • How do I know they're reliable?
Definition
• What is the nature of the problem/issue?   • What exactly is the problem/issue?   • What kind of a problem/issue is it?   • To what larger class of things or events does it belong?   • What are its parts, and how are they related?   It also may be useful to ask the following critical questions of your own research and conclusions: • Who/what is influencing my definition of this problem/issue?   • How/why are these sources/beliefs influencing my definition of the issue?

Stasis Questions
Quality
Is it a good thing or a bad thing?
How serious is the problem/issue?
Who might be affected by this problem/issue (stakeholders)?
What happens if we don't do anything?
What are the costs of solving the problem/issue?
It also may be useful to ask the following critical questions of your own research and conclusions:
Who/what is influencing my determination of the seriousness of this problem/issue?
How/why are these sources/beliefs influencing my determination of the issue's seriousness?
Policy
Should action be taken?
Who should be involved in helping to solve the problem/address the issue?
What should be done about this problem?
What needs to happen to solve this problem/address this issue?
It also may be useful to ask the following critical questions of your own research and conclusions:
Who/what is influencing my determination of what to do about this problem/issue?
How/why are these sources/beliefs influencing my determination of what to do about this issue?
Source: Adapted from Purdue Owl Resource on Stasis Theory, http://owl.english.purdue.edu/owl/resource/736/1.

Using Stasis Questions

To illustrate the use of stasis questions, a team of writers working together to compose a report on racism in America might use the stasis questions to talk through information they will later use in their report. In the following sample dialogue, team members disagree about what actions are racist.

> "Flying the Confederate battle flag is racist."
> "Flying the Confederate battle flag is *not* racist."
> "Yes, it is, because it represents the Confederate states that supported slavery, and it's generally accepted that slavery in America was racist."
> "Flying the Confederate battle flag is not racist, because it's a part of American history and Southern heritage."

These two team members disagree about whether or not flying the Confederate battle flag is a racist act. This sort of disagreement might lead to a complete breakdown of group work if common ground cannot be found.

In this example, the team members go on to agree that some people still exhibit the Confederate battle flag (*fact*) on their vehicles and on their clothes, but that the flag is also displayed in museums (*fact*). They go on to agree that the issue is still very important to some people since a number of American states have recently debated the flag in legislatures and assemblies (*quality*).Moreover, group members note that a number of legal suits have been filed for and against the display of the flag in public places, so it's clear the issue still matters to a lot of people (*quality*).

In this sense, the team members have achieved stasis on two of the four stases—*fact* (people still display the flag, though in different places) and *quality* (it's a very important issue). Where the team members disagree, however, is in the stases

of *definition* (is the display of the flag "racist"?) and *policy* (what should we do about this?).

Thinking about this disagreement using stasis theory allows people to build common ground so that parties who disagree can move toward resolution and action even if they can't agree on all levels. For example, team members who disagree about whether or not flying the Confederate battle flag is racist might still be able to agree on what to do about it.

> "Ok, we disagree about whether flying the flag is racist, but we can agree that flying the flag is probably protected under the First Amendment to the United States Constitution—that flying the flag is protected by our freedom of speech."
> "Yeah."
> "So, people are free to display the flag on their vehicles, on their clothes, and on their property, as well as in museums. But, state legislatures and assemblies will have to debate and vote on whether or not the flag can be displayed on publicly funded property or in public symbols, such as state flags and seals."
> "That sounds pretty democratic. Sure."

Not every team situation is going to end this amicably; however, by using the stasis questions to help keep the dialogue going—on a reasonable course—team members can find common ground and work toward action that is acceptable to most, if not all, of the group members.*[1]

Stasis Theory and Kairos

As you will remember from Chapter 3, the *kairos* of an argument is the context, opportune moment, or point in time in which the rhetor, the audience, the issue, and the current situation provide opportunities and constraints for an argument. If you keep kairos in mind as you analyze an issue, you take advantage of timeliness. For example, if you want to write an argument about the death penalty, you might consider that United States courts are increasingly questioning the validity of eyewitness testimony, evidence which has been the deciding factor in many death penalty cases.

As part of your use of stasis theory, consider the four questions in relation to kairos:

1. How do recent developments (new facts) or the local situation affect the issue? Will it change your audience's perception of the facts?
2. Does the current situation affect your audience's definition of the issue? Is it defined differently by an audience in this location than elsewhere?
3. Have recent events made the issue more or less important to your audience? Is it more or less important in your location than elsewhere?
4. Do recent events, locally or widely, affect the need or lack of need for action, in your audience's perception?

As a rhetorician, it is important for you to be aware of the history of a controversy. But it is equally important to have an awareness of the kairos of the argument. Such an awareness enables you to adopt a "ready stance" and adjust your argument, so that it reflects an awareness of your audience's position and interests, as well as contemporary developments in the issue. Such a flexible stance may afford you an opportunity to be persuasive that you might otherwise miss.

1* Allen Brizee, "Stasis Theory for Teamwork," *Purdue Owl,* April 17, 2010, http://owl.english.purdue.edu/owl/ (Accessed October 3, 2011).

Activity 7.2 **Explore:** Identify the Defense in a Television or Film Courtroom Drama

As your instructor directs, watch a courtroom drama on television or film and decide what defense the defendant's attorney is offering. Report your conclusion to your small group or the class. Then, after you have discussed the stasis questions, identify which of the four questions the attorney in the drama is focusing upon as the crux of the defense. Discuss with your group or the class.

Activity 7.3 **Explore:** Use Stasis Theory to Explore Your Topic

Choose an issue that interests you and answer all the stasis questions in the table on pages 117-118, both for your position and for the opposing argument. Elaborate with three or four sentences for each subquestion that is particularly relevant to your topic. Is your issue at stasis for any of the questions? Report to your group or to the class.

Activity 7.4 **Explore:** Evaluate a Public Debate

Locate a public debate that has been reported recently in newspaper editorials, television programs, or other media that can be analyzed by using stasis theory.   In a paper of 350 to 500 words, do the following:
- Describe the context (kairos).
- Identify the sides of the argument and their principal points.
- Decide which stasis question each side is primarily addressing.
- Determine whether or not the issue is at stasis and explain your answer.
- Include a citation in MLA or APA format for your source or sources.

Activity 7.5: **Compose:** Use Stasis Theory to Analyze a Case

Professors Vijay Govindarajan and Christian Sarkar launched a competition on the *Harvard Business Network* blog for designs to build $300 houses for the poor. Word of the competition spread quickly, and a wide variety of people began to write about the competition—in editorials in *The New York Times*, the *Economist,* and in a companion blog, http://www.300house.com/blog.

Your Task: Read the four articles written about the $300 house competition that appear on the following pages. Discuss them in class and in small groups. In particular, note that Matias Echanove and Rahul Srivastava write in their *New York Times* op-ed essay, "Hands Off Our Houses," that the idea of a $300 house is impractical and will fail in places such as Mumbai, India. In contrast, "A $300 Idea that Is Priceless," the editorial from the *Economist*, praises the design competition for initiating an "explosion of creativity." Work through the stasis questions, with one side of the controversy being those who support this design initiative. The other side would be those who foresee problems in applying this idealistic initiative in the real world, a viewpoint that is expressed in "Hands Off Our Houses."

Write a paper of approximately 750 words in which you do the following:

- Briefly present the idea of the design competition.
- Summarize the arguments of those in favor of the initiative.
- Explain the reservations expressed in "Hands Off Our Houses."
- Identify a stasis point, if one exists, and explain why you think the sides have common ground on that particular stasis question.
- Discuss whether the discovery of common ground might allow individuals involved in this debate to talk to one another and work toward solutions for the problem of substandard housing in slums worldwide.
- As your instructor directs, cite your sources in APA or MLA style.

Reading 7.1

The $300 House: A Hands-On Lab for Reverse Innovation? by Vijay Govindarajan Published in the HBR Blog Network.

David A. Smith, the founder of the Affordable Housing Institute (AHI) tells us that "markets alone will never satisfactorily house a nation's poorest citizens . . . whether people buy or rent, housing is typically affordable to only half of the population.

The result? Smith points to a "spontaneous community of self-built or informally built homes—the shanty towns, settlements, and ever-expanding slums that sprout like mushrooms on the outskirts of cities in the developing world."

We started discussing the issue, examining the subject through the lens of reverse innovation.

Here are five questions Christian and I asked ourselves:

1. How can organic, self-built slums be turned into livable housing?
2. What might a house-for-the-poor look like?
3. How can world-class engineering and design capabilities be utilized to solve the problem?
4. What reverse-innovation lessons might be learned by the participants in such a project?
5. How could the poor afford to buy this house?

Livable Housing. Our first thought was that self-built houses are usually built from materials that are available—cardboard, plastic, mud or clay, metal scraps and whatever else is nearby. Built on dirt floors, these structures are prone to collapse and catching fire. Solution: replace these unsafe structures with a mass-produced, standard, affordable, and sustainable solution. We want to create the $300-House-for-the-Poor.

Look and Feel. To designers, our sketch of this house might be a bit of a joke, but it's useful nonetheless to illustrate the concept, to get started. We wanted the house to be an ecosystem of products and solutions designed around the real needs of the inhabitants. Of course it would have to be made out of sustainable, green materials, but more crucially, it would have to be durable enough to withstand torrential rains, earthquakes, and the stress of children playing. The house might be a single room structure with drop-down partitions for privacy. Furniture—sleeping hammocks and fold-down chairs would be built in. The roof would boast an inexpensive solar panel and battery to light the house and charge the mobile phone and tablet computer. An inexpensive water filter would be built in as well.

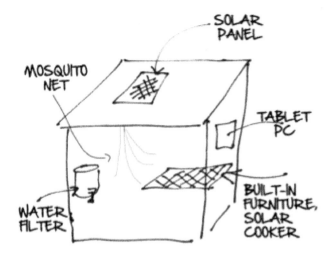

THE $300 HOUSE-for-the-POOR

In effect, the house is really a one-room shed designed around the family ecosystem, a lego-like aggregation of useful products that "bring good things to life" for the poor.

World-Class Design. Our next question was: "Who will do this?" We decided that it would have to be a collaboration between global design and engineering companies and non-profits with experience solving problems for the poor. The usual suspects ran through our minds—IDEO, GE, TATA, Siemens, Habitat-for-Humanity, Partners In Health, the Solar Electric Light Fund, the Clinton Global Initiative, the Gates Foundation, Grameen. Governments may play an important part in setting the stage for these types of cross-country innovation projects.

The Reverse Innovation Payoff. Participating companies will reap two rewards. First, they will be able to serve the unserved, the 2.5 billion who make up the bottom of the pyramid. Second, they create new competencies which can help transform lives in rich countries by creating breakthrough innovations to solve several problems (scaled housing for hurricane victims, refugees, and even the armed forces).

A House of One's Own: Affordability. To move beyond charity, the poor must become owners of their homes, responsible for their care and upkeep. The model of social business introduced by Muhammad Yunus resonates strongly with us. Micro-finance must surely play a role in making the $300 House-for-the-Poor a viable and self-sustaining solution.

Of course, the idea we present here is an experiment. Nevertheless, we feel it deserves to be explored. From the one-room shacks in Haiti's Central Plateau to the jhuggi clusters in and around Delhi, to the favelas in São Paulo, the problem of housing-for-the-poor is truly global.

We ask CEOs, governments, NGOs, foundations: Are there any takers?

Reading 7.2

Hands Off Our Houses by Matias Echanove and Rahul Srivastava Published in *The New York Times*.

Mumbai, India

Last summer, a business professor and a marketing consultant wrote on The Harvard Business Review's website about their idea for a $300 house. According to the writers, and the many people who have enthusiastically responded since, such a house could improve the lives of millions of urban poor around the world. And with a $424 billion market for cheap homes that is largely untapped, it could also make significant profits.

The writers created a competition, asking students, architects and businesses to compete to design the best prototype for a $300 house (their original sketch was of a one-room prefabricated shed, equipped with solar panels, water filters and a tablet computer). The winner will be announced this month. But one expert has been left out of the competition, even though her input would have saved much time and effort for those involved in conceiving the house: the person who is supposed to live in it.

We work in Dharavi, a neighborhood in Mumbai that has become a one-stop shop for anyone interested in "slums" (that catchall term for areas lived in by the urban poor). We recently showed around a group of Dartmouth students involved in the project who are hoping to get a better grasp of their market. They had imagined a ready-made constituency of slum-dwellers eager to buy a cheap house that would necessarily be better than the shacks they'd built themselves. But the students found that the reality here is far more complex than their business plan suggested.

To start with, space is scarce. There is almost no room for new construction or ready-made houses. Most residents are renters, paying $20 to $100 a month for small apartments.

Those who own houses have far more equity in them than $300—a typical home is worth at least $3,000. Many families have owned their houses for two or three generations, upgrading them as their incomes increase. With additions, these homes become what we call "tool houses," acting as workshops, manufacturing units, warehouses and shops. They facilitate trade and production, and allow homeowners to improve their living standards over time.

None of this would be possible with a $300 house, which would have to be as standardized as possible to keep costs low. No number of add-ons would be able to match the flexibility of need-based construction.

In addition, construction is an important industry in neighborhoods like Dharavi. Much of the economy consists of hardware shops, carpenters, plumbers, concrete makers, masons, even real-estate agents. Importing pre-fabricated homes would put many people out of business, undercutting the very population the $300 house is intended to help.

Worst of all, companies involved in producing the house may end up supporting the clearance and demolition of well-established neighborhoods to make room for it.

The resulting resettlement colonies, which are multiplying at the edges of cities like Delhi and Bangalore, may at first glance look like ideal markets for the new houses, but the dislocation destroys businesses and communities.

The $300 house could potentially be a success story, if it was understood as a straightforward business proposal instead of a social solution. Places like refugee camps, where many people need shelter for short periods, could use such cheap, well-built units. A market for them could perhaps be created in rural-urban fringes that are less built up.

The $300 house responds to our misconceptions more than to real needs. Of course problems do exist in urban India. Many people live without toilets or running water. Hot and unhealthy asbestos-cement sheets cover millions of roofs. Makeshift homes often flood during monsoons. But replacing individual, incrementally built houses with a ready-made solution would do more harm than good.

A better approach would be to help residents build better, safer homes for themselves. The New Delhi–based Micro Homes Solutions, for example, provides architectural and engineering assistance to homeowners in low-income neighborhoods.

The $300 house will fail as a social initiative because the dynamic needs, interests and aspirations of the millions of people who live in places like Dharavi have been overlooked. This kind of mistake is all too common in the trendy field of social entrepreneurship. While businessmen and professors applaud the $300 house, the urban poor are silent, busy building a future for themselves.

Reading 7.3

The $300 House: A Hands-On Approach to a Wicked Problem by Vijay Govindarajan with Christian Sarkar Published in the *HBR Blog Network*

When *The New York Times* printed "Hands Off Our Houses," an op-ed about our idea for a $300 House for the poor, we were both delighted and dismayed—delighted because the $300 House was being discussed, and dismayed because authors Matias Echanove and Rahul Srivastava, co-founders of the Institute of Urbanology, didn't seem to have read the series of blog posts about our idea.

Nearly every criticism the authors levy in their op-ed is answered in 12 blog posts, a magazine article from January/February 2011, a video interview, and a slideshow that integrated community and commentary, which were published between last October and this May.

In critiquing our vision, the authors cite Micro Homes Solutions as "a better approach." In fact, the leaders of that venture were invited several months ago to contribute a blog post to our series as a way of joining the discussion and helping us understand what they've seen on the ground there. They declined to be part of the conversation.

The authors also write that students who tried to write a business plan to serve the poor and who visited poor urban areas of India found "the reality here is far more complex than their business plan suggested."

Yet a fundamental tenet of our project and the blog series about it is that slums present complex challenges that can't be fixed with a clever shack alone. Rather than creating an echo chamber of rah-rah rhetoric, we told blog authors to focus on one of the many knotty issues that Echanove and Srivastava cite in their critique. From the start we asked: What are the complexities of financing these homes? How do you get energy and infrastructure into such dwellings? How do you get corporations to invest in a significant way? We acknowledged that we didn't have the answers. "Just because it is going to take longer than it should doesn't mean we should walk away," wrote Seth Godin in one of the posts. "It's going to take some time, but it's worth it."

The op-ed suggests that the $300 House doesn't acknowledge that "space is scarce" in urban poor areas. Yet, Sunil Suri wrote in a post on the urban challenge that "slums by their nature are located where land and space are limited." Suri proposed potential solutions, including innovative materials, new ways of thinking of the construction process, and building up.

The authors also say that "one expert has been left out of the challenge . . . the person who is supposed to live in it." But a post in the series on the co-creation challenge from Gaurav Bhalla addressed this squarely. "It will be unfortunate if the house were to be designed by those who will never live in it," wrote Bhalla. "Investments need to be made understanding the daily habits and practices of people for whom the house is being designed." Bhalla used the case study of the chulha stove, co-created by businesses, NGOs, and slum dwellers, to make his point. We are also bringing students to India and Haiti to do ethnographic research that will inform development of a $300 House, and when prototypes are developed, they will be deployed and tested with those who will live in them.

Echanove and Srivastava also state that a $300 House "would have to be as standardized as possible to keep costs low. No number of add-ons would be able to match the flexibility of need-based construction." While we agree that a one-size-fits-all approach will not work, we disagree that a $300 House would be inflexible. Core tenets from a blog post about the overall design challenge of creating a $300 House by Bill Gross include "give your customers options" and "make it aspirational." And David Smith's entry on the financial challenge shows that flexibility can be born out of financing options as well. A need-based approach alone also ignores the scale of the problem we are facing. "Triple the U.S. population by three. That's how many people around the world live on about a dollar a day," Godin writes. "Triple it again and now you have the number that lives on $2. About 40% of the world lives on $2 or less a day." In any situation where scale is required, so is some level of standardization.

The most puzzling critique in the op-ed was that "construction is an important industry in neighborhoods like Dharavi. Much of the economy consists of hardware shops, carpenters, plumbers, concrete makers, masons, even real-estate agents. Importing prefabricated homes would put many people out of business, undercutting the very population the $300 house is intended to help."

In fact, our contest's design briefing said these dwellings should be "self built and/or self-improvable." It also stated that the design should rely as much as possible on local materials, which of course would be harvested and crafted by local workers. Our goal is to increase demand for local trades, not drive them away. And the idea that jobs would disappear belies the fact that with progress comes new jobs; teachers for the kids who can now go to school; health care professionals for the families that can now afford check-ups; technology professionals who could service solar panels or internet access devices; farmers who could manage shared crop spaces in the neighborhoods. The $300 House project is a housing ecosystem project.

Finally, Echanove and Srivastava state that "The $300 house could potentially be a success story, if it was understood as a straightforward business proposal instead of a social solution."

We disagree completely. We do support other applications for low-cost housing—bringing these dwellings back to the industrialized world for hurricane relief, for example, would be a reverse innovation success story. However, trying to pigeonhole ideas as either "for good" or "for profit" is an outmoded way of thinking.

The authors have an implicit negative view on business. For them, profit seems to be a dirty word. For us, good business and social innovation are one and the same. The rising tide of New Capitalism, what Michael Porter calls "shared value" and what Umair Haque calls "thick value," is perhaps the most important reaction to the corruption and greed that spurred the most recent global economic crisis. The *Economist* was right when it suggested that this is a "can do" moment in history.

Our goal is neither to start yet another charity—one of our advisers, Paul Polak, tells us that "you can't donate your way out of poverty"—nor to start just another business. Rather we must encourage existing businesses to find ways to create new, scalable markets; to get NGOs to share their on-the-ground expertise; and to force governments to make it as simple as possible to work across the hybrid value chain in order to make such a project a reality and begin the process of instilling dignity in and creating options for individuals who now don't have either.

We are happy that Echanove and Srivastava share our passion for the problem of affordable housing, which is a wicked problem. We simply disagree with the idea that if it's a market, it can't also be a socially progressive solution. Trying to categorize the regeneration of slums as either a business problem or social problem is like trying to categorize a flame as either heat or light. It is both, always.

Reading 7.4

A $300 Idea that Is Priceless from Schumpeter, a column in the *Economist* Applying the world's business brains to housing the poor.

Friedrich Engels said in "The Condition of the Working Class in England," in 1844, that the onward march of Manchester's slums meant that the city's Angel Meadow district might better be described as "Hell upon Earth." Today, similar earthly infernos can be found all over the emerging world: from Brazil's favelas to Africa's shanties. In 2010 the United Nations calculated that there were about 827m people living in slums—almost as many people as were living on the planet in Engels's time—and predicted that the number might double by 2030.

Last year Vijay Govindarajan, of Dartmouth College's Tuck School of Business, along with Christian Sarkar, a marketing expert, issued a challenge in a *Harvard Business Review* blog: why not apply the world's best business thinking to housing the poor? Why not replace the shacks that blight the lives of so many poor people, thrown together out of cardboard and mud, and prone to collapsing or catching fire, with more durable structures? They laid down a few simple guidelines. The houses should be built of mass-produced materials tough enough to protect their inhabitants from a hostile world. They should be equipped with the basics of civilized life, including water filters and solar panels. They should be "improvable," so that families can adapt them to their needs. And they should cost no more than $300.

Mr. Govindarajan admits that the $300 figure was partly an attention-grabbing device. But he also argues that it has a certain logic. Muhammad Yunus, the founder of Grameen Bank, has calculated that the average value of the houses of people who have just escaped from poverty is $370. Tata Motors has also demonstrated the value of having a fixed figure to aim at: the company would have found it more difficult to produce the Tata Nano if it had simply been trying to produce a "cheap" car rather than a "one lakh" car (about $2,200).

The attention-grabbing certainly worked. The blog was so inundated with positive responses that a dedicated website, 300house.com, was set up, which has attracted more than 900 enthusiasts and advisers from all over the world. On April 20th Mr. Govindarajan launched a competition inviting people to submit designs for a prototype of the house.

Why has a simple blog post led to such an explosion of creativity? The obvious reason is that "frugal innovation"—the art of radically reducing the cost of products while also delivering first-class value—is all the rage at the moment. General Electric has reduced the cost of an electrocardiogram machine from $2,000 to $400. Tata Chemicals has produced a $24 purifier that can provide a family with pure water for a year. Girish Bharadwaj, an engineer, has perfected a technique for producing cheap footbridges that are transforming life in rural India.

Another reason is that houses can be such effective anti-poverty tools. Poorly constructed ones contribute to a nexus of problems: the spread of disease (because they have no proper sanitation or ventilation), the perpetuation of poverty (because children have no proper lights to study by) and the general sense of insecurity (because they are so flimsy and flammable). Mr. Govindarajan's idea is so powerful because he treats houses as ecosystems that provide light, ventilation and sanitation.

Numerous innovators are also worrying away at this nexus of problems. Habitat for Humanity, an NGO, is building durable houses of bamboo in Nepal. Idealab, a consultancy, is on the verge of unveiling a $2,500 house that will be mass-produced in factories, sold in kits and feature breakthroughs in ventilation, lighting and sanitation. Philips has produced a cheap cooking stove, the Chulha, that cuts out the soot that kills 1.6m people a year worldwide. The Solar Electric Light Fund is demonstrating that you can provide poor families with solar power for roughly the same cost as old standbys such as kerosene and candles.

Profits and other problems

These thinkers, like the advocates of the $300 house, must solve three huge problems to succeed. They must persuade big companies that they can make money out of cheap homes, because only they can achieve the economies of scale needed to hit the target price. They need to ensure sufficient access to microloans: $300 is a huge investment for a family of squatters living on a couple of dollars a day. And they need to overcome the obstacle that most slum-dwellers have weak or non-existent property rights. There is no point in offering people the chance to buy a cleverly designed house if they have no title to the land they occupy. Solving these problems will in turn demand a high degree of co-operation between people who do not always get on: companies and NGOs, designers and emerging-world governments.

However, the exciting thing about the emerging world at the moment is a prevailing belief that even the toughest problems can be solved. And a similar can-do moment, in the late 1940s, offers a striking historical precedent for the application of mass-production techniques to housing: as American servicemen flooded home after the second world war to start families, Levitt & Sons built Levittowns at the rate of 30 houses a day by mass-producing the components in factories, delivering them on lorries and using teams of specialists to assemble them.

Some emerging-world governments are beginning to realize that providing security of tenure is the only way to deal with the problem of ever-proliferating slums. And big companies that face stagnant markets in the West are increasingly fascinated by the "fortune at the bottom of the pyramid." Bill Gross of Idealab reckons the market for cheap houses could be worth at least $424 billion. But in reality it is worth far more than that: preventing the Earth from becoming what Mike Davis, a particularly gloomy follower of Marx and Engels, has termed a "planet of slums."

Other Invention Strategies

Great myths have grown up around writers who can supposedly sit down, put pen to paper, and write a masterpiece. If these myths had developed about any other type of artist—a musician or a painter—we would scoff about them and ask about the years of study and practice those artists had spent before they created their masterpieces. Since all of us can write to some degree, perhaps it seems more feasible that great authors simply appear magically amongst us. Alas, it is not so; like all talented artists, good writers must learn their craft through consistent and continuous practice. Similar to how the ancient Greeks used **topoi** (a strategy or heuristic made up of questions about a topic which allows a rhetor to construe an argument) to generate raw material for their compositions, many writers today use the following invention strategies as prewriting activities.

Freewriting

One practice method developed in the 1970s and often attributed to Peter Elbow, author of *Writing without Teachers*, is called freewriting. This method is just what it sounds like—writing that is free of any content restrictions. You simply write what is on your mind. This method is freeform, but there is some structure—you must set a time limit before you begin, and once you begin, you must not stop. The time period is usually 10 to 20 minutes, and you must keep your pen or pencil moving on the page—no hesitations, no corrections, no rereading. Don't worry about spelling, or punctuation, or grammar—just download onto the paper whatever comes to mind. It will seem awkward at best; some have said it is downright painful. But after a few weeks practice, you will realize it is effective and a wonderful individual method of getting at your thoughts on a subject.

Invisible Freewriting

If you just cannot stop paying attention to your spelling and grammar, or if you find yourself always stopping to read what you have written, you can freewrite invisibly. To do this, you will need carbon paper and a pen that is retracted or out of ink. You sandwich the carbon paper, carbon side down, between two sheets of paper and write on the top sheet with your empty pen. You cannot see what you are writing, but it will be recorded on the bottom sheet of paper. If you prefer to work on the computer, you can easily modify this technique by taping a blank sheet of paper over the monitor while you type.

Focused Freewriting

When freewriting, you are writing without sticking to any particular topic. You are exploring many ideas and your sentences may roam from your day at work, the letter you just got from your sister, or a story you read in the paper about a man who tracks the nighttime migrations of songbirds. With focused freewriting, you are trying to concentrate on one particular subject. You can write the name of that subject at the top of the page to remind you of your topic as you write. The rules are the same as the other types of freewriting, but you are focusing on one question or idea and exploring it in depth.

One drawback of focused freewriting is that students sometimes confuse it with a different step in the writing process, drafting. Remember that freewriting is "invention" work, intended only to help you explore ideas on paper. Drafting takes place only after you have explored, analyzed, and organized those ideas. Freewriting helps you think and write critically about a topic while drafting occurs once you have done the critical thinking necessary to come up with a unified, cohesive, and organized plan for an essay.

Listing/Brainstorming

This method of mapping is the least visual and the most straightforward. Unlike freewriting, where you write continuously, with listing you write down words and/or phrases that provide a shorthand for the ideas you might use in your essay, much as you would a grocery or "to-do" list. Brainstorming is a bit looser. Lists usually follow line after line on the page; brainstorming consists of words and phrases placed anywhere you want to write them on the page.

Clustering

When you think of a cluster, you think of several like things grouped together, often with something holding them together. Peanut clusters, a type of candy, are peanuts joined together with milk chocolate. Star clusters are groupings of stars, like the Pleiades or the Big Dipper, connected by their relative positions to each other in space. You can create clusters of like ideas by grouping your ideas around a central topic on a blank sheet of paper.

Organizing or Arranging

The "invention" process is intended to get our ideas out of our heads and onto a piece of paper, but rarely do these ideas arrive in the most logical or effective order. Take some time (an hour or so for a short essay) to analyze your inventions. Place all the ideas in a logical order, and join similar ideas. Next, look for your most significant point, the most important thing you want to say about your subject. This may become your tentative thesis. Then identify which of the other items on your list will help you communicate your point and delete items that are irrelevant to your thesis.

When I was working at Berkeley's College Academic Support Center, I often tutored second-language learners who struggled with sentences that had awkward constructions. Sometimes, I would say to a student, "What is it you're trying to say here?" The student inevitably could state the point orally with accuracy and clarity. I would then say to the student, "Write down what you just said." The student would write it down with pen and paper. Then I'd say, "Okay, pretend you're the professor. Which do you think is the easier sentence to understand: what you wrote or what you typed?" The student would say, "What I wrote. Whenever I type, I'm always afraid of what the professor will say."

Craig Wynne says, "When jumping out of an airplane, you don't have time to think about consequences. You just have to do it....The same principle applies to writing."

Around that time, I read an article in *Writer* magazine entitled "Forget the Rules and Take a Leap," by an author named Deanna Roy. In this article, Roy had been suffering from writer's block, and she found that skydiving was a way for her to release her thoughts without fear of saying the "wrong thing." So I decided to put this idea into practice myself for the purposes of teaching my students about overcoming their inhibitions when it came to writing.

When jumping out of an airplane, you don't have time to think about consequences. You just have to do it. You can see from the photo, jumping wasn't an easy thing for me to do, but afterwards I was glad I had gone through with taking that leap.

The same principle applies to writing. You need to find a way to write without thinking about whether your words are spelled correctly or whether the professor won't like the idea. Those thoughts get in the way with your writing process. Some students can write with that kind of freedom on a computer, but others find that with the computer comes an uninvited editor who looks over their shoulder and criticizes. Yet, they can escape that editor by talking out their thoughts and then writing with pen and paper. Whatever works. This doesn't mean that writing is ever going to be easy. It's just easier if you can get your thoughts down on a piece of paper before that internal editor starts looking for errors.

A professor named Peter Elbow developed a process called freewriting, which helps writers take that leap from thoughts into words. To freewrite, you put your pen to paper and just write. You don't want to think about whether something is spelled incorrectly or whether the professor will like an idea. Freewriting is the chance for you to get your ideas down on paper (or on the computer). When you freewrite, you don't stop. You just write. Even if you have an idea you think sounds completely stupid or off-the-wall, just write it down. You never know. Sometimes, those "silly" ideas could contain something you might be able to use for your assignment. When I start a project, I begin by letting all my ideas out in words in a row, even if they don't sound quite right. Professor Elbow remarked that freewriting results in a lot of words that are garbage. That's true. However, eventually, I come to words that express an idea I like. In order to get to the point of liking my words, I have to take that leap onto the page. Eventually, I have to worry about grammar, structure, and the end product, but not while I'm freewriting.

Activity 7.6 **Explore:** Consider "Take a Leap into Writing"

1. How do you write most easily? On a computer? With pen and paper? Share your experience getting words onto a page.
2. What do you think of Wynne's comparison of writing to skydiving? What do the two things have in common?
3. Do you have an internal editor that keeps you from writing freely? Can you describe your editor? What does it do?

Activity 7.7 **Compose:** Focused Freewriting

1. Write your topic at the top of a blank sheet of paper.
2. Write a list of at least 10 aspects or characteristics of your topic.
3. Choose two or three items from your list and do a focused freewriting on each item for five to eight minutes.
4. Add more items to your list if you have discovered new ideas during your freewriting.

Activity 7.8 **Collaborate:** Begin with What You Know

In your small group, make a list of controversial topics that you already have some knowledge about because of personal experience or course work. For example, one of you may be among the millions of Americans without health insurance or you may know someone else in this position. If so, you probably know about some of the failings of the American health care system. Alternatively, you may have lost a job during the 2009 recession or been unable to find a job when you needed one. If so, you probably have some thoughts about the efforts of the federal government to deal with the economic crisis. These personal connections with controversial issues give you a starting point for research on a topic. Share your group's list with the class.

Expand Your Personal Knowledge through Observation

Close observation for descriptive detail can enhance almost any topic. If you are writing a paper on the effectiveness of recycling in your community, you might take a trip to your community's processing area for recycled glass. There you could gather information through observing the glass recycling process. You also might be able to conduct short, informal interviews with the employees about the process.

You may need to call to get permission to visit certain places. You'll need to identify yourself and your topic. Usually you can get permission to visit and observe.

However, if you cannot get permission to visit an area, you can ask your contact if there is a similar area nearby. Again, look at your research questions before you visit to decide which questions might be answered by your observations. For example, if you have read about recycling centers in other communities, during your visit to the local center, you could observe the similarities and differences in their procedures. Good writers always gather more detail than they actually use so they have choices about what to include.

The key to successful observation is tuning the senses. Can you remember what your room smelled like when you woke up this morning, the first thing you saw when you opened your eyes, the way your sheets or blanket felt against your skin, the sounds in the room after you turned off your alarm, or the taste of the orange juice or coffee you had with breakfast? Our minds are trained to ignore seemingly unimportant information, so if you can't remember any sensory details from your morning, you're not alone. When conducting an observation, however, those sensory responses are an important part of your research. Sitting in the place you're observing, freewrite for at least five minutes on each of the senses: touch, taste, smell, sight, and sound. You might even freewrite on each of the senses from several different vantage points, depending on the size of the place or the event you're observing. Take notes on the responses given by those you speak with.

Within fifteen minutes of leaving the place you have been observing, take a few minutes to read over your notes and write a few overall impressions or add details you missed in your description. Look again at your research questions and decide which ones have been answered by your visit.

Activity 7.9 **Explore:** Observation Exercise

In this exercise, describe your classroom. Alternatively, go to another setting such as a museum, restaurant, or library and describe that space and the people in it.

- How large is the space, approximately? Describe the shape of the room, and the color and texture of the walls, the ceiling, and the floor.
- How is the space furnished? Describe the color, shape, and style of the furnishings.
- What about representing the other senses? Is the room silent or noisy? Does it have a characteristic smell? Describe.
- How many people are in the room? What are they doing? Describe their ages, general style of dress, and possessions such as computers, backpacks, or purses.
- Pick two or three people that stand out in some way from the other occupants and write a sentence or two about each, describing what it is about each person that caught your attention.

Reading 7.6

BMW 1M: Miniature, Mighty and Miles of Fun by Dan Neil Dan Neil, auto columnist for The Wall Street Journal, reviewed the new BMW Coupe in his weekly column "Rumble Seat." As you read the article that follows, pay attention to how the author uses details from both personal knowledge and close observation to enrich his writing.

Typically, car makers will choose a special color for the introduction of a special vehicle, known in the biz as the "launch color." In the case of the 1M Coupe—the Motorsports division variant of BMW's beastly looking 135i—the launch color is a sort of burnt tangerine, a phrase that also describes my own mental citrus after a weekend behind the wheel.

A bratty little barrel-racer of a car, with a spirit that seems to want to bite through the bit, the 1M Coupe is quick, playful, aggressive and laugh-out-loud fun to drive; indeed, it's as much fun as the law will allow. For BMW fanboys, I gather, that's just the problem.

A little history is in order: The M division began in the 1970s building highly tuned versions of the Werks' production cars, with more powerful engines, bigger brakes, more athletic legs and edgier electronics. Some of these cars have been, simply, epic. The M3 that I imprinted on was a '96 Euro-spec yellow coupe. That car is, to this day, the best handling five-seater I've ever driven.

Bratty Little Barrel Racer

(Note to Bavaria: Bring back the narrow-section steering wheel. And stop hogging all the good scenery.)

To describe the pleasures of that M3—known to the geek squad as the E36 model—is to define a kind of atavism that the Bimmerphiles pine for. Those cars were relatively simple (in-line six, manual transmission and spare amenities), with beautifully quick and sensitive steering and an easy progressiveness that meant you could let the rear end slide around without fear of losing it, catching the car with a dab of throttle and counter-steer. It wasn't the fastest car in the world but it was such a sheer limbic pleasure to drive, to wheel, to wield, to control. That's it: a sense of mastery. You got out of that car wearing a cape and a big S on your chest.

Most of all, that car was lightweight. That E36 coupe weighed about 3,200 pounds. By contrast, the current model-year M3 (E92) weighs fully 500 pounds more on a 2.4-inch-longer wheelbase. And while the current M3 has vastly more go-fast hardware—including a 414-horsepower V8, optional dual-clutch gearbox, cybernetic brakes and the M Variable Differential Lock (sounds like an outlawed wrestling hold, doesn't it?)—a certain something, call it a dynamic lucidity, has been lost.

And the fanboys feel betrayed. They whine, they fume, they wear black. You'd think Rudolph Valentino had just died or something. Why does the M3 have to be so heavy? What part of Ultimate Driving Machine does BMW itself not understand?

But everyone's favorite M3 of yore didn't have to have a monster stereo, navi, power seats, umpteen airbags or five-star crash structure. The M3 so fondly remembered has been essentially optioned up and regulated out of existence. Unless BMW discovers the formula for Flubber, that car isn't coming back.

And the bloat isn't confined to the weight scales. The current M3 is also punitively pricey, starting at $61,075 (with gas-guzzler tax) and luxed-out to nearly $70,000. More fanboy despair. Oh, Rudy!

To these disconsolate few, the news last year that the M division was going to hot up the 135i coupe (the E82 platform, in nerd-speak) must have sounded like salvation. The numbers were there. Not quite 3,400 pounds, with a twin-turbo 3.0-liter in-line six delivering 335 hp and 332 pound-feet of torque—with brief computer-summoned overboost of 369 pound-feet—and the sole choice of a six-speed manual transmission, the 1M Coupe sounded like more than just a cool car. It promised a return to form, an end to a kind of despised lavishness, a cure for what ails the BMW brand.

2012 BMW 1M Coupe

Base price: $47,010
Price as tested: $49,000 (est.)
Powertrain: Twin-turbo 3.0-liter in-line six cylinder with variable valve timing; six-speed manual transmission; rear wheel drive with variable differential lock
Horsepower/torque: 335 hp at 5,900 rpm/332 pound-feet at 1,500–4,500 rpm (369 pound-feet at overboost)
Length/weight: 172.4 inches/3,362 pounds
Wheelbase: 104.7 inches

EPA fuel economy: 19/26 mpg, city/highway
Cargo capacity: 8 cubic feet

Now that the car is here, is it? You know, it is, sort of.

To boil it down a bit, the 1M Coupe is the smaller car with the mighty M3's dirty bits, less 400 pounds. The same highly evolved suspension componentry, the same massive brakes behind the same stick-with-a-grip 35-series, 19-inch tires and wheels, the same electronically controlled rear differential, and the same M-tuned dynamics control, which allows drivers to color outside the lines safely at the track. And yes, you can turn the electronic interventions off. But once the nannies are dismissed, be advised, the car has a measure of the old-school, free-gimbaling character of the early M's. In other words, it can get away from you. Me? Oh, please. You'd like that, wouldn't you?

The 1M is certainly track-day ready, with a dry-sump engine-lubrication system with its own heat exchanger as well as a radiator for the heavy-duty six-speed transmission. The car I drove had a brake warning light come on—I think the 14-inch cross-drilled brakes got a little too warm after being lapped at Laguna Seca for a half-hour or so—but they never failed to haul the car down with a precise and determined yank rearward.

Here, at last, is a man's clutch—heavily weighted, with a smooth, precise uptake—and slick-shifting gearshift to go with it. Pedal position is just about perfect for heel-and-toe footwork.

Serene and smooth at low speeds, but with an increasingly impatient growl from the quad exhaust as the revs build, the 1M does several dynamic things particularly well. First, at corner exits, it pulls like hell, like it has deployed some magical torque spinnaker. BMW gives the 0–60 acceleration at 4.7 seconds, but the way this thing gets on the cam in second and third gear will bring a tear to your eye. Like my favorite M3 of olden days, the car is not unnervingly fast but it's hugely willing. This thing hits redline faster than one of the Real Housewives of Atlanta.

Second, it has splendid cornering grip, and the corner-to-corner transitions happen without a lot of heaving, rolling or rebound to unsettle the car or cause you to correct your line. The 1M Coupe has impeccable cornering manners, and the M Sport Seats lock you in driving position.

Third, it trail-brakes like a dream. Turn in to a corner with the brakes on and ease off the binders. The car's rear end slides gracefully to the outside, the world swivels and now you're looking at corner exit. Dig in the spurs, up come the revs. Hi-yo, Silbern, away!

So what could possibly be wrong? Well, for one thing, the 1M Coupe is a total buttaface, one of the ugliest, most disturbingly wrong car designs in modern history. The addition of all the massive wheel arches, lip spoilers, aero mods and the so-called Air Curtain front spoiler helps not at all. This car is the last revenge of former BMW styling head Chris Bangle. Jeez, put a flag over its head and drive for glory.

Second—at least to the fanboys—it's still too heavy, despite the fact it's actually 77 pounds lighter than the standard 135i. But I checked the trunk for lead bars and found none, and I found very little in the way of depleted uranium in the cabin.

I can only conclude that, for some old-schoolers, nothing BMW makes will ever be light enough again. That's too bad. This thing's a tangerine dream.

Activity 7.10 **Explore:** Find Artistic and Inartistic Proofs in a Reading

Much of Dan Neil's column, "BMW 1M: Miniature, Mighty and Miles of Fun," comes from his own personal experience and observation. For example, his description of the car as a, "bratty little barrel-racer of a car, with a spirit that seems to want to bite through the bit," is his own evaluation or thought and, thus, an artistic proof. So is the first sentence, "Typically, car makers will choose a special color for the introduction of a special vehicle, known in the biz as the 'launch color.'" That information comes from his long experience with reviewing cars. Also, his remark that the brake light came on in the car he drove is his observation.

However, the information that the car has "a dry-sump engine-lubrication system with its own heat exchanger as well as a radiator for the heavy-duty six-speed transmission" may have come from the manufacturer's promotional literature.

For this activity, go through the reading and highlight (or underline) the parts that you think come from Dan Neil's own knowledge or observation. These are the artistic proofs. Information he has obtained from other sources (such as the car company) would be inartistic proofs. If you aren't sure whether or not a sentence is his own knowledge or observation, make a note of that in the margin. Discuss this as a class.

Activity 7.11 **Compose:** Write a Product Review

Choose a new product in a category you know well, such as a computer or an MP3 player, and write a review as if you were a columnist for a newspaper, magazine, or blog. Using the techniques explained in this chapter, do prewriting to elicit what you know about the product and the product category. Then, observe the product and try it out, so that you can review its positives and negatives. If you need specific information that you do not know, consult the product advertising, packaging, or instruction manual.

Like Dan Neil's auto product review, you can use vivid language and insider slang in order to provide an enjoyable experience for your reader. Remember, however, that this is an argument. You need to evaluate whether the product is a good or bad selection for its target audience and why.

Activity 7.12 **Compose:** Write on Your Blog

Choose a controversial topic and speculate in your blog whether or not that topic is at a stasis point for any of the stasis questions.

Activity 7.13 **Compose:** Write in Your Commonplace Book

In your commonplace book, freewrite about how you do invention. What methods do you use to extract from your mind what you already know about a subject (what Aristotle would call artistic proofs)?

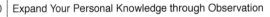

8
Writing Rhetorically

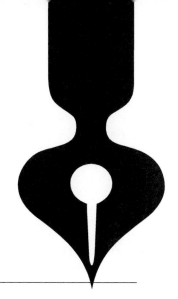

Praxis in Action: *How I Write* by Matthew Harding

Matthew Harding points out that writing can be daunting even for experienced writers.

Writing can seem very daunting at times, especially when you have a major writing assignment that's worth as much as a test. It should be easy since you know about the assignment way ahead of time, but somehow the time ends up getting away from you because it's hard to get started. You end up both stressing about the paper and trying to write it at the last minute. One way that I reduce the pressure of a writing assignment is to start writing long before the paper is due, giving myself enough time to work on it.

If I tell myself that I am only going to write a certain amount at a time, say a page a day, it is less intimidating to write. While this method may seem drawn out, it works. Whenever I come back to the paper the next day, I always review what I have already written, so I can be sure I keep the topic in mind. This way, I avoid burning myself out, getting my ideas confused, or losing track of the topic and, ultimately, rushing to finish by the end. This allows me to come to my paper with a fresh perspective and new ideas with every installment I write. Once I finish that day's work I feel good because I am getting the paper done while also giving it my best effort, which also greatly reduces the stress of having to write it.

Through Writing, Enter the Conversation

Cicero's famous work, *On the Ideal Orator*, is not a treatise or handbook about how to be an e-ffective rhetorician. Instead, it is a dialogue, a conversation. The setting is a villa outside Rome belonging to Lucius Licinius Crassus, and the time is 91 CE, an era of dangerous unrest in the Roman Empire. Prominent and respected citizens gather with Crassus to escape, for a while, the political crisis developing in the city. Crassus and his guests settle at leisure under a wide, spreading plane tree, not only to enjoy its shade but also to pay homage to Plato's *Phaedrus*, which similarly took place under a plane tree, though in Greece. They take time this day to dialogue about the attributes of an ideal orator. The purpose of the arguments they present to each other is not to win out over the others but, conversing together, to come to knowledge. It is not a trivial pursuit. Cicero reveals what his characters do not know—soon they will all die horribly as part of the civil unrest in Rome, violence traceable to the failure of leaders to resolve their differences in nonviolent dialogue.

Throughout ancient times, dialogue appears alongside rhetoric. It was through dialogue that rhetoricians such as Aristotle, Isocrates, and Cicero taught their students rhetorical skills. Today, in the writing classroom, group discussion or pairs dialogue is also part of the teaching process. A rhetorical text, too, is a conversation with previous texts, responding to ideas they have presented. In addition, arguments include paraphrases and quotes from others' compositions, making them part of the conversation. Moreover, writers composing texts must anticipate their audiences' reactions—questions they might ask or objections they might raise—so responses to these questions and objects can be included in the argument. This process of responding to audiences in advance continues the conversation.

Organize Your Essay

All texts are conversational, a characteristic reflected in the format or organization. In ancient times, orators began a speech by attracting the audience's attention in what was called the *exordium,* which we would call the opening or introduction. Next, they provided background information in a *narratio* (narration), followed by an *explication* in which they defined terms and enumerated the issues. During the *partition* they would express the thesis or main issue to be discussed, and in the *confirmation* they would provide evidence to support the thesis. Opposition arguments would be addressed in the *refutatio,* and the composition would be wrapped up with a *peroratio* or conclusion. The order of these different elements was not rigid in ancient times, nor is it today. Sometimes one or more sections were eliminated if they were not needed, but then, as now, an effective text included most of these elements. For example, if your audience is very familiar with a particular subject, you may not need to define terms, as you would with an audience who was unfamiliar with the material.

As did the ancient Greeks and Romans, when you write an argument, you begin with an introduction that gains your audience's attention and presents your thesis; likewise, you end with a conclusion that ties together what you have said or presents a call to action. However, you have a choice of several formats for what happens between that introduction and conclusion. Following are three prominent alternatives; your choice of which to use depends on your purpose and the type of evidence you have.

- Created by Stephen Toulmin, the **Toulmin model** for persuasion grew out of the 20th century emphasis upon empirical evidence and is *most effective for arguments that rely on evidence from scientific studies, surveys, or other data.* His model requires six elements. First, rhetors present a claim or statement that they want the audience to accept. Then, they back up the claim with data and facts, what Aristotle would have called inartistic proofs. A warrant links these data to the claim, explaining why the data make the claim valid. Backing provides additional support for the argument, while a counterclaim acknowledges any objections or weaknesses in the argument. And, finally, the rebuttal responds to any counterclaims, removing possible objections to the argument.

- The **Rogerian** (or common ground) **argument** is named for psychologist Carl Rogers. It is *most effective for arguments that attempt to establish common ground between opponents* on an issue. Rogerian argument begins with an introduction that states the problem to be considered. Second, in a much different move than the Toulmin pattern, the rhetor states the opposing argument in neutral language to demonstrate that he or she understands the other side's position, as well as instances when it may be valid. The assumption is that, since the rhetor has been willing to pay attention to the other side's position, they will, in fairness, listen as the rhetor states his or her own position, as well as discusses the instances when it is preferable. The Rogerian argument ends on a positive note, describing how the rhetor's position could, at least in some instances, benefit the opposition.

- The **general modern format** for argument is one that will probably be familiar to you from previous English classes. It is a *format that you can use when your argument does not fit neatly into either the Toulmin or Rogerian patterns*. Moreover, you can adapt it to serve the needs of your argument. It is the standard five-paragraph essay modified for presenting an argument, and, like that pattern, it can be expanded to accommodate longer essays. Similar to the five-paragraph essay, you begin with an introduction that attracts your audience's attention and states your thesis. Then two or three sections each present major points that support your thesis. The next section presents a counterargument, which anticipates audience questions or objections and is followed by a rebuttal of the counterargument. Finally, a conclusion ties the argument together, perhaps by reflecting back to the introduction or issuing a call for action.

Notice that all of these formats include an attempt to dialogue with the audience. In the Toulmin model, the warrant, in particular, is designed to help the audience make the logical link between the claim and the data offered as evidence. In a Rogerian argument, the rhetor carefully and in emotionally-neutral language demonstrates that he or she has been listening to the opposition and can even restate their argument fairly. The arguments produced via these models, even if they do not immediately convince, will not worsen the situation. The aim of well-intentioned rhetors is not to convince at any cost but to continue the conversation until reasonable solutions can be found. For a comparison of the different argument formats, see table 8.1.

Like the ancient Greeks, you will begin with an opening and end with a conclusion. However, in between the bookends of your essay, you have more flexibility to adapt the basic format than did the Romans.

Write a Thesis Statement

A **thesis** may be a sentence or a series of sentences, or in a few cases it may be implied rather than stated explicitly; but a thesis is at the heart of any piece of writing. If a reader cannot identify your thesis, the meaning of your text is not clear. How do you develop a thesis? First, you determine your occasion for writing—who is your audience, what is your purpose, and what special circumstances are there (if any)? Then you write a working thesis that makes an assertion or claim about your topic, something that will be affected by your audience and purpose. For example, if you

Table 8.1

Argument Formats: A Comparison			
Ancient Roman	**General Modern Format**	**Toulmin Model**	**Rogerian Argument**
Standard pattern the ancients modified to suit the argument.	Good all-purpose format that can be adapted for the needs of the argument.	Good for an argument that relies on empirical evidence such as scientific studies or data collection.	Good when the object is consensus or compromise, so that opponents can work together while retaining their positions.
Introduction— Exordium Attracts the interest of the audience and identifies the argument.	Introduction Attracts the interest of the audience through its opening strategy and states the thesis.	Claim Presents the overall thesis the writer will argue.	Introduction States the problem to be solved or the question to be answered. Often opponents will also agree there is a problem.
Background or narration—Narratio Details the history or facts of the issue.	First main point Supports the thesis.	Data Supports the claim with evidence.	Summary of opposing views Describes the opposing side's arguments in a neutral and fair manner.
Definition—Explication Defines terms and outlines issues.	Second main point Supports the thesis.	Warrant (also known as a bridge) Explains why or how the data support the claim. Connects the data to the claim.	Statement of understanding Concedes occasions when the opposing position might be valid.
Thesis—Partition States the particular issue that is to be argued.	Third main point Supports the thesis.	Counterclaim Presents a claim that negates or disagrees with the thesis/claim.	Statement of position Avoids emotionally charged language, and identifies position.
Proof—Confirmation Develops the thesis and provides supporting evidence.	Counterargument Acknowledges the opposing argument or arguments.	Rebuttal Presents evidence that negates or disagrees with the counterclaim.	Statement of contexts Describes the specific contexts in which the rhetor's position applies/ works well.
Refutation or opposition—Refutatio Addresses the arguments opposing the thesis.	Rebuttal of counterargument Refutes the opposing argument or arguments.	Conclusion Ties together the elements of the composition (if not included with the rebuttal).	Statement of benefits Presents benefits that may appeal to the self-interest of readers who may not yet agree with you; shows how your position benefits them. Ends on a positive note.
Conclusion—Peroratio Reiterates the thesis and may urge the audience to action.	Conclusion Ties together the elements of the composition and gives the reader closure. May summarize the essay and include a call to action.		Conclusion Ties together the elements of the composition (if not included in the statement of benefits).

are writing a research paper about the advantages and disadvantages of biodiesel fuel, your claim may be stated differently depending on whether your audience is an English class or a chemistry class. In the latter, you might need to use technical language that would be unfamiliar to your English professor.

Working theses are statements that develop and change as essays are written; they are basic frameworks that provide a connection for the ideas you have decided to convey to your reader. Later, after you have completed a draft of your text, examine your working thesis. If needed, rewrite your thesis so that it states the main idea of your essay in a clear and engaging fashion. Consider the following examples of thesis statements.

> The United States should implement a guest worker program as a way of reforming the illegal immigration problem.

> Nuclear power should be considered as part of a program to reduce the United States's dependence on foreign oil.

Compose an Introduction

Experienced writers have different methods of creating a good introduction. One writer who tends to discover his paper as he goes along swears the best way to write an introduction is to write the entire paper and then move the conclusion to the beginning of the essay and rewrite it as the introduction. Another writer lets the paper sit around for a few days before she writes her introduction. A third always writes two or three different introductions and tries them out on friends before deciding which to use. However you choose to write the introduction, make sure it is interesting enough to make your reader want to read on.

The introduction to your essay is an invitation to your reader. If you invite readers to come along with you on a boring journey, they won't want to follow. In magazine and newspaper writing, the introduction is sometimes called a *hook* because it hooks the reader into reading the text. If a magazine writer does not capture the reader's

Essay Starters. If, after you have done extensive invention (prewriting and research), you still find it intimidating to face the blank computer screen, try one of the essay starters below. These are phrases to get the words flowing. Then, later, after you have written a rough draft, go back and revise the beginning. Delete the essay starter and, in its place, write a real introduction. As you probably know, you do not need to say, "In my opinion," because what you write in your essay, unless you attribute it to someone else, is your opinion. See the section in this chapter on writing introductions.

In my opinion . . .

I agree . . .

I disagree . . .

Studies show . . .

Experts say . . .

My paper is about . . .

I am writing this essay because . . .

In the beginning . . .

attention right away, the reader is not likely to continue. After all, there are other and possibly more interesting articles in the magazine. Why should readers suffer through a boring introduction? Depending on the topic and pattern of your essay, you might employ one of the following techniques to hook your readers and make them want to keep reading:

- An intriguing or provocative quotation
- A narrative or anecdote
- A question or series of questions
- A vivid sensory description
- A strongly stated opinion

Your introductory paragraph makes a commitment to your readers. This is where you identify the topic, state your thesis (implicitly or explicitly), and give your readers clues about the journey that will follow in the succeeding paragraphs. Be careful not to mislead the reader. Do not ask questions you will not answer in your paper (unless they are rhetorical questions). Do not introduce a topic in your introduction and then switch to another one in your paper.

Although the introduction is the first paragraph or so of the paper, it may not be the first paragraph the writer composes. If you have problems beginning your essay because you cannot immediately think of a good introduction, begin with the first point in your essay and come back to the introduction later.

If you have problems writing anything at all, consider the suggestions offered in the following essay.

Reading 8.1

The Truth about Writer's Block by Judith Johnson Judith Johnson suggests in this essay, first published in *Huffington Post Books,* that there is no such thing as writer's block. She suggests what writers experience is the ebb and flow of the writing process.

I don't choose to experience "writer's block" which I see as simply a matter of faulty perception. It is a mislabeling of a very natural part of the ebb and flow of the writing process. To say "I have writer's block" is to judge a temporary or permanent absence of writing momentum and productivity as wrong and therefore to see oneself as a failure in some way. The process of writing is an intricate interplay of conscious and unconscious dynamics and what actually lands on the page is a small part of it all. When we label and judge that process, we interfere with its natural flow and take a position of againstness with ourselves. It's all in how you look at it.

When a writer declares that he or she is experiencing writer's block, it is like grabbing hold of a fear (Fantasy Expectation Appearing Real) and fueling it with emotional distress. A way to reframe this is to simply trust that what appears to be a dry spell is a normal part of the process of being a writer and that either you need time to be away from the writing focus or that the process is largely unconscious at that time. Each writer has to make peace with this by finding their own particular rhythm and honoring that. For example, what works for me is not to have any rigid writing schedule, but rather to let the words come to me—and they always do—sooner or later. When working on a deadline, whether self-imposed or not, I never lose sight of the deadline, it is always there, but I don't beat myself up with it if time keeps passing and nothing is getting on paper. I'll notice that the topic is alive in me—turning this way and that finding its way to the paper. It takes a lot of trust to let this be. So far, it has never failed me.

I have lots of books and articles and projects on the back burner and no fear of running out of things to write about. I know that each piece of writing has a life of its own. For example, I have a poem that I started at the age of 16 that rumbles around in my head from time to time looking for its ending. I know it will end someday, but hasn't so far. That's not a problem to me—just a reality. I also keep what I call a "dump" file for each project and whether I am actively working on it or not, I capture ideas and information there.

In addition to building a strong bond of trust with yourself, here are some other keys to maintaining a good relationship with yourself as a writer:

Just Do It: There is a point at which every writer just has to sit down and write. Whether you write for five minutes or five hours straight doesn't matter, but if you are going to be a writer, you have to sit down and write.

Write with Freedom and Abandon, Then Edit Ruthlessly: It is important to give yourself permission to write whatever comes up without any judgment. Just focus on capturing your thoughts and ideas—forget about grammar, structure and eloquence. Just get a hold of whatever comes up. Then, just as Michelangelo described the sculpting process as discovering a statue inside every block of stone, each writer must ruthlessly revise and refine a piece of work until pleased with it.

Get Out of Your Own Way: If you get into a pattern of negativity and beating up on yourself when writing, find a way to be more loving with yourself and do not feed the negativity.

Patience: Writing takes enormous patience. As with any other art form, you are constantly revising and refining your work. For an artist the equation is never time is money, but rather "do I feel complete with this piece? Is it my best effort given the time I have available?"

Flexibility, Cooperation and Balance: There is always some level of agitation just under the surface that propels a writer forward giving momentum to the working process. But there are always other forces at work and writing is only one of many activities in an individual's life. Finding your own rhythm and being willing to cooperate with the other elements of life that often seem to intrude on the writer's solitary endeavor are like moving between shooting the rapids and gliding along on calm waters, never quite knowing which is going to present itself and when. Experience teaches us all to go with the flow and somehow that seems to yield maximum inner peace and outward productivity.

Keeping a Sense of Humor and Humility: I've learned never to take myself too seriously as a writer. I do my best and need to laugh at myself from time to time when I give too much importance to what I write. If people get value from what I write, that's great and positive feedback is extremely gratifying. However, while writing is ultimately about communication, I find it very funny that I don't write to communicate, but rather because I simply need to write—I am compelled to do so. If the end product of my

endeavors is of value to others, that's great, but the solitary process of engaging in the art form itself is entirely for me and I think that is pretty funny.

Letting Go of the Illusion of Control: A really good writer is never in control of the writing process. You may find that having a rigid schedule works well for you or you might be someone who writes when the spirit moves you to do so. Either way, a good writer taps into the wellspring of human consciousness and like love, you can't make that happen on demand.

Is writing challenging? Absolutely! However, it is a great way to learn some profound lessons in life and to be of service to others.

Activity 8.1 **Explore:** Discuss "The Truth about Writer's Block"

How does Judith Johnson choose to reframe the concept of writer's block?

Johnson makes recommendations to deal with the "absence of writing momentum." Which of her suggestions makes the most sense to you? Which makes the least sense to you?

What do you think? Is there such a thing as "writer's block"?

Combine Your Ideas with Support from Source Materials

A research paper, by definition, makes use of source materials to make an argument. It is important to remember, however, that it is *your* paper, *not* what some professors may call a "research dump," meaning that it is constructed by stringing together · research information with a few transitions. Rather, you, as the author of the paper, carry the argument in your own words and use quotes and paraphrases from source materials to support your argument. How do you do that? Here are some suggestions:

- After you think you have completed enough research to construct a working thesis and begin writing your paper, collect all your materials in front of you (photocopies of articles, printouts of electronic sources, and books) and spend a few hours reading through the materials and making notes. Then, put all the notes and materials to the side and freewrite for a few minutes about what you can remember from your research that is important. Take this freewriting and make a rough outline of the main points you want to cover in your essay. Then you can go back to your notes and source materials to flesh out your outline.

- Use quotes for the following three reasons:

  1. You want to "borrow" the ethos or credibility of the source. For example, if you are writing about stem cell research, you may want to quote from an authority such as Dr. James A. Thomson, whose ground-breaking research led to the first use of stem cells for research. Alternatively, if your source materials include the *New England Journal of Medicine* or another prestigious publication, it may be worth crediting a quote to that source.

2. The material is so beautifully or succinctly written that it would lose its effectiveness if you reworded the material in your own words.

3. You want to create a point of emphasis by quoting rather than paraphrasing. Otherwise, you probably want to paraphrase material from your sources, as quotes should be used sparingly. Often, writers quote source material in a first draft and then rewrite some of the quotes into paraphrases during the revision process.

- Introduce quotes. You should never have a sentence or sentences in quotation marks just sitting in the middle of a paragraph, as it would puzzle a reader. If you quote, you should always introduce the quote by saying something like this: According to Dr. James A. Thomson, "Stem cell research. . . . "

- Avoid plagiarism by clearly indicating material that is quoted or paraphrased. See the appendix (at the end of the book) for more information about citing source material.

Support Your Thesis

After you have attracted the interest of your audience, established your thesis, and given any background information and definitions, you will next begin to give reasons for your position, which further develops your argument. These reasons are, in turn, supported by statistics, analogies, anecdotes, and quotes from authorities which you have discovered in your research or know from personal knowledge. Ideally, arrange your reasons so that the strongest ones come either at the beginning or at the end of this portion of the paper (points of emphasis) and the weaker ones fall in the middle.

Answer Opposing Arguments

If you are aware of a contradicting statistic or other possible objection to your argument, it may be tempting to ignore that complication, hoping your audience will not notice. However, that is exactly the worst thing you can do. It is much better to anticipate your audience's possible questions or objections and address them in your discussion. Doing so prevents you from losing credibility by either appearing to deceive your audience or being unaware of all the facts. Also, acknowledging possible refutations of your position actually strengthens your position by making you seem knowledgeable and fair-minded.

Vary Your Strategies or Patterns of Development

When composing your essay, you have many different strategies or **patterns of development** available to you. You may write entire essays whose sole strategy is argumentation or comparison and contrast, but more often, you will combine many of these different modes while writing a single essay. Consider the following strategies or patterns of development:

- *Analysis* entails a close examination of an issue, book, film, or other object, separating it into elements and examining each of the elements separately through other writing modes such as classification or comparison and contrast.
- *Argumentation* involves taking a strong stand on an issue supported by logical reasons and evidence intended to change a reader's mind on an issue or open a reader's eyes to a problem.
- *Cause and effect* is an explanation of the cause and subsequent effects or consequences of a specific action.
- *Classification* entails dividing and grouping things into logical categories.
- *Comparison and contrast* examines the similarities and differences between two or more things.
- *Definition* employs an explanation of the specific meaning of a word, phrase, or idea.
- *Description* uses vivid sensory details to present a picture or an image to the reader.
- *Exemplification* makes use of specific examples to explain, define, or analyze something.
- *Narration* uses a story or vignette to illustrate a specific point or examine an issue.

Write a Conclusion

After they have read the last paragraph of your essay, your readers should feel satisfied that you have covered everything you needed to and you have shared an insight. You may have heard the basic rules: A conclusion cannot address any new issues, and it should summarize the main points of the essay. Although these are valid and reliable rules, a summary is not always the best way to end an essay. The prohibition against new ideas in the final paragraph also might limit certain effective closures like a call to action or a question for the reader to ponder.

One effective technique for writing a conclusion is to refer back to your introduction. If you began with a narrative anecdote, a sensory description, or a question, you can tie a mention of it to your ending point. Or, if you are composing an argumentative essay, you might choose to summarize by using an expert quote to restate your thesis, giving the reader a final firm sense of ethos or credibility. You might also end with a single-sentence summary followed by a suggestion or a call to action for the reader. Another effective way to end an argument can be a paragraph that suggests further research.

A conclusion doesn't have to be long. As a matter of fact, it does not even need to be a separate paragraph, especially if your essay is short. If your closing comments are related to the final paragraph of the essay, one or two sentences can easily be added to the final body paragraph of the essay.

Consider Elements of Page Design

Professors now take it for granted that you word-process your paper using a professional looking typeface such as Times Roman. However, producing your text on a computer with Internet access gives you the option to do much more—including adding one or more images and other page design elements. Several of the assignments in this chapter offer you the opportunity to be creative with your project presentation. Even if you are required to submit your project in standard MLA or APA essay formats, however, you can still include one or more images, and it is important to consider where you place the images.

Some simple guidelines will help you design effective documents:

- Use space as a design element. Do not overcrowd your pages. Place material so that important parts are emphasized by the space around them.
- Rarely (if ever) use all capital letters. Words in all caps are hard to read, and on the Internet all caps is considered shouting.
- Use headings to group your information and make your pages easy to skim. Readers often like to skim pages before deciding what to read. Indeed, many people will skim all the headlines, headings, and photo captions first, before reading the body text of any section.
- Put important elements in the top left and lower right parts of the screen. English readers are trained to read from left to right, so our eyes naturally start at the upper left-hand corner of the screen. Our eyes, when skimming, don't flow line by line, but move in a Z pattern, as illustrated in the following diagram (see figure 8.1).

Figure 8.1

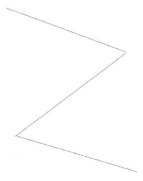

Eye movement when skimming a page

If you want to include a photo in your research paper, for example, you should put it either in the top left or the bottom right corner of the page, points of emphasis in the Z pattern. Today, with a sophisticated word processing program such as Microsoft Word, it is easy to import an image, size it, and move it to the desired place on a page. Once you have imported an image, you can click on it, hold your cursor at a corner, and enlarge or shrink the image by dragging the cursor. Also, by clicking on the image, you can activate the dialogue box that allows you to specify having the text run tightly around the image. Then you can easily move the image around on the page until you have placed it in a pleasing spot. Alternatively, Microsoft Word provides document templates that you can use for newsletters, brochures, and other types of projects.

If you look closely at figure 8.2 on the next page, you may notice that the text surrounding the image does not seem to make any sense (though it is actually Latin). That's because the text is Lorem ipsum text, sometimes called placeholder or dummy text, which designers use to create page layouts before they have the real text from writers. If you want to try using Lorem ipsum yourself, just do a search on the Internet for that name, and you will find sites that provide paragraphs of the nonsense words that you can utilize as placeholder text.

Figure 8.2

Including Images in Your Projects: Copyright Implications

United States copyright law includes a provision called "fair use" that allows copyrighted images to be used for educational projects. However, copyright laws are complicated, and the implications of using digital images is still being determined in the courts. Clearly, if you take the photo yourself, you own the copyright. Many photographers post photos on websites such as Flikr.com and give permission for "fair use" of the images on the Internet, so long as their work is credited. Others, however, post their work for viewers to enjoy but do not allow it to be copied. Scanning a photo from a published work and using it once for a class project falls more clearly under the spirit of the "fair use" law than does putting such an image up on the Internet. If you are doing a web page or blog project that includes images, be sure to contact the copyright owner to obtain permission.

Activity 8.2 **Compose:** Write a Research-Based Argument Paper

The Purpose of the Assignment
Writing a research paper gives you the opportunity to practice key academic writing skills, including locating and utilizing research materials, prewriting, drafting, and revision. It also requires you to take a position on a topic, create an argument, and support it with quotes and paraphrases from authoritative sources.

Purpose as a Writer
Your purpose as a writer is to convince readers to consider your argument carefully, and, if possible, to persuade them to agree with your point of view. To do this, include appropriate background material and definitions, as well as a consideration of opposing arguments.

Topic
Your topic should address a current issue about which you can take and support a position in the paper length your instructor specifies. Choose your topic carefully, as it should be one that engages your interest and enthusiasm.

Audience
Unless your instructor specifies otherwise, you can assume that your audience has general awareness of your issue but is unfamiliar with scholarly sources on the topic.

Sources
To do your research, you will need to utilize recent and credible sources that include a mix of recent books, scholarly articles, public speeches, and news articles. You may also use interviews, observation, and personal experience, if they are relevant to your topic. Sources will need to be cited in the text and in a works cited page or references page, according to MLA or APA style.

Information that you gather from your sources should support the argument you have created. A research paper is not an assignment in which you take information from sources and simply reorganize it into a paper. The expectation for this course is that you will use your sources to create an argument that is distinctly your own.

Thesis
Your essay should have a clear thesis that takes a position on an issue that can be supported within the word limitations of the assignment.

Rough Draft
As directed by your instructor, bring two copies of your rough draft essay to class for peer editing. The draft should have your sources credited in the text and should have a works cited page or references page.

Final Draft

Submit your final draft in MLA or APA format in a folder with your rough draft and copies of all of your source materials with the location of quotes or paraphrased material highlighted. If you are using material from a book or books, copy enough of the text before and after your quotes or paraphrases so that your instructor can determine the context of the material being quoted.

Reading 8.2

Film Review: *The Hangover* (2009) by Owen Gleiberman This film review by Owen Gleiberman appeared in EW.com. As you read the review, decide what you think is the author's position. How does he support his argument?

Going to Las Vegas for a "wild" bachelor party is now the ultimate middle-class hedonist cliché. It's not just that the jaunt has been done so often, in the movies as well as in life. It's that there's a contradiction embedded in the lure of the Vegas bacchanal. Men—and women too, of course—go there to be as reckless as humanly possible. But the naughtiness is so *organized* that there's not much recklessness left in it. Sure, you can craps-table your way to financial ruin, but the lap dances, the glorified college drinking binges, the ritualized ordering of hookers: It's all about as spontaneous as a shuffleboard tournament on a cruise ship.

The fun of *The Hangover*—what makes it more than just one what-happens-in-Vegas romp too many—is that the film completely understands all this. The four comrades who drive from Los Angeles to the Nevada desert to prepare for the wedding of Doug (Justin Bartha) aren't daring or cool; they aren't born swingers. They're an unglamorous Everyguy quartet, doing what they all think they're supposed to do. They're probably imitating Vegas movies as much as those films imitated reality.

Phil (Bradley Cooper), the one who's good-looking enough to strut into a casino like he owns it, is a junior-high teacher devoted to his wife and kid; Stu (Ed Helms), the group dweeb, is an anxious-eyed dentist who's like the 21st-century version of *American Graffiti*'s Terry the Toad, with a fascist girlfriend (Rachael Harris) who treats him like a slave; and Alan (Zach Galifianakis), so brick-stupid he qualifies as more nutzoid than dorkish, is a pudgy, bearded runt who stands up in the group's cruising convertible and shouts "Road trip!" That's an inside nod to the fact that Todd Phillips, the movie's director, made *Road Trip* as well, though it also indicates that these four think they're living inside a stupid teen comedy.

They arrive at their hotel, and the film then cuts to the next day, when they wake up in their trashed villa. There's a tiger in the bathroom, and a baby in the cabinet. Stu is missing his top right incisor; the groom is nowhere to be seen. And the thing is, none of them remembers . . . anything. *The Hangover* is structured, basically, as one long morning-after *OMG what have I done?*, and the kick of the film is that the discovery of what the characters have, in fact, done becomes the perfect comeuppance to their tidy fantasy of Vegas bliss. A light-buttered comic nightmare, like Martin Scorsese's *After Hours* (or Peter Berg's scandalous, overlooked *Very Bad Things* with things not nearly so bad), *The Hangover* is a riff on what the stuff you do when you're *really* out of control says about you.

The surprises in this movie are everything, so without giving much away, I'll just say that a Vegas chapel figures into the mix. So does a crowbar-wielding Asian gangster (Ken Jeong) who might be the epicene brother of Long Duk Dong in *Sixteen*

Candles. There's also a juicy run-in with Mike Tyson. *The Hangover* has scattered laughs (many in the cathartically funny end-credit montage), but overall it's more amusing than hilarious. The most deftly acted character is Stu, played by Helms with a realistic alternating current of horror and liberation. As Alan, Zach Galifianakis makes blinkered idiocy a cartoon rush, though a little of him goes a long way. I wish Phillips, working from a script by the knockabout team of Jon Lucas and Scott Moore (*Ghosts of Girlfriends Past*), had nudged the characters closer to being a true shaggy-dog Apatow-style ensemble. You're always a little too aware that they're types. But it's fun seeing each of them have the "fun" they deserve.

Activity 8.3 **Collaborate:** Discuss Review of The Hangover

1. Owen Gleiberman says that the "wild" bachelor party in Las Vegas has become a cliché. Is this true? What other films portray bachelor parties in Las Vegas?
2. What is different about the Vegas bachelor party in *The Hangover*, according to the review?
3. What is Gleiberman's thesis? What evidence does he offer to support his thesis?
4. Does the review make you want to see the movie, if you haven't? How so?

Activity 8.4 **Compose:** Write a Film Review

In this assignment, you are a film critic. Write a review that could appear in a newspaper, magazine, or blog. Your style and tone will be dictated by your audience, so identify the publication just under the title of your review by saying something like this: "Written for Undergroundfilms .com." Be sure to read several reviews published in your chosen media outlet.

1. Select a film you would like to review. Films that are social commentaries are particularly good for reviewing. It does not have to be a serious movie, but it should be one that makes you think about some social trend or historical event.
2. After you decide on a film, learn about its context. Who are the director, producer, and primary actors? What films have these individuals worked on before? Have they won awards? Are they known for a certain style? Read and annotate other reviews of the film, marking sections that you might paraphrase or quote to support your opinions.
3. What about the historical event or social context? Can you learn more about it to see if the film presents a reasonably accurate picture of that time and place (a kairos)? Is it based on a book? If so, what kind of a job does it do creating the world of the book?
4. Is the film persuasive? Does the film appeal to ethos, pathos, or logos? In what way?
5. Create a working thesis that makes an argument about the film. You can modify this thesis later, but it helps to identify early on what you want to argue.

6. Use some of the invention strategies in Chapter 4 to help you articulate what proofs you can use to support your argument.
7. Near the beginning of your draft, briefly summarize enough of the film that your review will be interesting to those who have not seen it. However, don't be a "spoiler." Don't ruin the film for potential viewers by giving away the ending.
8. Organize your essay into three main points that support your thesis and at least one counterargument that complicates or disagrees with your argument.
9. Write a compelling introduction that uses one of the approaches discussed in this chapter. You want your reader to be interested in what you have to say. For example, you might begin with a startling quote from the film or a vivid description of a pivotal scene.
10. Be sure to include specific examples and colorful details. These are essential to make your review interesting to the reader.

Activity 8.5: **Compose:** Write an Op-Ed Argument

The Op-Ed Project (www.theop-edproject.org) is an online initiative to "expand the range of voices" submitting op-ed essays to media outlets. According to its statistics, 80 to 90 percent of op-ed pieces are currently written by men, which is something it endeavors to change by helping women and members of other underrepresented groups develop the skills to get published in top media markets. Whether you are male or female, you may belong to an underrepresented group that is not having its voice heard as part of the national conversation about issues.

Tips for Op-Ed Writing from the Op-Ed Project

1. **Own your expertise.** Know what you are an expert in and why—but don't limit yourself. Consider the metaphors that your experience and knowledge suggest.

2. **Stay current**. Follow the news—both general and specific to your areas of specialty. If you write about Haiti, read the Haitian press. If you write about pop culture, read the media that cover it.

3. **The perfect is the enemy of the good**. In other words: write fast. You may have only a few hours to get your piece in before the moment is gone. But also . . .

4. **Cultivate a flexible mind.** Remember that a good idea may have more than one news hook; indeed, if the idea is important enough it can have many. So keep an eye out for surprising connections and new news hooks—the opportunity may come around again.

5. **Use plain language**. Jargon serves a purpose, but it is rarely useful in public debate, and can obfuscate–sorry, I mean cloud–your argument. Speak to your reader in straight talk.

6. **Respect your reader**. Never underestimate your reader's intelligence or overestimate her level of information. Recognize that your average reader is not an expert in your topic and that the onus is on you to capture her attention–and make the argument compel.

An op-ed is an opinion piece printed in a newspaper, magazine, blog, or other media outlet. The name derives from earlier times in print journalism when these opinion pieces would be printed on a page opposite the editorial page. Op-eds are written by individuals not affiliated with the publication, as opposed to editorials that are written by the publication's staff.

This assignment asks you to write an op-ed piece suitable for submission to a major newspaper or other media outlet. It does not require you to submit your text. That is up to you.

For this assignment, you need to do the following:

1. Read op-eds that appear in the major regional newspaper or other media outlet for your city, such as the *Chicago Tribune,* the *Washington Post,* or the *Arizona Republic*. The Op-Ed Project provides a list of the top 100 U.S. media outlets on its website. Read several op-eds to get a sense of the topics and style of the articles that the newspaper or other media outlet prints.
2. Notice that op-eds are not academic writing. They must be well-researched, but they also generally are written in a more casual and engaging style than traditional academic writing. You must first attract your audience's attention in order to present your case. Analyze how each op-ed you read captures the reader's interest.
3. Choose a topic that is timely and of interest to the readers of the publication that you choose. Research that topic using some of the tools in the research chapter of this textbook.
4. The length and structure of your op-ed should follow the pattern of pieces recently published in your publication.
5. Keep your audience in mind—the readers of the publication.
6. Follow the basic op-ed structure recommended by the Op-Ed Project, reprinted below.
7. Read the "Tips for Op-Ed Writing from the Op-Ed Project," in the sidebar.

(*Note*: A *lede* (or lead) is a journalism term that means the beginning of your article that catches your reader's attention and establishes your topic.)

Basic Op-Ed Structure from the Op-Ed Project

(*Note*: This is not a rule—just one way of approaching it.)

Lede (around a news hook)

Thesis (statement of argument—either explicit or implied)

Argument (based on evidence, such as stats, news, reports from credible organizations, expert quotes, scholarship, history, and first-hand experience)
- 1st Point
  - Evidence
  - Evidence
  - Conclusion

- 2nd Point
  - Evidence
  - Evidence
  - Conclusion
- 3rd Point
  - Evidence
  - Evidence
  - Conclusion

Note: In a simple, declarative op-ed ("policy X is bad; here's why"), this may be straightforward. In a more complex commentary, the 3rd point may expand on the bigger picture (historical context, global/geographic picture, mythological underpinnings, etc.) or may offer an explanation for a mystery that underpins the argument (e.g., why a bad policy continues, in spite of its failures).

"To Be Sure" paragraph (in which you preempt your potential critics by acknowledging any flaws in your argument and address any obvious counterarguments)

Conclusion (often circling back to your lede)

Activity 8.6 **Compose:** Write on Your Blog

Write an informal review of a film you have seen recently. What did you like and what did you dislike? Would you recommend the film to a friend?

Activity 8.7 **Compose:** Write in Your Commonplace Book

Find a piece from the Opinion/Editorial section of your local newspaper that interests you. If you were going to write a letter to the editor in response, what might you say?

The Casebook: In 2011, two professors launched a competition on the *Harvard Business Network* blog for designs to build $300 houses for the poor. Word of the competition spread quickly, and a wide variety of people began to write about the competition—in editorials in *The New York Times* and the *Economist* and in a companion blog, http://www.300house.com/blog.

Your Task: In Chapter 4 you read four articles about the $300 house competition. Read and discuss them in class and in small groups. Make a list of the different positions being argued in these texts and what evidence the writers offer to support their opinions. Then construct your own short research-based argument about the design competition or an op-ed essay (as your instructor specifies) agreeing with one of the positions or developing your own.

9
Revising
Rhetorically

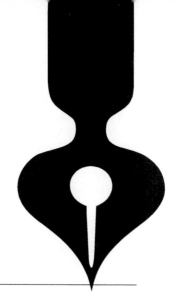

Praxis in Action: *How I Revise*
by Amber Lea Clark

Amber Lea Clark says that one important part of her revision is setting her paper aside for a few hours or overnight and then looking at it with fresh eyes.

Revising is an essential part of the writing process. One of the first things I do when I revise a paper is read with organization in mind. How is my introduction? Does my argument make sense? Did I transition well between points? Next, I look for words and phrases I have repeated too many times and look for other ways to say what I'm trying to say.

For me, a very necessary part of the revision process is reading the paper out loud to see how it flows. I look for any awkwardly worded sentences. It also helps me find typos and misused words. If I'm in a lab setting, I read very quietly, just mouthing the words. I might get a couple of funny looks but I don't care, it is a must when it comes to the revising process for me.

One of the best things to do in the revising process is set your paper aside and come back to it several hours or a day later. This requires some planning and an attempt not to procrastinate too much. Doing this allows me to look at my paper again with fresh eyes and see what I might have left out or want to say differently.

My mother always told me to have someone else give me feedback on my papers before I turn them in. This is valuable advice. I always have someone look over my papers and try to help others when they need someone to look at their papers. I ask the person who is proofing my paper to look for typos but also any sentences that do not make sense as they are worded. Is my argument coming through clearly?

Also, I always run my paper through the computer's spell check and grammar check. The computer will flag things as grammatically wrong that aren't, so I don't follow everything it says; but the computer also finds errors I haven't. Oh, be sure to spell the proper names right!

Revision Is Part of the Writing Process

In ancient times, the focus of the rhetor was upon the presentation of oral arguments in the form of speeches and students trained to perform in pressured situations before a law court or assembly. Though a speaker might spend time in preparation, most speeches were one-time opportunities. If the words were not well-chosen and well-spoken the first time, there was no second chance to influence an audience.

With modern written documents, a composition does not have to be perfect when the words first appear on the page. A document is not truly finished until it is transmitted to an audience, and, even then, important documents are often circulated in draft stages to colleagues for comments before they are presented to an audience.

Many writers claim that revising is the most rewarding step in writing, the time when they have words on a page to work with and can manipulate them to create a composition that communicates effectively. Yet, many students feel that their first drafts should stay exactly the way they've written them because these writings are truest to their feelings and experience. They are sure they have made their point clearly. In reality, a first draft often leaves the reader scratching his or her head and wondering what it was the writer meant to say. To communicate effectively, a writer must learn to interact with his reader to ensure he has communicated his message clearly.

Begin Revision by Rereading

The first step of revising is rereading. This step can be simple, if you are reading something written by someone else. When it is your own writing, it becomes infinitely more difficult. After all, you know what you meant to say—you know the research behind the writing and why you chose certain words or phrases. You even know how every sentence is supposed to read—even though you may have left out a word or two or three—and your mind can trick you into seeing the missing words right where they belong. Unfortunately, the reader does not have your understanding, and communication can break down. You need to learn to read your own work critically, as if it were written by a stranger. One of the first aids in this process is to read your work aloud. You can often hear stumbling blocks quicker than you can see them.

You can also learn to read your own work more objectively by reading and commenting on other writers' work. Look at the structure of essays, at the way the writers use transitions and topic sentences, and at the sentence structure and choice of words. As you learn to see how good writers put ideas and words together, you will begin to think about the readings in a more thorough manner—thinking of alternative, perhaps even better, ways to express the message of each essay. You will also learn to read your own work with a more critical eye.

Qualities of Effective Writing

Reading the work of some professional writers, you may have developed the idea that the best writing is writing that is difficult to understand, writing that sends the reader to the dictionary with every sentence, or writing that uses many technical or specialized terms. Often, we think something difficult to read must be well written. Although it is sometimes difficult to read about topics that are new to us because we're learning new vocabulary and struggling with complex ideas, it simply is not true that the best writing is hard to read. Indeed, the most effective writing, the kind of writing you want to produce in your classes, is simple, concise, and direct.

Keep It Simple

Simple means "unadorned" or "not ornate." *Writing simply* means saying something in common, concrete language without too much complication in the sentence structure. Writing simply doesn't mean you have to use only short or easy words. It doesn't mean that all your sentences will be simple sentences. It doesn't mean that you can't use figures of speech or intricate details. Simple writing means that you try to get your point across in a direct and interesting way. You aren't trying to hide your ideas. Instead, you are trying to amplify those ideas and begin an intelligible conversation with your reader.

Rely on Everyday Words

When writing about computers or other technical subjects, it's tempting to use **jargon** or specialized words you might use when talking to others with the same knowledge, interest, and background. When writing for a limited audience whose members are familiar with technical terms, a bit of jargon might be acceptable. However, most of the writing you will do in college and later in the workplace will address a larger audience. You will want to avoid the use of highly technical terms, acronyms, and abbreviations.

If it seems that the writers in this text use many big words or technical terms, stop for a minute to consider the original audience for each of the essays. Consider how your vocabulary grows each year as you read, discuss, and consider new ideas. The everyday words of a tenth grade student will probably be fewer in number than

♦ William Safire's Rules for Writing

William Safire, long-time language enthusiast, political columnist, and contributor to "On Language" in the New York Times Magazine, has a little fun with grammar rules and myths.

- Remember to never split an infinitive.
- The passive voice should never be used.
- Do not put statements in the negative form.
- Verbs has to agree with their subjects.
- Proofread carefully to see if you words out.
- If you reread your work, you will find on rereading a great deal of repetition can be avoided by rereading and editing.
- A writer must not shift your point of view.
- And don't start a sentence with a conjunction. (Remember, too, a preposition is a terrible word to end a sentence with.)
- Don't overuse exclamation marks!!
- Place pronouns as close as possible, especially in long sentences, as of 10 or more words, to their antecedents.
- Writing carefully, dangling participles must be avoided.
- If any word is improper at the end of a sentence, a linking verb is.
- Take the bull by the hand and avoid mixing metaphors.
- Avoid trendy locutions that sound flaky.
- Everyone should be careful to use a singular pronoun with singular nouns in their writing.
- Always pick on the correct idiom.
- The adverb always follows the verb.
- Last but not least, avoid clichés like the plague; seek viable alternatives.

the everyday words of a junior in college. Similarly, the everyday words of a college freshman will be different from the everyday words of a computer professional with three years of work experience. Use words that are comfortable and familiar to you and your readers when you write, and you will write clear, effective essays.

Use Precise Words

We sometimes assume that the reader will know what we mean when we use adjectives like "beautiful," "quiet," or "slow." However, the reader has only his or her own ideas of those adjectives. You can make your writing more interesting and effective by adding concrete details to give the reader an image that uses at least two of the five senses.

You can use details from all of the senses to make your writing even more concrete and precise. What are some of the sensual qualities of the experience or thing? Can you compare it to another thing that your readers may be familiar with to help them understand it better? Can you compare it to something totally unlike it? Can you compare it to a different sense to surprise readers and help them understand the image you are trying to create?

A good way to practice your ability to write original concrete images is to expand on a cliché. A **cliché** is an overused saying or expression. Often, clichés begin as similes that help make images more concrete. They become clichéd or overused because they lose their originality or they don't contain enough detail to give us the entire picture. Choose a cliché and write a sentence that expands the cliché and uses the senses to create a clear picture of the thing described. You might try some of the following clichés:

> She is as pretty as a picture.
> It smelled heavenly.
> It was as soft as a baby's bottom.
> His heart is as hard as stone.
> It tastes as sour as a pickle.
> We stared at the roaring campfire.
> We listened to the babbling brook.

Precise details allow us to experience the world of the writer. We leave our own views and perceptions and learn how someone else sees the world. We learn what "quiet" is like for one writer and what "beautiful" means to another. Fill in the gaps between your words and ideas with vivid images and your writing will become more interesting and more effective.

Be Concise

Rid your writing of excess words and leave only that which makes your meaning clear and concrete. Becoming aware of several common problems can help you make your writing more concise. When you begin a sentence with either "it is" or "there is," you transfer all the meaning of the sentence to the end of the sentence. This is known as a **delayed construction**. You have delayed the meaning. The reader must read on to find out what "it" or "there" refer to. They don't get anything important from the beginning of the sentence.

Examine the following sentences:

> It is important to change the oil in older gasoline engines.

There is an apple on the table.
There isn't anything we need to fear except our own fear.

We can rewrite these sentences, making them more concise, by deleting the "there is" or the "it is" and restructuring the sentence.

Changing the oil in older gasoline engines is important.
An apple is on the table.
We have nothing to fear but fear itself.

Notice that the second group of sentences is shorter and the important information is no longer buried in the middle. Revising this type of sentence can make your writing more concise and get information to the reader more effectively.

If you think you may be guilty of using "it is" and "there is" (or "it's" and "there's") too often, you can use most word processing programs to seek these constructions out. Use the "search" or "find and replace" tool that's found in the Edit portion of your pull-down menu. Type "it is" and ask your computer to find every place you use this construction in your document. When you find a sentence that begins with "it is," revise the sentence to make it more concise. Do the same with "there is," "it's," and "there's." After you become more aware of these errors by correcting them, you'll find that you notice the errors before or as you make them. You will begin to write more concisely, and you'll have fewer delayed constructions to revise.

You can also make your writing more concise by avoiding common wordy expressions. Sometimes when we're nervous about writing or insecure about our knowledge of a topic, we try to hide that insecurity behind a wall of meaningless words, such as in the following sentence:

At this point in time, you may not have the ability to create a web page due to the fact that you've avoided using computers for anything other than playing Solitaire.

This sentence is full of deadwood phrases that add no meaning to the sentence. If we take out the unneeded words, we have this sentence:

You may not be able to create a web page because you've only used your computer to play Solitaire.

Your computer may have a grammar checker that will identify some commonly used wordy expressions. If your computer doesn't have a grammar checker, or if your instructor has asked you not to use the grammar checker in your computer, you can still learn to revise the wordiness out of your paragraphs. Use the computer to separate a paragraph of your writing into sentences. As you scroll through the paragraph, hit the hard return or "Enter" key on your keyboard twice every time you find a period. Once you have separated the sentences, look at each sentence. What is the important idea in the sentence? What words are used to convey that idea? What words don't add any meaning to the sentence? Delete words that don't convey meaning, and revise the sentence to make it more concise.

Use Action Verbs

Action verbs are words that convey the action of a sentence. They carry much of our language's nuance and meaning. Many inexperienced writers use only "to be" verbs: *am, is, are, was, were, be, been,* and *being*. If you use too many of these verbs, you risk losing much of the power of language. If I say someone is coming through the door, I've created a picture of a body and a doorway. If I say someone marches or slinks through the door, I've added information not only about movement but also about the quality of that movement. I've given my subject the attitude of a soldier or a cat. For example, consider this sentence written by Howard Rheingold:

> Thirty thousand years ago, outside a deceptively small hole in a limestone formation in the area now known as southern France, several adolescents shivered in the dark, awaiting initiation into the cult of toolmakers.

By using the verb "shivered," especially when accompanied by the words "in the dark," Rheingold paints a word picture much more vivid than he would have conveyed with the use of a "to be" verb. Using interesting verbs can enliven your writing.

If you want to focus upon using more action verbs, skim through your essay and circle all the "to be" verbs. Read the sentences with circled "to be" verbs more closely, and choose several to rewrite using active verbs in place of the "to be" verbs. You won't be able to do this for every sentence, but replace them where you can and your writing will become more lively, more concise, and more effective.

Fill in the Gaps

When we write, we sometimes forget that we are writing to an audience other than ourselves. We expect that our readers are people just like us, with our experiences, memories, and tastes. Because we have assumed they're so much like us, we expect our readers to be able to read more than what we've written on the page. We expect them to read our minds. We may leave large gaps in our essays, hoping the reader will fill in exactly the information we would have included.

If I'm writing an essay about my childhood in the South and I say it was always so hot in the summer that I hated to go outside, I might think my reader knows what I mean by hot. However, there are many different ways to be "hot." In east Texas where I grew up, the hot was a sticky hot. Eighty degrees made me long for a big glass of sweetened iced tea with lots of ice. The heat made my clothes cling. Sweating didn't help because the sweat didn't dry. I spent the day feeling as if I'd never dried off after my morning shower. In New Mexico, I never really felt hot unless the temperature got above 110 degrees. At that point, the heat would rush at me, making it difficult to breathe. I would open the door to leave the house, and it felt as if I had opened the oven door to check on a cake. If I say I was hot in the summer without describing how heat felt to me, my reader may not get the message I'm trying to convey. Don't expect your reader to know what you mean by "hot" or by any other general description. Instead, take a minute to add details that will fill in the gaps for the reader.

Speak Directly

To *speak directly* is to say, up front, who is doing what. Sometimes we don't tell the reader who is completing the action or we tell them too late. Let's look at the following sentences:

> The steak was stolen from the grill.
> The decisive battle was fought between the Confederate and the Union armies in Vicksburg, Mississippi.
> The red truck has been driven into the side of the green car.

Although we might be able to guess who the actors are in each of the sentences, the first and last sentences don't tell us directly. Even if the reader can guess that it was a dog who stole the steak from the grill or my neighbor who drove the red truck into the side of the green car, the reader has to stop and figure out who is doing what before he or she can read on. This slows the reader down and diminishes the effectiveness of your writing.

Language professionals call this **passive voice**. The action comes before the actor. Note that sometimes, as in the first and last sentences above, the writer doesn't mention the actor at all. To identify passive verbs in your writing, look for verbs coupled with another action word that ends in "-ed" or "-en" such as "was stolen" or "was forgotten."

Find the action and the actor in the sentence to make sure that they are in the most effective order. The most effective sentence order is actor first, then action. If the sentence does not specify the actor but leaves it implied, chances are that it is a passive sentence. For example, read this sentence: "The red truck was driven into the green car." It does not say who the driver was, and thus it is a passive sentence.

Rewriting some of your sentences to eliminate use of the passive voice will make your writing stronger and more interesting.

President Barack Obama has won high marks for his verbal eloquence, as illustrated by this cartoon published in the *International Herald Tribune*. His 2004 Keynote Speech at the Democratic National Convention and his best-selling book, *The Audacity of Hope,* helped propel him to national prominence.

Activity 9.1 **Explore:** When You Reeeaaallly Want to Describe Something

This activity requires a thesaurus or access to the Visual Thesaurus website (http://www.visualthesaurus.com).

1. Strunk and White's *The Elements of Style*, in an entry on "Misused Words and Expressions," says,

   "*Very*. Use this word sparingly. Where emphasis is necessary, use words strong in themselves."

   With a partner, paraphrase and discuss this Strunk and White writing tip.

2. To demonstrate Strunk and White's advice in (1) above, revise the following sentence, getting rid of the adverb "very."

   Julie is very pretty.

   No, don't say, "Julie is beautiful." Make a list of more precise and vivid words that could be used instead. Refer to a thesaurus (or the Visual Thesaurus website) to find words such as "stunning" and so on.

3. As a class, brainstorm other intensifying adverbs such as "awfully" or "extremely" that you tend to use as words of emphasis (in writing or in everyday speech) and list those words on the board.

4. In pairs again, compose a short paragraph of two or three sentences about a subject or event (e.g., a tornado, a celebrity sighting, a sports event, a news event, a concert, etc.) and intentionally use as many common or trite intensifying words as possible.

5. Exchange the short paragraph you composed in (4) above with another pair of classmates. Revise the other partnership's dialogue with the use of a thesaurus. The revised dialogue should not contain any "intensifiers" or trite words of emphasis. Replace such words and phrases with more powerful and concise language. For example, "I was really happy to see the Hornets win. They totally beat the Giants," could be revised to read (with the help of more concise and powerful words): "I was euphoric to see the Hornets thrash the Giants."

6. Read your "before" and "after" dialogues to the class.

   Afterward, discuss which words were eliminated and how the words that replaced those intensifiers changed the tone and/or meaning of the dialogue.

Source: Adapted from a lesson plan, "When You Reeeaaallly Want to Say Something," from the Visual Thesaurus website, http://www.visualthesaurus.com/cm/lessons/1450.

Remember to Proofread

It is understandably difficult to find the errors in an essay you have been working on for days. A few tricks used by professional writers might help you see errors in your essay more clearly.

With pencil in hand, read the essay aloud, slowly—and preferably to an audience. When you are reading aloud, it is more difficult to add or change words, so you tend to catch errors you would not see reading silently to yourself. Plus the reactions of your audience may point out areas where future readers may become confused or lose interest.

Another trick is to read the essay backwards, sentence by sentence. This forces you to look at sentence structure and not at the overall content of the essay. If you are working on a computer, another way to accomplish this is to create a final edit file in which you hit the hard return twice at the end of every question or statement. You might even go so far as to number the sentences so they look more like grammar exercises. Then look at each sentence individually.

Reading 9.1

Grammar Girl's Top Ten Grammar Myths by Mignon Fogarty, quickanddirtytips.com In this blog entry by Mignon Fogarty, she offers her top-ten list of grammar mistakes and misunderstandings.

10. **A run-on sentence is a really long sentence.** Wrong! They can actually be quite short. In a run-on sentence, independent clauses are squished together without the help of punctuation or a conjunction. If you write "I am short he is tall," as one sentence without a semicolon, colon, or dash between the two independent clauses, it's a run-on sentence even though it only has six words.

9. **You shouldn't start a sentence with the word "however."** Wrong! It's fine to start a sentence with "however" so long as you use a comma after it when it means "nevertheless."

8. **"Irregardless" is not a word. Wrong!** "Irregardless" is a bad word and a word you shouldn't use, but it is a word. "Floogetyflop" isn't a word—I just made it up and you have no idea what it means. "Irregardless," on the other hand, is in almost every dictionary labeled as nonstandard. You shouldn't use it if you want to be taken seriously, but it has gained wide enough use to qualify as a word.

7. **There is only one way to write the possessive form of a word that ends in "s." Wrong!** It's a style choice. For example, in the phrase "Kansas's statute," you can put just an apostrophe at the end of "Kansas" or you can put an apostrophe "s" at the end of "Kansas." Both ways are acceptable.

6. **Passive voice is always wrong. Wrong!** Passive voice is when you don't name the person who's responsible for the action. An example is the sentence "Mistakes were made," because it doesn't say who made the mistakes. If you don't know who is responsible for an action, passive voice can be the best choice.

5. **"i.e." and "e.g." mean the same thing. Wrong!** "e.g." means "for example," and "i.e." means roughly "in other words." You use "e.g." to provide a list of incomplete examples, and you use "i.e." to provide a complete clarifying list or statement.

4. **You use "a" before words that start with consonants and "an" before words that start with vowels. Wrong!** You use "a" before words that start with consonant sounds and "an" before words that start with vowel sounds. So, you'd write that someone has an MBA instead of a MBA, because even though "MBA" starts with "m," which is a consonant, it starts with the sound of the vowel "e"— MBA.

3. **It's incorrect to answer the question "How are you?" with the statement "I'm good." Wrong!** "Am" is a linking verb and linking verbs should be modified by adjectives such as "good." Because "well" can also act as an adjective, it's also fine to answer "I'm well," but some grammarians believe "I'm well" should be used to talk about your health and not your general disposition.

2. **You shouldn't split infinitives. Wrong!** Nearly all grammarians want to boldly tell you it's OK to split infinitives. An infinitive is a two-word form of a verb. An example is "to tell." In a split infinitive, another word separates the two parts of the verb. "To boldly tell" is a split infinitive because "boldly" separates "to" from "tell."

1. **You shouldn't end a sentence with a preposition. Wrong!** You shouldn't end a sentence with a preposition when the sentence would mean the same thing if you left off the preposition. That means "Where are you at?" is wrong because "Where are you?" means the same thing. But there are many sentences where the final preposition is part of a phrasal verb or is necessary to keep from making stuffy, stilted sentences: "I'm going to throw up," "Let's kiss and make up," and "What are you waiting for" are just a few examples.

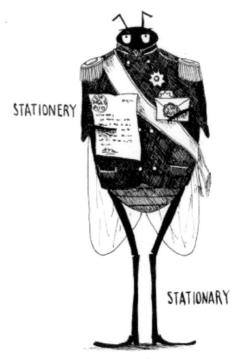

STATIONERY

STATIONARY

Stationary means "fixed in place, unable to move;" *stationery* is letterhead or other special writing paper. (Hint: *Station**e**ry* with an *e* comes with an **e**nvelope.) Examples: Evan worked out on his *stationary* bike. The duke's initials and crest appeared atop his personal *stationery*.

© The Huffington Post

Eminent means "distinguished or superior"; **imminent** means "impending, sure to happen." Also, **eminent** domain is the right of a government to take over private property for public use. Examples: The rain was **imminent**; it would arrive soon, soaking the **eminent** dignitaries on the stage. (Think of **imminent** and **impending**, which both begin with the same letters.)

© The Huffington Post

Reading 9.2

Top Ten Distractions for Writers, or Any Job Really by Sam Scham The following list, "Top Ten Distractions for Writers, or Any Job Really," by Sam Scham, was published in the Yahoo Contributor Network.

When you have a set goal in mind, whether it is for personal or work reasons, so many other things can become easy distractions. For writers in particular, life seems to get in the way. There are other pressing matters that we have to worry about.

1. **The Internet**
   The Internet is a very huge distraction these days. For writers who do research online for their great idea, it is easy to stumble upon different links and steer away from the main point in focus. If you find yourself doing this, try to limit the time you do research therefore getting off the Internet earlier and allow more time for writing.

2. **The Radio**
   Music can help a writer generate ideas and feelings. Listening to the radio can be a distraction if you leave it on for too long. If you are like me, you are able to write the best in silence. You need to be able to hear yourself think. If you are listening to the radio and it is hard to turn away from it, listen to it in segments. Listen to

some music and when a commercial comes on, mute the radio and start writing. Maybe, before you know it, you will forget that you were ever listening to the radio.

3. **The Television**

   The television and the radio are similar in many ways. For one, it is hard to turn off, especially if you are in the middle of a show that you want to finish. But then, you see a commercial for what is coming up next and you are intrigued to watch it. At the end of the current show, turn off the TV and get writing. Soon, you will not notice the absence of the picture box.

4. **Own Procrastination**

   You want to sit down and write, but at the same time you don't, you have no motivation. The solution is to take a day off, do not think of it at all. Work on any other pressing matters like home chores or calling up an old friend that you've been meaning to catch up with. On the next day, wake up and get writing. Just jump right into it and it will be like you never took a break.

5. **Other People**

   Especially if you live with family or friends other people always being around can be a huge distraction. In order to solve this, find out when everyone will be out and fit in time to write while they are gone. If that just doesn't work with your everyday schedule, find a nice place outside or at the local library where you can work in peace without other people bugging you.

6. **Other Responsibilities**

   Work, chores, walking the dog; these everyday responsibilities are tiring and at the end of the day you just cannot get the energy to write. Try writing in the morning, even if it is just for a few minutes. Get the best out of what you got and do not get discouraged.

7. **Telephones**

   With cell phones these days, you can be getting texts at every minute either from friends or social networks. When you are writing, the best way to refrain from your cell phone is by turning it completely off and leaving it somewhere out of sight so that you are not tempted to check it.

8. **Outdoor Activities**

   Especially on a really nice day, you may want to forget the writing and spend some time outdoors. That is completely fine. Enjoy life to the fullest. If you end up not writing for the day, remember that there is always tomorrow. But be careful not to put it off for too long and too often. If you really want to spend time outside, take the writing with you and kill two birds with one stone.

9. **Everyday Needs**

   You need to eat sometime and when you work and do everything else, cooking can really tire you out and make you not want to write. On those days, try to make simple meals if you absolutely do not want to order out. There is nothing wrong with having a bowl of cereal for dinner.

10. **Being Bored**

    We all get bored sometimes, even of our own writing. Take a break. Do not work on writing your big project, but work on something else. A day or two later go back to that big project and start working on writing it again and if you are still bored, put it to the side again. At least you cannot say that you did not try.

Activity 9.2 **Compose:** Write a List of Your Writing Habits

As you write an essay assigned by your instructor, keep notes about your writing process. What distracts or keeps you from writing? What works well when you write? What kind of prewriting do you do? What are the best (or worst) conditions for you when you write?

Organize your notes about your writing process into a theme such as "Best Places to Write" or "Ways to Avoid Procrastinating." As Sam Scham does, write two or three sentences about each of your writing habits.

Gain Feedback by Peer Editing

Your instructor may schedule class periods for peer workshops. These workshops are opportunities for you to get responses from your readers. Often, you will be divided into groups of three or four students and you will be given a list of questions to answer about your peers' essays. Your peers will get copies of your essay, and they will give you comments as well. The first peer workshop can be a difficult experience. It is never easy to take criticism, constructive or not. Taking criticism in a small group is even more difficult. There are several things you can do to make your peer groups more productive.

When Your Essay Is Being Reviewed

1. Write down everything the reviewers say. You think you will remember it later, but often you will forget just that piece of advice you need. More importantly, writing while the reviewers speak is an effective way to keep the channels of communication open. It is hard to come up with a defense for your paper if you are busy writing.
2. Save your comments until all the reviewers are done. If you have specific questions, write them in the margins of your notes. If they ask you questions, make a note to answer them when everyone is done. If you allow yourself to speak, you will be tempted to start defending your essay. Once you start defending your essay, two things happen. First, you stop listening to the comments. Second, you offend your reviewers, making it less likely that they will give you honest criticism in the future.
3. The first comment you should make to your reviewers is "Thank you." The second comment can be anything but a defense. Your readers are only telling you how they have interpreted your essay. They are giving you their opinions; you do not have to make the changes they suggest.
4. Save all the comments you get on your essay. Set them aside for a day or so. Then make the changes that you think will make your essay better.

When You Are the Reviewer

1. Read an essay through, at least one time, just to browse the content of the essay. Appreciate the essay for what it does well. Try to ignore any problems for now.

You will get back to them the second time you read and begin your comments in the margins. Every essay will have at least one thing about it that is good.

2. Always begin your comments with a sincere discussion of what you like about the essay.

3. Be specific in your comments. Your peers will probably understand you better if you say, "The topic sentence in paragraph four really sets the reader up for what the essay accomplishes in paragraph four. But I can't really find a topic sentence for paragraph six, and the topic sentences in paragraphs two and three could be improved." Note how this statement gives a positive response and then identifies specific places where the author can improve the essay. This works much better than a generalized statement like, "Topic sentences need work."

4. Be descriptive in your comments. It is often helpful for students to hear how you are reading their essays. "Paragraph five seems to be telling me . . . " or "I got the feeling the essay's overall message is . . . " are good ways to start descriptive sentences.

5. Realize that you are analyzing a paper and not a person. Directing your comments toward the essay, "Paragraph nine doesn't really have anything new to add, does the paper need it?" sounds better to the listener than "You repeat yourself in paragraph nine. Do you really need it?"

Independent Reviewing (See Editing Policy, Chapter 3)

If your instructor does not require peer editing, you can ask someone to review your essay. Choose someone you trust to give you an honest opinion. It might not be effective to ask a parent, spouse, or girlfriend/boyfriend to give you a critique if you know they are going to like anything you write, just because you wrote it. It might be better to ask another student who has recently had an English class or one of your current classmates. In exchange, you might offer to look over their work. Remember, you learn to read your own essays better by reading other peoples' essays more critically.

Sample Questions for Peer Review

When you have revised your paper several times, have someone answer these questions regarding its overall content, paragraph development, and word choice and sentence structure.

Overall Content

1. What is the thesis or main point of the essay? Where does the writer state this main point? If the main point is implied rather than stated, express it in a sentence. Does the main point give a subject and an opinion about the subject? How might the writer improve his/her thesis?

2. What is the purpose of this essay? What are the characteristics of the audience the writer seems to be addressing (formal, fun-loving, serious, cynical, laid-back, etc.)?

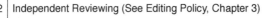

Paragraph Development

1. Do each of the paragraphs in the essay work to support the main point of the essay? Which paragraphs seem to wander from that main point? What other information needs to be added to develop the main point?
2. List two places in the essay where the writer uses vivid sensory details. How effective are those details? Are they used to support the thesis of the essay? Identify two places in the essay where the writer needs more effective details. What kind of details might he or she include?
3. What grade would you give the introduction? How does it draw the reader into the essay? What specific things can the writer do to make the introduction more inviting?
4. Which paragraph do you like the best? Why? Which paragraph in the essay do you like the least? Why? What can the writer do to improve his/her paragraphs?
5. What grade would you give the conclusion? How does it provide closure for the essay? What specific things can the writer do to make the conclusion more effective?

Word Choice and Sentence Structure

1. Are adequate transitions used between the paragraphs? Find an effective paragraph transition and identify it. Why does it work? Find two places between paragraphs that need more or better transitions. What can the writer do to improve these transitions?
2. Are a variety of sentences used? Where might the writer vary the sentence structure for better effect? What two sentences in the essay did you find most effective? Why?
3. Are there any words that seem misused or out of place? What positive or negative trigger words are used? Do they enhance the message of the essay or detract from it?

Activity 9.3 **Compose:** Peer Editing of Sample Student Essay

As your instructor directs, either individually or in groups, peer edit one of the following sample student papers and then answer the questions regarding overall content, paragraph development, and word choice and sentence structure listed in the above section, Sample Questions for Peer Review. Then discuss your peer editing in your small groups, comparing your answers to those of others in your group.

Sample Student Essay for Peer Editing, Profile Assignment

Longing for Better Days

As she sits in her cramped room in Amman, Jordan, watching the recent news, Aysha Mustafa, 92, is saddened by the world she lives in today. As she places her wrinkled hands on her lap and begins to recall a time when things were pleasant, tears begin to flow down her cheeks. Those times are long gone she says. Aysha moved from Palestine to Jordan after the sudden death of her husband in 1995. Moving here was tough she says, "It was hard to leave my country." Aysha's story goes back 60 years ago, where she lived in her homeland Palestine. She recalls her childhood as being peaceful and joyous. She smiles as she describes memories of her and her brother riding in the back of her father's wagon. "Life was good," she says. Although her family had very little to live on, she was still happy.

Like many Palestinians, Aysha still dreams to one day return back and live in her homeland Palestine, where she longs to rekindle sweet memories there. "Jordan is fine she says but I rather live on the land that is mine." As we sit in the living room watching the crisis in Gaza in January 2009, Aysha begins to wipe the tears from her sad yet hopeful eyes, and reiterates with a sigh in her voice, "May God be with them." The appalling images of young children being killed by Israeli rockets leave 92 year old Aysha in distress. How many more men, women and children will die before both sides reach an agreement she questions? As her grandson flips through the channels, he crosses upon the Al-Jazeera news that announces that the number killed in Gaza has reached the disturbing number of 781. She suddenly lowers her head and gazes into space. . "It kills me to see my people getting killed like this," she stutters trying to hold back tears.   The Israeli and Palestinian conflict has been going on for more than 60 years now. Many innocent civilians of both sides have been killed due to this grotesque war.

Despite all of this, it is people like Aysha that still carry hope that one day they will return back to their homeland and live in peace and harmony. Aysha's wish like many others is for all Palestinians to live a life of security and freedom, freedom to make their own choices and decisions on their own land. Aysha struggles to explain how as a child she used to run around in the fields freely, fearing no one or anything. "The feeling of freedom is indescribable," she says. "I was free to walk and go as I pleased, with no blockades to hold me back."

Today however, boys and girls in Palestine do not share the same luxury that Aysha experienced before the occupation. It is heart breaking watching this old yet strong willed woman recalling her childhood memories. Suddenly, Aysha begins to hold her chest and breathe heavily; her grandson approaches her and gives her her heart medicine. He explains that talking about such a personal and stressful topic leaves his grandmother feeling tired and overwhelmed. She has a weak heart, "My days are getting shorter," she says. Aysha is an inspiration, throughout this interview she kept calm and never   wavered or seemed weak. One would think she would be vulnerable to everything surrounding her, but on the contrary she was full of wisdom. When asked what she hoped for, she said with a confident tone, "My people will see better days than this; I know this for a fact. They will be happy again; mothers will no longer be forced to bury their children. The day of justice and freedom is near, I can feel it." As she said this, Aysha seemed certain that this war will not last very long.

Many Palestinians have the same hopes as Aysha, they too are confident that the day will come when their people will believe in security again.

Aysha is one of many Palestinians who shares the same dream as millions, which is a liberated and a prosperous Palestine. As she stands up and leans on her cane she says, "We want our rights, we want justice, we want freedom on our land, and we want Palestine."

Aysha's final words were that she prays that once her soul rests, she hopes to be buried next to her husband's grave on the holy land of Palestine.

Sample Student Essay for Peer Editing, Rhetorical Analysis Assignment

Rhetorical Analysis of President Reagan's
"Challenger Speech"

FIVE, FOUR, THREE, TWO, ONE, WE HAVE LIFT OFF! THE SPACE SHUTTLE CHALLENGER HAS CLEARED THE LAUNCH PAD. This was supposed to be a glorious day in American history, a mile stone in the United States Space Program. Instead this day quickly turned into one of the most horrific scenes witnessed live by the American public, which included thousands of school children, who watched from the comfort and safety of their classrooms.

On January 28, 1986, the space shuttle Challenger was scheduled for launch in Florida. It would mark the second flight by the United States Space program and it was the first educational launch program. On this particular flight there was to be a teacher on board, she was the first teacher on a space shuttle as a result of a special program from NASA. Although there were some clear concerns regarding whether the shuttle should launch, NASA officials gave the green light and the mission moved forward. Within seconds of lift off, the space shuttle Challenger burst into flames and disintegrated in mid flight, instantly killing all seven passengers aboard. The nation was shocked, especially thousands of young children who eagerly watched the live coverage on television. Within hours of the explosion President Ronald Reagan went on live television and addressed the nation from the White House. President Reagan was scheduled to address the nation on that particular day to report on the state of the Union, instead he went on television and paid tribute to the Challenger Seven. President Reagan delivered one of the most inspirational, and motivational speeches of his tenure as the President of the United States. It is a speech, like all great speeches, that would out live his presidency, and be regarded as one of the great speeches of our time.

The nation stood still, not knowing what to make of the days events. In such times of sorrow people tend to need support, guidance, and reassurance. The American people needed someone to follow, a shoulder to lean on, a vision of the future, a leader. President Reagan went on live television and paid tribute to the "Challenger Seven" in a speech from the White House. President Reagan sat alone behind a large desk surrounded in the background by family pictures. President Reagan used his ethos as a credible individual; he was the leader of the free Nation. He gave the speech from the White House, which is clearly recognized by the American public as a symbol of power and security. The image of him sitting behind a great desk flanked by pictures of family and loved ones borrowing once again from their ethos. This was a

not only the President of the United States delivering this speech, this was a husband, a father, and a son too.

The occasion for the speech was obvious: The Nation had just witnessed seven brave individuals perish before their very eyes. These brave souls were, husbands, sons, daughters, fathers, and they had paid the ultimate sacrifice for mankind. President Reagan portrayed all of these different roles played by each of the "Challenger Seven" from behind that desk. As the speech proceeded, President Reagan was careful to not down play the Challenger incident, but he appealed to logos, or logic, by saying "But we have never lost an astronaut in flight. We've never had a tragedy like this one." Here he used pathos to emphasize the severity of the incident while at the same time letting the nation know that there have been other brave astronauts who have also paid the ultimate price for the visions and progress of mankind. President Reagan throughout his speech used his words very carefully and with great insight. His words and the double meaning or relation to the events of the day made a huge impact on the delivery and acceptance of his speech by the American public. As he stated "Your loved ones were daring and brave, and they had that special grace, that spirit that says, Give me a challenge, and I'll meet it with joy." As one can see, President Reagan is using the word challenge here, this is a direct reference to the space shuttle Challenger.

President Reagan goes on to address the thousands of children who also witnessed the event, addressing the emotion or pathos of the occasion. He states, "And I want to say something to the schoolchildren of America who were watching the live coverage of the shuttle's take-off. I know it's hard to understand, but sometimes painful things like this happen. It's all part of the process of exploration and discovery. It is all part of taking a chance and expanding man's horizons. The future doesn't belong to the fainthearted; it belongs to the brave. The Challenger crew was pulling us into the future, and we'll continue to follow them." Here President Reagan's audience is the children, who in turn are the future of the nation. By saying that the Challenger was taking them towards the future, he is saying what everybody already knows. The children are the future of the nation and he is telling them that they must continue to move forward, for one day they will be the leaders of the country.

President Reagan's message is very clear: This was a tragedy, yet we as a nation must continue to move forward in order to honor the memory of the "Challenger Seven." President Reagan, utilizing logos, then mentions the NASA employees in his speech. Here he does not blame or degrade the space program or its employees. Instead he praises there hard work and dedication to the American people and the space program. He does not speculate on the cause of the explosion nor does he address any issues related to who is to blame. He completely omits any negative or accusatory comments in his speech. This was a very tactful and extremely intelligent move by Reagan. He knew the American public had many questions regarding the explosion. He also knew that those questions needed to be answered and that it was his responsibility to provide those answers to the nation. Yet on this day, and in this speech, it was not the right time to do so.

President Reagan in closing his speech borrows from the ethos of the past when he stated "There's a coincidence today. On this day three hundred and ninety years ago, the great explorer Sir Francis Drake died aboard ship off the coast of Panama… a historian later said, He lived by the sea, died on it, and was buried in it. Well, today, we can say of the Challenger crew: their dedication was, like Drake's complete."

President Reagan's speech on the space shuttle Challenger served several purposes. First, it paid tribute to the seven astronauts who lost their lives in the explosion. Second, it provided the nation with a much needed reassurance that everything was going to be all right. And although this was terrible accident and set back for our country, he also left no doubt that the Nations commitment to NASA and the space program would not only survive, but continue to advance forward into the future.

Sample Student Essay for Peer Editing, Short Op-Ed Argument

Women in Combat

It is without a doubt that most of us have seen, read, or even heard about women in foreign countries, specifically the Middle East, being victims of sexual discrimination in male dominated work. But, would anyone possibly imagine, that even at a smaller scale, it occurs right here right now. This op-ed piece focuses on women in combat. While some countries do allow women to fight in combat, it seems archaic that the leader of the free world and by many referred as the #1 nation in the world, that we still bar women from certain roles in the military.

The most common fallacies believed by many include, women's enervated strength. Or, there psychological structure is so that they are considered nurturers not murderers. The most archaic mentality yet is that women are a distraction to men. The list can go on, but the above seems to be the most common misconceptions.

The case against the strength of a woman seems irrefutable. No one can argue that in general men are stronger than women. But there are many factors to be considered in arguing the rebuttal. For instance, the double standards set by our military. The annual Physical fitness test clearly subordinates the female's potential physical ability. A study conducted in Great Britain by the Ministry of Defense concluded that "women can be built to the same levels of physical fitness as men of the same size and build" (Shepard, 2007). How can we expect a woman to perform closer to a man's standards when we delude her understanding of what it really takes to achieve physical fitness? Would it be any different if we took a male chef and only taught him how to cook appetizers, then graded him for the entire meal including entre and desert?

Psychological structure is also a hot topic. Women are nurturers, not murderers. Kingsley Browne, author of Co-Ed Combat, The New Evidence Why Women shouldn't Fight the Nation's Wars, made a diluted attempt to answer this question by stating "There are large differences in men and women and willingness to take Physical risks. For example something like 93% of work place deaths are men" (Traders Nation, 2007). While men seem quite capable to murdering, Browne failed to cite that women are also capable of committing heinous crimes, as evidenced by the 2.1 million women serving sentences in American Prisons for violent crimes (Shepard, 2007).

Psychological Structure is an important factor in wars, as Browne reiterates. "Women's greater fear of death and injury and greater aversion to physical risks are likely to affect their combat performance negatively" (Arron, 2007). Clearly not all women are cut out for combat. But if we use this formula, it is also evidenced that not all men are cut out for combat. It is said that over 100,000 men panicked at the thought of going to the Vietnam War and fled the country to avoid the draft (Shepard, 2007). Surely any veteran of any War would consider this a perfect paradigm of a coward?

Another myth is that, women are a distraction to men. While the idea may rain ring true one could also conclude that any soldier, male or female, that is so easily distracted may be a danger not only to themselves but also to the unit they serve. While this conclusion does not rectify that argument, it does show the weak rationales that women face. Furthermore this mentality sends society the message that it's acceptable to punish/exclude women from full participation due to men's personal failings. Since World War One female nurses have served on the front line, and it has never been documented that women distract men (Jericho, 2008, p. 8).

This topic clearly incites emotions from opponents and proponents of women in combat. Women deserve attention to the matter starting with the Pentagon ensuring our women are properly trained and given the tools to succeed. But the story doesn't begin there, it begins at home. If we cannot treat a boy and a girl the same when growing up, why should we expect anyone to treat them any different as adults. How many times do we see a girl with a dole while the father teaches the son to hunt? Or watch a father rough house with his son, while the mother teaches her daughter how to apply makeup? Give your sister the tools and she will build you a bridge.

References

Arron. (2007). *The Clock Stopped*. Retrieved from: http://thestoppedclock.blogspot. com/2007/12/cowardly-untrustworthy-women.html

Jericho, J. (2008). *Effectiveness of the Sex Discrimination Act*. Retrieved from: http://www.aph.gov.au/Senate/committee/legcon_ctte/sex_discrim/submissions/ sub02.pdf

Sheppard, c. (2007). *Women in Combat. Strategy Research Project*. Retreived from: http://www.carlisle.army.mil/usawc/Registar/policies.cfm

Traders Nation. (2007). Retrieved from: http://www.youtube.com/ watch?v=1VgAd3WdaD0

Activity 9.4 **Compose:** Write on Your Blog

Choose one of your previous blog postings, and revise it using the suggestions provided in this chapter.

Activity 9.5 **Compose:** Write in Your Commonplace Book

Choose one of the readings in this chapter that you think could be improved, and write in your commonplace book about how it could be changed. Give specific examples.

10
Researching
Rhetorically

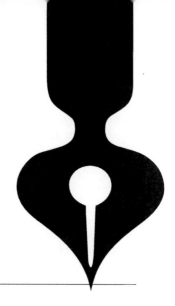

Praxis in Action: *How I Do Research* by Jane Concha

Jane Concha uses the Internet, online databases, and librarians when conducting research for a paper.

You have your topic and you're ready to go. But now you think, "Where do I go from here?" I have definitely been there. Sometimes, I am so nervous that I don't even research until the last minute, thinking that the Internet would grant me some great sources. Unfortunately, that *never* works.

What I have now realized is that research takes time; with patience and a clear path, I have always managed to find sources that are geared to my topic and add depth to my paper.

To start, I brainstorm ideas of where I want to go with my research. Sometimes, a quick search on Google can help give me some hints on where to start. For example, if I choose to write on the desert in El Paso, a quick search can help me find the name of the desert, the type of climate, and the habitat. From there, I could easily go on the library database and search the keywords I have based on my online search.

I like to use online databases from my library website like Jstor and Academic Search Complete (EBSCO) because I can access print articles from my computer, and that satisfies professors who require that you have a certain number of print sources.

However, I'd recommend to fellow students that it's a good idea to get over their fear of actually going to the library in person except to use the computers or have study dates. Yes, you may be able to access articles and even books (Google Books, etc.) from your computer, but the library does have one great advantage—the research ninjas called librarians. These are people to cultivate, not once but throughout your academic career. They can help you find sources you wouldn't have thought of and can be invaluable when you can't find that essential bit of information.

Even when websites look useful, I'm careful with a *.com* website because those sites usually get their information from research that is easily accessible on a database or information that is slanted toward a certain point of view. However, I do like *.gov* websites because they usually have great statistics I can add to my paper.

Once I find my sources, I pick out the ones that I don't want and discard them. I usually don't look at anything over five years old. I also reject information that pertains to my topic, but is too boring to be interesting to my reader.

Once I'm done finding great sources, it is a lot easier to write my paper.

Research Provides Inartistic Proofs

As discussed in Chapter 7, ancient Greeks began the writing process with invention, a stage in which they searched their memories for data related to the topic at hand. This information constituted artistic proofs, knowledge that rhetors invented from their own minds, emotions, and observation. However, rhetors also supplemented their invented proofs with information that was gleaned from other sources such as the testimony of witnesses, evidence given under torture, and written contracts. Yes, evidence given under torture was considered a legitimate proof. None of these inartistic proofs were generated from the rhetor's mind or "invented." As such, the Greeks considered these sources of information to be inartistic proofs.

Today, the range of inartistic proofs available to writers and speakers is vastly expanded—scientific studies, opinions from authorities, videotapes of events, government documents, and so on. You can locate these in the traditional way— library books and print periodicals—but more likely you will begin your search with the Internet, a resource the ancients could not have imagined. However, as in ancient times, it is still the task of today's rhetor to locate available resources, sift through them to locate those that are relevant, evaluate their reliability and validity, and incorporate them into a text to support an argument.

Researching rhetorically, the title of this chapter, refers to making use of your ethos or credibility as a writer by incorporating your expert knowledge because of everyday experiences and the subjects you have studied. It also involves maximizing as well as"borrowing" the credibility of source materials you quote or paraphrase in your text. When you quote or paraphrase an expert, your paper gains authority that it would not otherwise have. For example, if you are the parent of a child with attention deficit hyperactivity disorder (ADHD), your experiences caring for that child and interacting with the health care and educational systems, as well as the reading you have done to seek out effective treatment, qualifies you to speak with authority about what it is like to raise such as child. If you are writing a paper about educational options for children with ADHD, you can cite some of your own experiences, but you will also want to quote or paraphrase opinions of authorities about the best ways to provide a quality educational environment for these children. These opinions of experts can be found in books, periodicals, and possibly government documents, and including them will increase your power to convince an audience.

You Do Research Every Day

Although the words "research paper" sound imposing to many students, research is really a natural part of your experience. You do research every day, often without being aware of the process, whether it is determining the calorie count of a serving of sugar-free ice cream or calculating the dollar amount you will spend on gasoline for a weekend trip. The information- gathering you do for a research paper builds on the informal research skills you already have by adding additional places to look for information and additional tools to use in that search.

How do you go about finding the best reference sources to support your general knowledge? A key factor to keep in mind is the credibility of each of the sources you choose. Citing information from a source written in the last three years is generally more credible than a source published ten years ago because the information is obviously more current. Peer-reviewed journals and books published by reputable publishers are probably the most credible sources. Information from a news magazine such as *Time* has more credence than material found in popular magazines such as *Glamour* or *People,* which are designed for entertainment rather than covering the news. Indeed, many instructors will forbid the use of Wikipedia as a source, not because all the information is inaccurate (because it is not) but because the reader has no way of evaluating whether information is correct or not since the entries were written by volunteers and the content has not been vetted by a reputable publisher or other authoritative organization.

Don't be reluctant to ask for help. Your instructor may be willing to suggest resources on your topic, as will librarians. Instructors may refer you to specific books or authors. Others may demonstrate a journal search for you, in the process finding you valuable sources. As noted by Concha in the chapter opener, librarians can be valuable allies in your search, as their job is to serve your needs as a library patron. If you ask for help, a librarian will often run a search for you in the online catalog or may even walk with you into the stacks to find appropriate source materials.

Primary and Secondary Research

If you've ever purchased a major consumer product, say a computer, chances are you already knew quite a bit about what was available before you took out your charge card. For example, many of your friends probably have computers as well as definite opinions about what brands and models are preferable. Perhaps you already own a computer and like it so much that you want to upgrade to the next model or maybe you have complaints about its performance. Still, before you made your purchase, you probably did some research on the Internet, reading product specifications and reviews. Maybe you tried out a computer or two at the local Apple Store or another retailer. If you went through this sort of process before buying a computer or another consumer product, you already know the basics about primary and secondary research.

Primary research involves personal interaction with your subject. Interviews with people on the scene of an event and questionnaires are all primary sources. Novels, poems, diaries, and fictional films are also primary sources because they stand alone and are not interpreting anything else. To return to the computer purchase analogy, when you visited the Apple Store or other retailers to examine computers, you were doing primary research. When you looked at product reviews in magazines, you were doing secondary research. Similarly, when you read a *Time* magazine article that analyzes climate change and quotes prominent experts in the field, you are conducting secondary research.

A little later in this chapter, Activity 10.1 asks you to interview someone who has had an unusual life experience and write a profile of that person. You may be able to gather all the information you need for this assignment by doing an interview, though it might be a good idea to revisit the observation exercise (Activity 7.10) in Chapter 7. If you know the person personally, you can also utilize that prior knowledge.

Other writing assignments ask you to combine your own experience or primary research with information gained from secondary research in books or periodicals. For example, you might be asked to write an essay about recycling. You can include your own experience with recycling or visit a recycling center in your community and report what you see. You can also support this primary research with secondary research in books or periodicals in which authorities offer facts and opinions about the effectiveness of recycling. In addition, you can interview an authority on recycling, perhaps a professor or chairperson of a community committee, as an additional secondary source.

You may notice that many magazine articles or books refer to other books, statistical studies, or additional evidence but do not document sources in the text or give a bibliography. In this course, however, your instructor will probably ask you to document outside references following the Modern Language Association (MLA) or American Psychological Association (APA) format. The purpose is to train you in academic writing, which differs from journalism or popular writing in that all sources are credited both in the text and in a works cited page. Documentation also benefits those who read your essays and might want to use the same sources for additional research of their own. It is, therefore, not a check against plagiarism but an important tool for other researchers.

Reading 10.1

Bringing History to Life with Primary Sources by Alexander A. Aimes In this article, Alexander A. Aimes argues that primary sources add depth and help bring a research topic to life.

History sometimes bores because of the way it is taught. Often, educators merely present students with information they are supposed to remember, rather than encourage students to explore historic documents and draw conclusions. As a Museum Studies intern at Mystic Seaport, a maritime history museum in Mystic, Connecticut, I worked with other interns to create history education programs targeted at high school audiences. We presented students with primary sources and asked them to think critically about the documents, to develop their own ideas about history.

My favorite program we developed related to the Temperance Movement, a mid-nineteenth century social reform movement that aimed to put an end to alcohol consumption. Members of the Greenman family, prominent shipbuilders and storeowners who lived in Mystic, became involved in Temperance as the movement gained national momentum. We traced the development of their beliefs through historic documents relating to their business and civic activities. For example, we showed students pages from the 1840s account books of the family-owned Greenman General Store that had frequent references to the sale of alcohol. By the 1850s, those references had vanished. Also, we gave students newspaper articles from the 1870s in which the Greenmans publicly stated their support of Temperance, indicating the passion with which the Greenmans advocated against alcohol. The text of the education program encouraged students to discover the Greenmans apparently stopped selling alcohol, a decision that affected the company's profits, *before* their public announcement of their change in attitude toward alcohol.

Students going through the educational program realized they would not know this fascinating detail, which hints the Greenmans were willing to lose company revenue in support of their beliefs, if they had not scrutinized account books from the 19th century. Moreover, we asked students to think about whether they could cite negative evidence—that is, the *absence* of liquor sales in the 1850s account books—as sufficient grounds for assuming the Greenmans changed their business practices by that decade? What other evidence would help support this conclusion—an open ended question students can answer in a variety of ways.

Focusing on historical evidence allows us to ask deeper questions about our conclusions. The questions we encouraged the students at Mystic Seaport to think about show the debatable nature of historical conclusions based on primary sources. While applied here to a museum activity, this strategy of poring over primary sources can be used in almost any research context. Original documents get us as close as possible to whatever subject we are studying. They also add depth to our interpretations by encouraging critical analysis of sources.

Interviews

Depending on your topic, your community probably has some excellent sources sitting behind desks at the nearest college, city hall, or federal office building. If you are looking into the environment, you could contact the Environmental Protection Agency, an attorney who specializes in environmental law, a professional employee of the park system or the Bureau of Land Management, a college professor who works in the natural sciences, or a group in your area dedicated to beautification and restoration efforts. If you don't know anyone connected with these organizations, a look in the yellow pages or blue government pages of the phone book should give you the information you need.

When you contact the person you'd like to interview, identify yourself and your reason for wanting to speak with him or her. Most people are happy to assist college students in their research, and almost everyone is flattered by the attention. If your first choice refuses, ask him or her if they know anyone who might be knowledgeable about your topic and available for an interview. When you get a positive response, arrange an hour and a location convenient for both of you. If the interview is scheduled more than a week from the initial contact, you can write a letter confirming your appointment, or you can call the day before the scheduled interview to confirm the time and location.

Once you've scheduled the interview, make a list of questions you will ask your interview subject. There are two types of questions you can ask your subject: open and closed. **Open questions** such as the following leave room for extended discussion because they don't have a yes, no, or specific answer:

> Could you tell me about the most positive experience you've had with [topic]?
>
> When did you decide to study [topic]?
>
> What's the most negative experience you've had with [topic]?

Questions like these allow for extended discussions. Even if it seems your subject has finished his or her response to the question, let a few moments of silence pass before you ask another question. Silence can be uncomfortable for some people, and he or she might feel compelled to expand on the response to your question in interesting ways.

Closed questions are useful for gathering specific information. Questions such as "When did you graduate?" and "How long have you been involved in [topic]?" are closed questions. Although closed questions are important to an interview, be sure

they're balanced by questions that allow your subject room to talk and expand on his or her ideas.

Before the interview, confirm the exact location of your appointment. If you are unfamiliar with the planned meeting place, go by the day before to make sure you can find it. Take several pens or pencils with you to the interview in addition to a writing tablet with a stiff back. If possible, use a recorder to record the interview, but be sure to ask your subject if it is okay. Most people will allow recording, if you assure them that the recording is only for your use in collecting information for your research paper. If you are using a recorder, test its operation before you get to the interview location so you won't have any surprises when you're with your subject or discover later that the machine was not working.

Although you've prepared a list of questions to follow, don't be afraid to ask a question that isn't on your list. If your subject mentions briefly an experience that seems relevant to your topic, you might want to ask him or her more about that experience, even though it isn't on your list of questions. Indeed, the best way to interview may be to read over your questions just before you meet your subject, then not refer to them during the interview. Before you leave, however, look over your list to see if you have missed any questions of importance.

Remember to let lulls in the conversation work for you by drawing your interview subject into further explanations or illustrations of previous comments. If you interview a talkative person who strays from the topic, try to steer him or her back to the questions you've prepared, but if you can't, don't worry. You'll probably get useful information anyway. Be courteous and attentive. Even if you're recording the interview, take notes. It makes both the subject and the interviewer feel more comfortable and serves as a backup, should your recording not work.

Within 15 minutes after leaving the interview, jot down some notes about your subject's appearance; the sights, sounds, and smells of the place where you conducted the interview; and any overall impressions of the meeting. Make sure you have the date and location of the interview in your notes because you will need it for documentation on your works cited page.

Activity 10.1 **Compose:** Write a Profile of a Person

Write a profile of a person that is unusual in some way. Your profile should include description, quotes, and whatever background explanations are needed to provide a context, so that the story flows logically from one element to another. The length should be approximately 750 to 1,000 words. Answering the following questions will help you elicit information you need to write your profile.

1. **History**—What is the history of the person? Does the history affect the present?

2. **Qualities**—What qualities make this person worth writing about? Can you give examples that *show* the qualities?

3. **Values and standards**—What does the subject believe in most strongly? How does this shape his/her actions? Can you give specific examples?

4. **Impact**—How does the subject affect those around him or her? This may include both positives and negatives. Give examples.

5. **Description**—Write a physical description of the person, including any unusual aspects that make the person stand out in a crowd. Describe the setting where you interviewed the person or where the person works or lives.

Secondary Research Sources Expected by Professors

You have been assigned a research paper or project. What does your professor expect? First of all, you need to understand the assignment: What specifically does your professor want you to research? Do you have instructions about what kinds of sources your professor wants? Are restrictions put on what Internet or database sources you can use? Possibly, your instructor has specified that you need to use books, journals, major magazines and newspapers, and certain web-based information. This means that you are to use reputable sources to obtain a balanced, impartial viewpoint about your topic. So, how do you find these sources?

Neither you nor your professor should be surprised that you can find enough material for your research paper through the Internet, even if your professor says you can use only print sources. Your library has full-text databases such as Jstor and Academic Search Complete (EBSCO) that will provide you with PDF images of actual journal pages, not web pages. Moreover, Google and other online libraries have the full-text versions of many book chapters or entire books.

However, in many cases the latest books in a field are not online, so you need to venture into the actual library building to find some of the best sources for your research. This is also true of primary sources such as letters and maps. Moreover, librarians can aid you in finding the research materials you need.

Consider the following secondary research sources:

Books: In these days of easy-to-find resources on the Internet, students may wonder why they should bother with books at all. However, scholarly books treat academic topics with in-depth discussion and careful documentation of evidence. College libraries collect scholarly books that are carefully researched and reviewed by authorities in the book's field. Look for recently published books rather than older books, even if they are on your topic. Academic books or well-researched popular books often have bibliographies or lists of additional references at the end of the book. These lists are useful for two reasons: First, if such lists of books are present, it is a good clue this is a well-researched book, and, second, it gives you a ready list of other possible resources you can consult for your research project.

Scholarly journals: Just having the word "journal" in the title does not mean it is a journal. *Ladies Home Journal,* or *The Wall Street Journal,* for example, are not journals. Your instructor means peer-reviewed journals in which the authors have documented their sources. Peer-reviewed means that articles have been reviewed by experts in the field for reliability and relevance before being published. Your library should have print indexes to journals in which you can look up your topic. You may also be able to find journal articles—sometimes in full text—through the online databases offered by your college library.

Major magazines and newspapers: These publications report the news based on the actual observation of events and interviews with experts and also present informed editorial opinions. Examples are magazines such as *Time* and *Fortune* and newspapers such as *The New York Times,* the *Boston Globe, The Wall Street Journal,* and the *Washington Post.* You can locate full-text articles directly from the online versions of major print magazines and newspapers. Often, these publications charge a fee for articles not published recently. However, you can often find the same articles free through one of your library databases.

Special interest publications: These are periodicals that focus on a specific topic but are written for a wider audience than scholarly journals. Authors of articles base their articles on interviews with experts, recent scholarly books and journals, and other reputable sources. Examples include *Psychology Today* and *Scientific American.*

Government documents: Government documents present a wealth of information for many contemporary events and issues. Your library may be a federal depository, which means that users can locate many federal documents onsite. If so, you can look up government sources in the online library catalog. Government documents are also available through online databases.

Encyclopedias: Encyclopedias can be useful to browse when you are looking for topics. They are also helpful for providing background information such as dates when events occurred. However, most instructors prefer that you do not use encyclopedias as sources in your paper. This is particularly true for Wikipedia, the online encyclopedia that is assembled by volunteers who have specialized knowledge on topics and, thus, has no systematic vetting of the contents. However, Wikipedia entries often include bibliographies which can be useful in pointing you to books, articles, or other websites that can be used as references.

Web pages: The problem with web-based information is that anyone with some knowledge of computers can put up a website on the Internet. Thus, information from websites must be carefully evaluated as to author, publishing organization, etc. One way to deal with this problem is to find web information through librarian-generated indexes and search engines that are designed to screen websites for credibility (see the section titled "Find Internet Information," which appears later in this chapter).

As you use the categories above to find secondary sources for your paper or project, realize that your topic influences your choice of reference materials. If you are writing about a literary topic such as Shakespeare's *Othello,* you will find a number of relevant books and journal articles. If your topic is more contemporary, such as the current status of the country's housing market, you may be able to find some books or journal articles for background information, but you will need to use recent magazine and newspaper articles to find the latest information.

As you examine your sources, remember that gathering the information should help you discover what you think about your topic, not just what others think. This will enable you to create a paper based on *your* ideas and opinions, with source materials supporting your position.

Employ Computerized Library Catalogs

Public Access Catalogs (PACs) or computerized catalogs, accessed through the Internet, have replaced card catalogs. A library computerized catalog provides bibliographical information about the library's collection, including thousands of books, photos, videos, journals, and other items. Generally, catalogs can be accessed by any of the following methods: keyword, subject, author, title, or call number. You may also find books that are available in digital form through the catalog. In addition, on the library home page, you will find links to other information and services such as database searches, interlibrary loans, and course reserves.

Types of Computerized Searches

Conducting a computerized search involves accessing the library's catalog using one of the following search methods:

- **Keyword**—Unless you know the author or title of a book, keyword is the best type of search because it finds the search word or words anywhere in the bibliographical citation.
  - Example: water quality
- **Title**—Type the exact order of words in the title.
  - Example: History of the United Kingdom
- **Author**—Type the author's name, putting the last name first. You don't need to include a comma.
  - Example: Miller Henry J.
- **Subject**—Type the exact Library of Congress subject heading.
  - Example: Spanish language—Grammar, Historical
- **Call Number**—Type the exact call number.
  - Example: B851.P49 2004

If you have a general topic, you probably want to use the keyword search, for subject search actually refers to the exact Library of Congress subject-search designations, and, unless you use the precise search terms specified by that classification system, you may not get the results you want. The use of keywords, however, will lead you to hits on your topic. Then, once you have found one book that is in your topic area, you can examine the screen for Library of Congress subject headings and click on those to browse for more books.

An invaluable resource of any library is the Interlibrary Loan department. Here you can request books your library does not own, as well as journal articles from periodicals not in the library's collection or obtainable through the library's databases. Books and articles are obtained for you by the staff on a minimal or no-fee basis. This is extremely helpful because you can request books you find in bibliographies. However, it generally takes seven to ten days to obtain books through an interlibrary loan, so you need to plan well in advance. To request an item, you simply go to the Interlibrary Loan department in your library or fill out a form on the library's website.

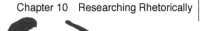

Activity 10.2 **Explore:** Locate Books on Your Topic

Using the online card catalog at the library, locate three books about your topic. Write down the titles, authors, publishers, dates of publication, and catalog numbers. Now, go to the stacks and find the books. While you are there, find two other books nearby on the same topic. Check the table of contents and index to see if they contain information you can use.

Utilize Electronic Library Resources

College and university libraries increasingly rely on databases to provide digital versions of articles published in journals, magazines, newspapers, and government documents, as well as other publications and materials. Generally, the databases are available to students and faculty through the Internet via the library home page, though a library card and a password may be required for off-campus access.

Library databases make use of online forms similar to those of a library computerized catalog. Searches are by subject, title, author, and name of publication. Advanced search features are available. Some databases provide the full-text versions of articles published in newspapers, journals, and magazines. Others give publication information only, such as title, author, publication, date of publication, and an abstract of the article. Popular databases include Lexis-Nexis, Academic Search Complete (see figure 10.1), Periodical Archive Online (ProQuest), Project Muse, and JSTOR.

Figure 10.1

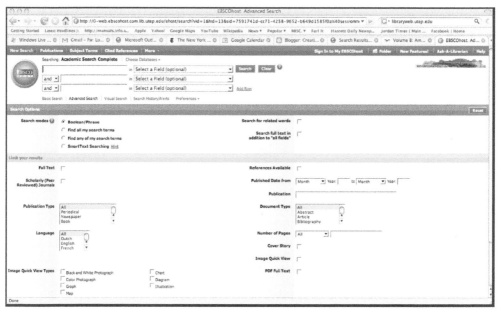

Activity 10.3 **Explore:** Locate Newspaper and Magazine Articles

Go to your library's online databases and choose one that relates to your topic. Then access it and type in your topic. Try using various key words. Jot down titles, authors, and publication information concerning any articles that look interesting. If full-text versions are available, save them to your computer or disk drive or e-mail them to yourself. If not, find out if your library has a hard copy version or microfilm of the articles.

Find Internet Information

The World Wide Web is an incredible resource for research. Through it, you can find full texts of pending legislation, searchable online editions of Shakespeare's plays, environmental impact statements, stock quotes, and much, much more. Finding credible research sources is not always easy. Anyone with an Internet connection and a little knowledge can put up a web page and claim to be an expert on a chosen topic. Therefore, information from the Internet must be scrutinized with even more diligence than print sources. For example, if you enter the word "environment" in one of the keyword search engines, you may receive thousands of "hits," or sites that relate to that topic from all over the world. How do you sift through all of that feedback in order to find information relevant to your topic? It is a problem that has not been completely solved on the Internet.

However, the search engine Google now provides Google Books, http://books.google.com, which offers the full-text versions of millions of books, though usually not the full text of the entire book unless the book is no longer copyrighted. Also, Google Scholar, http://scholar.google.com, provides access to scholarly papers, though if your library has computerized databases (see figure 10.2), it will likely have a more extensive collection available to you. Also, the Directory of Online Open Access Journals, http://www.doaj.org, enables you to search online journals that offer free access.

Figure 10.2

Click on the menu bar on the left side of the Google.com search page to find links to Google Books and Google Scholar. Google Books offers the full-text versions of millions of books, though usually not the full text of the entire book unless the book is no longer copyrighted. Also, Google Scholar, at http://scholar.google.com, provides access to scholarly papers, though not always full text.

One of the best ways for students to find Internet resources is through indexing projects sponsored by major libraries. In the case of each directory/search tool, librarians have personally reviewed and selected websites that are of value to academic researchers, including both students and faculty. These indexing websites may be organized by subject area, in addition to having keyword search engines. Thus, you might quickly locate the most authoritative websites without having to wade through masses of sites looking for the reliable ones. The following websites offer links to a variety of reputable sources:

IPL2: Information You Can Trust, http://www.ipl.org (see figure 10.3)

Infomine, http://infomine.ucr.edu

IPL2: Information You Can Trust is a public library on the Internet. It offers links to resources by subject, newspapers and magazines, and special collections created by the Internet Public Library.

Government documents also can be found easily through the Internet and are indexed at a variety of sites, including these:

FirstGov, http://www.firstgov.gov
Thomas Legislative Information, http://thomas.loc.gov
Federal Citizen Information Center, http://www.pueblo.gsa.gov/
FedWorld.Gov, http://www.fedworld.gov/

Activity 10.4 **Explore:** Find a Journal Article in Google Scholar

Go to Google Scholar either through Google.com or directly at http://scholar.google.com and search for a journal article on your chosen topic. If the Google link does not offer you full text, then go to the index of electronic journals on your college library website and search for the journal. Likely, your library will offer a database that provides full text for the article. Note: The advantage of this method of finding journal articles is that Google Scholar indexes articles from journals available in many different databases.

Evaluate Sources

Many people tend to believe what they see in print. They may think that if information is in a book or a news magazine, it must be true. If you read critically, however, you know that all sources must be evaluated. With the Internet, perhaps even more than with print texts, it is important to evaluate your sources. Here are some guidelines to consider when evaluating sources.

- **Who is the author?** This question is equally important, whether the source in question is a book, a magazine, or a website. If you have the dust jacket of the book, the back flap will quickly provide you with essential information to screen the author. In the short biographical sketch, usually included along with a photo, you can learn the author's academic credentials and university affiliation, what previous books the author has published, and other qualifications that the publisher thinks qualifies the author to write this particular book. If there is no dust jacket (as is often true with library books), you can try to find information about the author through an Internet search engine or a reference text such as *Contemporary Authors*. A magazine or journal will often provide brief biographical information at the end of the article or on a separate authors' page. If the text is on a website, determining the authorship is more complex, as authors often are not named. In that case, you are forced to rely on the credibility of the entity publishing the website. Many websites have a link called something like "About Us" or "Mission Statement," and that page will give you some idea about the motivations of the entity sponsoring the site. Is it selling something? Is it part of an organization that has a political agenda? These are things to keep in mind when considering the bias of the site's content.

- **For what audience is the text written?** Determining this may require some detective work. In the case of a book, the preface or introduction may give you some clues. With magazines and journals, consider the demographics of the readership. With a website, a little clicking around in the site and a look at the kind of texts, graphics, and advertising used (if any) should tell you what readers the site is designed for.

- **What sources does the author rely upon?** If you are working with an academic text, the sources should be clearly cited in the text by author and page number, footnotes, or endnotes. If it is a more popular book or article, sources are acknowledged less formally; however, a credible author will still make an effort to credit sources. For example, an article might say, "According to the March issue of the *New England Journal of Medicine*. . . . "

- **Does the text have an obvious bias?** Ask yourself if the argument is logical and if sources are mentioned for any statistics or other evidence. Are any opposing viewpoints discussed fairly? Does the author engage in name calling (a clear sign of bias)? Are there obvious holes or contradictions in the argument? For most purposes, you are looking for texts which do not appear to have been written with a biased agenda. However, in some cases, the opposite is true. If you are looking for a political candidate's position on a certain issue, then reading the candidate's book or going to the candidate's website will provide you with a biased viewpoint but one which you can analyze for the purposes of your paper. When dealing with information from sources with an obvious agenda, though, you must be careful not to represent the material as unbiased in your text.

- **What do others think of the text?** For a book, you can look for a review in *Book Review Digest* or *Book Review Index*, two publications you can find in the reference section of the library. Also, *The New York Times* and other newspapers review prominent popular books. Most magazines and newspapers print letters to the editor, which may offer comments on controversial articles. The Scout Report, which can be found at the *Scout Project*, http://scout.wisc.edu, reviews selected websites. If you locate a review of your text, you can cite the review in your research paper to provide additional evidence of the text's credibility.

Activity 10.5 **Explore:** Locate and Evaluate a Source

Locate one source (book, magazine or newspaper article, or website page) which you think would be a credible source for a research paper. For that source, answer the questions in the Evaluate Sources section above.

Activity 10.6 **Explore:** Evaluate a Website

Go to the Internet and look up a website related to a topic you are researching. Answer these questions as fully as you can.

1. Who is the author of this source? Is the author credible on this topic? Why or why not?
2. What does the text focus on? Is it thoughtful and balanced, or does it seem one-sided? What gives you that impression?
3. When was the website last updated?
4. What is the purpose of this site? Is it to provide information? Or is it trying to persuade readers to accept a particular point of view?
5. How professional is the tone, and how well-designed is the site? How carefully has it been edited and proofread? Are there any grammatical and spelling errors that compromise its credibility?
6. What kinds of links does the site provide? Do they add to the website's credibility or detract from it?

Avoid Plagiarism

Plagiarism is defined as follows by the Writing Program Administrators (WPA), a group of English professors who direct college composition programs: "In an instructional setting, plagiarism occurs when a writer deliberately uses someone else's language, ideas, or other original (not common-knowledge) material without acknowledging its source." A keyword here is "deliberately." Instructors, however, may have difficulty distinguishing between accidental and deliberate plagiarism. The burden is upon you as the writer to give credit where credit is due. These are some examples of plagiarism:

- Turning in a paper that was written by someone else as your own. This includes obtaining a paper from an Internet term paper mill.
- Copying a paper or any part of a paper from a source without acknowledging the source in the proper format.
- Paraphrasing materials from a source without documentation.
- Copying materials from a text but treating it as your own, leaving out quotation marks and acknowledgement.

The guidelines provided in table 10.1 can help you identify when it is appropriate to give credit to others in your writing.

Table 10.1

Choosing When to Give Credit	
Need to Document	**No Need to Document**
• When you are using or referring to somebody else's words or ideas from a magazine, book, newpaper, song, TV program, movie, web page, computer program, letter, advertisement, or any other medium. • When you use information gained through interviewing another person. • When you copy the exact words or a "unique phrase" from somewhere. • When you reprint any diagrams, illustrations, charts, and pictures. • When you use ideas given to you by others, whether in conversation or through e-mail.	• When you are writing your own experiences, your own observations, your own insights, your own thoughts, or your own conclusions about a subject. • When you are using "common knowledge"— folklore, common-sense observations, or shared information within your field of study or cultural group. • When you are compiling generally accepted facts. • When you are writing up your own experimental results.

The Online Writing Lab (OWL) at Purdue University provides an excellent handout on avoiding plagiarism, including the information about when to give credit to sources in the table above.
See http://owl.english.purdue.edu.

Activity 10.7 **Collaborate:** Plagiarism Exercise

In this exercise you will intentionally plagiarize a text. Then you will collaborate with a partner to produce a text that paraphrases and cites sources.

1. With a partner, choose a public figure currently in the news. On your own, write a brief bio of the individual you have both chosen, intentionally quoting extensively from one source without using quotation marks or citing the source.
2. Exchange your text with your partner by e-mail. Now, paste into Google or another search engine a sentence or long phrase copied in your partner's text, putting the copied text in quotation marks. Search. Repeat until you are able to identify the source of the text that your partner has intentionally plagiarized. Your partner should follow the same exercise using your text.
3. Finally, back in class, work with your partner to compose a brief bio of the individual that paraphrases these texts (and others, if needed).

4. Turn in the final version, along with the plagiarized versions. Describe your experience in trying to locate the source of your partner's plagiarized text.

Reading 10.2

Anatomy of a Fake Quotation by Megan McArdle In this article, originally published in *The Atlantic,* Megan McArdle tells the story of how a fake Martin Luther King, Jr. quote was created and posted on the Internet.

Yesterday, I saw a quote from Martin Luther King Jr. fly across my Twitter feed: "I mourn the loss of thousands of precious lives, but I will not rejoice in the death of one, not even an enemy."—Martin Luther King, Jr. I was about to retweet it, but I hesitated. It didn't sound right. After some Googling, I determined that it was probably fake, which I blogged about last night.

Here's the story of how that quote was created.

It turns out I was far too uncharitable in my search for a motive behind the fake quote. I assumed that someone had made it up on purpose. I was wrong.

Had I seen the quote on Facebook, rather than Twitter, I might have guessed at the truth. On the other hand, had I seen it on Facebook, I might not have realized it was fake, because it was appended to a long string of genuine speech from MLK Jr. Here's the quote as most people on Facebook saw it:

> I will mourn the loss of thousands of precious lives, but I will not rejoice in the death of one, not even an enemy. Returning hate for hate multiplies hate, adding deeper darkness to a night already devoid of stars. Darkness cannot drive out darkness; only light can do that. Hate cannot drive out hate, only love can do that.

Everything except the first sentence is found in King's book, *Strength to Love,* and seems to have been said originally in a 1957 sermon he gave on loving your enemies. Unlike the first quotation, it does sound like King, and it was easy to assume that the whole thing came from him.

So how did they get mixed together?

Thanks to Jessica Dovey, a Facebook user, that's how. And contrary to my initial assumption, it wasn't malicious. Ms. Dovey, a 24-year-old Penn State graduate who now teaches English to middle schoolers in Kobe, Japan, posted a very timely and moving thought on her Facebook status, and then followed it up with the Martin Luther King, Jr., quote.

> I will mourn the loss of thousands of precious lives, but I will not rejoice in the death of one, not even an enemy. "Returning hate for hate multiplies hate, adding deeper darkness to a night already devoid of stars. Darkness cannot drive out darkness; only light can do that. Hate cannot drive out hate, only love can do that." MLK Jr.

At some point, someone cut and pasted the quote, and—for reasons that I, appropriately chastened, will not speculate on—stripped out the quotation marks. Eventually, the mangled quotation somehow came to the attention of Penn Jillette, of Penn and Teller fame. He tweeted it to his 1.6 million Facebook followers, and the rest was Internet history. Twenty-four hours later, the quote brought back over 9,000 hits on Google.

The quote also went viral on Twitter, and since the 140-character limit precluded quoting the whole thing, people stripped it down to the most timely and appropriate part: the fake quote. That's where I saw it.

The speed of dissemination is breathtaking: mangled to meme in less than two days. Also remarkable is how defensive people got about the quote—though admirably, not Penn Jillette, who posted an update as soon as it was called to his attention. The thread for my post now has over 600 comments, and by my rough estimate, at least a third of them are people posting that I need to print a retraction, because of the nonfake part of the quotation. But I didn't quote that part; I was only interested in the too-timely bit I'd seen twittered.

Even more bizarrely, several of these readers, who clearly hadn't read too closely, started claiming that I had retroactively edited the post to make them look like idiots, even going so far as to scrub all the versions in RSS readers so that they, too, showed that I was talking about the truncated version. Even if you think I am the sort of low scoundrel who would do such a thing, this seems like a lot of work for not much reward. I'm not sure whether it's even possible to completely scrub an RSS feed, but even if it were, I'd have had to notify my bosses, who tend to frown on retroactive editing.

Meanwhile, several other people began confabulating a provenance for it. *Obviously*, he was talking about Vietnam, and what sort of moral midget couldn't understand that? This even though the latest citation for the true part of the quote was a book published in 1967, which would have been written earlier than that, when U.S. casualties in Vietnam were still relatively low. Moreover, the ambiguity with which the antiwar movement viewed the North Vietnamese makes "enemy" a hard fit.

It is, of course, not strange that people might look for possible confirming facts. What's strange is that they were sure enough of themselves to make fun of anyone who disagreed. Yet several other people on the comment thread had linked to a version of the quotation from 1957. I am second to no one in my admiration for Dr. King. But I do not think that he prefigured Vietnam by seven years.

Which only illustrates why fake quotes are so widely dispersed. Though one commenter accused me of trying to make people feel stupid for having propagated the quote, that was hardly my intention—we've all probably repeated more fake quotations than real ones. Fake quotations are pithier, more dramatic, more on point, than the things people usually say in real life. It's not surprising that they are often the survivors of the evolutionary battle for mindshare. One person actually posted a passage which integrated the fake quotation into the larger section of the book from which the original MLK words were drawn.

We become invested in these quotes because they say something important about us—and they let us feel that those emotions were shared by great figures in history. We naturally search for reasons that they could have said it—that they could have felt like us—rather than looking for reasons to disbelieve. If we'd put the same moving words in Hitler's mouth, everyone would have been a lot more skeptical. But while this might be a lesson about the need to be skeptical, I don't think there's anything stupid about wanting to be more like Dr. King.

Ms. Dovey's status now reads: "has apparently gone back in time and put her words into one of MLK's sermons. I'm somewhere between nervous and embarrassed and honored . . . I really hope I haven't said anything he wouldn't agree with . . . Only what I feel in my heart."

A lot of us were feeling the same thing—and I think it's clear from his writings that MLK would have too. There's no reason to be embarrassed about that.

Activity 10.8 **Collaborate:** Discuss "Anatomy of a Fake Quotation"

1. How was the fake quotation created? How did it spread on the Internet?
2. Note the speed and the reach of the fake quote. What does Megan McArdle suggest the story of this fake quote says about why fake quotes can become so widely disbursed?
3. What is your reaction to this story of the fake quotation?

Activity 10.9 **Compose:** Prepare an Annotated Bibliography

An annotated bibliography is a list of bibliographical citations with a few sentences or a paragraph for each entry that offers explanatory information or critical commentary about the source. Many instructors request an annotated bibliography as a step in writing a research paper because it is an indication of the scope and direction of your research.

1. Select 10 quality sources about your topic. These should be, as your instructor directs, a mix of books, scholarly journal and magazine articles, government documents, and selected texts from websites.
2. Skim the text of each source and read portions more closely that seem relevant to your topic.
3. Write a bibliographical citation for each source in MLA style. (See the appendix that follows this chapter for MLA style samples.)
4. Write a few sentences for each source in which you do the following:
   (a) Summarize the content and purpose of the source.
   (b) Explain how you might use the source in your research paper.

Sample Annotated Bibliography on the Federal Aviation Administration User Fees

Horne, T. A. (2007, February). User Fee Debate. *AOPA Pilot Magazine,* 50, 27.

The author of this article is an experienced, commercial rated pilot that has flown for over 30 years. He also sits on the Aircraft Owners and Pilots Association (AOPA) board. This article explains what the Federal Aviation Administration (FAA) has proposed and what it means to pilots. Congress is cutting the budget for the FAA and in turn wants to impose fees for anyone who flies into a controlled airspace. This would have a very tragic effect on general aviation. This is huge because if anyone is flying anywhere around a decent-sized city, they are going to fly through these airspaces. Also, the FAA wants to charge for approaches into airports and landing on airport runways. This is bad because all of these charges would add up to more than $200. This would discourage people from flying, making them sell their aircraft. This would slowly dissolve the general aviation industry. I can use this article to explain what is going on and why the government wants to charge these fees.

Boyer, P. (Director) (2007, October 6). AOPA's Reasonable Analysis of User Fee Issues at AOPA Expo. *AOPA Expo 2007.* Lecture conducted from AOPA, Hartford, CT.

This lecture was given by the president of AOPA, Phil Boyer. He spoke of the fees that the FAA is trying to impose and what they would mean for general aviation pilots. He explains that the fees that the FAA wants are directed toward general aviation and not toward the airlines. He also gave some examples of what would be better for everyone, if the FAA really is in a crisis. This source is important because it provides an explanation and breakdown of these user fees and gives some examples of what could be put in place of these proposed fees.

Fact Sheet—Impact of Administration's Financing Proposal on General Aviation. (2007, April 23). *FAA: Home.* Retrieved March 2, 2011, from http://www.faa.gov/news/fact_sheets/news_story.cfm?newsid=8747.

This website is the official FAA website that has all of its information. This one fact sheet lists all the facts and myths related to this issue. It goes over what the FAA wants to put into place and where and when it will happen. It brings up all of the more important issues regarding the topic, but leaves some out as well. For example, nowhere in the sheet does it say anything about controlled airspace fees, which is one of the biggest fees it would implement. It does mention another, which is the fuel tax hike. This would weaken general aviation because a lot of pilots cannot afford higher fuel prices. This will be important to have a government agency's point of view on the topic.

AOPA Online: What's the FAA's user fee proposal? (2006, November 30). *AOPA Online: Aircraft Owners and Pilots Association.* Retrieved March 2, 2011, from http://www.aopa.org/whatsnew/newsitems/2006/061130userfees.html.

This website is the official website for AOPA, which is a foundation that protects flying and everything related to aviation. This article goes over what the user fees would be, but it goes into greater detail about what the fuel prices would be after the legislation is put into place. Fuel is needed for all flights and is already expensive. What the government wants to do in addition to implementing user fees is to put more tax on fuel. This would make it much harder for the average pilot to afford flying his/her aircraft. This is beneficial to the argument because it focuses on one of the major fees that the FAA would implement: the fuel hikes.

User Fees—NBAA Calls Proposed FAA Budget a 'Sweetheart Deal' For the Airlines. (2006, November 30). *California Pilots Association.* Retrieved March 2, 2011, from http://www.calpilots.org/index.php?option=com_content&view=article&id=1141&catid=45:pre-2008-archived-articles&Itemid=81.

Cal Pilots is an organization similar to the AOPA, but it has a defined area. It is also very concerned with this issue. The article is from the NBAA which is the National Business Aviation Association. The article explains that the airline industry is getting it easy with this proposal. It says that the government is trying to move fees from the airlines to general aviation. The problem with this is that the airline industry can handle it, general aviation cannot. General aviation includes every aspect of aviation excluding the airlines and the military. The majority of general aviation pilots are your everyday, fly-for-fun kinds of people. These people cannot afford all the fees that would be put into place. This would destroy the industry. This is important because it ties the airline industry into the argument.

Network, A. (2009, October 12). Aero-TV: AirVenture Meet the Boss—Randy Babbitt Tackles User Fees. Retrieved from http://www.youtube.com/watch?v=J14ut3O_j3M.

This video is from AirVenture, which is a fly-in expo. Randy Babbitt is one of the head officials for the FAA and he explains that the FAA needs money to meet the needs of the industry. He says that the planes now are more efficient, making them use less fuel which means that the fuel tax in effect now is less effective. He goes on to explain that the FAA needs to make up this deficit, but it does not know exactly where it is going to come from. This is important because it is a government official who is explaining the situation the FAA is in and what he thinks will happen.

Wald, M. L. (2006, March 7). F.A.A. Seeks New Source of Revenue in User Fees. *The New York Times*. Retrieved March 2, 2011, from http://query.nytimes.com/gst/fullpage.html?res=9507E0D91531F934A35750.

Matthew L. Wald is a journalist for *The New York Times*. In the article, he interviews some very influential people in the aviation industry. Another important fact about him is that he is also a general aviation pilot. This article explains that because of the drop of airline tickets that the FAA needs to find new ways to make money because the tax implemented on tickets is not getting the job done. It says that the FAA is going to tax the users of the air traffic control system. This article is important because it gives specific numbers on how much the FAA is in debt and what the budget proposal is.

Activity 10.10 **Compose:** Compare and Contrast Media

Your instructor will select an article on a topic or event that is currently in the news. Find another article on the same subject either from the same news outlet or another major news source (*The New York Times, The Wall Street Journal, CNN, Time*, etc.). Compare and contrast how the reporting of the event is similar or different in the two texts. Note: You are not to write a report on the content of the articles themselves; instead, identify the author's perspective in each text and how it influences how the news is portrayed to readers.

Look for opinions, adjectives with positive or negative connotations, facts or evidence presented, the tone of the headline, and the text itself. Also consider the target audience.

Organize your observations in a one- to two-page report with a clear thesis that presents your evaluation of the two texts.

Activity 10.11 **Compose:** Write on Your Blog

In your blog, write a summary and a response to a source you might use to research your topic. Is it useful for your research? Why or why not?

Activity 10.12 **Compose:** Write in Your Commonplace Book

Copy a quote from a source that you think makes a critical point about the argument paper you are writing. Then comment about the quote—what does it mean and why is it important?

11

Reading Across
the Curriculum

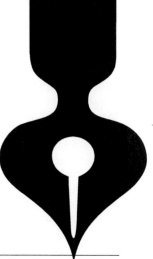

> Let us read with method, and propose to ourselves an end to which our studies
> may point. The use of reading is to aid us in thinking.
>
> —Edward Gibbon

> The more that you read, the more things you will know. The more that you learn,
> the more places you'll go.
>
> —Dr. Seuss, *I Can Read With My Eyes Shut!*

Reading is essential for learning—in more ways than you may think. Reading provides you with an understanding of vocabulary, grammar, sentence structure, and text structure. The more you read and the more varied you are in your reading, the more authentic language input you give your brain to absorb and process, allowing you to foster the development of a broader vocabulary, richer sentence variety, and rhetorical maturity. Reading also provides you with opportunities for cultural inquiry and awareness, including an introduction to the specialized writing you will be reading in your chosen field. Most of all, though, reading allows you to obtain content information about subjects that you are studying in depth.

Just as with writing, reading can be broken down into two areas that will help you focus on becoming the best college-level reader that you can be: reading to learn and learning to read. The reading-to-learn approach focuses on how you, as a reader, can locate and analyze complex ideas and then use this knowledge to craft your opinion. The learning-to-read approach involves basic strategies that you may have learned in high school or other courses; however, the focus at this stage is learning which of these strategies is most useful for each assigned reading and which ones work best for you.

> **♦ Did You Know?** The 2008 ACT's High School Profile Report noted only 53 percent of the students who took the ACT were ready for college-level reading requirements. In addition to reading readiness for college, employers identified reading and writing as top deficiencies of new employees.
>
> —James Pelech and Susan T. Hibbard,
> *Evaluating the Effectiveness of Reading Strategies for*
> *College Students: An Action Research Approach*

Reading to Learn

When you read to learn, you are reading to comprehend and retain information more effectively than when you read for fun. Just as with the writing-to-learn approach discussed in Chapter 1, one of the tenets of reading to learn is for you to use reading to make your thoughts more visible to yourself, so you can organize and analyze them effectively. Whether it is a general education course or a course in your major, your instructor will usually assign reading to help you understand lecture material or prepare you for writing assignments or exams.

To be a successful writer or test-taker, you need to be able to read varied and extensive material with a high command of understanding. Some reading assignments may be low risk, such as previewing material prior to a lecture, and some may be of a higher risk, such as reading research essays that you will critically evaluate in terms of their usefulness for your own research paper. Whatever the risk, the main purpose behind any assigned course reading is to make you more comfortable with thinking critically about key concepts. How you share these ideas with yourself, your instructor, your classmates, or any other type of audience is discussed more fully in Chapters 1 and 2, which focus on writing.

To be an effective reader, you should be an active reader. You need to bring all your knowledge to the forefront and use it as you process new material for understanding. Good readers engage with the text as if in a conversation, asking questions and searching for answers as they read. They observe how they are interacting with the text by taking notes or keeping track of main concepts and important information. One of the most important ways for you to become an effective reader—one who is able to observe details, recall facts, and come to conclusions—is to learn and apply strategies that will help you process what you read. These reading strategies are critical if you are to become an active and effective reader.

Learning to Read Effectively

> Reading is not magic. It is the consistent application of a range of comprehension strategies.
>
> —Erika Daniels, *The Power of Strategies Instruction*

Different disciplines may have diverse classes, distinct types of information, and discipline-specific types of writing, but they all include reading. When you are assigned reading in a course, you are a scholar, and scholarly reading is quite different from reading for pleasure. You must become a critical reader to be an effective scholarly reader. One component of being critical involves asking questions about not only the assigned reading, but also about why the reading was assigned. The first step to becoming a critical reader is to engage with the reading by being an active reader. Be sure to understand why your instructor has assigned this particular reading. The following questions will help you understand the purpose.

- How does this reading fit in with the objectives of the course?

- How does this reading address the themes of the course?
- How does this reading relate to what is currently being covered in the course?
- Is the reading a critical part of an assignment that will follow?

Once you understand why a reading has been assigned, consider how your instructor wants you to read, process, and analyze the reading. If you are not certain, it is a good idea to ask your instructor how you should manage the assigned reading and process it for understanding. The time you allocate to the reading will depend on how much you want to absorb from the reading. Use these questions to determine how you want to read; the further down the list, the more time it will take you to process the reading for full understanding:

- Was this reading assigned for entertainment?
- Was this reading assigned to grasp a certain message?
- Was this reading assigned to find an important detail?
- Was this reading assigned to answer a specific question?
- Was this reading assigned to be evaluated?
- Was this reading assigned to apply its concepts to something else?

You must also be an active reader to be an effective reader. To think as you read, use active reading strategies, which improve comprehension, retention, and recall. Your high school teachers may have shared some strategies with you for becoming an active, engaged reader; therefore, some of these strategies may be familiar to you. Whether the following are new to you or not, it is a good idea to have an arsenal of strategies that work for you when you are assigned a reading in class. Consider the reading process to be like the writing process, with a separation into three primary areas: prereading, reading, and postreading. Depending on what kind of reader you are, you should be able to choose at least a few strategies in each area to improve your critical reading skills.

> The research shows that [readers] who struggle tend not to ask questions at any time as they read—before, during, or after. . . . They're inert as they read. They read—or I should say they submit to the text—never questioning its content, style, or the intent of the author.
> —Ellin Oliver Keene and Susan Zimmermann, *Mosaic of Thought*

Strategies for Prereading

1. Know your discipline's common organization for articles and books. Each field has its own practice, and knowing yours will help you know where to find abstracts or conclusions that will help you review the material.
2. Read the preface and introduction. Oftentimes, the author or editor will present or review important points or even each chapter for you.
3. Preview and predict what the reading will be about.
   a. Look at the table of contents, and review the headings and subheadings for the assigned reading.
   b. Write a short journal entry that describes what you know about the topics that are listed in the headings.
   c. Draft some questions you have about the topic.

    d.   <u>Use</u> a K-W-L chart by creating columns headed with "What I Know," "What I Want to Know," and "What I have Learned." Fill in the first two columns prior to reading and the last after you finish.

4.   Skim and scan the reading before you start fully reading. Look at how many pages the reading is, how many sections there are, how long the sections are, and what types of headings and subheadings there are.

5.   Create reading goals and develop a plan to split up what you need to read or what has been assigned. You can do this in a journal, on notebook paper, on your calendar, or in the table of contents.

6.   Choose specific times to read that work for you, and plan enough time to finish a full section. Find out how many pages you can read in an hour, count up your assigned reading, and then make a realistic plan.

Strategies as You Read

1.   Read for 30 to 45 minutes, and then review what you have read before taking a short break. An effective strategy is to read for 30–45 minutes, review for 5 minutes, and take a break for 5 minutes.

2.   Read section by section. It is best to stop when there is a natural break in the reading material. This will help later when you organize your notes, since they will already be focused on one section at a time.

3.   Circle new terms and underline their definitions. Use a circle or some other graphic tool to help you note new terms as you read and note them later as you return to review the reading. If the term is not defined in the text, look it up and note the definition near the term in the reading, if possible. Consider creating a "terms" page at the beginning of your notebook or binder, and note both the term and its definition when you first encounter them.

4.   Annotate your text. Draw attention to main ideas or important points by underlining, highlighting, circling, or using asterisks or other graphic reminders. Use a pen or pencil, rather than a highlighter; you'll have less chance of marking excessively.

> **Tip:** If you are marking too much, it means you aren't able to select main points and important details. Highlighting more than 20 percent of the text means highlighting isn't working for you.

5.   Read difficult sections out loud, or take turns reading out loud with a classmate. This will help you process the important information in more than just one way since it adds the audio element to the visual.

6.   Create a bulleted list of main ideas as you read, or use an informal or formal outline method. You might also use a cluster approach to keep notes about related ideas together.

7.   Create a timeline to keep track of dates, especially when reading literature or when reading about history.

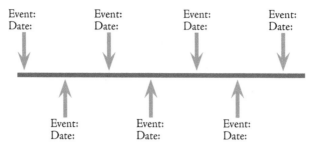

Event: Event: Event: Event:
Date: Date: Date: Date:

Event: Event: Event:
Date: Date: Date:

8. Draw helpful pictures or diagrams in your notes, especially when you want to depict relationships between one character or idea to another.

9. Visualize different sections or ideas by using different colored pens, pencils, or highlighters. Take notes as you read.

10. Write down questions next to the material as you read. Or keep a detailed Reader's Notebook with questions, and be sure to include the page number of the material to which they refer.

11. Use information management software to take notes, add tags to highlight related ideas, and then organize your notes into folders. Information management software is available for most computer platforms and is an easy way to search through your notes. (See Box 11.1.)

Box 11.1

Information Management Software		
AllMyNotes Organizer	KeyNote	Qiqqa
AudioNote-Notepad	KNote	SilverNote
BasKet Note Pads	Memonic	Tiddly-Wiki
Catch Notes	Microsoft OneNote	Tomboy
CintaNotes	MyInfo	TreeDBNotes
Evernote	MyNotex	WikidPad
Gnote	Notee	Windows Journal
Jarnal	Okular	XLnotes
Keeppy	PDF Studio	Xournal
KeepNote	Personal Knowbase	Zim

Strategies for Postreading

1. After reading, write to learn by using journals, graphic organizers, or other options.

2. Read particularly challenging sections again, or reread as needed to answer study questions.

3. Answer reading questions that your instructor has given you, or check the end of the chapter or the book's website for helpful questions.

4. Mark information in your notes that connects to your instructor's lectures or other class materials. Bring your reading notes to class, and highlight any information from the book that your instructor covers again in class or asks questions about.

5. Turn your linear notes into a chart, table, outline, or any other graphic that will help you process the information more quickly. Check out the many different types of

graphic organizers at http://www.thinkport.org/technology/template.tp. See Figure 11.1 for one example of a Venn diagram.

Figure 11.1 Venn diagram

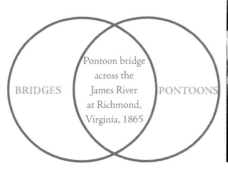

6. Use the *shrinking outline* method. Immediately after reading, write in a journal as much information as you remember or think is important. Then, go through what you've described, making it more concise by taking out things you've repeated or that are not as important as others. Then, go through the information one more time, and create a concise, abstract-like description of what you read.

7. Create a concise statement about the reading topic. While riding on an elevator for a few floors, try to come up with a brief statement of what the reading was about before the elevator stops, or you might apply this strategy as you walk up a few flights of stairs.

8. Use special strategies for difficult material.
   a. Reread. Sometimes rereading is all it takes to grasp something you didn't understand the first time.
   b. Stop reading after each paragraph or section, and write your notes or rephrase what you have read using your own words.
   c. Discuss the reading with a classmate, create a study group, or go see your instructor during office hours.
   d. Create a flow chart of how ideas in each section or paragraph relate to each other.
   e. Take a break from your reading and return when you are refreshed. Sometimes, a cup of coffee or a good night's sleep will help you understand what was eluding you.

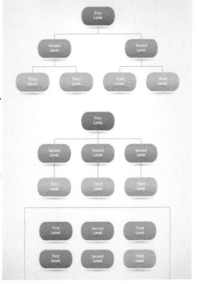

You may have also learned a reading and studying technique in high school that constructed all of the reading steps into one model, such as the SQ3R, SQ4R, or PQRST methods. If you break down these models, they follow the same prereading,

reading, and postreading pattern described earlier, but you may want to add other strategies from the list above when you build your own reading model. Here's a brief breakdown of these methods:

S   ⇨ SURVEY
Q   ⇨ QUESTION
3R ⇨ READ, RECITE, REVIEW

S   ⇨ SURVEY
Q   ⇨ QUESTION
4R ⇨ READ, RECITE, RELATE, REVIEW

P   ⇨ PREVIEW
Q   ⇨ QUESTION
R   ⇨ READ
S   ⇨ SELF-RECITE
T   ⇨ TEST

Reading researchers stress that students should choose reading strategies that fit their personalities, reading levels, and time constraints. Once you choose what strategies work for you, it is best to make using them a habit as you read for your courses. Use an organizer like the one in Figure 11.2 to track your reading strategies.

Figure 11.2 Sample Strategies Organizer

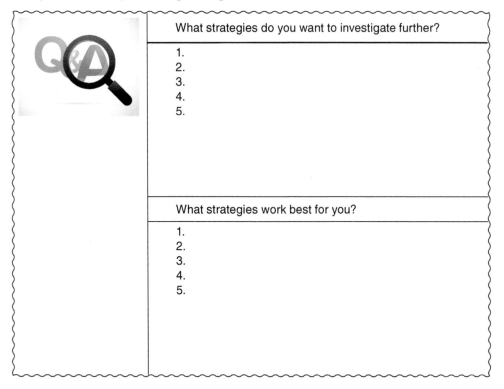

What strategies do you want to investigate further?

1.
2.
3.
4.
5.

What strategies work best for you?

1.
2.
3.
4.
5.

Read More About It

Adler, Mortimer J. *How to Read a Book.* New York, NY: Touchstone, 1972. Print.

Buckner, Aimee. *Notebook Connections: Strategies for the Reader's Notebook.* Portland, ME: Stenhouse, 2009. Print.

Eagleton, Terry. *How to Read a Poem.* Indianapolis, IN: Wiley-Blackwell, 2006. Print.

Frank, Marjorie. *Graphic Organizers for Any Subject: Any Level.* Nashville, TN: Incentive Publications, 2007. Print.

Hennings, Dorothy Grant. *Reading with Meaning: Strategies for College Reading.* New York, NY: Longman, 2004. Print.

Smith, Brenda D. *The Reader's Handbook: Reading Strategies for College and Everyday Life.* New York, NY: Longman, 2009. Print.

Reading 11.1

How to Mark a Book by Mortimer Adler

You know you have to read "between the lines" to get the most out of anything. I want to persuade you to do something equally important in the course of your reading. I want to persuade you to "write between the lines." Unless you do, you are not likely to do the most efficient kind of reading.

I contend, quite bluntly, that marking up a book is not an act of mutilation but of love.

You shouldn't mark up a book which isn't yours. Librarians (or your friends) who lend you books expect you to keep them clean, and you should. If you decide that I am right about the usefulness of marking books, you will have to buy them. Most of the world's great books are available today, in reprint editions, at less than a dollar.

There are two ways in which one can own a book. The first is the property right you establish by paying for it, just as you pay for clothes and furniture. But this act of purchase is only the prelude to possession. Full ownership comes only when you have made it a part of yourself, and the best way to make yourself a part of it is by writing in it. An illustration may make the point clear. You buy a beefsteak and transfer it from the butcher's icebox to your own. But you do not own the beefsteak in the most important sense until you consume it and get it into your bloodstream. I am arguing that books, too, must be absorbed in your bloodstream to do you any good.

Confusion about what it means to own a book leads people to a false reverence for paper, binding, and type—a respect for the physical thing—the craft of the printer rather than the genius of the author. They forget that it is possible for a man to acquire the idea, to possess the beauty, which a great book contains, without staking his claim by pasting his bookplate inside the cover. Having a fine library doesn't prove that its owner has a mind enriched by books; it proves nothing more than that he, his father, or his wife, was rich enough to buy them.

There are three kinds of book owners. The first has all the standard sets and best-sellers—unread, untouched. (This deluded individual owns wood-pulp and ink, not books.) The second has a great many books—a few of them read through, most of them dipped into, but all of them as clean and shiny as the day they were bought. (This person would probably like to make books his own, but is restrained by a false respect for their physical appearance.) The third has a few books or many—every one of them dog-eared and dilapidated, shaken and loosened by continual use, marked and scribbled in from front to back. (This man owns books.)

Is it false respect, you may ask, to preserve intact and unblemished a beautifully printed book, an elegantly bound edition? Of course not. I'd no more scribble all over a first edition of "Paradise Lost" than I'd give my baby a set of crayons and an original Rembrandt! I wouldn't mark up a painting or a statue. Its soul, so to speak, is inseparable from its body. And the beauty of a rare edition or of a richly manufactured volume is like that of a painting or a statue.

But the soul of a book can be separated from its body. A book is more like the score of a piece of music than it is like a painting. No great musician confuses a symphony with the printed sheets of music. Arturo Toscanini reveres Brahms, but Toscanini's score of the C-minor Symphony is so thoroughly marked up that no one but the maestro himself can read it. The reason why a great conductor makes notations on his musical scores—marks them up again and again each time he returns to study them—is the reason why you should mark your books. If your respect for magnificent binding or typography gets in the way, buy yourself a cheap edition and pay your respects to the author.

Why is marking up a book indispensable to reading? First, it keeps you awake. (And I don't mean merely conscious; I mean wide awake.) In the second place, reading, if it is active, is thinking, and thinking tends to express itself in words, spoken or written. The marked book is usually the thought-through book. Finally, writing helps you remember the thoughts you had, or the thoughts the author expressed. Let me develop these three points.

If reading is to accomplish anything more than passing time, it must be active. You can't let your eyes glide across the lines of a book and come up with an understanding of what you have read. Now an ordinary piece of light fiction, like, say, "Gone with the Wind," doesn't require the most active kind of reading. The books you read for pleasure can be read in a state of relaxation, and nothing is lost. But a great book, rich in ideas and beauty, a book that raises and tries to answer great fundamental questions, demands the most active reading of which you are capable. You don't absorb the ideas of John Dewey the way you absorb the crooning of Mr. Vallee. You have to reach for them. That you cannot do while you're asleep.

If, when you've finished reading a book, the pages are filled with your notes, you know that you read actively. The most famous active reader of great books I know is President Hutchins, of the University of Chicago. He also has the hardest schedule of business activities of any man I know. He invariably reads with a pencil, and sometimes, when he picks up a book and pencil in the evening, he finds himself, instead of making intelligent notes, drawing what he calls "caviar factories" on the margins. When that happens, he puts the book down. He knows he's too tired to read, and he's just wasting time.

But, you may ask, why is writing necessary? Well, the physical act of writing, with your own hand, brings words and sentences more sharply before your mind and preserves them better in your memory. To set down your reaction to important words and sentences you have read, and the questions they have raised in your mind, is to preserve those reactions and sharpen those questions.

Even if you wrote on a scratch pad, and threw the paper away when you had finished writing, your grasp of the book would be surer. But you don't have to throw the paper away. The margins (top and bottom, as well as side), the end-papers, the very space between the lines, are all available. They aren't sacred. And, best of all, your marks and notes become an integral part of the book and stay there forever. You can pick up the book the following week or year, and there are all your points of agreement, disagreement, doubt, and inquiry. It's like resuming an interrupted conversation with the advantage of being able to pick up where you left off.

And that is exactly what reading a book should be: a conversation between you and the author. Presumably he knows more about the subject than you do; naturally, you'll have the proper humility as you approach him. But don't let anybody tell you that a reader is supposed to be solely on the receiving end. Understanding is a two-way operation; learning doesn't consist in being an empty receptacle. The learner has to question himself and question the teacher. He even has to argue with the teacher, once he understands what the teacher is saying. And marking a book is literally an expression of your differences, or agreements of opinion, with the author.

There are all kinds of devices for marking a book intelligently and fruitfully. Here's the way I do it:

1. Underlining: of major points, of important or forceful statements.
2. Vertical lines at the margin: to emphasize a statement already underlined.
3. Star, asterisk, or other doo-dad at the margin: to be used sparingly, to emphasize the ten or twenty most important statements in the book. (You may want to fold the bottom corner of each page on which you use such marks. It won't hurt the sturdy paper on which most modern books are printed, and you will be able to take the book off the shelf at any time and, by opening it at the folded-corner page, refresh your recollection of the book."
4. Numbers in the margin: to indicate the sequence of points the author makes in developing a single argument.
5. Numbers of other pages in the margin: to indicate where else in the book the author made points relevant to the point marked; to tie up the ideas in a book, which, though they may be separated by many pages, belong together.
6. Circling of key words or phrases.
7. Writing in the margin, or at the top or bottom of the page, for the sake of: recording questions (and perhaps answers) which a passage raised in your mind; reducing a complicated discussion to a simple statement; recording the sequence of major points right through the books. I use the end-papers at the back of the book to make a personal index of the author's points in the order of their appearance.

The front end-papers are, to me, the most important. Some people reserve them for a fancy bookplate. I reserve them for fancy thinking. After I have finished reading the book and making my personal index on the back end-papers, I turn to the front and try to outline the book, not page by page, or point by point (I've already done that at the back), but as an integrated structure, with a basic unity and an order of parts. This outline is, to me, the measure of my understanding of the work.

If you're a die-hard anti-book-marker, you may object that the margins, the space between the lines, and the end-papers don't give you room enough. All right. How about using a scratch pad slightly smaller than the page-size of the book—so that the edges of the sheets won't protrude? Make your index, outlines, and even your notes on the pad, and then insert these sheets permanently inside the front and back covers of the book.

Or, you may say that this business of marking books is going to slow up your reading. It probably will. That's one of the reasons for doing it. Most of us have been taken in by the notion that speed of reading is a measure of our intelligence. There is no such thing as the right speed for intelligent reading. Some things should be read quickly and effortlessly, and some should be read slowly and even laboriously. The sign of intelligence in reading is the ability to read different things differently according to their worth. In the case of good books, the point is not to see how many of them you can get through, but rather how many can get through you—how many you can make your own. A few friends are better than a thousand acquaintances. If this be your aim, as it should be, you will not be impatient if it takes more time and effort to read a great book than it does a newspaper.

You may have one final objection to marking books. You can't lend them to your friends because nobody else can read them without being distracted by your notes. Furthermore, you won't want to lend them because a marked copy is a kind of intellectual diary, and lending it is almost like giving your mind away.

If your friend wishes to read your "Plutarch's Lives," "Shakespeare," or "The Federalist Papers," tell him gently but firmly, to buy a copy. You will lend him your car or your coat—but your books are as much a part of you as your head or your heart.

From *The Saturday Review of Literature,* July 6, 1941.

12
Writing in Arts and Humanities

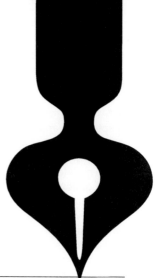

Architecture, Art, English, Film, History, Music, Philosophy, Theater, and Theology

> Good composition is like a suspension bridge—each line adds strength and takes none away.
>
> —Robert Henri

Purposes of Writing in the Arts and Humanities

Arts and *humanities* are general terms representing a variety of academic disciplines that focus on questions that have preoccupied us as humans since the dawn of thought. Even without absolute answers, these questions may concern us on a daily basis: What is love? How is love depicted? Is there a higher being? Why are there hate and pain in this world? Is there a place in the world for everyone? Writers in the arts and humanities pose and try to answer such questions of human existence, and the answers are not like the definitive ones that might occur in other disciplines such as the sciences or business.

Four general types of writing are used in the arts and humanities: creative, theoretical, interpretive, and analytical. Those who do creative writing place their focus on narrative and character development for fictional works, such as novels (*Bridge to Terabithia*), plays (*A View from the Bridge*), poetry ("The Bridge Builder"), and short stories ("An Occurrence at Owl Bridge"). Those who do theoretical writing attempt to create generalized and abstract overarching views of how or why something is true, such as Milton literary scholar Robert Bridges's prosodic analysis of Milton's *Paradise Lost* and other works, which helped him

The Rolling Bridge by Thomas Heatherwick

©wikimediacommons.org

create a theory about Milton's work. Those who do interpretive writing try to discover meaning in a text or in the process of reading a text, such as a student who writes about how the erratic time sequencing in "An Occurrence at Owl Creek Bridge" creates a special meaning of its own. And those who do analytical writing examine the components or form of the text by breaking it down into its parts, such as an architect describing how the octagonal bridge over London's Grand Union Canal works.

Interpretive writing and analytical writing overlap in many ways since both interpretive and analytical writers are interested in examining texts for patterns, looking at how language is used, and searching for clues that are in the text as well as clues that are missing in the text.

As a writer in the arts and humanities, you may be asked to do any of these types of writing; however, the majority of the writing done in the humanities is motivated by interpreting and analyzing texts. In most writing situations, you will be asked to closely and critically read whatever text you are studying and then draw your own conclusions based on your interpretations. The arts and humanities text you will be studying may be oral, visual, or written. It may be a piece of music or a poem, a film or a painting, a play or a novel. It may be an architectural artifact, such as a bridge, or a theological event, such as a sermon.

When you write about the arts or humanities, you may be writing for many different types of courses within this discipline. This chapter is designed to help you meet your writing goal as you consider the purpose behind your communication and what conventions of the field are expected as you investigate the text or artifact under consideration. In addition, this chapter offers guidelines that you can transfer to any writing you do after you graduate. Remember, most employers today are looking for new hires who can communicate effectively through oral and written language. Knowing the conventions of your field can help you secure employment, as well as help you showcase your communication skills throughout your career.

Types of Writing Assignments in the Arts and Humanities

A word after a word after a word is power.

—Margaret Atwood

In the arts and humanities, choosing the appropriate form or format is often the first step in beginning your writing. Since various types of writing assignments exist, learning those that are appropriate for the fields within the arts and humanities discipline is essential. This section includes some common genres of writing assignments you may be asked to use in an arts and humanities course and some additional types of writing genres that you may be asked to create in a job related to the arts and humanities. First, though, review Table 12.1, which highlights some common writing activities and genres for a variety of fields within the discipline of arts and humanities.

Table 12.1

Common Writing Genres in Arts and Humanities Fields								
	Art	Architecture	English	Film	History	Music	Philosophy	Theater	Theology
Class notes	√	√	√	√	√	√	√	√	√
Journals	√	√	√	√		√	√	√	√
Peer reviews or responses	√	√	√	√		√		√	
Summaries			√		√		√		√
Book reviews			√		√		√		√
Writing-to-Learn invention exercises			√						
Sketchbook	√	√							
Exhibition design	√								
Statement of directorial concept						√		√	
Fiction			√						
Poetry			√					√	
Plays			√					√	
Proposals	√	√	√	√		√		√	
Editorials			√						
Oral presentations	√	√	√	√	√	√	√	√	√
PowerPoint, Prezi, or other digital presentations	√	√	√	√	√	√	√	√	√
Professional reports	√	√		√		√		√	
Response/ Reflection essays	√	√	√	√		√	√	√	√

Common Writing Genres in Arts and Humanities Fields									
	Art	Architecture	English	Film	History	Music	Philosophy	Theater	Theology
Review or critique	√	√	√	√		√		√	√
Descriptive essays	√	√	√			√	√	√	√
Narrative essays			√	√			√		√
Comparative essays	√	√	√	√	√	√	√	√	√
Interpretative essays	√	√	√	√		√		√	√
Analysis essays	√	√	√	√	√	√	√	√	√
Argumentative essays	√	√	√	√	√	√	√	√	√
Visual essays	√	√	√	√	√			√	
Primary source analysis	√	√	√	√	√	√	√	√	√
Research notes			√		√		√		√
Literature reviews			√		√		√		√
Annotated bibliographies			√		√		√		√
Research papers	√	√	√	√	√	√	√	√	√
Essay exams	√	√	√	√	√	√	√	√	√
websites			√						
Conference presentations			√		√		√		√

Below we discuss some of the most common writing assignments and genres for the arts and humanities. This is not an exhaustive list, and your instructor or employer might ask you to write in a genre that is not given here. If so, use that form or genre, and read the section in this chapter on Writing Effectively in the Arts and Humanities on page 215.

Review or Critique

A review or critique briefly describes a text and explains its merits for readers so they can decide whether they want to experience the text for themselves. Remember that a text can be written, visual, or oral—this means that this genre can be useful in most subfields of the arts and humanities. As a student in an art or architecture course, you might critique a painting or a building; in a history or philosophy course, you might review a book in the subject area of a research paper; in a film or theater course, you might review a movie or a play that you have seen for class, and so on. In presenting your review or critique, be sure to go beyond the first impression you take from reading, viewing, or listening to the text. In your review, you will discuss a few key points about the text, rather than describe everything that the author or artist created. No matter the academic field, you should always include these three pieces of information: (a) identify the text and its creator, (b) include a brief summary of the text, and (c) include your evaluation. Depending on the assignment or your field, the review or critique might also expand to include some or all of the following parts:

- An informative title that identifies the title of the text or work and its creator
- A summary of essential content and main ideas
- A description of the creator's theme, purpose, and methods of development
- A brief biography of the creator, including information about other texts or works
- A description of how the text or work relates to other texts or works in the field
- Your evaluation of the text or work, with evidence supporting your opinions
- Short quotations or visuals from the text or work that represent the theme of the piece and the creator's style and tone

Most reviews or critiques are shorter than essays, around one to two pages. Some instructors might ask you to write a review or critique essay, in which case you will want to look at both this section and the section on writing essays in this chapter.

Oral Presentation for Class or a Conference

Most fields in the arts and humanities will require you to give an oral presentation at some point. If you have never given an oral presentation before, you might be quite anxious. To alleviate any anxiety, prepare for your presentation effectively by clearly identifying the content you want to present, organizing it into a well-defined outline, and creating a handout for your audience (if the assignment, your instructor, or your employer permits). Your first step in the process of developing the oral presentation is to recognize and organize the content you want to present. Here are some questions that will help as you think about the preparation and content of your talk.

- How much time do I have for my talk, and how much information will fit within my time limit?
- What types of supporting materials can I use? This might be restricted by the assignment or your instructor.
- What types of technology and software are available for me to use?
- What is the thesis, main idea, or main argument of my presentation?
- What are the key points related to my thesis, main idea, or main argument?
- How can I limit my focus to only three or four key points to help my audience process all the information?
- What examples (oral, written, or visual) will I use to support the key points? How will I present these examples?
- What examples will be the most relevant for my particular audience?
- What strategies will I use to help the audience follow my presentation?

> **Tip:** Use signposts within your presentation to guide the reader through key points, supporting ideas, and different segments. Common signposts include the following:
> - Using numbers, such as *First, The first point, My third example*, and so on
> - Using parallel structures, such as *My first quotation comes from, My second quotation comes from*, and later in the talk, *My last quotation comes from*
> - Using strict chronological order when presenting information, such as giving supporting evidence that is organized from oldest to newest or vice versa
> - Using organizational words—such as *In conclusion*—to remind your audience where you are in your presentation

After clarifying the content you will cover in your presentation, you will want to carefully organize the material. Here are some hints to assist you in preparing the introduction, body, and conclusion of your oral presentation.

Introduction

- Begin with an attention getter, such as an interesting quotation or statistic.
- State the focused topic or intention of your presentation (e.g., *I will be discussing two philosophical movements today*).
- Provide an outline or plan of what you will discuss (e.g., *I will be comparing these two movements by focusing on three elements: X, Y, and Z*).
- Pass on any significant background information that might be needed to process the material you will be discussing.

Body

- Present the information, following the outline or plan you presented in the introduction.
- Include just enough evidence to clearly support your points and not overburden your audience.
- Use signposts that help your audience process the information you present.

Conclusion

- Announce clearly to your audience that you are beginning your conclusion (e.g., *In conclusion, . . .*).
- Restate the main points very briefly.
- State the importance of the information you have presented.
- Ask your audience to imagine themselves taking action, or invite them to ask you questions or share their ideas.

Finally, you will need to decide whether you will memorize your talk, read your material from a script, or use an outline to help you deliver your information. If you are preparing an oral presentation for a class, read the assignment thoroughly to see if you do indeed, have a choice or if your instructor requires only one of these options. If you are presenting at a conference, make sure you understand the conventions of your field. For example, if you present on a literary topic either in English or foreign language studies at the annual Modern Language Association conference, you most likely will be expected to read from a script. However, if you present at the same conference on a linguistics or composition topic, you most likely will be expected to have a helpful handout and a presentation using technology, such as PowerPoint slides or a Prezi demonstration.

All three types of oral presentation methods can be effective, but each has its pros and cons, so if you have a choice, it is up to you to decide which one feels the most comfortable for you. Memorizing your talk can make it seem that you are an expert in your field, but it can also be uncomfortable if you experience anxiety or forget your material. Reading from a previously written script will ensure that you do not forget to discuss all the points you planned on, but it might also prevent you from interacting effectively with your audience since your eyes will be down when you read. Using an outline to guide your talk showcases your expertise and allows you to make eye contact with your audience, but it also requires you to memorize a great deal of the material. Whichever delivery method you choose, be sure to practice your presentation multiple times, by yourself and in front of a practice audience, so you will be more fully in control of the timing and delivery of your material.

Digital Presentation

Oral presentations can often be more effective and interesting if you use technology to support the delivery of your information. If you are giving an oral presentation for a class, check the assignment to see whether you can use technology within your presentation. Some instructors may even assign a digital presentation on its own, rather than an oral presentation, especially if they are preparing you to share information with peers at conferences or workshops. Two of the more common digital visual aids in the arts and humanities are PowerPoint and Prezi.

PowerPoint

Using Microsoft PowerPoint is an easy and helpful way to add a professional touch to a presentation. PowerPoint provides a variety of templates that can be used to quickly format your presentation, or you can design your own templates or slides. Figure 5.1 presents a typical PowerPoint slide. If you choose to use PowerPoint, use it wisely by following some of these important guidelines:

Learn how to compose slides effectively

- Keep the design basic so it does not distract from the content.
- Create a slide template that allows room for visuals or website addresses.
- Choose an easy-to-read font size and type.
- Decorate slides in a professional manner.
- Decide that content is always the primary concern. Do not let the design restrict or distract from your message.

Be consistent

- Use the same font type on all slides.
- Use the same font size for headings/subheadings/examples.
- Use no more than five or six colors for the entire presentation.
- Create a frame for images, and use this frame throughout the presentation.

- Choose a way of highlighting important information (such as bolding, underlining, changing font color), and do it the same way throughout the presentation.

Add text

- Use key words only. Do not use full sentences.
- Use the text as an outline or supplement to your oral presentation. Do not read from your slides.
- Balance text with images, and do not overwhelm the slide.

Add images

- Use images to help your audience visualize the material. Do not decorate with them.
- Create your own images, rather than overusing stock or comedic clip art.
- Balance images with text, and do not overwhelm the slide.

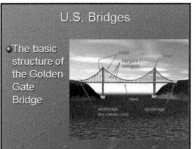

Figure 12.1 Sample PowerPoint Slide

Consider your audience

- Use text and images that fit their expertise and expectations.
- Highlight the material you are introducing to them.
- Use font types and sizes that will be viewable by all in the audience.
- Provide a handout of printed slides and enough room for the audience to take notes.
- Avoid "Death by PowerPoint"—be sure that what you choose to present is of interest to your audience.

Practice your presentation

- Use a timer so your talk will fit within the required time limit.
- Know the technology you will be using, and try it out in the room in which you will be presenting.
- Use the PowerPoint presentation as an outline to help present your ideas smoothly.
- Maintain eye contact with the audience.
- Speak naturally—not too quickly or slowly.

Prezi

Prezi (http://prezi.com) is online presentation software. Like PowerPoint, it allows you to present information digitally to an audience by using template designs. However, by using Prezi, you can also highlight information more by using its nonlinear presentation functions that allow you to zoom in and out, embed multimedia elements, and graphically organize your material. Prezi is available online for free if you want to use only its basic functions. Be sure to check out the upgraded version if you want to have even more options. By using the same basic guidelines as given above for PowerPoint presentations, especially those related to design and audience, you can create an informative and interesting presentation. For a sample Prezi presentation, that covers how to create an effective Prezi presentation, visit http://prezi.com/c9pdlrpx3pr6/copy-of-presentation-on-presentations. A sample Prezi slide is shown in Figure 12.2.

Figure 12.2 Sample Prezi

Essay or Research Paper

A variety of long-form genres are used across the fields of arts and humanities. You might be assigned a critical analysis essay in a music, art, or theater course in which you must choose an element or some elements to analyze and discuss. In a history course, you might be assigned a comparative essay, in which you are asked to compare two events or two time periods. Or you might be asked in a film or English course to write a response essay, in which you use a film to trigger personal memories that you then relate. Whatever essay type or genre you are asked to write, the basic structure includes an introduction, body, and conclusion with the presentation of an explicit or implied thesis in the introduction. In a personal essay, your thesis can be informational or argumentative; in this type of essay, your own personal experience is given as support throughout the essay. In an essay that requires you to engage with a primary source or text, such as a song or a short story, your thesis can be informational or argumentative, depending on what essay genre you are writing. In this type of essay, you can use your own experience, ideas from the primary source, or quotations from the primary source as support for your thesis. For an essay that requires you to form your thesis or argument and use evidence as support, you use primary or secondary sources within the body of your essay to support the thesis with evidence, take at least a small part of the essay body to engage with some counter-evidence, and then conclude the essay. See the section on Writing Effectively in the Arts and Humanities (page 215) for more details on how to write different types of essays and what types of evidence you might want to use in your essay.

Personal essay genres, as described above, most likely include only your own thoughts or opinions. Generally, these types of essays are shorter because the support you include comes from your own experiences, rather than from sources outside yourself. Although we can describe some essay genres as personal, these same genres can also be used with primary or secondary sources. Table 12.2 illustrates how some essay genres can be used with personal experience alone or in combination with primary or secondary sources. Since many fields of study exist within the arts and humanities, it is best to consult with your instructor about any essay genre that is assigned.

Table 12.2

How Essay Genres Can Be Used			
	Personal experience	Primary source	Secondary source
Descriptive essay	√	√	
Narrative essay	√		
Reflection/Response essay	√	√	
Review or Critique essay	√	√	√
Summary essay		√	√
Comparison/Contrast essay	√	√	√
Interpretive essay	√	√	√
Analysis essay	√	√	√
Argumentative essay	√	√	√
Visual essay	√	√	√
Research paper (informative or argumentative)		√	√

The research paper is a longer form of the essay, and it requires a much longer and in-depth research process, along with a sophisticated and critical level of inquiry. As part of the research paper process, you locate and use secondary sources, such as peer-reviewed articles, in order to assess and support your own thesis or argument. Research papers can be informational, such as a 15-page paper in a philosophy course, in which you present the life and theories of a particular philosopher. Research papers can also be argumentative, such as a 10-page paper in a different philosophy course, in which you make an argument that the film *The Bridge* is an inaccurate representation of the philosophical trolley problem. The format of the research paper parallels that of an academic essay. Thus the format described below represents both short essays and longer research papers. For more information on using primary and secondary sources for essays and research papers, see the section later in this chapter entitled Know the Kinds of Evidence Used in the Arts and Humanities.

Basic structure of an essay or research paper in the arts and humanities

Introduction

- Use an attention getter or hook, such as a quotation or a startling statistic to engage the reader immediately.
- Appeal to the reader's *ethos* (emotional side) or *logos* (logical side).
- Provide a frame or context for your topic by narrowing it down to a specific point by the end of the introduction.
- (Optional) Provide a question that relates to the specific topic of your essay, setting up the answer to this question as the thesis of the essay.
- Provide a thesis or argument (this can be written or implied).

Body

- Provide evidence that supports your thesis or argument.
- If there might be an opposing view to your argument or thesis, present it here, but also include some evidence against the opposing argument.

Conclusion

- Give the essay a sense of completeness by doing the following:
- Stressing the importance of the thesis
- Answering the question, "So what?"
- Showing how the points and evidence you have presented strongly support the thesis
- Echoing the introduction and reminding readers that you have brought them full circle
- Giving the reader something to remember
- Inviting the reader to apply something from the essay to herself or her own life
- Raising a question that the reader can think about after he finishes your essay
- Asking the reader to use the information from your essay and make a prediction for the future

Literature Review

The literature review paper is used to show the reader that you have read and understand the major published works (also known as the *literature*) within a particular field or about a particular question. Some instructors give a literature review as a stand-alone assignment, but it is often assigned in conjunction with a longer work, such as a research paper or thesis. What we provide here is appropriate for many fields within the arts and humanities, but be sure to consult the assignment and your instructor about which specific format to use and which types of sources are acceptable.

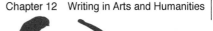

Before you begin to gather sources to review, be sure to have a specific topic that you are researching or a clear argument for which you are gathering sources. Treat the literature review as a formal assignment and use a clear and academic voice and tone. Here are some hints to follow as you collect sources and prepare to create the literature review:

- Focus your research by narrowing your topic and creating an in-progress thesis. The thesis may change as you do your research and read your sources, but having one at the start of the literature review will help you collect only relevant sources.

- Read your sources critically, keeping careful and complete notes on the important information you want to include in the literature review. Be sure to use a system that allows you to mark summaries, paraphrases, and quotations you want to use.

- Choose effective sources that will fit both the literature review and any further assignment:
  - Avoid duplication of information.
  - Identify areas of controversy.
  - Record additional questions your sources raise.
  - Highlight gaps in sources and find other sources that fill in the missing information.

> **Tip:** In the literature review, be sure to synthesize sources and information. Do not just describe what one source says and then what the next source says and so on.
>
> The format for the literature review may be specialized according to your field or your teacher's instructions. However, what follows is a basic outline of what a literature review includes. Design your literature review in a way that reflects topics or subtopics on which the source authors (dis)agree, or relates these topics back to your argument. Use signposts that show relationships among the sources or between the sources and your argument. Transitional expressions such as these can be useful as signposts: again, also, conversely, however, in addition, moreover, nevertheless, on the other hand, and similarly.

Basic structure of the literature review in the arts and humanities

Introduction

- Make it short and clear, giving a blueprint to what main topics and arguments will be covered.
- Explain the order in which you will present the literature and why you have selected this order. Typical organizational patterns include:
  - Moving from general to specific.
  - Arranging according to topics.
  - Classifying via type of theory, research, or research method.
  - Structuring with an organizational pattern that fits your sources, thesis, topic, or field.
- Give the purpose of the review.

Body

- Group authors who share opinions or views.
- Compare and contrast authors with different views.
- Discuss and critique author methodology.
- Highlight excellent studies.
- Highlight gaps in research done previously.
- Show how your study relates to previous studies.
- Show how your study relates to the literature in general.

Conclusion

- Give an overall summary of what the literature says.
- Recap sources or studies that are significantly related to your own research or argument.
- Show an understanding of how the sources you have reviewed relate to your original argument, the overall field of your research, or any future research you plan on doing or would consider doing.

Annotated Bibliography

The annotated bibliography is an organized list of sources (articles, books, journals, periodicals, websites, and so on) with each source having a brief note or annotation that follows. In the annotations, you summarize the content of the source, remark on the source's usefulness for your research, evaluate the validity and reliability of the source's method or conclusions, and present your reactions to the source.

The format of an annotated bibliography can vary across fields, courses, and instructors. If you are required to prepare an annotated bibliography for a course, be sure to read the assignment thoroughly and ask your instructor about the specific format required. Generally, in the arts and humanities, the bibliographic information of the source is written in Modern Language Association (MLA) documentation style; for more information on MLA documentation style, see Chapter 14. The annotations for each source are written in paragraphs, and the length can vary from a few sentences to a few pages, depending on the course assignment and how the annotated bibliography will ultimately be used. If you are asked to write only summaries, the annotations will be rather short; if you are asked to add an evaluation for each source, the annotation will be longer.

Sample Student Annotated Bibliography

Chin-Cheng Eric Lin

Dr. Dubek

English 1020

3 August 2011

Annotated Bibliography

Beef: It's What's For Dinner. Beef Industry Council and Beef Board-Commercial. 1993. Youtube.com. Youtube, 2005. Web. 31 July 2011. Subtle advertising is the key in this commercial. While the focus is a tight shot around the dishes made from beef, the hands and headless bodies tell of the gender assigned to the specific dishes. From these brief images we associate the kabob and the steak sandwich as man food whereas the sirloin citrus salad is associated with women and children's food. These subtle imageries linger and form our subconscious so that as men or women, we are then prone to look for these offerings at our next dining experience.

"Mein Coming Out." *Happy Endings.* ABC. WKRN, Nashville, 20 April 2011. Television. The exploits of six friends in their late twenties is the premise of the sitcom. In this particular episode, the gay character, Max, is in a quandary over whether to continue to lie to his parents or face the music and come out. Deciding to enlist the help of Jane, a married female friend within the group, Max and Dave, another single male character in the group, attends dinner with Max's parents. As they approach Max's parents, we are told that they actually think that Dave is the gay one. This misunderstanding is backed just as Dave is about to deny his homosexuality; the waiter brings the drinks to the table with 2 scotches and a daiquiri. Dave then responds, "Really guy? That's your timing?" The intent here, following the stereotype that men drink scotch while women, or in this case gays, drink daiquiris.

Sobal, Jeffrey. "Men, Meat, and Marriage: Models of Masculinity." *Food & Foodways* 13 (2005): 135-158. *Academic Search Premier.* Sun. 31 July 2011. In exploring the differences between food choices, Sobal relates to the complexities derived especially in terms of marriage. As food influences our identity, we come to identify foods as either masculine or feminine. Where men identify with a meat-centric diet, women do not. As such, in marriage, a compromise must be formed. Focusing on the selection of meat in dining, Sobal explores what it is to be a man culturally. She then applies that definition to marriage and how it then creates turmoil as the two sexes attempt at a compromise. This singular masculinity is defined and in compromise, Sobal attempts to expand on masculinity and define "Multiple Masculinity" to the meat-centric man.

"To See or Not to See?" Science Channel. July 24, 2011. Television. Focused on our sense of sight, the program explores the various situations and circumstances where sight affects us. In particular, we are introduced to the physiology of sight and the processes by which our brain adapts its information to memory. We also see research into the extraordinary, where lack of sight is replaced by other senses such as sound. Of particular interest is the closeness to which we associate color with taste. In this segment, the researchers introduce a group of highly trained culinary students to color liquids with contrasting tastes that are not commonly associated with their familiar colors. Some examples of these pairings are yellow liquid to strawberry flavor or red liquid to lime flavor. Upon tasting these liquids, the student-chefs are asked to identify these liquids. The results are surprising. Even with the refined tastes of the chefs, the liquids are all misidentified. Where yellow should have been strawberry, it is identified as lime or citrus in flavor. This experiment shows that our sense of sight not only influences our senses and memory, it is in fact dominant over our sense of taste.

When Harry Met Sally . . . by Nora Ephron. Dir. Rob Reiner. 1989. MGM, 2001. DVD. A film about the meeting and relationship turmoil between two individuals different in occupation and life is the main focus of the story line. The question of what makes a man so different from a woman is explored. We see the male character Harry Burns, played by a rough and unrefined Billy Crystal, an active, on-the-go basketball referee walking through life living the typical man's dream—with pragmatic social commentaries in love and life to physical activities of batting cages and poker nights with the guys. While the female character Sally Albright, played by the always lovable and refined Meg Ryan, embodies the typical emotional and cunning yet seductive woman. The film is filled with gender stereotypes and has produced many iconic scenes, one of which is the restaurant scene in which we see Sally act out a scene of sexual climax. It is at this scene which we see the epitome of social stereotypes not only in life but also more subtly in food. On the table, we see the typical meal of the man, Harry, which is a heavily stacked pastrami sandwich of which he is engulfing with gusto. Meanwhile, Sally's meal consists of an equally heavily stacked turkey sandwich except, wait; she removes most of the meat prior to eating it diminutively. This scene subconsciously encourages us to further identify and empathize with our respective gender characters.

Writing Effectively in the Arts and Humanities

> To make our communications more effective, we need to shift our thinking from "What information do I need to convey?" to "What questions do I want my audience to ask?
>
> —Chip Heath

Know the Audience(s) in the Arts and Humanities

Many people writing in the arts and humanities are writing for their peers or colleagues: peers in university courses, fellow researchers, employers and employees, team members, and project managers. They may be presenting at conferences or workshops, writing journal or magazine articles, or sharing through newsletters, blogs, and websites. They may be communicating with more general, inexpert audiences through their websites and blogs, newsletters, newspaper articles and editorials, and community talks or presentations. It is important to always know who you are writing for in order to determine whether your narrative should be written

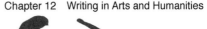

in the first or third person (See Figure 12.3). Before you begin to write, ask yourself the following questions:

- Who are your primary readers?
- Who else might read your writing or listen to your presentation?
- What will the members of your audience already know about your topic or text?
- What will you need to define or explain?
- Will your audience be predisposed to agree or disagree with your point of view?
- What do you want this audience to do or believe?
- What kinds of evidence will be most convincing for this audience?

In addition, if you are writing for a course, you need to be aware that your instructor is also part of your audience. It is always best to consult your instructor about whether she wants to be included as part of your knowledgeable audience—and if that is the case, it is a good idea to learn how much your instructor knows about the topic. Likewise, if you are writing for your job, you need to be aware that your employer is also part of your audience.

Figure 12.3 Point of View Flow Chart

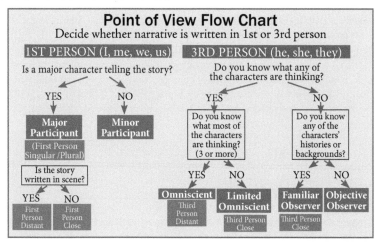

Know the Questions to Ask in the Arts and Humanities

> A prudent question is one-half of wisdom.
>
> —Francis Bacon

As a student, you may be assigned research questions or writing goals. Often, however, you will have to make a decision about these questions or goals. You can begin your writing preparation by asking yourself what you want to know more about and what you need to understand better in order to complete the assigned task or goal. One of the first factors you should consider is the type of arts and humanities writing you will be doing. Be sure to fulfill the assignment by providing the type of writing required.

Questions for interpretive writing

1. **Why** did the events occur? Or, **why** was the artifact created?
2. **Why** is the event or artifact significant to the author/creator or reader?

In interpretative writing, you are seeking to explain something, usually an event or an artifact. Your answers to these questions about your interpretations will show how you have explored your own thoughts or delved into the thoughts or mind of the creator of the text or artifact. In interpreting a piece of literature, music, or art, you try to determine the meaning of the piece, as though you are explaining it to yourself.

Questions for analytical writing

1. **What** is the issue (question, or problem) addressed by the author? Or, **what** is the artifact made by the creator?
2. **Why** is the issue (question, problem) or artifact important to the author/creator or reader?
3. **Who** does the issue or artifact impact?
4. **How** does the issue or artifact impact those affected?

Basically, in analytical writing, you are preparing a detailed examination or study of an issue, question, problem, or artifact that impacts others or yourself. The goal of the writing is to determine the issue's or artifact's nature, structure, or essential features. Your analysis should be systematic and methodical; in effect, you are breaking up a complex whole into its basic elements, such as analyzing a piece of music by breaking it down into its verses, bridges, and chorus. In an analytical paper written for an English class, you can use an ordered, logical structure to break down or resolve an argument. You can use the same type of logical structure for a paper in a philosophy, history, theology, or language class. In a music, architecture, or art class, you most likely will give a critical description of the piece under consideration by focusing on its structure and giving a synopsis of the piece.

> **Tip:** If you find yourself in analysis paralysis with an inability to analyze a situation or issue effectively, you are most likely using an overly analytical approach or have an excess of information. Possible cures for analysis paralysis include simplifying your thesis or argument or outlining your paper to determine which information is the most important to use and which information can be discarded.

Know the Kinds of Evidence Used in the Arts and Humanities

> Doing research [only] on the Web is like using a library assembled piecemeal by pack rats and vandalized nightly.
>
> —Roger Ebert

A common organizational pattern of interpretative or analytical writing includes presenting your claim, providing support from the text or artifact, and then discussing how the support corroborates or proves your claim. This type of organization can be repeated multiple times, depending on how many claims you make in your interpretation or analysis. For instance, if you want to break a text down into two parts for your analysis, you might decide to have two major parts of your essay. However, you might also take that same text and decide to take the piece as a whole but discuss five different possible interpretations of the piece.

Using primary sources

Since most arts and humanities writing is either interpretive, analytical, or a combination of both, and since the supporting evidence for this type of writing is most often textual or visual, your main focus will usually be on the text or artifact you are interpreting or analyzing. The text or artifact about which you are writing is considered your primary source, and this primary source can be presented in a written, visual, or audio format. Common primary sources in the arts and humanities are provided in Table 12.3.

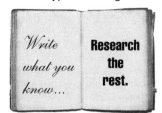

Write what you know... **Research the rest.**

Table 12.3

	Common Primary Sources in the Arts and Humanities
Art	Paintings, sculptures, folk art, quilts, blown glass, drawings, prints, sketches, photographs, carvings, computer and digital graphics, architecture, ceramics, mosaics, silk screens, lithographs, collages, furniture
English	Plays, poems, short stories, novels, nonfiction, creative nonfiction, autobiographies, biographies, fables, myths, folktales, fantasies, legends, ballads, jokes, satires, parodies, farces, monologues, essays, literary criticism, diaries, journals, travel literature, newspapers, magazines, comic books, graphic novels
Film	Scripts, recordings, photographs, feature films, television movies, media industry trade papers, film reviews, fan magazines, editorials, advertisements, film trailers, press kits, lobby cards, film clips, prints, slides, scene shots, publicity stills, archives, background music, documentaries, mockumentaries, filmographies, festival and exhibition programs, interviews
History	Archives, birth certificates, obituaries, marriage certificates, death certificates, political papers (such as the Declaration of Independence), census records, military records, diaries, letters, personal papers, coins, stamps, photographs, reports, literature, maps, advertisements, pamphlets, posters, laws, family Bibles, wills, deeds, school report cards, financial records, ledgers, board meeting minutes, tax and voter lists, department reports, police records, court records, oral histories, stories, anecdotes, films, paintings
Modern languages	Plays, poems, short stories, novels, nonfiction, creative nonfiction, autobiographies, biographies, fables, myths, folktales, fantasies, legends, ballads, jokes, satires, parodies, farces, monologues, essays, literary criticism, diaries, journals, travel literature, newspapers, magazines, comic books, graphic novels
Music	Songs, raps, opera, symphonies, suites, overtures, concertos, background, canons, ballads, carols, fugues, etudes, impromptu, marches, oratorios, sonatas, rondos, requiems, serenades, verses, refrains, choruses, hymns, variations, cycles, movements
Philosophy	Religious texts, pamphlets, letters, diaries, scholarly works, lectures, contemporary criticism, archives, journals, memos, manuscripts, newspaper articles, photographs, minutes of conferences or agencies
Theology	Religious texts or theological works in original language, translated religious texts or theological works, scholarly works, church records, lectures, contemporary criticism, archives, diaries, letters, journals, memos, manuscripts, newspaper articles of current events, photographs, government records, birth and death certificates, minutes of conferences or agencies

Using Secondary Sources

Anyone else who has written about your primary source or topic is considered a secondary source. Your instructor, usually through the assignment, will indicate whether you should focus only on the primary source or also use secondary ones. You should also think about how and where you can locate secondary source information. The type of writing you do to achieve your communication goals should guide your research approach and topics.

The key to writing an effective interpretation or analysis in the arts and humanities is to cite enough evidence to make your point but not to overload the paper with massive amounts of material from secondary sources. By focusing your topic and providing support in a concise manner, you will retain your own voice but also show that you are able to uphold your thesis or argument through the use of examples from the primary text or secondary sources. A good rule of thumb is not to use more sources than the number of pages in your essay or research paper.

Secondary sources include both general and specific sources. It is often wise to consult general sources as you brainstorm and then focus on a specific thesis or argument. General secondary sources such as dictionaries and encyclopedias, either in print or online, are a good place to begin brainstorming about your topic, but they are typically not considered valuable secondary sources to use within an essay or research paper.

In fact, these types of sources are sometimes referred to as *tertiary sources* (see Figure 12.4) to distinguish them from the types of secondary sources that are most useful in supporting arguments. In the arts and humanities, secondary sources that can be used successfully as effective supporting evidence include scholarly books and journals, which should preferably be peer reviewed, which means the article has been read and reviewed by others in the field. Secondary sources are written by authors who evaluate, analyze, or interpret original information. For instance, if you are writing a three-page essay about the novel, *The Monkey Bridge*, you might list the following sources in your Works Cited

Figure 12.4 Example of a Tertiary Source

breeches	brim
firemen behind the barrel. —**breech delivery** birth of baby with the feet or buttocks appearing first. **breeches** pl. n. trousers extending to just below the knee. **breed** v. **breeding, bred**. produce new or improved strains of (domestic animals or plants); bear (offspring); produce or be produced, breed trouble. —n. group of animals, etc. within a species; kind or sort. —**breeder** n. —**breeding** n. result of good upbringing or training. **breeze** n. gentle wind —v. move quickly or casually, —**breezy** adj. windy, casual, carefree. **brethren** pl. n. Old-fashioned (used in religious contexts) brothers. **breve** n. a note in medieval mensural notation equal to one-half or one-third of a longa.	has just been or is about to be married. —**bridesmaid** n. girl who attends a bride at her wedding. **bridge** n. a structure for crossing a river etc.; platform from which a ship is steered or controlled; upper part of the nose; piece of wood supporting the strings of a violin etc. —v. build a bridge over (something). —**bridgehead** n. fortified position at the end of a bridge nearest the enemy. **bridge** n. card game based on whist. **bridle** n. headgear for controlling a horse. —v. put a bridle on (a horse); restrain. —**bridle path** path suitable for riding horses. **brief** adj. short in duration; using few words; concise, succinct. —n. a short and concise statement or written item; a writ summoning one to answer any action.

Works Cited

Cao, Lan. *The Monkey Bridge*. New York: Penguin Books, 1998. Print.

Coward, Harold G. "Psychology and Karma." *Philosophy East and West* 33.1 (1983): 49–60. Print.

Reichenbach, Bruce R. "Karma, Causation and Divine Intervention." *Philosophy East and West*. 14.1 (1989): 135–149. Print.

Schinto, Jeanne. "Review: Invisible Scars." *The Women's Review of Works* 14.10 (1997): 26–27. Print.

Primary versus secondary sources

Although you might think that sources can always be clearly categorized as either primary or secondary, the distinction can sometimes be subjective and based on the context in which you are using the source. For example, an archive of letters from Benjamin Franklin may be considered a primary source for a historian to study in detail, interpreting or analyzing the content and form of the letters. However, that same archive of letters could also be considered a secondary source for someone in literature to study how Franklin responded to Thomas Paine's work *Common Sense*.

> Facts are stubborn things; and whatever may be our wishes, our inclinations, or the dictates of our passions, they cannot alter the state of facts and evidence.
>
> —John Adams

Qualitative versus quantitative supporting evidence

Although writers in the various fields of arts and humanities can use both quantitative and qualitative data in order to make arguments or support their claims, qualitative data are more the norm when interpreting or analyzing a text. Quantitative data, though not as common, can also be used to make arguments or support claims, especially in humanities areas other than English. Both types of data come from primary research regarding the text or artifact in question, as well as secondary research from other published resources. Common types of qualitative evidence used in arts and humanities writing include textual or other examples, definitions, testimonies, and stories or narratives. For example, if you are writing about the painting *Scholar on the Bridge*, you might use a quotation from Maxwell Hearn, the author of *How to Read Chinese Paintings*, to support your own ideas. Common types of quantitative evidence include facts and figures presented as numbers within the text or a combination of numbers, and visuals, such as charts and graphs in the text or in appendixes. If you are writing about patterns within a text or are attempting to demonstrate causal relationships, you need to present the methods you used to arrive at the quantitative data that you are presenting, including any mathematical formula used for transcribing or coding of the text. If statistical or quantitative analysis is used in arts and humanities writing, the mathematical component is often simple arithmetic or percentages. For example, you might want to compare two bridges in the San Francisco area: the Bay Bridge and the Golden Gate Bridge. In this case, you could use a simple pie chart to provide a comparison of the number of cars driving over each bridge daily. As the pie chart in Figure 12.5 clearly reveals, the Bay Bridge has much more traffic.

Figure 12.5 Comparison of car travel across two San Francisco bridges

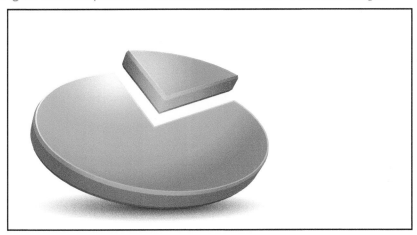

If you use established statistical tests to present quantitative data, be sure to acquaint yourself with the statistical packages available at your institution or required in your field. Two statistical packages used in the arts and humanities are SAS (Statistical Analysis System) and SPSS (Statistical Package for the Social Sciences), which are usually more familiar to social scientists. And, finally, always double-check the accuracy of your data before using it to support your arguments.

The most common type of qualitative data used in the arts and humanities to support an argument is a summary, paraphrase, or quotation from a secondary source. Qualitative data are nonnumerical and may include introspective evidence; testimonials from authors or critics; comments from focus groups, interviews, and surveys; or stories and observations from experts or ordinary people acquainted with the topic. Expert testimony often carries more weight with readers, so be prepared to explain an expert's credentials or qualifications. Ethnography is another type of qualitative research that arts and humanities writers might use to reflect the knowledge or systems within a particular (sub)cultural group. This type of research might be used by a compositionist (one who studies writing) who is investigating how certain groups create or organize their writings, or it might be useful to an historian who is interested in analyzing the artifacts of a particular group or time period. The resulting field report is descriptive in nature and allows the researcher/writer to explore cultural aspects of the humanities.

You may also use a combination of both quantitative and qualitative data—for example, percentages (quantitative) that show how often a particular word or phrase is used in a text alongside comments (qualitative) from readers that indicate how this amount of use affects their interpretation of the text. When possible, use multiple sources and types of evidence. The most important question to ask yourself is this: What kind of evidence is needed to support my claim or to make it persuasive to my intended audience?

You must be careful to present both qualitative and quantitative evidence in an ethical manner. Withholding evidence or not giving the full picture because you think it hurts your argument is unethical and presents inaccurate results. You should make sure that the evidence you use, no matter what kind, actually supports the claim you are making. For example, the evidence you present should avoid leaps in logic and

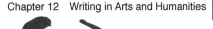

inaccurate cause-and-effect arguments. See Table 12.4 for a summary of the different types of qualitative and quantitative supporting evidence.

Table 12.4

Types of Supporting Evidence	
Qualitative	Quantitative
Analogical Anecdotes Intuition Judgment of an expert Personal experience Testimonials	Physical Scientific results Statistics

Know the Writing and Style Conventions used in the Arts and Humanities

> Persistent, disciplined study can be shown as well in a personal narrative as in a lab report, so . . . academic writing is not restricted in style or voice, although disciplines and subfields of disciplines do vary in customary ways of thought and in traditional modes of expression.
>
> —Chris Thaiss and Terry Myers Zawacki,
> in *Engaged Writers, Dynamic Disciplines*

The writing genres and hints that we have shared so far are appropriate across many fields within the arts and humanities. Other general writing guidelines and stylistic conventions are shared across the entire discipline, and we give some of these here to help you recognize them. However, as you review the following guidelines, be aware that when you take specific courses, you always need to follow the assignments or consult with your instructors, in case the specialized writing or genre guidelines vary from the general norm presented here.

A good writer in the arts and humanities presents relevant content to the reader in a format that is easy to understand and appropriate to the field. To achieve this, you need to be attentive to both global elements of writing (content, organization, and style) and local characteristics of writing (format, grammar, and mechanics). The following guidelines present suggestions that will strengthen your writing on both the global and local levels.

Conventions about Content

Rhetorical triangle: As a writer, you always want to situate the message you are presenting through your writing. This means that whenever you write, you are aware of who your audience (the reader) is, what you want them to understand (the message), why you are presenting your message (the purpose), and what field you are presenting your message in (the context). At the university level, most of the writing you will do is academic in nature.

Thesis: The type of writing that you do helps determine what type of thesis you will write. Academic genres, such as the ones presented earlier in this chapter, tend to have a strong thesis at their center. Most of the common genres in the arts and humanities include either interpretative writing or analytical writing, and using a strong thesis makes each of these types of writing stronger. As well-known composition scholar Andrea Lunsford suggests, everything is an argument. However, a strong thesis (or argument)—one that shows clearly what is at the center of the entire paper—can be either implied or explicit in the introduction.

Support: Whether you write a personal essay or one that includes primary or secondary sources, you will always include supporting evidence for whatever thesis or argument you make. In a personal essay, such as for an assignment that asks you to reflect on your favorite piece of art or music, you will make your claim(s) and then provide support with specific and vivid details from either your life or the piece to which you are reacting. In an argumentative research paper, such as for an assignment that asks you to use five sources, you will make your claim and then provide support with specific details from your primary or secondary sources. For more information on using primary and secondary sources, see the section Know the Kinds of Evidence Used in the Arts and Humanities earlier in this chapter.

Conventions about organization

Title: Since using a title on a piece of writing is an arts and humanities convention, creating a good one is often overlooked. Do not make that mistake. In your courses, a good title is important because it can catch the reader's interest, help the reader predict what the content of the paper is, and reflect the tone of the writing or the voice of the writer. In addition, as you transfer your writing to upper-level courses or to the workplace, having an effective title with key terms that enable a quick computer or Web search makes your writing much more accessible to your intended audience.

> **Tip:** Always create your own titles. Do not use the titles of other works as the title of your paper. For instance, if you write a paper about the book *Intelligent Design: The Bridge Between Science and Theology*, do not use the book title as your paper's title. Add something about the topic of your paper, such as "Investigating the politics of *Intelligent Design: The Bridge Between Science and Theology*."

Attention getter: Always include an attention getter in the introduction to your review, essay, or research paper. This is an arts and humanities convention that gives you a chance to entice the reader into reading your paper thoroughly and with interest. An attention getter is usually a few sentences near the beginning of the introduction; it should lead smoothly into introductory information that then leads into the thesis. One of the best strategies for creating an effective attention getter is to give a startling anecdote, fact, or statistic. The more you can surprise, shock, or scare your reader, the more likely it is that he will want to continue to read your paper. Another common and effective strategy is to give a quotation from an expert or someone who you are betting will either interest your reader or make your reader mad. Some writers make the mistake of using a question as their attention getter. A question is a good lead-in to a thesis, but usually it is not striking or interesting enough to be used as an attention getter.

Introduction, body, and conclusion: In the arts and humanities, a recognized format of most genres is to have an understood introduction, body, and conclusion.

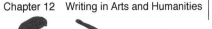

Conventions about style

Across the arts and humanities, it is most common to use style and documentation conventions that are from the Modern Language Association (MLA), which publishes the *MLA Handbook for Writers of Research Papers*, now in its seventh edition. Be sure to have a copy on hand for those times when you may have a style or documentation question. Below are some style questions that might arise as you write in the arts and humanities.

> **Tip:** In some fields, such as history, style and documentation information from *The Chicago Manual of Style*, 16th edition, is more relevant than the *MLA Handbook*.

Q: What general writing style is common in the arts and humanities?

A: In formal assignments, use a formal objective writing style, rather than a conversational style. Avoid slang and contractions, and be concise in your descriptions. However, you should also avoid the other extreme of using overblown or pompous language that may alienate your reader or make your writing hard to understand. Avoid giving human feelings or actions to nonhuman beings, especially written elements. For example, rather than saying, *The chapter states that the bridge was faulty*, say: *In 1981, Thompson stated that the bridge was faulty.*

Q: Which verb tense should I use?

A: In general, use the appropriate tense for the appropriate action: use present tense for present actions, past tense for past actions, and future tense for future actions. Pay attention to verb tenses, and be consistent. However, when referring to authors and their words or quotations, use the present tense: *C. B. Bridges says that it is important to cross the bridge when he comes to it.* or *C. B. Bridges suggests, "Crossing a bridge when I come to it is always an interesting prospect."* And, when referring to the narrative or storyline (for a literary text, film, or television show) in a paper for an English course, use what is called the <u>literary present tense</u> to describe what is happening: *Then, Nash Bridges takes the bandit by the arm and throws him into the San Francisco Bay.*

Q: When should I use third person?

A: When writing formal academic papers, in general, use third person (she, he, her, him, they, them) unless the assignment asks you for your personal opinion or story. For personal stories, or if the assignment or teacher instructs you to do so, use first person (I, me, my). Research papers are usually written in third person.

Q: Should I use active or passive voice?

A: It is conventional wisdom to use active voice to a greater extent in the arts and humanities. For instance, use *Moby Dick chased down the boat* rather than *The boat was chased down by Moby Dick.* However, use passive voice if it is appropriate for the context or if you are not sure who the subject of the sentence is. For example, use *The house was sold* instead of *Someone sold the house.*

Q: Is there a list of words or phrases I should avoid when writing academic pieces in the arts and humanities?

A: Stylistically, be as concise as you can when writing academic papers by avoiding weasel words, such as *I think, I believe, In my opinion, I know that it is true that,* and *Being that;* vague words, such as *good, bad, incredible, literally, people, they,* and *there;* or clichés or overused expressions, such as *a stitch in time saves nine, life is for the living,* and *as easy as pie.*

Q: How should I refer to authors within my essays?

A: The first time you present an author or his or her work, give the author's full name, such as *Thomas H. Winters proposes that we see the rose as a living being.* After that, use only the author's last name: *Winters also sees the bedroom as a symbol for a lonely death.*

Q: How can I avoid sexist language in my writing?

A: You can avoid language that marginalizes your reader by avoiding gendered pronouns, such as *she, he, him,* and *her,* and making them plural (*they, them*) instead. Also, do not assume that a job can be filled by only one gender or another; you can do this by avoiding labels such as *stewardesses, mailmen,* and *chairman,* and changing them to more neutral descriptions: *flight attendants, mail carriers,* and *chair.*

Conventions about Formatting

The format of your essays or other genres can vary across fields, so it is best to check with your instructor or refer to your textbook for the appropriate format for your assigned writing. That way, you will know whether an essay needs a cover page, preferred margins, and so on.

Conventions about Using Sources

In the arts and humanities, it is common and appropriate to use summaries, paraphrases, and quotations from primary and secondary sources as supporting evidence in your papers. A good rule of thumb is to use one source per page assigned. That is, if you are assigned a paper that is about 10 pages long, use around 10 sources. However, check the assignment carefully for any restrictions or requirements for sources. If you are using the *MLA Handbook* as your guide for documentation style, you will cite each summary, paraphrase, and quotation you use. Using the MLA documentation style involves using parenthetical (in-text) citations and a Works Cited page. When you want to add bibliographic or explanatory notes to a paper, MLA allows footnotes and endnotes but discourages extensive use of them. For more information on using sources and following MLA format, please see Chapter 14.

Conventions about Grammar, Spelling, and Mechanics

To be a successful writer, not only do you need to follow the stylistic and format conventions for your field, but you must also be aware of grammatical issues that can distract your reader from your message. The most common problems in writing involve a lack of sentence variety and an inadequate grasp of how to punctuate different types of sentences. Readers can become bored or irritated if they have to wade through

sentences that they have difficulty understanding. Learning about the four different types of sentences (simple, compound, complex, and compound-complex) and how to punctuate them correctly can improve the flow of your paper and enhance the delivery of the content you want the reader to understand.

Spelling words correctly and using the appropriate word form are also important cues to your readers that you care about the topic, the paper, and them. Spend some time looking up correct spellings or word forms when you edit your work, and do not automatically accept everything your computer grammar and spell checkers tell you to do. You ultimately want your words to represent *you*, and leaving choices to your computer does not always represent you well.

Know the Appropriate Documentation Style Used in the Arts and Humanities

MLA, the documentation style recommended by the Modern Language Association, is typically used by scholars in the arts and humanities. However, instructors in some fields, such as history, may use *The Chicago Manual of Style*. Knowing which documentation style is preferred in a course or in your field is an important first step in knowing how to choose, incorporate, and cite sources. Always follow the guidelines dictated by your assignment, by your employer, or by the academic journal to which you are submitting your work.

The Internet and You: Using Internet Videos in First-Year Composition
Holly T. Hamby, Middle Tennessee State University

What: A variety of Internet video resources can invigorate your teaching practices and provide new avenues for critical inquiry, particularly as these videos can be considered as multimodal texts, which students can reflect upon and analyze and then respond to in writing. Included in this presentation: Internet-only animation, archived media from America's past (including propaganda cartoons), music videos, video collages (mash-ups) unique to the Internet, and the "reality" YouTube video phenomenon. These videos also utilize students' familiarity with some Internet characters (and retro characters in these videos, such as Bugs Bunny) and forms of text, which can be a gateway to teach students to understand, interpret, and analyze American issues and varieties of rhetoric.

    Why: Internet videos in a variety of genres can be used in low-risk writing activities that segue into class discussions about global course concerns. These videos have distinct pedagogical purposes for both expository writing and research and argumentative writing.

- The videos can help students understand the importance of the rhetorical triangle and certain rhetorical strategies in their own writing/creation of a multitude of "texts."
- The videos often highlight dialectical and language concerns students have in writing, and more specifically, finding their writing voice(s).
- These videos also often present various arguments, both sound and not so sound, which help students to understand the principles of argument, and move into persuasive writing techniques in expository writing and later progress to argumentative strategies in research and argument.

Theoretical Support:
Mary Louise Pratt's Contact Zone theory (and the adapted Pop Culture Zone theory).

    These Internet videos, as a part of popular Internet culture, provide a contact zone for students and teacher to explore and grapple with language and writing, which in turn leads to practical writing techniques students use on high-risk writing assignments, as well as to the larger global concerns of the expository writing course.

But, I *can't* use this! I don't have a Master, Smart, or Computer Classroom:
Solution: Send the link/URL to students through e-mail, or post on D2L. Then, transform these in-class writing assignments to homework writing assignments. The students can watch these videos at their own leisure and come to class with their written responses, prepared for class discussion.

I. "You're my best friend" description activity Based on a clip from the show *The Marvelous Misadventures of Flapjack*. Clipped on YouTube: <http://www.youtube.com/watch?v=um1wt5UDdY0>

Summary: In this clip, Flapjack sings a short and sweet song to his best friend, Cap'n Knuckles, followed by a little ditty composed for a random "little old lady" who is in the audience. While this is a current cartoon on Cartoon Network that is apparently intended for children, it is very offbeat and populated with often grotesque characters that embody the "other." (For example, in another episode, Flapjack apparently falls in love with a girl, but it turns out he just has a parasitic infection of heart-shaped tick creatures that make him think he's in love). It proves both familiar and unfamiliar to students, who are sometimes unsettled by the characterization.

(I'm including this, although it's available on DVD, because this particular clip has been edited for the Internet to highlight one part. Also, it brings up questions of plagiarism, ownership of texts, and how that works with the Internet).

Activity: This cartoon could be used to teach students how to write descriptions, which I would generally present near the start of my expository writing course.

1. Students are asked to view the cartoon and write down what phrases Flapjack uses to describe both characters.

2. Then, each student pulls from a container a slip of paper on which a noun is written. They are then given 5–10 minutes to compose their own short song in homage of their noun. They are asked to try and describe the most important characteristics of their noun in their song.

3. The students can then be put in small groups, where they share their songs with each other! As the group hears each person's song, they are asked to write down what descriptions the songwriter is using. Often the students are eager to perform their songs for the whole class, and the teacher uses the group's impressions of how their group-mates described their nouns to segue into a broader discussion of how to use description in more formal writing.

II. "My Humps" Style and Tone Comparison Activity
Original, by the Black Eyed Peas:
   http://www.youtube.com/watch?v=iEe_eraFWWs
Parody, by Alanis Morissette:
   http://www.youtube.com/watch?v=pRmYfVCH2UA

This activity engages students about style and tone, not to mention irony, in either model writing or their own writing. First, the teacher would need to define and discuss what we mean by *style* and *tone* in writing, and how we can analyze our own writing to determine what types of style and tone we are using and should perhaps use in future writings. These videos also usually lead to discussions of rhetoric, particularly what arguments are being made in each about appropriate behavior for men and women a'courtin.

Students should listen to a snippet of the original song and respond with a description of the style and tone (in writing). Then, the second version is played, and the students are asked to repeat the exercise (once again, by in-class writing). Then the whole class shares their observations. The point of this fun exercise is to clue students in to how to "read" style and tone differences, why these characteristics are important to understanding/interpreting texts, and how to use these style and tone changes in their writing for different audiences and purposes.

Sample Student Interpretive Essay

Name/
Instructor/
Course/
Date—double
space, align
at left and top
margin

Elizabeth Burton

Dr. Laura Dubek

English 3000

15 December 2010

Title—
centered

"Put a Ring on It":
Female (Dis)Empowerment in *The Taming of the Shrew* and American Popular
Culture

Note that the
author puts
quotations
around this
part of the
title because
it is the name
of a song.
Normally,
titles will not
take quotation
marks.

Attention-
getter opens
the essay

Gazing through the cultural lens of the increasingly malleable gender roles of modern
society, it may be difficult to imagine a world similar to that of Shakespeare's *The
Taming of the Shrew*—a world where gender roles are non-negotiable. In
Shakespeare's day, the domestic life was the domain of the "submissive wife," while
the external world of commerce was the domain of the "masterful husband" (Dolan
13). A woman knew "her place" and a man monitored her closely to ensure that she
remained there. The two spheres and their keepers traditionally were never to be
intermingled or exchanged. Such mingling of spheres only occurred when a woman's
failure to fulfill her "wifely duties" necessitated her husband's use of authority, which
commonly manifested itself in the form of physical violence or verbal abuse, in order
to restore her to her rightful subservient position within the relationship, household
and community (Dolan 13).

This set of disturbing social norms perhaps comes as a shock to modern minds
that, since infancy, have benefitted from movements toward racial and gender equality
in mid-twentieth century America. In the current "progressive" culture, women can
do anything from working as CEOs of Fortune Five Hundred companies to burning
their undergarments in protest against traditional patriarchal values—or both
concurrently. These women frequently work outside the home in occupations of their
own choosing, raise children without the aid of "father figures," and hold
authoritative positions within their families regardless of their marital statuses.
However, these two seemingly contradictory societies may not be as far removed from
each other as they initially appear. Katharina Minola of Shakespeare's *Shrew* has
quite possibly met her match in the most unlikely of places—twenty-first century
American popular culture. Within the presently overpopulated constellation of
homogenous female pop stars, there is one, Beyoncé Knowles, who shines above the

Thesis
statement—
this sets up
the paper up
as a literary
analysis that
compares and
contrasts two
works.

rest. Although these two women come from seemingly dissimilar cultures, they share
a common goal and, more importantly, a common means by which they seek to obtain
this goal: Both Katharina and Beyoncé benefit from artfully employing the male-
constructed feminine stereotypes of their respective societies in order to acquire
power within those societies.

Within her community, there is little debate regarding Katharina's long-standing
status as a shrew. Her demeanor satisfies all of the necessary requirements: she is

Topic
sentence that
provides the
overall focus
of the following
paragraph.

excessively talkative, loud, assertive, and often hostile. In short, she is the stereotypical "bossy woman" (9). However, as Frances Dolan reveals, a shrew is more than just an outspoken woman; she is "a woman refusing to submit to a man's authority and aggressively asserting her independence"—a woman who "strive[s] for mastery" (10). Although Katharina aims for mastery, her straightforward approach is unsuccessful because her overt assertion of dominance only serves to perpetuate her own submission. She fails to realize that her reputation within her patriarchal society is dependent on the reports of men with whom she interacts. In this way, Katharina unintentionally bestows upon men the power to turn their personal opinions of her into public facts. As a result, men portray her as "the devil," the enemy of her society, because her ideals, and thus her behavior, threaten the highly regarded patriarchal tradition (*Shr* 3.2.146).

After the utter failure of Katharina's initial approach, she finds her "occasion for revenge" by turning to her only other option—marriage (2.1.35-36). When Hortensio taunts her about the unlikelihood that she should ever find a willing mate, she boldly asserts:

> I' faith, sir, you shall never need to fear;
>
> Iwis it is not halfway to her heart.
>
> But if it were, doubt not her care should be
>
> To comb your noddle with a three-legged stool,
>
> And paint your face, and use you like a fool. (1.1.61-65)

If Katharina must resort to marriage, she will triumph over her new husband and make a fool of him by whatever means necessary. Her plan of attack can best be evidenced by her first encounter with the unfortunate "fool" Petruchio (2.1.250).

> PETRUCHIO: Myself am moved to woo thee for my wife.
>
> KATHARINA: Moved? In good time! Let him that moved you hither
>
> > Remove you hence. I knew you at the first
> >
> > You were a movable.
>
> PETRUCHIO: Why, what's a movable?
>
> KATHARINA: A joint stool. (2.1.190-194)

In this exchange, the adaptations of the word *move* seem to emphasize physical action; however, Katharina's wordplay actually hints at the refinement of her strategy. Rather than attempting to physically dominate her husband, she will mentally mold him into her desired product. For instance, the noun *movable* may be interpreted as both "one easily changed or dissuaded" and "an article of furniture" (Dolan 79). In this case, Katharina claims ownership of both meanings. She employs the interpretation that a *moveable* is a joint stool in order to outwardly insult Petruchio by comparing him to furniture while she secretly divulges her scheme to carefully whittle him down into a stool (or fool)—a joint stool being a "well-fitted stool made by an expert craftsman" (79). Katharina, the craftsman, utilizes Petruchio, that which is crafted, as a prop in order to enhance the believability of her performance.

Sidebar annotations:

The author uses a short quotation from *Taming of the Shrew* and incorporates it effectively into a sentence that begins with her own words. Note how the line from a play is documented in the parenthetical citation at the end of the line.

The author uses a block-by-block comparison, discussing *Taming of the Shrew* first and then "Put a Ring on It" next, both in blocks of multiple paragraphs.

Compare this long quotation and how the documentation is placed to the short quotation in the previous paragraph.

The author italicizes any particular word that she is defining or discussing.

Once married, Petruchio delivers his notorious "She is my goods, my chattels" proclamation and announces to his servants that he has "politicly begun [his] reign" over Katharina, which will undoubtedly be a success (*Shr* 3.2.219-4.1.157). Although Petruchio intends to kill his wife "with kindness" by depriving her of basic sustenance, Katharina finally demonstrates her mastery over him during the "sun and moon" confrontation when she tames him with her amiable disposition: "And be it moon, or sun, or what you please;/And if you please to call it a rush candle,/Henceforth I vow it shall be so for me" (4.2.177-4.5.13-15). By submitting to Petruchio, Katharina gains her independence through the guise of dependence. Petruchio believes he has successfully changed her into the ideal gentlewoman when, in fact, she has tricked him into accepting the authenticity of her reformation.

Katharina's subtle, yet satisfying victory culminates in her final Oscar-worthy performance at Bianca's wedding reception.

> Fie, fie! Unknit that threatening, unkind brow,
>
> And dart not scornful glances from those eyes
>
> To wound thy lord, thy king, thy governor.
>
> It blots thy beauty as frosts do bite the meads,
>
> Confounds thy fame as whirlwinds shake fair buds,
>
> And in no sense is meet or amiable.
>
> A woman moved is like a fountain troubled,
>
> Muddy, ill-seeming, thick, bereft of beauty; (5.2.140-147)

The focus of this speech has traditionally been placed on Katharina's complete lack of shrewish qualities, on her obedience to Petruchio, and on her instruction of other women to follow the example she has set with her own behavior. Although the latter may be correct, Katharina's behavior, and consequently her instruction, is often misinterpreted as the promotion of submission. In this context, *moved* is commonly interpreted as a synonym for *angry*, which suggests that Katharina intends to criticize the supposed hostility of her female audience (Dolan 137); however, the reemergence of the word *moved* implies Katharina's continuation of her previous wordplay. In her speech, Katharina furtively hints that a woman changed, or altered, is not a thing of beauty. As she dominates her clueless audience with her captivating tongue, which was once considered only to emit "meaningless noise," she instructs the other women not to begrudgingly submit to their husbands but instead to apply her method in order to obtain subliminal control (17). Thus, Katharina reveals Petruchio's perceived taming of her as a farce cleverly orchestrated by her via the usage of time-honored social traditions to her own advantage. Simply stated, Katharina succumbs under her own terms.

Much like Katharina, Beyoncé Knowles has obtained power in modern culture by way of her own devices; however, unlike Katharina, Beyoncé has managed to escape the stigma of being labeled a shrew. Although she appears to be an unlikely candidate for "shrewhood," a quick review of Dolan's definition of a shrew will prove most enlightening because Beyoncé *is* "a woman refusing to submit to a man's authority and aggressively asserting her independence." Throughout the first decade of the twenty-first century, Beyoncé achieved success by relentlessly promoting herself as *the* image of modern female empowerment and independence—as a "Survivor" ("Survivor"). Even Beyoncé's public abandonment of her surname—forced upon her at birth in compliance with an archaic patriarchal practice—exudes defiance against a male-centered society. One superficial glance at her song lyrics clues the reader into the explicit nature of her message: I am a self-sufficient woman, and you can (and should) be one too. Her song "Independent Women Part I" is quite possibly her most obvious assertion of dominance.

> I buy my own diamonds and I buy my own rings
>
> Only ring your celly when I'm feelin' lonely
>
> When it's all over please get up and leave
>
> Question: Tell me how you feel about this
>
> Try to control me, boy, you get dismissed
>
> Pay my own fun, oh, I pay my own bills ("Independent")

In order to extinguish any doubts listeners might still harbor about the legitimacy of her declaration of independence, she then proceeds to list her material possessions and continually brags, "I've bought it" and "I depend on me" ("Independent"). In the form of a conveniently concise and catchy phrase, Beyoncé has effectively armed the modern shrews of the world with their newest mantra: "I've bought it" (also known as the lengthier and less popular "I don't need a man to provide for me").

Perhaps more puzzling than Beyoncé's success as an updated version of Shakespeare's shrew is her simultaneous compliance with and perpetuation of the male-conceived standards of feminine beauty and behavior. In addition to her provocative clothing, voluminous hair and overstated makeup, her songs "Bills, Bills, Bills" and "Crazy in Love" reveal Beyoncé's submission to gender-biased ideals. In the former, she warns a potential suitor that he has no chance to date her unless he can pay her "telephone" and "automo' bills" ("Bills"); while in the latter, she confesses to a man, "Got me hoping you'll page me right now, your kiss/Got me hoping you'll save me right now" ("Crazy in Love"). This embarrassingly intimate confession begs the question, "Save you from *what*, Beyoncé? His own *absence?*" Her plea for a man to "save" her supports the classic view of woman as damsel-in-distress who not only desires but needs a prince to ensure her continued existence. At this point, one might ask, "What happened to your previous "Survivor" mentality?" Just as Katharina betrays her coveted principles by allowing Petruchio to publicly tame her, Beyoncé contradicts her own image of female empowerment in order to reinforce sexist ideologies by claiming that a woman's financial and emotional successes are dependent on the presence of a capable man in her life. Meanwhile, without so much as the appearance of a skeptically elevated eyebrow, her devoted female followers digest this blatant inconsistency in personal beliefs, and Beyoncé gains an entirely new set of listeners or, perhaps more accurately described, viewers from the male population.

> The author refers back to the previous block about Katharina here to link this section of the paper to the last.

Although Beyoncé's two attitudes about gender roles appear to be incompatible, her identification with these patriarchal ideals allows her to manipulate her audience in order to advance her independent lifestyle and to assert her dominance over the aforementioned audience as it grows larger and larger each year. Once again, she returns to her initial status as an undercover shrew. In one of her latest successes, "Single Ladies (Put a Ring on It)," Beyoncé embraces her incongruous, yet simultaneous roles as both empowered individual and objectified sex symbol. While repetitively expressing admiration for "all the single ladies," or independent women of the world, she informs the men of the world, "If you liked it, then you should have put a ring on it" ("Single Ladies"). Beyoncé's mastery of her audience is evident in her ability to praise self-sufficient women while also encouraging their compliance with the cultural institution of marriage. Furthermore, remaining true to her ambiguous form, she *demands* that men take the dominant role in relationships by putting "a ring on it." In this respect, Beyoncé takes her cues from Katharina by taming men while allowing them to think they possess absolute power. They remain oblivious to the fact that, in actuality, she *bestows upon them* this power. Inadvertently paying tribute to Katharina's wordplay, Beyoncé's use of "ring" also suggests ambiguity in meaning because the word may be understood literally as a wedding ring or figuratively as a means by which men seek to trap or tie down women. Beyoncé also seems to imply a third kind of ring—the metaphorical circus ring in which she performs daily her delicate balancing act between sovereignty and acquiescence.

Although their cultures come wrapped in different packages, when the casings are removed, Katharina Minola of Shakespeare's *The Taming of the Shrew* and Beyoncé Knowles, the shining star of American popular culture, undoubtedly confront the same fundamental societal injustices. Once the motives behind their manipulative behaviors have been established, the focus must necessarily shift from *why they* do it to *what it* does to them. What are the effects of this deception on the deceiver? By using the patriarchal system against itself in order to reclaim their own individuality, these women actually risk losing themselves because they compromise their own belief systems in defense of those very same beliefs. It is no coincidence that only until Katharina relinquishes her right to speak can she finally be heard. Consequently, as Hortensio appropriately proclaims, "The field has been won," but who declares the victory (*Shr* 4.5.23)? The women who covertly control a sexist system by submitting to it? Or the men who retain their precious patriarchal practices, ironically assisted by the women who seek to control that system rather than to dismantle it? By playing the puppet, the shrew becomes the puppeteer; however, confined by the necessity to conceal her duality, she creates a new form of oppression for herself as she is destined to perform the traditional show of the previous master and thus to preserve the interests of those whom she claims to despise.

Works Cited

Dolan, Frances E. *The Taming of the Shrew: Texts and Contexts*. Boston, Massachusetts: Bedford Books of St. Martin's Press, 1996. Print.

Knowles, Beyoncé. "Bills, Bills, Bills." *The Writing's on the Wall*. Columbia, 1999. CD.

---. "Crazy in Love." *Dangerously in Love*. Columbia, 2003. CD.

---. "Independent Women, Part I." *Survivor*. Columbia, 2001. CD.

---. "Single Ladies (Put a Ring on It)." *I Am... Sasha Fierce*. Columbia, 2008. CD.

---. "Survivor." *Survivor*. Columbia, 2001. CD.

Shakespeare, William. *The Taming of the Shrew*. *The Taming of the Shrew: Texts and Contexts*. Ed. Frances E. Dolan. Boston, Massachusetts: Bedford Books of St. Martin's Press, 1996. Print.

This entry is for a print book and follows the MLA format.

When two (or more) entries in a row are by the same person or group, use three hyphens in a row followed by a period in all entries after the first.

Heading centered

This entry is for a song from a CD and follows the MLA format. Be sure to put the type of recording (CD, MP3 file, or LP).

1) Place the first line of each entry flush to the left margin. Each line after that in the entry will be indented.

2) Do not forget to alphabetize the list of sources.

3) Double space all entries.

WORTH A THOUSAND WORDS:

The Impact of the Brady Photographs in the Civil War

Patrick Murphy

HST 304: The American Civil War

Dr. Peter Knupfer

August 18, 2011

It is the iconic picture of Gettysburg: the dead Confederate sniper in Devil's Den. The deceased is lying on his back, almost as if he were asleep. His rifle is standing where he fell, behind the tall rock wall sandwiched between two massive boulders. His hat has fallen by his feet. It is a haunting, moving scene. It is also a blatantly staged one. The body's position is parallel to the wall; for the hat to have fallen where it did, the body's angle would have had to have been different. Moreover, the rifle would not have been neatly leaning against the wall so much as fallen over the body. Finally, the rock wall is considerably taller than the man appears to be. He could not, under any circumstances, have died where he is photographed.[1] But accuracy was of little importance to Alexander Gardner, the cameraman. In the Civil War, photographers were not motivated to document the results of engagements, though their pictures served that purpose to an extent. Instead, it seems they were far more interested in capturing the emotions and spirit of the battles.

Currently, any news photographer or photojournalist who "doctors" a photo taken of an event immediately loses credibility, possibly their job, and their chances of restoring either. The idea of "posing" smacks of falseness and separation from reality rather than a reflection of it—studio photographers use it to make people look more attractive or intelligent or professional than they actually are. News photographers are supposed to take snapshots of reality, so that the audience can understand the truth about the subject being captured on camera. And yet, we find Mathew Brady and his team of photographers taking staged photos of the dead and passing them off as authentic at every battlefield they were at, save Antietam. Further, judging from the fact that they constitute a large and important collection in the National Archives, not only were they not stigmatized, they were applauded. How is it that these three fathers of photojournalism (Brady, Gardner, and Timothy O'Sullivan) were elevated for work that would get a modern photographer fired from the news circuit?

Perhaps, to the 19th century audience, Brady's men did capture a certain reality of war that had not been in the public eye. The dominant American mindset early in the war was that combat was a grand game, a test of values. Officers, especially Southern ones, were culled from the upper classes and thought of as highly chivalrous. Among the 14 rebel generals listed by the New York Times in July 1861 were an Episcopal bishop, a former Secretary of War, a former governor, a Congressman, and a former ambassador.[2] Those who died, without exception, did so bravely and for the "right reasons," and each side was convinced that the righteousness of their respective causes would be enough to win the war.[3]

Newspaper articles reinforced these beliefs. Reporters following the Army asserted at Bull Run that a mere 20,000 Federal troops were gallantly engaged against a swarm of 90,000 rebels, and nearly carried the day anyway (actual combat strengths

1. Alexander Gardner. *Dead Confederate Soldier in Devil's Den.* July 1863. Photograph. Library of Congress, Washington, D.C. http://memory.loc.gov/ (accessed June 21, 2011).
2. Thomas Summerhill. "Week Two: Amateurs at War." History 304: The American Civil War, Online. Accessed May 23, 2011; "Generals in the Rebel Army," *New York Times,* July 21, 1861, http://www. proquest.com.
3. Thomas Summerhill. "Week Two: Amateurs at War." History 304: The American Civil War, Online. Accessed May 23, 2011.

were less lopsided: 28,450 Union, 32,230 Confederate). Every Federal action was done "gallantly," as was every death of a Union soldier. The tone of these articles from Northern reporters insinuates the Confederates, who frequently hid behind cover, were less masculine, less heroic, and less noble than their Union counterparts.[4]

This kind of reporting had two effects on the public mind. First, readers were given a simple, "us vs. them" slant to the war, which allowed the audience to dehumanize the opposing side. Second, it fed the belief that chivalry and a worthy cause could, on the battlefield, trump an enemy's superior numbers, firepower, and generalship. This reporting style continued unchallenged for over a year, until a group of men, armed with cameras, began following the Army.

The images they took altered the course of public opinion and changed the way news was reported. Brady and his photographers, through the posed pictures of casualties, were able to drain romanticism out of the conflict and subdue its glorification. The tragedy of the conflict, blithely skipped over by the newspapers, screams out from the Brady photographs. Photographers like Brady were able to balance the nobility of the Federal cause found in the papers with the raw realism of combat and the underlying heartbreak of civil war. They illustrated the gruesome side of war while the papers, especially the Republican ones, reminded readers of what it all was supposedly for. The effect was that two different messages were communicated—one romantic, the other realistic. By 1864, this turn to realism was beginning to have an effect on the public's perception of the war. This was also true of northern sentiment toward southerners in general, making Lincoln's reconciliation plans more palatable in contrast to those of the revenge-hungry Republican Congress.

The photograph taken by O'Sullivan of the dead near McPherson's Woods is a fine example of bringing the war's brutality to the public's attention. Four Union soldiers lay close together on the ground, mangled by musket balls, as if they fell while advancing in formation.[5] Up through the end of the war, infantry tactics had hardly changed since Napoleon. Men fought shoulder to shoulder in the open, or on horseback. Such tactics were viewed as proper and manly. However, they also led to alarmingly high casualty rates. After Bull Run, one Union officer reported that of the one thousand men and officers of his regiment, only he and 200 others survived the engagement.[6] The photograph helps give the statistics a horrifying visual. For the audience, chivalry and a righteous cause provided little solace when the visuals were so graphic.

A similar photo by Gardner gives us another haunting visual. Taken near the "Slaughter Pen" by Little Round Top, Southern infantrymen, presumably of Hood's division, are strewn across the boulders and cuts at the base of the hill, gunned down as they advanced against what was left of Sickles's corps.[7] Picturing what a battle

---

4. "Retreat of Gen. McDowell's Command from Mannassas: Full Details of the Engagement," *New York Times*, July 23, 1861, http://www.proquest.com.
5. Timothy O'Sullivan. *Bodies of Federal Soldiers, Killed on July 1, near the McPherson Woods*. Photograph. Library of Congress, Washington D.C. http://memory.loc.gov/ (accessed June 22, 2011).
6. "Retreat of Gen. McDowell's Command from Mannassas: Full Details of the Engagement," *New York Times*, July 23, 1861, http://www.proquest.com.
7. Gardner. *Slaughter Pen at the Foot of Little Round Top*.

may look like can be difficult, but photographers were able to give the audience a visual reference point to contrast with the melodramatic newspaper descriptions. Consequentially, those same papers began reporting more accurately.

The battle at Peach Tree Creek in 1864, as reported by the once-hyperbolic *New York Times*, recorded the attack by Hardee's corps in a more modest manner when compared to earlier accounts. Here the *Times* actually gives credit to Southern soldiers for a "furious charge." The reporter also telegraphed more accurate casualty figures: 3,000 Confederate dead and wounded to 1,500 Union.[8] The sober, factual reporting is more like what we would see today, and nothing like the reports from Bull Run a mere three years before.

At the battle of Franklin in November 1864, southern newspapers were still running melodramatic articles where the rebels nearly carried the day with a mere handful of casualties, in spite of being grossly outnumbered. This suggests a discrepancy between the papers each side had published.[9] The northern papers were growing more realistic in their reporting as more of Brady's battlefield photographs were displayed, while the southern ones remained essentially propaganda. It is also important to note that the South did not have a corps of battlefield photographers following their armies, where the Union armies had Brady's men in the camps. Thus the impact of civil war photographers cannot be overlooked because as northern newsmen continued to produce battlefield accounts they were inevitably held accountable by the existence of visual evidence.

The photographs of the Confederate dead, especially in such areas as Spotsylvania Court House and Gettysburg, had an effect on northern attitudes toward the Administration's reconstruction plans by the end of the war. These gruesome pictures of "the enemy" possibly were key to softening the North's stance towards the South as the war was concluding. Looking at the photographs of the dead, only the caption enables the reader to tell which side the deceased was on. This served to further engender sympathy for southern soldiers. The various photos O'Sullivan took at Spotsylvania Court House of a dead Confederate feature a body dressed in a uniform so dark it could well have been blue as easily as gray. His rifle changes position in the photos, as does the camera angle, but the man is just as difficult to identify.[10] A Gardner photograph of a dead Confederate at the foot of Round Top is also only identifiable as Southern by its caption.[11] These photographs were intentionally designed to inspire feelings of pity and pathos in its viewers—the pictured dead could just as easily have been one's son or nephew or neighbor, thus strengthening the link between the rank and file southerner with one's own flesh and blood. The "us vs. them" dynamic that defined the war's reporting for four years was in this way almost totally transformed by the end of 1864.

The *New York Times* noted in 1865 that the "common people of the South... are deserting the standards of the perjured traitors who betrayed them . . ." and

8. "Details of the Battle: From Sherman's Army," *New York Times*, July 27, 1864. http://www.proquest.com.
9. "The Battle of Franklin—Hood's Army," *Daily Richmond Examiner*, December 7, 1864. http://infotrac. galegroup.com.
10. O'Sullivan. *Bodies of Confederate Soldiers near Mrs. Alsop's House.*
11. Gardner. *Dead Confederate Sharpshooter at the Foot of Round Top.*

demonstrates how many northern papers later accepted the southern people (in contrast to southern leadership).[12] As a result, in combination with the relative success of the Free State constitutions signed in Arkansas and Louisiana, there was a sense in the North that the Southern people were returning to the Union voluntarily—even if their state governments were not.[13]

By humanizing the South through photos of the dead, Brady's outfit contributed to making Lincoln's plan for post-war reconciliation more acceptable to Northern civilians. Harsher methods of reconstruction, such as the Wade-Davis bill, were increasingly seen as gratuitous torture of a beaten people. The *New York Times* stated that this particular bill and its sponsors intended " . . . to satisfy wounded arrogance, and to destroy [the Southern people]."[14] The paper also points out that Lincoln thought it unconstitutional as well. Until the president's death in 1865, there was little call for more suffering—there was enough death captured by Brady's photographs.

In a way, then, it seems that staging photos of the dead as Brady's men repeatedly did was an act of service to the country. They shook the civilian population out of the sort of careless romanticism that made throwing away the lives of soldiers seem acceptable. They reminded the viewer that even our wartime enemies are human and should be treated with dignity, not ground into a humiliating submission to make ourselves feel better. While neither Brady, O'Sullivan, or Gardner would probably retain a photojournalist's or publisher's position with a news organization today, they did bring home certain realities of the conflict that simply photographing the end results of battles may have missed. They told the story of the war in terms of its emotions, its high drama, and its deep tragedy. Robert E. Lee famously commented that "it is well that war is so terrible, lest we grow too fond of it." Brady's photographs made viewers agree.

Bibliography

"Details of the Battle.: From Sherman's Army," *New York Times*, July 27, 1864. http://www.proquest.com.

"From Washington.: Proclamation by President Lincoln. His View on Reconstruction," *New York Times*, July 10, 1864. http://www.proquest.com.

Gardner, Alexander. *Dead Confederate Sharpshooter at the Foot of Round Top*. July 1863. Photograph. Library of Congress, Washington, D.C. http://memory.loc.gov/ (accessed June 21, 2011).

---. *Dead Confederate Soldier in Devil's Den*. July 1863. Photograph. Library of Congress, Washington, D.C. http://memory.loc.gov/ (accessed June 21, 2011).

---. *Slaughter Pen at the Foot of Little Round Top*. July 1863. Photograph. Library of Congress, Washington, D.C. http://memory.loc.gov/ (accessed June 21, 2011).

12. "Jeff Davis' Army," *New York Times*, January 18, 1865. http://www.proquest.com.
13. "From Washington: Proclamation by President Lincoln. His View on Reconstruction," *New York Times*, July 10, 1864. http://www.proquest.com.
14. "The Wade Manifesto: The President's Action on the Reconstruction Bill of Congress," *New York Times*, August 18, 1864. http://www.proquest.com.

"Generals in the Rebel Army," *New York Times*, July 21, 1861, http://www.proquest.com.

"Jeff Davis' Army," *New York Times*, January 18, 1865. http://www.proquest.com.

O'Sullivan, Timothy. *Bodies of Confederate Soldiers near Mrs. Alsop's House.* Photograph. Library of Congress, Washington D.C. http://memory.loc.gov/ (accessed June 22, 2011).

---. *Bodies of Federal Soldiers, Killed on July 1, near the McPherson Woods.* Photograph. Library of Congress, Washington D.C. http://memory.loc.gov/ (accessed June 22, 2011).

"Retreat of Gen. McDowell's Command from Mannassas: Full Details of the Engagement," *New York Times*, July 23, 1861, http://www.proquest.com.

Summerhill, Thomas. "Week Two: Amateurs at War." History 304: The American Civil War, Online. Accessed May 23, 2011.

"The Battle of Franklin—Hood's Army," *Daily Richmond Examiner*, December 7, 1864. http://infotrac.galegroup.com

"The Wade Manifesto: The President's Action on the Reconstruction Bill of Congress," *New York Times*, August 18, 1864. http://www.proquest.com.

Emma Kallstrom

Dr. Charles Wolfe

English 4440

13 April 2010

"They knew how to live with nature and get along with nature":
The Martian Secret to a Successful Civilization

Twentieth-century Americans witnessed stunning scientific discoveries, such as the atomic bomb and the space age, frightening political maneuvering stemming from America's sense of superiority and the Cold War, and continued social strife in racial tension and religious intolerance. These scientific, political, and social phenomena clearly influenced Ray Bradbury's *The Martian Chronicles*. The development of the V-2 weapon, capable of reaching heights of 100 miles, during World War II marked the beginning of the space age. After the war ended, rocket-powered weapons development led naturally to space exploration programs ("History"). In addition, the Cold War ensued due to the rivalry and weapons buildup between the United States with its Western allies and the Soviet Union with its communist supporters (Snead). In *The Martian Chronicles*, Bradbury takes rocket technology and space exploration, combines them with the power struggle between the atomic-weapon-wielding superpowers, and imagines potential consequences played out in both the Earth and Martian arenas. Although the novel treats a variety of social and political ills, often bizarrely juxtaposed, a discernible story arc emerges regarding the relationship between successful civilizations, living in harmony with the environment, and careful management of technology. *The Martian Chronicles* travels from the Martians' harmonious coexistence with nature and technology through mankind's destructive and self-destructive disregard for such harmony to the final realization that humans must adopt the Martian philosophy in order to survive and succeed as a civilization.

The standard for living in harmony with nature and science is established in the second chapter, "Ylla," in which the lifestyle of a typical Martian couple is described. The description of the house evokes a serene, peaceful environment of fruit-bearing walls and creek-inlaid floors. Everything about the house has been designed to complement the Martian climate. For example, being farther from the Sun than Earth, the Martians have found a way to get as much sunlight as possible: The house "turned and followed the sun, flower-like" throughout the day, but to withstand the cold of night, it "clos[ed] itself in, like a giant flower, with the passing of light" (Bradbury 2, 5). Because the climate is also mostly dry, the Martians have invented ingenious ways to harness their limited water supply to provide necessary humidity: Within the home, a "gentle rain sprang from the fluted pillar tops, cooling the scorched air, falling gently on [Ylla]. On hot days it was like walking in a creek. The floors of the house glittered with cool streams" (Bradbury 2-3). The Martians have remained in control of their technology, using their impressive technological advances to enhance their harmonious relationship with nature. They sleep on clouds of chemicals that support and conform to their bodies overnight and gently lower them down to the floor in the morning. Books are fashioned from durable metal, eliminating the need for wasteful, polluting paper production. One of Mr. K's books sings of "ancient men [who] had carried clouds of metal insects and electric spiders into battle" (Bradbury 2), which reveals that at one time, Martian history had resembled that of war-prone Earth. However, at some point, Martians took control of their destiny, and the civilization as a whole endured successfully as indicated by the fact that the Ks' ancestors had lived in that same house before them for the past ten centuries.

Unlike their Martian counterparts, few Earth men appreciate the advantages of a peaceful, natural existence as illustrated in chapter seven, "—And the Moon Be Still as Bright." After three failed missions before them, the fourth expedition lands on Mars only to find a dead planet. The crew's cavalier attitude clearly shows the typical Earthman's, or more specifically, the typical American's, insensitivity to the loss of life or culture as long as their goal is achieved. They revel in their success despite the discovery that a nearby Martian city's population was decimated as recently as a week ago. Crewmember Biggs especially lacks respect for Mars or its lost civilization: he pollutes a canal by throwing wine bottles into it and later vomits the effects of that wine all over the beautiful ancient tile in the Martian city the team investigates. Of the sixteen surviving crewmembers only Spender and Captain Wilder understand the reverence that Mars deserves.

Spender, an archaeologist, is keenly interested in learning as much as possible about the Martians and their culture. His mind reels at the news that the Martians were senselessly destroyed by chicken pox:

> Chicken pox, God, chicken pox, think of it! A race builds itself for
> a million years, refines itself, erects cities like those out there, does
> everything it can to give itself respect and beauty and then it dies. . . .
> [I]t has to be chicken pox, a child's disease, a disease that doesn't even
> kill *children* on Earth! It's not right and it's not fair. . . . It doesn't fit the
> architecture; it doesn't fit this entire world! (Bradbury 51)

Having rejected the mission, Spender wanders off to study the Martian artifacts on his own and begins to feel a connection with them. Through his research, he discovers the key to the Martians' way of life and the point at which the Mars and Earth philosophies diverge:

> They knew how to live with nature and get along with nature. . . . Man
> had become too much man and not enough animal on Mars too. And
> the men of Mars realized that in order to survive they would have to
> forgo asking that one question any longer: *Why live?* Life was its own
> answer. Life was the propagation of more life and the living of as good
> a life as possible. . . . They quit trying too hard to destroy everything, to
> humble everything. They blended religion and art and science because,

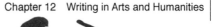

at base, science is no more than an investigation of a miracle we can
never explain, and art is an interpretation of that miracle. They never let
science crush the aesthetic and the beautiful. (Bradbury 66-67)

Spender recognizes the value of living in harmony with nature and science. He
anticipates and loathes the effect colonists from Earth will have on Mars, knowing
that they will destroy Mars just as they have been destroying and continue to destroy
Earth.

While Capt. Wilder understands Spender's argument, he feels more responsibility
to the mission and adopts a more optimistic attitude about Earth's relationship with
Mars. He openly hopes that Earth will learn from Mars and use the knowledge to
improve its civilization: "[O]ne day Earth will be as Mars is today. This will sober
us. It's an object lesson in civilizations. We'll learn from Mars" (Bradbury 55). His
doubt and inner struggle become apparent, however, during his pursuit of Spender
through the Martian wilderness. During their temporary truce-protected discussion,
Spender tries to sway Wilder to his point of view, but Wilder keeps his focus on the
mission. Nevertheless, he swears to do all he can to provide future archaeologists with
adequate opportunity to investigate thoroughly the Martian ruins in order to preserve
the culture as much as possible. Apparently, he does try to keep his promise because
in chapter 24, it is revealed that Wilder had been shipped off to Saturn, Neptune, and
Pluto for the twenty years following the fourth expedition to prevent his interference
in the colonization program on Mars.

Following the success of the fourth expedition, colonization of Mars begins in
earnest, confirming the Earthmen's insistence on molding the environment to suit
them instead of learning to adapt to their surroundings. In chapter nine, "The Green
Morning," colonist Benjamin Driscoll, having fainted upon arrival because of the thin
air, vows to fight "a private horticultural war with Mars" (Bradbury 75) and plants
thousands of tree seeds and sprouts. By doing so, he effectively changes the climate of
Mars, adding rich oxygen to the atmosphere. The next chapter, "The Locusts," finds
90,000 colonists "beat[ing] the strange world into a shape that was familiar to the
eye, . . . bludgeon[ing] away all the strangeness" (Bradbury 78). The transformation of
Mars to adhere to Earth standards is evident in chapter 13, "Interim," in which Tenth
City, built of imported Oregon pine and California redwood, so accurately resembles
a replica of an Iowa town that one might believe "a whirlwind twister of Oz-like
proportions had carried the entire town off to Mars to set it down without a bump"
(Bradbury 88). Spender's prophecy that "We'll rip [Mars] up, rip the skin off, and
change it to fit ourselves" (Bradbury 54) has been fulfilled; Earthmen have changed
the face of Mars.

The physical landscape is not the only item on the Earthmen's agenda; soon, their
ideology takes over as well, further emphasizing their disharmony with their new
surroundings. They begin with the basics—renaming towns with familiar Earth
names:

The old Martian names were names of water and air and hills. They
were the names of snows that emptied south in stone canals to fill the

empty seas. . . . And the rockets struck at the names like hammers, breaking away the marble into shale, shattering the crockery milestones that named the old towns, in the rubble of which great pylons were plunged with new names . . . , all the mechanical names and the metal names from Earth. (Bradbury 102-03)

This renaming of places had also been predicted by Spender: "[W]e'll give them new names, but the old names are there, somewhere in time, and the mountains were shaped and seen under those names. The names we'll give to the canals and mountains and cities will fall like so much water on the back of a mallard" (Bradbury 54). After the renaming is accomplished and Mars becomes comfortably familiar, officials arrive to impose the same laws and regulations that govern Earth's society. The Earthmen take complete control of Mars despite the existence of real Martians as confirmed by sporadic sightings of a few who have survived the Disease (chicken pox epidemic). In this way, amid the frenzy of colonization, the Martian culture is eradicated by the settlers from Earth.

The Earthmen's vision dominates Mars; however, an occasional settler understands the uniqueness of Mars and feels a natural harmony with it. Pop, the gas station owner in chapter eleven, "The Night Meeting," has the right attitude towards his strange new home:

We've got to forget Earth and how things were. We've got to look at what we're in here, and how *different* it is. I get a hell of a lot of fun out of just the weather here. It's *Martian* weather. Hot as hell daytimes, cold as hell nights. I get a big kick out of the different flowers and different rain. . . . I'm just experiencing. If you can't take Mars for what she is, you might as well go back to Earth. Everything's crazy up here, the soil, the air, the canals, the natives . . . . Well, that's Mars. Enjoy it. Don't ask it to be nothing else but what it is. (Bradbury 79)

Pop's acceptance of Mars is so rare that it is not equaled again until the end of the book. Before then, however, the colonists witness the distant explosions and depart en masse for Earth, leaving a few individuals stranded on Mars. Genevieve Selsor, introduced in chapter 23 ("The Silent Towns"), willfully chooses to stay behind. She finds solace in her isolation on deserted Mars—she can eat whatever and whenever she wants without facing society's criticism for being overweight. Eventually, Genevieve meets Walter Gripp, who was left behind unintentionally. Although he is desperately lonely, Walter cannot accept Genevieve—the last woman on Mars—as a companion and opts instead for a life of isolation. By the time Capt. Wilder returns in chapter 24 ("The Long Years"), Walter has become so acclimated to Mars that he refuses passage back to Earth. Capt. Wilder encounters another forgotten colonist, former crewmember Hathaway from the fourth expedition. Even though Hathaway cannot bear the loneliness of his existence and creates a robotic family to keep him company, he does choose to live in the Martian wilderness instead of in the town built by the Earthlings. This handful of individuals represents the very small minority of people who accept Mars for what it is.

Finally, one family rejects Earth values permanently and embraces the Martian way of life unequivocally. They have seen the destruction caused by letting technology get out of control in the form of atomic war on Earth: The desolation following the Great War is depicted in Chapter 25, "There Will Come Soft Rains," which coincides with the family's emigration. This family determines to shed all vestiges of Earth—its technology, laws, and ideals—and start a new, improved civilization on Mars. They choose an authentic ancient Martian city in which to dwell and start their new lives. The father symbolically burns his important papers from Earth (government documents, religious doctrines, financial records, war propaganda, and world map) as he explains to his young sons what went wrong with Earth:

> I'm burning a way of life. . . . Life on Earth never settled down to doing anything very good. Science ran too far ahead of us too quickly, and the people got lost in a mechanical wilderness, like children making over pretty things, gadgets, helicopters, rockets; emphasizing the wrong items, emphasizing machines instead of how to run the machines. Wars got bigger and bigger and finally killed Earth . . . [T]hat way of life proved itself wrong and strangled itself with its own hands. (Bradbury 179-80)

Their capitulation to the Martian way of life is complete when the children ask their father when they will see real Martians, and he poignantly shows them their own reflections in the canal.

In *The Martian Chronicles*, Ray Bradbury explores the future of mankind if it were to follow its current course of space exploration, the development of atomic weapons, and international power struggles. His fictional hypothesis emphasizes the destructive tendencies of humans and warns them of the disastrous outcome that is likely to occur. He does offer a glimmer of hope, however, suggesting that by learning to live in harmony with the environment, effectively blending nature and science, mankind may yet save itself.

Works Cited

Bradbury, Ray. *The Martian Chronicles*. New York: Bantam, 1979. Print.

"History of Technology." *Encyclopaedia Britannica Online*. Encyclopaedia Britannica, 2010. Web. 30 Mar. 2010.

Snead, David L. "Cold War." *Dictionary of American History*. Ed. Stanley I. Cutler. 3rd ed. Vol. 2. New York: Scribner's, 2003. N. pag. *Gale U. S. History in Context*. Web. 4 Apr. 2010.

Activities

Welcome to the Conversation

Discuss these questions with your classmates in class or via a class wiki or shared blog.

1. In general, what four types of writing are used in the arts and humanities?
2. What are the types of writing that are used most often in the arts and humanities?
3. If you have knowledge about a genre, what do you know?
4. What should you have before you begin your research and writing for a literature review?

Writing to Learn

1. **Summary**: Write a summary of an article or book chapter that deals with a topic related to an argument you are interested in using for a future research paper.
2. **Dialogue journal**: Create a dialogue journal page by drawing a vertical line from the top to the bottom of a piece of notebook paper. On the left, write three facts about an argumentative topic that you are interested in pursuing. For example, one of the facts you could write is "The Zhaozhou Bridge is the oldest standing bridge in China and the world's oldest stone segmental arch bridge." Now trade your dialogue journal with someone in class, and that person will write two questions about each of the facts you have written. For instance, next to the fact about the Zhaozhou Bridge, your classmate could write these questions: "When was the bridge built? What is the oldest bridge in the United States?"
3. **Reading journal**: Focus on a reading that you have done for class. In one page or less, summarize key ideas and people, and then respond to the reading's main points.

1. **Annotated bibliography**: Choose a general area of research and narrow your topic down to one about which you can make an argument. Find at least ten sources that you may be able to use to research your topic. Prepare a citation list of at least ten articles, books, book chapters, websites, and other documents. For each citation, add one or two paragraphs that describe, summarize, and evaluate the source.

2. **Literature review**: Focus your preliminary research for a research paper by narrowing down your topic and creating an in-progress thesis (that is, an argument that may be changed later after you do your literature review). Read at least five sources critically, taking notes on important information you may want to include in the literature review. Following the literature review genre format for your field, write a literature review.

1. **Digital presentation**: Choose a type of primary source that is commonly used in your particular arts and humanities field. For example, if you are a history major, you might choose census records or voter lists. Create a Prezi or PowerPoint presentation that introduces this type of primary source to your class/audience.

2. **Review, critique, or review essay**: Choose a primary text/source form your field, and write a review, critique, or review essay. Be sure to briefly describe the text/source before you explain its merits for your readers, so they can decide whether they want to experience the text for themselves. Remember to focus on a few key points rather than including everything that you know about the text/source.

Read More About It

Allosso, Salvatore F., and Dan Allosso. *A Short Handbook for Writing Essays in the Humanities and Social Sciences*. No City: Stay Outside the Box Publishing, 2011. Print.

Barnet, Sylvan. *A Short Guide to Writing About Art*. 10th ed. New York: Longman, 2010. Print.

Barnet, Sylvan, and William E. Cain. *A Short Guide to Writing About Literature*. 12th ed. New York: Longman, 2011. Print.

DeVoss, Danielle Nicole. *Understanding and Composing Multimodal Projects*. Boston: Bedford/St. Martin's, 2013. Print.

Ferguson, Marcia L. *A Short Guide to Writing About Theatre*. New York: Longman, 2007. Print.

Goodson, Patricia. *Becoming an Academic Writer: 50 Exercises for Paced, Productive, and Powerful Writing*. Los Angeles: Sage, 2013. Print.

Herbert, Trevor. *Music in Words: A Guide to Researching & Writing About Music*. New York: Oxford UP, 2009. Print.

Lange, Alexandra. *Writing About Architecture*. New York: Princeton Architectural Press, 2012. Print.

Marius, Richard, and Melvin E. Page. *A Short Guide to Writing About History*. 7th ed. New York: Pearson, 2010. Print.

O'Hair, Dan, Hannah Rubenstein, and Rob Stewart. *A Pocket Guide to Public Speaking*. 3rd ed. Boston: Bedford/St. Martin's, 2010. Print.

Rampolla, Mary Lynn. *A Pocket Guide to Writing in History*. 7th ed. Boston, MA: Bedford/St. Martin's, 2012. Print.

Vyhmesiter, Nancy Jean. *Your Guide to Writing Quality Research Papers: For Students of Religion and Theology*. 2nd ed. Grand Rapids, MI: Zondervan, 2008. Print.

13
Writing Effectively in Various Disciplines

Writing Effectively in Business

Know the Audience(s) in Business

People in business must write for a variety of audiences. Much of this writing is directed toward colleagues—bosses, employees, team members, project managers—people who are internal in the business. Likewise, much writing is directed outside the business, to past, present, or potential clients. People in business must communicate with others in their fields—industry experts, accreditation and licensing officials, professional colleagues, and competitors. Or they may be required to present at conferences or workshops, write journal or magazine articles, or share through newsletters, blogs, and websites. Additionally, they may need to communicate with more general, inexpert audiences through websites, blogs, newsletters, newspaper articles and editorials, and community talks or presentations. For these reasons, it is important to always know who you are writing for:

- Who are your primary readers?
- Who else might read your writing or listen to your presentation?
- What will the members of your audience already know about your topic?
- What will you need to define or explain?
- Will your audience be predisposed to agree or disagree with your point of view?
- What do you want this audience to do or believe?
- What kinds of evidence will be most convincing for this audience?

Know the Questions to Ask in Business

As a student, your research questions or writing goals may be assigned to you by your instructor. Often, however, you will have to make a decision yourself about these questions or goals. You can begin your writing preparation by asking yourself what you want to know more about and what you need to understand better in order to complete the assigned task or goal. You should also think about how and where you can locate this information. Do you need figures and statistics that already exist in a government database, such as the Census Bureau? Do you need to conduct your own market tests, interviews, or client surveys? Do you need to research government regulations or material costs? Perhaps you will need to locate models that show you how employees in your company have successfully approached this type of writing in the past. The type of writing required to achieve your communication goals should guide your research approach and topics.

Know the Kinds of Evidence Used in Business Arguments

Writers in the various fields of business use both quantitative and qualitative data in order to make arguments, support claims, and sell products. Both types of data come from primary research in the field or lab, as well as secondary research from other published resources. Common types of evidence used in business writing include facts and figures, examples, definitions, testimonies, and stories or narratives. Facts and figures, or quantitative data, are often presented as numbers within the text, or as a combination of numbers and visuals, such as charts and graphs in the text or in appendixes. You may need to present the methods you used to arrive at the numbers you present, including the mathematical formulas used or developed to test data, to look for or extend patterns, or to demonstrate causal relationships. Likewise, you may find it helpful or even necessary to use established statistical tests when presenting your quantitative data, so you should familiarize yourself with the computer software available at your institution or required in your field. Make sure your facts and figures are as up to date and accurate as possible.

Qualitative data are non-numerical and may include testimonials from clients; comments from focus groups, interviews, and surveys; and stories and observations from employers and employees, clients or customers. Expert testimony often carries more weight with readers, so be prepared to explain your expert's credentials or qualifications. When possible, use multiple sources and types of evidence. You may often use a combination of both quantitative and qualitative data—for example, percentages that show how many customers say they are pleased with your services alongside sample comments from satisfied customers.

The most important question to ask is this: What kind of evidence is needed to support my claim or to make it persuasive to my intended audience? Of course, you must also present evidence in an ethical manner. Withholding evidence or not giving the full picture because you think it hurts your argument is unethical and presents inaccurate results; this misuse of data will be detrimental in the long run. In addition, you should make sure that the evidence used, no matter what kind, actually supports the claim you are making (avoid leaps in logic and inaccurate cause-and-effect arguments, for example).

Know the Writing and Style Conventions in Business Writing

In the world of business, you only get one chance for a great first impression. The stakes are high—you are asking an investor for money, a customer for an order, or another executive for a partnership. Badly written letters, long rambling or emotional e-mails, or an obvious lack of spell-checking will brand you as a poor business risk before the message is even considered.

–Marty Zwilling, Cayenne Consulting
"Business Writing Style Is as Important as Content"

A good business writer communicates clearly, is aware of his or her audience, uses complete and thorough research (both primary and secondary), presents appropriate and accurate evidence for the goals of the writing, and uses the best format for the information and audience. To be a good business writer, you should accurately use the required documentation system and follow the basic tenets of all good writing—be organized, provide easy-to-read material, and make sure the material is grammatically correct. In addition, here are some specific conventions you may want to keep in mind when writing for business:

- Use short simple sentences.
- Use active voice. Also use verbs rather than nouns whenever possible.
  Example:
  The stockholders decided to change our organizational structure. Not, *The stockholders made a decision to change our organizational structure.*
- Write using second person or what some call the "you" viewpoint, which puts the reader's interests at the forefront. This point of view not only uses the words *you* and *your* to speak directly to the reader (the client or customer), it also stresses the benefit to the reader, not the company.

> **Tip:** An exception here may be when you have bad or negative news. Since you want to avoid being accusatory with clients, using the "you" viewpoint may mean adopting a passive or indirect style.
> For example: The budget should include matching funds from the agency (not, *Your budget does not indicate any matching funds from the agency*).

- Use words and sentence structures that fit your audience and your communication format. The company's instant messaging system may allow for more informal communication between co-workers; this same style would be inappropriate for a letter going out to potential customers.
- Avoid biased language that may offend your readers and damage your credibility. Language that makes assumptions or is based on stereotypes about gender, ethnicity, age, mental or physical (dis)ability, or sexual orientation is not effective. Often differences among people are not relevant to the discussion, so avoid bias by not mentioning them. When the differences are relevant, research the accepted usage or the appropriateness of a term or expression. In addition, you can often avoid bias or awkward phrasing by using plural forms.
  Example:
  All employees should submit an evaluation form. Not, *Every employee should submit his or her evaluation form.*

See Table 13.1 for some common terms that have a preferred form of expression in business.

Table 13.1

Forms of Expression in Business	
Yes	No
chair, chairperson	chairman, chairwoman
police officer	policeman, policewoman
an employee with a disability	disabled employee
significant others welcome	spouses welcome

- Design your business communication effectively. Many types of communication have very specific and stylized forms such as letters, memos, and résumés. Likewise, with items such as brochures, newsletters, flyers, or even websites, the visual design of a document may be just as important as the written content. Design elements to consider and learn more about include the effective use of the following:
  - White space: White space is used to frame the text and provide visual cues to the reader.
  - Color: The colors themselves as well as their placement can be important as they are used to highlight items, emphasize material, organize material, and guide the reader.
  - Font or typeface: Size, type, serif versus sans-serif, emphasis (underlining, italics, bold, and upper and lower case) can all affect readability and accessibility.
  - Arrangement: Headings, headers, and footers, text justification, lists, and columns are all used to organize material on the page and help guide the reader through the document.
  - Graphics: When integrating graphics, consider the proportion of image to text, the message or statement in the graphic, the graphic's connection to the text, the understandability of icons or global graphics, the purpose behind the graphic, and the relationship being shown in the graphic, as well as the words being replaced by the graphic.

Tip:

1. Graphics should always serve a specific function and should be as simple as possible.
2. Give each graphic a caption that clearly describes its content.
3. Figures and tables should be numbered chronologically below the graphic (e.g., Fig. 6-A, Fig. 6-B), and should be referred to in the text.
4. If your school, program, or company has a style guide, review it and use it.

- Write effectively in collaborative groups. Many businesses operate through the use of project teams and working groups. This cooperative model may require you to research and write collaboratively. Such groups are designed to bring together multiple areas of expertise, experience, and viewpoints as well as to share the workload, often with a goal of shortening the time to completion. As part of a team, you will be expected to contribute your knowledge, meet your deadlines, and give feedback to your team members.

- Be aware that many businesses operate in an international or global market, which means you may be writing for audiences with different rhetorical patterns, approaches to leadership, methods of persuasion, and styles of communication. They might even operate under different rules and regulations. In addition, you may be operating across technologies, general business practices, and time zones, as well as understandings of time.

Writing Effectively in Education

Know the Audience in Education

Audiences for writing in the education field may include colleagues in the profession, including teachers, administrators, superintendents, academics, and scholars; the lay public; local, state, and federal government; private testing or assessment companies; and private granting agencies and foundations. Most writing that you will do on a daily basis will focus on formal writing that is intended for your classroom or your colleagues, from lesson plans and research papers to assessment reports. People in the education profession also create oral presentations for conferences and other venues, textbooks, pamphlets, and important messages about the importance of education through popular media. Based on your specific focus, you may also write for the government and private agencies that are monitoring or funding your work, corporate employers, or regulatory bodies, such as a county school board or the Department of Education. In every case, it is essential that you analyze your audience and write with their interests in mind:

- Who are your primary readers?
- Who else might read your writing or listen to your presentation?
- What will the members of your audience already know about your topic?
- What will you need to define or explain?
- Will your audience be predisposed to agree or disagree with your point of view?
- What kinds of evidence will be most convincing for this audience?

Know the Research Questions to Ask in Education

As a student and as a professional, you will find that your research questions often spring directly from your work in the classroom. As a student, your instructor may assign your research questions or the conditions for your research. However, you may need to decide what research you want to pursue and how this research will impact your own growth as an educator.

Research topics might include studies of student populations across different schools, student responses to particular types of pedagogy, theoretical issues, and testing of assessments and interventions. The research question you decide on will form the basis for your project design and your final written product. Your research question is also your working hypothesis, the idea you will test through textual research and action research from your practice or observation; consequently, it will be described in your writing (see Table 13.2 for example).

Table 13.2

Research Questions	
What you want to know more about	**Your research question**
My students tend to become bored when I deliver course material only by lecture. Why? What other method could I use to engage them in the class?	How do teachers of a middle school physical science course improve student engagement through the technique of "flipping" the classroom?

Know the Kinds of Evidence Used in Education

> Scientific educational research is defined as the application of systematic methods and techniques that help researchers and practitioners to understand and enhance the teaching and learning process.
>
> — Marguerite Lodico et al

Researchers in education use quantitative and qualitative data to generate research questions and support their arguments. These types of data often come directly from the field, in the classroom or in observing a target population. While research can focus primarily on quantitative or qualitative approaches, a very effective process is "mixed-method" design, which calls for a mix of both quantitative and qualitative data sets. These research projects are systematic in their collection and evaluation of both kinds of evidence. Another common form of research in education is **action research**, which calls for you to examine an issue in your own teaching practice and school setting in order to fix what is problematic. This style, reminiscent of case studies and other writing discussed in this chapter, also calls for a mixed-methods approach, with both quantitative and qualitative data.

Research in the field of education uses two types of central reasoning, similar to how scientific research is structured across other fields.

- Inductive reasoning calls for the researcher to observe a situation, look for patterns or themes, and then use this analysis to argue for a specific generalization or conclusion about the subject under investigation. This type of reasoning is associated with **qualitative research**, which is when data is pulled from written or verbal narratives, such as classroom observations or student and teacher interviews.

Example:
After noticing that two science teachers have students who are performing at a higher level than other classes in the same grade level, you ask to observe their classes at different points through a unit. During the observation, you note that these teachers are team teaching, and have "flipped" their classes, putting the lectures and notes online for students to review at home, and spending valuable class time on active projects or experiments that illustrate the scientific principles under study. Your analysis leads you to argue that collaboration and the "flipping" pedagogical technique may be an important factor in increasing student involvement with curriculum, in turn resulting in better performance on assessment measures.

- Deductive reasoning is similar to the reasoning used in traditional scientific research projects, and is based on the traditional scientific method. This calls for the researcher to hypothesize based on a specific educational theory or a review of previous studies and then collect data to test the hypothesis. This is aligned with **quantitative research**, which focuses on data that can be interpreted numerically.

Example:
Paulo Friere's theory of critical pedagogy, which calls for educators to resist a "banking" model of education, may be used in advanced high school English curriculum to encourage active study of assigned texts in preparation for AP exams, and in turn influence students' scores. This will be done by allowing students to vote on choices of suitable texts to fulfill course and assessment goals, and then measuring changes in student scores on practice exams. (Note: this type of study would require some method of control, either with a control group of students to compare, and/or outside raters of the students' practice exams to avoid bias on the part of their teachers).

Know the Writing and Style Conventions in Education

If a man will begin with certainties, he shall end in doubts; but if he will be content to begin with doubts, he shall end in certainties.

—Francis Bacon

Writers in the education professions aim to communicate clearly, are aware of their audience, use complete and thorough quantitative and qualitative research, and utilize the format of each genre to highlight the most important aspects of the pedagogical or theoretical issues they are arguing for. Good writing in education follows the general basics of successful communication: effective organization, readability, correct grammar and mechanics, and adherence to the conventions of the chosen documentation style. There are also some specific conventions that you may want to follow as you write in education:

1. When using qualitative or quantitative evidence, you should be as objective as possible in your collection and presentation of the data. With qualitative data, it is important to remember how the human element affects how you handle the data. Because you are talking about your observations and interactions, many variables and variations exist and you will not be able to account for all of them, so it is important to use conditional terms as you talk about behaviors, motivations, and causes (e.g., *often* instead of *always, many* instead of *all*, the *participants* in this study rather than *students*).
2. Depending on the type of evidence and the method of data collection, you may decide to be objective (quantitative), or you might use first person and talk about yourself as a researcher or observer in the field. Make sure you check with your professor about expectations and follow the examples set in the models you read and review for class. Particularly with documents such as reflections, lesson plans, and class observations, you will likely use the first person.
3. If you are working from qualitative research, you will likely use direct evidence from research participants. These may be quotes from interviews, observations, or survey responses. However, you should also explain in your own words how this data serves as evidence for your argument. Also, APA style calls for you

to use the past tense when citing others' work, as well as events that you have observed in a classroom setting.

4. Avoid biased language that may offend your readers and will damage your credibility. Language that makes assumptions or is based on stereotypes about gender, ethnicity, age, mental or physical (dis)ability, or sexual orientation is not effective. If one of these variables is part of your research, tread carefully and investigate the most appropriate way to address these aspects of your study.

5. Audience is very important to consider when communicating in education. If you are writing for a more formal audience of colleagues or professors, or in an official capacity, you should use the more formal terminology and language expectations of the discipline. However, when writing for a more general audience, such as a memo to parents or a newspaper article, you should thoroughly explain any theoretical constructs and terminology that you use.

> **Tip:** You should also avoid the other extreme of using overblown or pompous language that will make your writing harder to read and may alienate your reader.

Know the Appropriate Documentation Style in Education

APA, the documentation style developed by the American Psychological Association, is most often used in education. It uses an author-date method of documentation for both in-text citations and the reference list at the end of the document. Putting the author's last name and the year of the publication in parentheses within the text as soon as the source is mentioned emphasizes the timeliness of the resource and lends credibility to the writer. Some majors, areas of study, or journals within the discipline may have their own documentation style guides, so always check to see what is appropriate for your purposes or your assignment.

Writing Effectively in Engineering

Know the Audience in Engineering

Many people writing in engineering are writing for their clients and co-workers. They are writing a wide variety of documents as discussed above in order to communicate their proposals, projects, research, and other aspects of their work. Engineers may also be writing for government and corporate audiences, including employers, granting agencies, and regulatory agencies. It is important to always know who you are writing for:

- Who are your primary readers?
- Who else might read your writing or listen to your presentation?
- What will the members of your audience already know about your topic?
- What will you need to define or explain?
- Will your audience be predisposed to agree or disagree with your point of view?
- What kinds of evidence will be most convincing for this audience?

Know the Research Questions to Ask in Engineering

As a student, your research questions or the conditions for your research may be assigned to you by your instructor. Often, however, you will have to create your question on your own. One place to begin is by asking yourself what you want to know more about, what you want to understand better, or what assumptions you need to test. You may ask how questions or why questions. Your final research question will guide both your research design and your writing. The research question is also referred to as the working hypothesis. It is the idea you will systematically test or analyze through the research process and describe through the writing process. Table 13.3 illustrates how this process can be used to arrive at a viable research question.

Table 13.3

Research Questions	
What you want to know more about:	**Your research question:**
Bridges continue to rust and decay and many will need to be rebuilt in the next few years. How can we build longer-lasting bridges?	What type of polymer materials are best suited for bridge building?
Is it possible to build bridges that can withstand natural disasters such as earthquakes and hurricanes? Would the use of flexible structures make bridges better able to withstand such disasters?	Which flexible structures are most viable for bridge building?

Know the Kinds of Evidence Used in Engineering Arguments

Engineers use both quantitative and qualitative data in order to make arguments and support their claims; they also build and test prototypes. They use data from primary research in the field or lab, as well as secondary research from other published resources, especially when others detail what they have tried—what worked and what didn't. Data are often presented in mathematical and/or scientific formulas; this includes the presentation of statistics in the text as well as through graphs, charts, and tables. In your writing, you may need to present the mathematical formulas you developed to test data, look for or extend patterns, or demonstrate results. Likewise, you may find it helpful, or even necessary, to use established statistical tests when presenting your quantitative data, so you should familiarize yourself with the computer software available at your institution or in your lab. Qualitative data may also be used in engineering because some experimental results must be described as well as measured. The most important question to ask is this: What kind of evidence is needed to test my claim or hypothesis? Your research should then be designed to help you accurately collect this type of data or evidence.

Know the Writing and Style Conventions in Engineering

An effective writer in engineering communicates clearly, is aware of the audience, uses complete and thorough research (both primary and secondary), presents appropriate and accurate evidence for the study, and uses the best format for the information and audience. Good writing in engineering also follows the basic tenets

of good writing in general: it is organized, easy to read, and grammatically correct, and accurately uses the required documentation system. In addition, here are some specific conventions you may want to keep in mind when writing about engineering:

- Use the terms and principles in the field in order to be understood. Avoid common or vernacular names, which may not be precise and can cause confusion. You should explain these engineering terms when writing for more general audiences.
  - Follow disciplinary rules for the use of names and formulas such as those for species, genes, chemicals, proteins, and procedures.
  - The use of abbreviations is common, but you should still write out the whole word or phrase the first time you use it, and put the abbreviation in parentheses. Then use the abbreviation consistently throughout the rest of the paper.
- Be as descriptive as possible so your reader can visualize the problem or solution, but avoid metaphorical language unless a comparison is used to make an abstract concept more concrete and thus more understandable.
- Use visuals strategically to illustrate points and present data—this includes the use of images, models, concept maps, photographs, tables, graphs, and charts.

> **Tip:** Tables and figures should be numbered consecutively in separate series (e.g., Table 10.1, Table 10.2; Figure 10.1, Figure 10.2). Tables should have titles, and figures should have legends or keys. Both should be understandable apart from the text even though they should also be referenced in the text. Often images have captions to help readers make sense of what they are seeing.

- Every equation, table, or figure should be discussed in the text. It should also be labeled with an appropriate, descriptive caption.
- Equations should be set apart in the text for ease of reading as well as emphasis. Equations should also be numbered and then explained in the text following the equation.

> **Tip:** Make sure all variables have been defined in the text.

- When listing equipment, give the manufacturer, model number, and serial number.
- Spell out numbers at the beginning of sentences or rephrase to move the number; spell out numbers 1–10 unless they are part of a series using Arabic numerals. Use the symbol ~ to mean "approximately equal to".
- Use headings and subheadings to divide your material into small, manageable chunks for the reader. These can also be used in your table of contents to guide your reader.
- Pay attention to verb tense and be consistent. Studies already completed should be presented in past tense; studies being proposed (e.g., in a grant proposal) should be in future tense; conditions that presently exist should be discussed in the present tense. Some engineering style guides use passive voice (e.g., an experiment was conducted) while others use first person, active voice (e.g., we conducted an experiment). Check with your professor, your company style guide, or previous issues of the journal or magazine to help you decide which form is appropriate for your context and purpose, and then be consistent throughout the text.

- Rarely use direct quotes from source materials. Instead rely on summaries and paraphrases.
- Be as objective as possible, avoiding emotional words and phrasing that will bias or unduly influence the reader. This includes avoiding sexist language and gendered expressions in your writing.

  Example:
  The new equipment was tested by *firefighters* in three different precincts; rather than, The new equipment was tested by *firemen* in three different precincts.

Know the Appropriate Documentation Style in Engineering

APA, the documentation style recommended by the American Psychological Association, and CMS, the documentation style outlined by the *Chicago Manual of Style*, are both used by engineers, depending on context. Likewise, many different areas or fields within engineering have their own documentation guides. For example, each of the groups or societies listed below has its own documentation style for use with its publications. These publications are widely read and published in by engineers.

> *IEEE: Electrical and Computer Engineering*
> *ACS: American Chemical Society*
> *MRS: Materials Research Society*
> *ASME: American Society of Mechanical Engineers*
> *BMES: Biomedical Engineering Society*

In choosing your documentation style, use the style required by your instructor or the journal to which you are submitting your paper, or consult the style set forth in your company's in-house style guide.

Writing Effectively in the Health Sciences

Know the Audience(s) in the Health Sciences

> [W]riting in the field of Public Health involves assessing a problem and addressing it rhetorically through writing, [recognizing] that simply providing information may not persuade an audience to change its behavior, that it is necessary to assume a more nuanced writer identity in order to have an impact upon an intended audience, and that the assumption of this identity constitutes a performance.
>
> —Clark and Fischbach

Audiences for health writing may include colleagues in the health professions, including physicians, nurses, public health officials, and other health care professionals; the lay public; local, state, and federal government agencies; and private agencies, insurance companies, and pharmaceutical companies. Most writing that you will do on a daily basis will focus on formal writing that is intended for colleagues, from charts, to research papers, to journal articles. Those in the health professions also write oral presentations for conferences and other venues, textbooks,

pamphlets, and important health messages to be shared via popular media. Based on your specific focus, you may also be writing for government or private agencies that are monitoring or funding your work, corporate employers, and regulatory bodies, such as the Food and Drug Administration or the Drug Enforcement Agency. In every case, it is essential that you analyze your audience and write with their interests in mind:

- Who are your primary readers?
- Who else might read your writing or listen to your presentation?
- What will the members of your audience already know about your topic?
- What will you need to define or explain?
- Will your audience be predisposed to agree or disagree with your point of view?
- What kinds of evidence will be most convincing for this audience?

Know the Research Questions to Ask in the Health Sciences

As a student and as a professional, you will find that your research questions will often spring directly from your work in the field, clinic, or laboratory. As a student, you may be assigned research questions or the conditions for your research. In other cases, you may need to decide what research you want to pursue.

Research topics might include studies of patient populations or potential populations, patient responses to health problems and complications, theoretical issues, and the testing of assessments and interventions. The research question you decide on will form the basis for your project design and your final written product. Your research question is also your working hypothesis—the idea that you will test through research, clinical practice, or observation, and consequently describe in your writing (see Table 13.4 for example).

Table 13.4

Research Questions	
What you want to know more about:	**Your research question:**
I've noticed that many of my patients who are overweight into middle age tend to have diabetes, but they usually prefer medication to lifestyle changes.	Which lifestyle interventions succeed at preventing or reversing the course of type 2 diabetes in older populations?

Know the Kinds of Evidence Used in Health Science Arguments

Scientists in the health profession use quantitative and qualitative data to generate research questions and support their arguments. These types of data often come directly from the field, either in clinical practice or in observing a target population. Quantitative data are often numerical and include statistics, charts, graphs, and other mathematical and scientific formulae. Accurate integration of numerical data will support your methods and help prove your results.

Qualitative data are non-numerical. For this reason, some believe these data are not as accurate since they rely on observation and description. However, qualitative data are important in many types of writing and research in the health sciences, particularly those projects focused directly on patient care and outcomes. With any sort of evidence, you must ask yourself whether or not it helps test or prove your hypothesis. What types of evidence are needed? To be effective, look for both types of evidence—both qualitative and quantitative—that will support and prove your research hypothesis.

Know the Writing and Style Conventions in the Health Sciences

I once heard a medical student claim that "writing has nothing to do with science." Of course, this is not true. No one would advance the profession if the results of research were not written and published. Ultimately, effective medical writing requires the same principles of logic, organization, clarity and precision that any science requires. Professionals of any kind must understand the importance of written communication and how it affects their status in the profession.

—Karl Terryberry

When writing in the health sciences, as in any other science, be precise and detailed. This is especially vital when you are writing direct-to-practice health care documents, such as charts and histories. Do not just state actions taken or other information vaguely, such as "changed I.V. fluid"; rather, record all relevant data that may be necessary to continue to evaluate and treat the patient, in this case which fluid was changed, the amount given, the time of the change, and why/on whose order the I.V. was changed. This preciseness also ensures readers that you are in compliance with care directives.

As with all science writing, objectivity is important. In your writing, remember to accurately and without bias observe your patient and precisely document your findings, keeping your own emotions from affecting your interpretation. Good writing in the health sciences demands an awareness of your audience, effective research, and careful choice of a format. In some cases, such as a public health message, appealing more directly to an audience's emotions may prove useful in getting your message across more effectively.

Good writing in any field follows the general basics of successful communication: it should be well organized, easy to read, logical, and grammatically and mechanically correct, and it should follow the conventions of the chosen documentation style. There are also some specific conventions that you may want to keep in mind as you write in the health sciences:

- Audience is very important to consider when communicating in the health sciences. If you are writing for more formal audiences of colleagues, professors, or in official capacities, you should use the scientific terms and principles of the field. However, when writing for a more general audience, such as in patient literature or digital sources of information, you should thoroughly explain these scientific terms and principles.
  - Follow the disciplinary rules per context and audience when using names and formulae, such as those for genes, medications, proteins, and procedures.
  - While it is common to use discipline-specific abbreviations, your writing may be read by an audience of practitioners from another discipline or a more general audience. You should still write out an entire word or phrase the first time that you use it, follow it with the abbreviation

in parentheses, and then use this same abbreviation consistently throughout the paper, chart, or project.

- Generally, you should use a more formal and objective writing style, avoiding slang and contractions. However, in other types of writing, particularly as part of public health outreach, a more conversational style may be appropriate in order to reach target audiences.

> Avoid the other extreme of using overblown or pompous language that will make your writing harder to read and may alienate your reader.

- Use visuals strategically to illustrate points and present data. This includes the use of images, models, concept maps, photographs, tables, graphs, and charts.

> Tables and figures should be numbered consecutively in separate series (i.e., Table 9.1, Table 9.2; Figure 9.1, Figure 9.2). Tables should have titles and figures should have legends or keys. Both should be understandable apart from the text. Other images may have captions to help readers make the connection between the image and the text.

- Spell out numbers at the beginning of sentences or rephrase to move the number. Spell out the numbers 1–10 unless they are part of a series that is using Arabic numerals. (There is sometimes an exception to this if the number is part of a commonly accepted name for a disease or disorder, e.g., type 2 diabetes. Always consult the style guide or your instructor in these instances). Use the symbol ~ to mean "approximately equal to."

Example:
"The prevalence of hypertension in type 2 diabetes is higher than that in the general population, especially in younger patients. At the age of 45 around 40% of patients with type 2 diabetes are hypertensive, the proportion increasing to 60% by the age of 75."

Turner, R., Holman, R., et al. (1998) Tight blood pressure control and risk of macrovascular and microvascular complications in type 2 diabetes: UKPDS 38. *British Medical Journal*, pp. 703–713.

- Pay attention to verb tense and be consistent. Studies already completed should be presented in past tense; studies being proposed (e.g., **in a grant proposal**) should be in future tense; conditions that presently exist should be discussed in the present tense.

> The sciences do not use the literary present tense that you may have been taught in a literature class. The literary present tense is reserved for fiction.

- Rarely use direct quotes from source materials; rely instead on summaries and paraphrases.
- In most health science writing, be as objective as possible, avoiding emotional words and phrasing that will bias or unduly influence the reader. This includes avoiding sexist language and gendered tropes in your writing. However, when writing materials to convince the public or another target audience to make lifestyle changes or adopt another health measure, it may be helpful for you to appeal to the *pathos*, or emotions, of your intended audience.

For example: You might encourage pregnant women to seek adequate prenatal care by presenting statistics of infant mortality rates, accompanied by pictures of healthy babies.

Know the Specialized Research Conventions in the Health Sciences

Research in the health sciences is generally empirical and often directly addresses outcomes of patient health, including not just the physical side of health, but the psychological and social aspects of health as well. Many research questions will focus on studying a specific variable or theory, which can then be applied in a practical setting. In outcomes-focused research, the patient is the first source: Is the patient satisfied with the results of a treatment or intervention? Has the patient's functionality or quality of life improved? When included as a part of evidence-based medicine, clinical research focuses directly on the treatments or interventions used by a health care provider for a particular patient or population.

You may be asked to conduct and write up several types of clinical research. Basic research calls for laboratory or field data to be used to influence theory. Applied research uses data to solve issues in practice. Translational research asks you to examine both how research influences practice and, in turn, how issues encountered in practice can lead to important research questions. These types of clinical research projects can also be categorized as experimental and observational, depending on the assignment and context.

Know the Appropriate Documentation Style in the Health Sciences

There are several documentation styles commonly used in the health sciences. APA, the documentation style of the American Psychological Association, is often used in writing specific to nursing, such as nursing case studies. CSE, the documentation style recommended by the Council of Science Editors, is also used by many in the medical fields. Occasionally, a journal will call for medical writing to be documented according to CMS, or the *Chicago Manual of Style*. However, many types of health writing and professional organizations also have their own documentation guides, such as that of the American Medical Association. CSE offers three different documentation options: the name-year option (also known as the "Harvard system"), which is similar to APA style, and two number formats—the citation-sequence option (also known as the "Vancouver system") and the citation-name option. You should use the style required by your instructor or the journal to which you are submitting your writing.

Writing Effectively in the Sciences

Know the Audience in the Sciences

Many people writing in the sciences are writing for their colleagues in order to expand scientific knowledge and continually advance our understanding in every scientific discipline from biology and chemistry to physics and geology. They are writing

journal articles to be read by other scientists and students, presenting their findings at conferences, publishing textbooks for students at a variety of school levels, and sharing scientific principles in popular magazines and books. Scientists may also write for government and corporate audiences, including employers, granting agencies, and regulatory agencies such as the Environmental Protection Agency or the Food and Drug Administration. It is important to always know who you are writing for:

- Who are your primary readers?
- Who else might read your writing or listen to your presentation?
- What will the members of your audience already know about your topic?
- What will you need to define or explain?
- Will your audience be predisposed to agree or disagree with your point of view?
- What kinds of evidence will be most convincing for this audience?

Know the Research Questions to Ask in the Sciences

As a student, your research questions or the conditions for your research may be assigned by your instructor. Often, however, you will have to develop your research questions on your own. One place to begin is by asking yourself what you want to know more about, what you want to understand better, or what assumptions you need to test. You may ask *how* questions or *why* questions. Your final research questions will guide both your research design and your writing. The research question is also referred to as the *working hypothesis*. It is the idea you will systematically test or analyze through the research process and describe through the writing process. Table 13.5 illustrates how this process can be used to create a viable research question.

Table 13.5

Research Questions	
What you want to know more about:	Your research question:
There are so many kinds of suntan lotion out there I don't know what to buy, but I really don't want to get burned when I go to the beach for spring break.	Is SPF 65 more effective at preventing sunburn than SPF 50?
MTA3 plays an important role in the pluripotency of mice ES cells; however, the role of MTA3 in induced pluripotency of human iPS cells is still unknown. Therefore, we want to determine the functional requirement for MTA3 in iPS cell generation.	Is MTA3 required in iPS cell generation?

Know the Kinds of Evidence Used in Science Arguments

Scientists use both quantitative and qualitative data in order to make arguments and support their claims. Both types of data come from primary research in the field or lab, as well as secondary research from other published resources. Quantitative data are presented in numbers and scientific formulas; this includes the presentation of statistics in the text as well as through graphs and charts. In your writing, you may need to present the mathematical formulas you developed to test data, look for or extend patterns, or demonstrate results. Likewise, you may find it helpful, or even necessary, to use established statistical tests when presenting your quantitative data, so you should familiarize yourself with the computer software available at your institution or in your lab. Qualitative data are non-numerical; because they rely on descriptions, many scientists find qualitative data less accurate or rigorous than quantitative data. However, both types have their place in the lab and in the field. Some experimental results must be described as well as measured. The most important question to ask is this: What kind of evidence is needed to test my claim or hypothesis? Your research should then be designed to help you accurately collect this type of data or evidence.

Know the Writing and Style Conventions in the Sciences

Reading, writing, and science are, or should be, inseparable. Many of the process skills needed for science inquiry are similar to reading skills, and when taught together reinforce each other. Examples of skills in common are predicting, inferring, communicating, comparing and contrasting, and recognizing cause and effect relationships. In language as well as science learning, students analyze, interpret and communicate ideas. These are skills needed to evaluate sources of information and the validity of the information itself, a key factor for scientifically literate citizens.

–Science Magazine

Good science writers communicate clearly, are aware of their audience, use complete and thorough research (both primary and secondary), present appropriate and accurate evidence for the study, and use the best format for the information and audience. Good writing in the sciences also follows the basic tenets of good writing in general, so it is organized, easy to read, grammatically correct, and accurately uses the required documentation system. In addition, here are some specific conventions you may want to keep in mind when writing about science:

- Use the terms and principles of the field in order to be understood; avoid common or vernacular names, which may not be precise and can therefore cause confusion. You should explain these scientific terms when writing for more general audiences.
  - Follow disciplinary rules for the use of names and formulas such as those for species, genes, chemicals, proteins, and procedures.
  - The use of abbreviations is common, but you should still write out the whole word or phrase the first time you use it, followed by the abbreviation in parentheses. Then use the abbreviation consistently throughout the rest of the paper.
- Use a more formal objective writing style rather than a conversational style. Avoid slang and contractions as well as metaphorical examples.

You should also avoid the other extreme of using overblown or pompous language that will make your writing harder to read and possibly alienate your reader.

- Use visuals strategically to illustrate points and present data. This includes the use of images, models, concept maps, photographs, tables, graphs, and charts.

> Tables and figures should be numbered consecutively in separate series (e.g., Table 10.1, Table 10.2; Figure 10.1, Figure 10.2). Tables should have titles, and figures should have legends or keys. Both should be understandable apart from the text. Other images may have captions to help readers make sense of what they are seeing.

- Spell out numbers at the beginning of sentences or rephrase to move the number. Spell out numbers 1–10 unless they are part of a series that is using Arabic numerals. Use the symbol ~ to mean "approximately equal to."

Example:
Of the 83 species of freshwater fish in southeastern Australia, half migrate at least once as part of their life cycle. Four notable long distance swimmers are the Mary River cod (30km), silver perch (570km), Murray cod (1,000km) and the golden perch, which has been recorded swimming a staggering 2,300km.

Fairfull, S. and Witheridge, G. (2003) Why Do Fish Need to Cross the Road? Fish Passage Requirements for Waterway Crossings. NSW Fisheries, Cronulla, 16 pp.

- Pay attention to verb tense and be consistent. Studies already completed should be presented in past tense; studies being proposed (e.g., in a grant proposal) should be in future tense; conditions that presently exist should be discussed in the present tense.

> Science does not use the literary present tense that you may have been taught in a literature class. The literary present tense is reserved for fiction writing.

- Use direct quotes from source materials sparingly. Instead, rely on summaries and paraphrases.

- Be as objective as possible, avoiding emotional words and phrasing that will bias or unduly influence the reader. This includes avoiding sexist language and gendered expressions in your writing.

Example:
talking about eggs as passive and sperm as aggressive because of cultural notions about female and male roles in reproduction and in human culture

- Avoid anthropomorphizing objects, giving human feelings or actions to nonhuman beings, or giving sensory experiences to inanimate objects.

Example:
"The Praying Mantis has lived among us for centuries. Their beauty and mystique stirs our curiosity. Long and slender, quick yet graceful they stand on top of the insect world as regal creatures of the fields even in all their many colors of camouflage."
From http://www.theprayingmantis.org/

Know the Appropriate Documentation Style in the Sciences

CSE, the documentation style recommended by the Council of Science Editors, is typically used by biologists, chemists, and those in many medical fields. However, many fields also have their own documentation guides, including the American Chemical Society and the American Medical Association. CSE offers three different documentation options: the name-year option, which is similar to APA style, and two number formats, the citation-sequence option and the citation-name option. You should use the style required by your instructor or the journal to which you are submitting your paper.

> CMS (the Chicago Manual of Style, is used by many journals, including some scientific journals, so you may need to be familiar with this documentation style as well.

Writing Effectively in the Social Sciences

Know the Audience in the Social Sciences

Many people writing in the social sciences are writing for their colleagues—their classmates, their fellow researchers, their employers and employees, and their team members and project managers. Likewise, social scientists are writing to patients and clients—past, present, and potential. They may also be communicating with others in their discipline—industry experts, government leaders, accreditation and licensing officials, and professional colleagues. They may be presenting at conferences or workshops, writing journal or magazine articles, or sharing through newsletters, blogs, and websites. These same social scientists may be communicating with more general, inexpert audiences through their websites and blogs, newsletters, newspaper articles and editorials, and community talks or presentations. As a social scientist, you always need to know who you are writing for:

- Who are your primary readers?
- Who else might read your writing or listen to your presentation?
- What will the members of your audience already know about your topic?
- What will you need to define or explain?
- Will your audience be predisposed to agree or disagree with your point of view?
- What do you want this audience to do or believe?
- What kinds of evidence will be most convincing for this audience?

Know the Questions to Ask in the Social Sciences

As a student, your assignment or research question may be assigned to you by your instructor. Often, however, you will have to formulate your research questions or goals for yourself. Typically, the social sciences ask how and why questions. One place to begin is by asking yourself what you want to know more about and what you need to understand better in order to complete an assigned task or goal. Starting with your own day-to-day life and interests will help you ask more interesting and useful questions. Preliminary research of existing literature may help you narrow and refine your questions. Find out what has already been said on your topic, where there are holes in the research, and perhaps where you disagree with what has already been said. Talking with others about your topic will also help; classmates, writing center consultants, and your professor are all good resources for helping you focus your research. Your final product and communication goals should guide your research approach and topic.

Know the Kinds of Evidence Used in Social Science Arguments

After you've formed your research questions, you'll want to think about how you can collect the information you need to answer the questions you have posed. As one instructor puts it, "You need to know how to marshal your evidence." Social scientists use both primary and secondary research and types of evidence. Primary research tools include interviews, focus groups, surveys, and observations. Perhaps you need to interview friends about local sports clubs or family members about holiday traditions. You may want to conduct surveys about students' study habits or spending habits. Perhaps you could use a focus group to learn more about why gamers prefer certain games over others. You might use observations to study a particular time and space, such as your local writing center for a day or parent behavior in the mall over the weekend. In many majors, social scientists choose to supplement the stories and first hand experiences they collect (i.e., their qualitative data) with quantitative data.

Statistics and figures, or quantitative data, are often presented as numbers within the text or as a combination of numbers and visuals, such as charts, graphs, and tables in the text or in appendixes. You may need to present in your writing the methods you used to arrive at the numbers you are presenting, including the mathematical formulas used or developed to test data, to look for or extend patterns, or to demonstrate causal relationships. Likewise, you may find it helpful, or even required, to use established statistical tests when presenting your quantitative data, so you should familiarize yourself with the computer software available at your institution or required in your field, such as SPSS in psychology and social work and Stata in economics. Make sure your secondary data sources are as up to date as possible and that your statistics are as accurate as possible.

In some disciplines, researchers and experts take sides on which is the best method for research in the field, qualitative versus quantitative. As Faigley and Hansen explain, "In anthropology, for example, physical anthropologists write articles that resemble those of natural scientists while cultural anthropologists sometimes write essays that resemble those of literary scholars" (140). The same is true with majors such as psychology and linguistics, which are often divided along clinical and cultural lines.

When possible, use multiple reliable sources and types of evidence in order to triangulate your data and validate your arguments for your readers. You may often use a combination of both quantitative and qualitative data—for example, percentages that show how many students play intramural sports alongside interview responses from students who play an intramural sport. The most important question to ask (and answer) is this: What kind of evidence is needed to support my claim or to make it persuasive to my intended audience? Of course, you must also present evidence in an ethical manner. Withholding evidence or not giving the full picture because you think it hurts your argument is unethical and presents inaccurate results. This misuse of data will be detrimental in the long run. In addition, you should make sure that the argument you present is clear and logical and is actually supported by the evidence.

Know the Writing and Style Conventions for Social Science Writing

Good writers in the social sciences communicate clearly, are aware of their audience, use complete and thorough research (both primary and secondary), present appropriate and accurate evidence for the goals of the writing, and use the best format for the information and audience. Good social science writing also follows the basic tenets of all good writing, so it is organized, easy to read, grammatically correct, and accurately and correctly documented. In addition, below are some specific conventions you may want to keep in mind when writing for the social sciences:

- Be as objective as possible in your presentation of evidence. Because you are talking about human behaviors, many variables and variations exist and you will not be able to account for all of them. Therefore it is important to use conditional terms as you talk about behaviors, motivations, and causes (e.g., often instead of always, many instead of all, the participants in this study rather than students).
  - Some majors such as psychology ask you to use the passive voice in order to keep the researcher/observer out of the text (e.g., No significant increase in aggressive driving was observed, rather than, *I observed no significant increase in aggressive driving.)*
- Other majors such as communication studies may ask you to use first person and to talk about yourself as a researcher in the field. Make sure you check with your professor about expectations and follow the examples set in the models you read and review for class.
- You will often use quotes from research participants, also referred to as informants, subjects, or even research partners, as evidence in your papers. These may be quotes from interviews, observations, or survey responses. However, you should also explain in your own words how these statements provide evidence for your argument.

> People say and argue things. Books, articles, or even quotes do not.   Likewise, the data or the evidence may indicate something. Be precise with your attribution. For example, *Leibowitz (2008) has argued that gephyrophobia, the fear of bridges, is related to other types of panic disorders. (Not: This essay shows that gephyrophobia, the fear of bridges, is a panic disorder.)*

- Always link your evidence, whether participant quotes, statistical data, or secondary sources, to your main argument or thesis. Guide your reader through your argument.
- Avoid biased language that may offend your readers and damage your credibility. Language that makes assumptions or is based on stereotypes about gender, ethnicity, age, mental or physical (dis)ability, or sexual orientation is not effective. In the social sciences, various identity markers may be the very subject you are writing about, making it even more important to be precise with your language and to not make assumptions about groups of people based on these various markers. Look into accepted usage or the appropriateness of a label, term, or expression. In addition, you can often avoid bias or awkward phrasing by using plural forms (e.g., All employees should submit an evaluation form, rather than, *Every employee should submit his or her evaluation form*).

Know the Appropriate Documentation System for Social Science Writing

APA, the documentation style developed by the American Psychological Association, is most often used in the social sciences. It uses an author-date method of documentation for both its in-text citations and its reference list at the end of the document. Put the author's last name and the year of the publication in parentheses within the text as soon as the source is mentioned; this emphasizes the timeliness of the source and lends credibility to the writer. Some majors, areas of study, or journals within the discipline may have their own documentation style guides, so always check to see what is appropriate for your purposes or your assignment.

Some organizations in the social sciences provide writing tips so that their members might better achieve their goals.

14

Documentation Styles Across the Curriculum

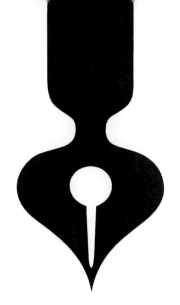

MLA

When you do research to find supporting evidence for your ideas or arguments, you need to credit your outside sources. Depending on what type of essay you are writing or which type of course you are writing for, you will need to choose a documentation style and continue with that style for the entire essay. Two of the most common styles, especially for freshman and sophomore students, are MLA (Modern Language Association) and APA (American Psychological Association).

If you write in composition, language, linguistics, and literature courses, you will often be asked to use documentation guidelines created by the Modern Language Association (MLA). The MLA Handbook for Writers of Research Papers, in its seventh edition, provides a full description of the conventions used by this particular community of writers. Updates to the MLA Handbook can be found at www.mla.org.

MLA guidelines require that you give both an in-text citation and a Works Cited entry for any and all sources you use. Using accurate in-text citations helps guide your reader to the appropriate entry in the Works Cited. For example, the in-text citation given below in parentheses directs the reader to the correct page of the book listed in the Works Cited.

In-text citation

The beam of a bridge can be made simply (Cortright 2).

Entry in Works Cited

Cortright, Robert S. *Bridging the World*. Wilsonville, Oregon: Bridge Ink Publishing, 2003. Print.

This section provides a general overview of MLA documentation style and an explanation of the most commonly used MLA documentation formats, including a few significant revisions since the previous edition of the MLA guidelines.

Using MLA In-Text Citations

In-text citations (also called parenthetical citations) point readers to where they can find more information about your researched supporting materials. When you use MLA documentation style, you need to indicate the author's last name and the location of the source material (page or paragraph number). Where this in-text information is placed depends on how you want to phrase the sentence that is summarized, paraphrased, or quoted. Be sure that the in-text citation guides the reader clearly to the source in the Works Cited, where complete information about the source is given.

The following are some of the most common examples of parenthetical citations.

1. Author's name in text

When using a parenthetical reference to a single source that is already named in the sentence, put the page number in parentheses at the end of the sentence before the period. Note that the period goes after the parentheses.

> Jean Holder (2010) discusses the problems associated with owning airlines in Jamaica: "We don't want to burn bridges" (63).

2. Author's name in reference

When the author's name is not included in the preceding sentence, put the author's last name and the page number in parentheses at the end of the sentence before the period. Note that there is no comma between the name and date in an MLA parenthetical reference, and also note that the period comes at the end of the sentence after the parentheses.

> There are potential issues associated with owning airlines in Jamaica (Holder 63).

3. No author given

When a work has no credited author, use a clipped version of the work's title.

> In a recent *Time* article, a list of 15 most popular bridges locates 10 bridges in the United States ("Popular Bridges").

4. Two or three authors given

When you use a source that was written by two or three authors, use all the names in the text of the sentence or in the citation.

> The Golden Gate Bridge is "unquestionably an American icon" (McDonald and Nadel 7).

> According to Proske and van Gelder, "bridges, as physical features, already existed for millions of years, created from geological formations by wind and water" (1).

5. Four or more authors given

MLA documentation style offers a choice when an item to be cited has four or more authors. You can either name all the authors or include only the first author's name followed by et al. (Latin for "and others").

> A variety of groups have been working together to "bridge the science and practice of the field of bereavement" and to use dialogue to close the divide between the two (Neimeyer, Harris, Winokuer, Thornton).

A variety of groups have been working together to "bridge the science and practice of the field of bereavement" and to use dialogue to close the divide between the two (Neimeyer, et al.).

6. Authors with the same last names

If your source material includes items by authors who happen to have the same last name, be sure to use each author's first name or initial in the parentheses.

> The history of bridges stretches back to the 13th century BC (S. Jones 63).

> Bridges can occur in nature (B. Jones 114).

7. Encyclopedia or dictionary unsigned entry

When you use an encyclopedia or dictionary to look up a word or entry, be sure to include the word or entry title in the parenthetical entry.

> According to *The Oxford English Dictionary*, the card game of Bridge was first referenced in the 1800s ("bridge").

8. Lines of verse (plays, poetry, or song lyrics)

For plays, give the act, scene, and line numbers that are located in any edition of the play. Separate the act, scene, and line numbers with periods. For example, the quotation below comes from *Much Ado About Nothing*, Act I, Scene 1, lines 255 and 256. The MLA also advises using this method with biblical chapters and verses. Be sure, though, that the sequence goes from largest unit to smallest unit.

> Don Pedro responds to Claudio by saying, "What need the bridge much broader than the flood?/The fairest grant is the necessity" (1.1.255-256).

Use a slash (/) to signify line breaks when you quote poetry or song lyrics, and put line numbers in the in-text citation instead of page numbers.

> Simon and Garfunkel famously sang about friendship, "I'm on your side/When times get rough/And friends just can't be found/Like a bridge over troubled water/I will lay me down" (5-9).

9. Indirect quotation

When you use a quotation of a quotation—that is, a quotation that quotes from another source—use the term "qtd. in" to designate the source.

> Smith has said, "I have always had an affinity toward bridges" (qtd. in Jones, par. 8).

Using Long or Block Quotations

Long or block quotations have special formatting requirements of their own.

1. Block quote of prose

If you quote a chunk of prose that is longer than four typed lines, you are using what is called a block quotation. Follow these MLA guidelines for block quotations:

1. If introducing the block quotation with a sentence, use a colon at the end of the sentence.
2. Begin the quotation on a new line.
3. Do not use quotation marks to enclose the block quote.

4. Indent the quote one inch from the left margin, but use the same right margin as the rest of the text.
5. Double space the entire quotation.
6. Put a period at the end of the quotation, and then add the parenthetical citation.

In an interview, Bridges explained:

> A large part of acting is just pretending. You get to work with these other great make-believers, all making believe as hard as they can. What I learned most from my father wasn't anything he said; it was just the way he behaved. He loved his work so much that, whenever he came on set, he brought that with him, and other people rose to it. (72)

2. Block quote of poetry, drama, or song lyrics

For songs and poems, be sure to give line numbers rather than page numbers and to use the original line breaks.

Simon and Garfunkel famously sang about the power of friendship:

> I'm on your side
> When times get rough
> And friends just can't be found
> Like a bridge over troubled water
> I will lay me down (5-9).

Adding or Omitting Words in a Quotation

1. When adding words to a quotation, use [square brackets] to point out words or phrases that are not part of the original text.

Original quotation: "When we entered the People's Republic of China, we noticed that the bridges were unique."

Quotation with added word: She said, "When we entered the People's Republic of China, [Dunkirk and I] noticed that the bridges were unique" (Donelson 141).

You can also add your own comments inside a quotation by using square brackets. For example, you can add the word *sic* to a quotation when you know that there is an error.

Original quotation: "When we entered the People's Repulic of China, we noticed that the bridges were unique."

Quotation with added comment: She said, "When we entered the People's Repulic [*sic*] of China, we noticed that the bridges were unique" (Donelson 141).

Omitting words in a quotation

Use an ellipsis (...) to represent words that you deleted from a quotation. The ellipsis begins with a space, then has three periods with spaces between them, and then ends with a space.

Original quotation: "As it stretches across the Golden Gate from San Francisco to Marin County, the bridge, with its suspended arc and majestic towers, dominates but does not overpower its natural setting."

Quotation with words omitted in middle of sentence: Donald McDonald and Ira Nadel, authors of *Golden Gate Bridge: History and Design of an Icon*, remark, "As it stretches across the Golden Gate from San Francisco to Marin County, the bridge . . . dominates but does not overpower its natural setting" (6).

If you omit words at the end of a quotation from a source and the sentence has a parenthetical citation at the end, use an ellipsis with no space before the ellipsis, then the quotation mark with no space before it, and then the parenthetical before ending the sentence with a period.

Original quotation: "As it stretches across the Golden Gate from San Francisco to Marin County, the bridge, with its suspended arc and majestic towers, dominates but does not overpower its natural setting."

Quotation with words omitted at end of sentence when there is also a parenthetical at the end of the sentence: Donald McDonald and Ira Nadel, authors of *Golden Gate Bridge: History and Design of an Icon*, remark, "As it stretches across the Golden Gate from San Francisco to Marin County, the bridge, with its suspended arc and majestic towers, dominates but does not overpower. . . " (6).

Citing Online Sources

In the MLA documentation style, online or electronic sources have their own formatting guidelines since these types of sources rarely give specific page numbers.

The MLA recommends that you include in the text, rather than in an in-text citation, the name of the person (e.g., author, editor, director, performer) that begins the matching Works Cited entry. For instance, the following is the recommended way to begin an in-text citation for an online source:

In a review of the film *Bridge to Terabithia,* Catsoulis says that the acting is "spectacular and the characters are enchanting" (par. 8).

If the author or creator of the website uses paragraph or page numbers, use these numbers in the parenthetical citation. If no numbering is used, do not use or add numbers to the paragraphs, pages, or parenthetical citation.

When the website does not number paragraphs:

In a review of the film *Bridge to Terabithia*, Catsoulis says that the acting is "spectacular and the characters are enchanting."

When the website numbers paragraphs:

In a review of the film *Bridge to Terabithia*, Catsoulis says that the acting is "spectacular and the characters are enchanting" (par. 8).

General Formatting Guidelines for the MLA Works Cited

If you cite any sources within a paper, be sure to include a Works Cited at the end of the paper. Here are some general formatting guidelines to follow when setting up a Works Cited.

1. Put the Works Cited at the end of your paper as a separate page.
2. Use one-inch margins on all sides.
3. Include any header used for the paper on the Works Cited.
4. Center the title Works Cited at the top of the page, using no underlining, quotation marks, or italics.

5. Place the first line of each entry flush left with the margin. Indent any additional lines of the entry one-half inch (or one tab).
6. Double-space the entries in the Works Cited; don't add any extra spaces between entries.
7. Alphabetize the Works Cited. Use the first major word in each entry, not including articles such as *a, an,* or *the,* to determine the alphabetical order. If the cited source does not have an author, alphabetize by using the first word of the title of the source.
8. Put author's last name first (e.g., Ebert, Roger). Use this reverse order (last name, then first) only for the first author's name. If there is more than one author, follow the first author's name with a comma, and add the other author names in the order of first then last names (e.g., Ebert, Roger, and Gene Siskel).
9. Use hyphens in place of the author's name for the second and subsequent works by the same author. Alphabetize the titles, use the author's full name for the first entry, and then use three hyphens to replace the author's name in all entries after the first.
10. Capitalize all words in titles except for articles, conjunctions, and short prepositions. Always capitalize the first word of a subtitle.
11. Use quotation marks for titles of shorter works, including articles, book chapters, episodes on television or radio, poems, and short stories.
12. Italicize the titles of longer works, including album or CD titles, art pieces, books, films, journals, magazines, newspapers, and television shows.
13. Give the edition number for works with more than one edition (e.g., *MLA Handbook for Writers of Research Papers*, 7th edition).
14. Use the word *Print* after print sources and *Web* for Internet or Web sources.

Formats for Print Sources

1. Books (includes brochures, pamphlets, and graphic novels)

Author's Name. *Title of Book*. Place of publication: Publisher, date of publication. Print.

> Holder, Jean. *Don't Burn our Bridges: The Case for Owning Airlines*. Jamaica: University of West Indies Press, 2010. Print.

2. Books with two or more authors

A comma is used between the author names, even if there are only two authors.
First Author's Name, and second Author's Name. *Title of Book*. Place of publication: Publisher, date of publication. Print.

> Dupre, Judith, and Frank O. Gehry. *Bridges: A History of the World's Most Famous and Important Spans*. New York: Black Dog & Leventhal Publishers, 1997. Print.

3. Two books by the same author

Use three hyphens and a period in place of the author name in the consecutive entries. Be sure the entries are in alphabetical order.

> McCullough, David. *The Epic Story of the Building of the Brooklyn Bridge*. New York: Simon & Schuster, 1983. Print.

> ---. *The Path Between the Seas: The Creation of the Panama Canal*, 1870-1914. New York: Simon & Schuster, 1978. Print.

4. Anthology or collection

Editor's Name(s), ed. *Title of Book*. Place of publication: Publisher, date. Print.

> Hummel, Heather, ed. *Bridges: An Anthology*. New York: PathBinder Publishing, 2008. Print.

5. Work within an anthology

Author's Name."Title of Work." *Title of Anthology*. Ed. Editor's Name(s). Place of publication: Publisher, date. Pages. Print.

> Schwartz, Susan E.B. "Gracie's First Multi-Pitch." *Bridges: An Anthology*. Ed. Heather Hummel. New York: PathBinder Publishing, 2008. 1-6. Print.

6. Article in a scholarly journal

Author's Name. "Title of the Article." *Journal Title* vol. number (date of publication): pages. Print.

> Adam, M.D., and J.P. Hayes "Use of Bridges as Night Roosts by Bats in the Oregon Coast Range." *Journal of Mammalogy* 81.2 (2000): 402-407. Print.

7. Article in a scholarly journal that uses only issue numbers

Author's Name. "Title of the Article." *Journal Title* issue number (date of publication): pages. Print.

> Clark, Robert. "A Tale of Two Bridges: Dangerous and Still Standing." *Leadership and Management in Engineering* 4 (Oct. 2008): 186-190. Print.

8. Article in a newspaper

Author's Name. "Title of Article." *Newspaper Title* Day Month Year: pages. Print.
Note: When citing English language newspapers, use the name on the masthead but be sure to omit any introductory article (*New York Times*, not *The New York Times*).

> Maeder, Jay. "In the Naming of a Bridge, a Lesson in Democracy Foiled." *New York Times* 18 Feb. 2011: 26. Print.

9. Article in a magazine

Author's Name. "Title of Article." *Magazine Title* Day Month Year: pages. Print.
Note: Use the day only if the magazine is published on a weekly or bi-weekly basis.

> Bukota, George. "Big Bridges; Local Spans Expanding and Receiving Facelifts." *Northwest Construction* 1 May 2004: 25. Print.

10. Review

Reviewer's Name. "Title of Review." Rev. of Title of Work, by name of author (editor, director, etc.). Journal or Newspaper Title Day Month Year: pages. Print.

> Holden, Stephen. "That Beautiful but Deadly San Francisco Span." Rev. of *The Bridge*, by Dir. Eric Steel. *New York Times* 27 Oct. 2006: E11. Print.

11. Article in a reference book

Author's Name. "Title of Article." *Title of Reference Book*. Ed. Editor's Name. Location: Publisher, date. Pages. Print.

> "Bridge." *New American Webster Handy College Dictionary*. Ed. Philip D. Morehead. New York: Signet, 2006. 99. Print.

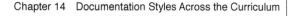

12. Religious works

Title of Work. Ed. Editor's Name. Place of publication: Publisher, date. Print.

> *Zondervan NIV Study Bible*. Fully rev. ed. Ed. Kenneth L. Barker. Grand Rapids, MI: Zondervan, 2002. Print.

Formats for Online Sources

1. Web publications

Author's Name (if author given). *Name of Page*. Name of institution or organization associated with the website. Date of posting/revision. Web. Date of access.

> *Services Locator*. United States Post Office. 2010. Web. 9 Feb. 2010.

2. Article on a website (including blogs and wikis)

Author's Name. "Article Title." *Name of website*. Name of institution or organization associated with the website. Date of posting/revision. Web. Date of access.
Note: If no author's name is given, begin the citation with the article title.

> "Building Big: Bridge Basics." PBS. 2001. Web. 9 Feb. 2012.

> Lamb, Robert and Michael Morrissey. "How Bridges Work." *HowStuffWorks.com*. 1 April 2000. Web. 9 Feb. 2012.

3. Online newspaper or magazine

Author's Name. " Title of Article." *Newspaper Title*. Day Month Year: pages. Web. Date of access.

> Eckholm, Erik. "Covered Bridges, Beloved Remnants of Another Era, Were Casualties, Too." *The New York Times* 2011: A20. Web. 9 Feb. 2012.

4. Online journal article

Author's Name. "Title of Article." *Title of Journal* Vol. Issue (Year): pages. Web. Date of access.

> Adam, M.D. and J.P. Hayes. "Use of Bridges as Night Roosts by Bats in the Oregon Coast Range." *Journal of Mammalogy* 81.2 (2000): 402-407. Web.

5. Article from an online service, such as General One- File or LexisNexis

Author's Name. "Title of the Article." *Journal Title* vol. issue (Date of publication): pages. Name of database or other relevant information. *Access Provider*. Web. Date of access.

> Starossek, Uwe. "Avoiding Disproportionate Collapse of Major Bridges." *Structural Engineering International* 19.3 (2009): 289-97. *ProQuest*. Michigan State University. Web. 9 Feb. 2012.

6. Article from an online reference work

Author's (or editor's) Name. "Title of Article." *Title of Reference Work*. Location, Date of publication (Day Month Year). Web. Date of access (Day Month Year).

> Alder, Phillip and Albert H. Morehead. "Bridge." *Encyclopedia Britannica*, 2012. Web. 2 Feb. 2012.

Formats for Other Commonly Used Sources

1. Television or radio program

"Title of Episode or Segment." *Title of Program or Series*. Name of network. Call letters and city of the local station (if applicable). Broadcast date. Medium of reception (e.g., Radio, Television). Supplemental information (e.g., Transcript).

> "Lost and Found." *Nash Bridges*. CBS. WSFO, San Francisco, CA. 19 Sept. 1997. Television.

2. Sound recording

Artist/Band. "Song Title." *Title of Album*. Manufacturer, year of issue. Medium (e.g., Audiocassette, CD, Audiotape, LP, Digital download).

> Simon & Garfunkel. "Bridge over Troubled Water." *Bridge over Troubled Water*. Columbia Records, 1969. LP.

3. Film

Title. Dir. Director's Name. Perf. Actor's Name(s) (if relevant). Distributor, year of release. Medium.

> *Quake Proof: Building the Perfect Bridge*. Dir. Dylan Weiss. Ex. Prod. Milt Weiss. Cry Havoc Productions, 2006. Film.

4. Advertisement

Name of product, company, or institution. Advertisement. Publisher date of publication. Medium of publication.

> SunChips. Advertisement. *Newsweek* 15 Jan. 2010: 33. Print.

> SunChips. Advertisement. NBC. 15 Jan. 2010. Television.

> Note the difference in how the citations for print and television advertisements are formatted.

5. Painting, sculpture, or photograph

Artist's Name. *Title*. Creation date (if known). Medium of Composition. Name of institution that houses the work or the individual who owns the work, City.

> da Vinci, Leonardo. *Mona Lisa*. c. 1503-6. Oil on Poplar. Louvre, Paris.

6. Interview

Interviewee's Name. Descriptive Title of Interview (e.g., Personal, Telephone, Webcam). Date of interview.

> Elbow, Peter. Interview. 1 Jan. 2009.

7. Lecture, speech, address, or reading

Author's Name. " Title of Speech." Relevant information of where speech was given. Date of presentation. Descriptive label (e.g., Lecture, Speech, Address, Reading).

> Gibson, Denise D. "Building Bridges: Professional Development Advising Teams." Annual Meeting of the Association of American Medical Colleges, Kansas City, MO. 25 Mar 1999. Address.

Sample Works Cited using MLA

Following is an example of how a completed Works Cited would look at the end of your paper.

Works Cited

Besner, Hilda F., and Charlotte I. Spungin. *Training for Professionals Who work with Gays and Lesbians in Education and Workplace Settings.* Washington D. C.: Accelerated Development, 1998. Print.

Condon, Frankie. "Beyond the Known: Writing Center and the Work of Anti-Racism." *The Writing Center Journal* 27.2 (2007): 19-38. Print.

Fletcher, Anne C., and Stephen T. Russell. "Incorporating Issues of Sexual Orientation in the Classroom: Challenges and Solutions." *Family Relations* 50.1 (2001): 34-40. Print.

Hanks, Janet and Frances Heller. "After the Sock Factory: Collaboration between Generations in the Writing Center." *Inquiry* 4.2 (1999): 62-68. Web. 21 April 2010.

Konstant, Shoshanna Beth. "Multi-sensory Tutoring for Multi-Sensory Learners." *The Writing Lab Newsletter* 16.9/10 (1992): 6-8. Print.

Martin, Patricia Yancey. "'Said and Done' versus 'Saying and Doing': Gendering Practices, Practicing Gender at Work." *Gender and Society* 17.3 (2003): 342-66. Print.

Miritello, Mary. "Teaching Writing to Adults: Examining Assumptions and Revising Expectations for Adult Learners in the Writing Class." *Composition Chronicle: Newsletter for Writing Teachers.* 9.2 (1996): 6-9. Web. 25 April 2010.

Villanueva, Victor. "Blind: Talking about the New Racism." *The Writing Center Journal* 26.1 (2006): 3-19. Print.

Wall, Vernon A., and Nancy J. Evans. *Toward Acceptance: Sexual Orientation Issues on Campus.* Alexandria: American College Personnel Association, 2000. Print.

APA

If you write an essay in the social sciences, you will usually be asked to use documentation guidelines created by the American Psychological Association. *The Publication Manual of the American Psychological Association*, in its sixth edition, provides a full description of the conventions used by this particular community of writers. Updates to the APA manual can be found at www.apastyle.org.

This section provides a general overview of APA documentation style and an explanation of the most commonly used APA documentation formats.

Using APA In-Text Citations

In-text citations (also called parenthetical citations) point readers to where they can find more information about your researched supporting materials. In APA documentation style, the author's last name (or the title of the work if no author is listed) and the date of publication must appear in the body text of your paper. The author's name can appear either in the sentence itself or in parentheses following the quotation or paraphrase. The date of publication can appear either in the sentence itself, surrounded by parentheses, or in the parentheses that follow the quotation or paraphrase. The page number always appears in the parentheses following a quotation or close paraphrase.

Your parenthetical citation should give enough information to identify the source that was used for the research material as the same source that is listed in your References list. Where this in-text information is placed depends on how you want to phrase the sentence that is summarized, paraphrased, or quoted. Be sure that the in-text citation guides the reader clearly to the source in the References list, where complete information about the source is given.

The following are some of the most common examples of in-text citations.

1. Author's name and date in reference

When making a parenthetical reference to a single source by a single author, use parentheses to enclose the author's last name + comma + year of publication. Note that the period is placed after the parenthetical element ends.

> When a teenager sleeps more than 10 hours per night, it is time to question whether she is having significant problems (Jones, 1999).

2. Author's name and date in text

In APA, you can also give the author's name and date within the sentence; write the author's full name and the date of the publication in parentheses.

> Jean Holder (2010) discusses owning airlines in Jamaica.

3. Using a partial quotation in text

When you cite a specific part of a source, give the page number, using p. (for one page) and pp. (for two or more pages).

> Jean Holder (2010) discusses the problems associated with owning airlines in Jamaica: "we don't want to burn bridges" (p. 63).

4. No author given

When a work has no credited author, use the first two or three words of the work's title or the name that begins the entry in the References list. The title of an article or chapter should be in quotation marks, and the title of a book or periodical should be in italics. Inside the parenthetical citation, place a comma between the title and year.

> In a recent *Time* article, a list of the 15 most popular bridges in the world locates 10 bridges in the United States ("Popular Bridges," 2010).

5. Two to five authors given

When you use a source that was written by two to five authors, you must use all the names in the citation. For the in-text citation, when a work has two authors, use both names each time the reference occurs in the text. When a work has three to five authors, give all authors the first time the reference occurs in the text, and then, in subsequent citations, use only the surname of the first author followed by *et al.* (Latin for "and others") and the year for the first citation of the reference in a paragraph.

> The idea that "complexity is a constant in biology" is not an innovative one (Sole & Goodwin, 1997, p. 63).

The last two authors' names in a string of three to five authors are separated by a comma and an ampersand (e.g., Jones, Smith, Black, & White).

> A variety of groups have been working together to "bridge the science and practice of the field of bereavement" and to use dialogue to close the divide between the two (Neimeyer, Harris, Winokuer, & Thornton, 2011, p. 3).

6. Six or more authors given

When an item to be cited has six or more authors, include only the first author's name followed by et al. (Latin for "and others"). Use this form for the first reference of this text and all references to this text after that. Note: be sure, though, to list all six or more of the authors in your References list.

> In Hong Kong, most of the signs on bridges are in Chinese and English; however, once you are in mainland China, English is rarely found on bridge signs, except in tourist areas (Li, et al., 2007).

7. Authors with the same last names

If your source material includes items by authors who happen to have the same last name, be sure to use each author's initials in all text citations.

> The history of bridges stretches back to the 13th century BC (S. Jones, 1999, p. 63).
>
> Bridges can occur in nature (B. Jones, 2003, p. 114).

8. Encyclopedia or dictionary unsigned entry

When you use an encyclopedia or dictionary to look up a word or entry, be sure to include the word or entry title in the parenthetical entry.

> According to *The Oxford English Dictionary,* the card game of Bridge was first referenced in the 1800s ("bridge," 2001).

9. Indirect quotation

When you use a quotation of a quotation—that is, a quotation that quotes from another source—use "as cited in" to designate the secondary source.

> Smith has said, "I have always had an affinity toward bridges" (as cited in Jones, 1990, p. 64).

10. Personal communication

Personal communications—private letters, memos, non-archived e-mails, interviews—are usually considered unrecoverable information and, as such, are not included in the References list. However, you do include them in parenthetical form in the text, giving the initials and surname of the communicator and providing as exact a date as possible.

> A. D. Smith (personal communication, February 2, 2010)
>
> J. Elbow (personal interview, January 6, 2009)

Using Long or Block Quotations

Long or block quotations have special formatting requirements of their own. A prose quotation that is longer than 40 words is called a block quotation. Follow these APA guidelines for block quotations.

1. If introducing the block quotation with a sentence, use a colon at the end of the sentence.
2. Begin the quotation on a new line.
3. Do not use quotation marks to enclose the block quote.
4. Indent the quote five spaces from the left margin, but use the same right margin as the rest of the text.
5. Double space the entire quotation.
6. Indent the first line of any additional paragraph.
7. Put a period at the end of the quotation, and then add the parenthetical citation.

In an interview, Bridges (2007) explained:

> A large part of acting is just pretending. You get to work with these other great make-believers, all making believe as hard as they can. What I learned most from my father wasn't anything he said; it was just the way he behaved. He loved his work so much that, whenever he came on set, he brought that with him, and other people rose to it. (p. 72)

Adding or Omitting Words in a Quotation

1. When adding words in a quotation, use [square brackets] to point out words or phrases that are not part of the original text.

> Original quotation: "When we entered the People's Republic of China, we noticed that the bridges were unique" (Donelson, 2001, p. 141).
>
> Quotation with added word: She said, "When we entered the People's Republic of China, [Dunkirk and I] noticed that the bridges were unique" (Donelson, 2001, p. 141).

You can also add your own comments inside a quotation by using square brackets. For example, you can add the word *sic* to a quotation when you know that there is an error.

> Original quotation: "When we entered the People's Repulic of China, we noticed that the bridges were unique" (Donelson, 2001, p. 141).
>
> Quotation with added comment: She said, "When we entered the People's Repulic [*sic*] of China, we noticed that the bridges were unique" (Donelson, 2001, p. 141).

2. Omitting words in a quotation

Use an ellipsis (. . .) to represent words that you delete from a quotation. The ellipsis begins with a space, then has three periods with spaces between them, and then ends with a space.

> Original quotation: "As it stretches across the Golden Gate from San Francisco to Marin County, the bridge, with its suspended arc and majestic towers, dominates but does not overpower its natural setting" (McDonald & Nadel, 2008, p. 6).
>
> Quotation with words omitted in middle of sentence: Donald McDonald and Ira Nadel, authors of *Golden Gate Bridge: History and Design of an Icon*, remark, "As it stretches across the Golden Gate from San Francisco to Marin County, the bridge . . . dominates but does not overpower its natural setting" (2008, p. 6).

If you omit words at the end of a quotation, and that is also the end of your sentence, you should use an ellipsis plus a period with no space before the ellipsis or after the period. Use an ellipsis only if words have been omitted.

> Original quotation: "As it stretches across the Golden Gate from San Francisco to Marin County, the bridge, with its suspended arc and majestic

towers, dominates but does not overpower its natural setting" (McDonald & Nadel, 2008, p. 6).

Quotation with words omitted at end of sentence: Donald McDonald and Ira Nadel, authors of *Golden Gate Bridge: History and Design of an Icon*, remark, "As it stretches across the Golden Gate from San Francisco to Marin County, the bridge, with its suspended arc and majestic towers, dominates but does not overpower. . . ." (2008, p. 6).

Citing Online Sources

In the APA documentation style, online or electronic sources have their own formatting guidelines since these types of sources rarely give specific page numbers.

The APA recommends that you include in the text, rather than in an in-text citation, the name of the person that begins the matching References list entry. If the author or creator of the website uses paragraph or page numbers, use these numbers in the parenthetical citation. If no numbering is used, do not use or add numbers to the paragraphs, pages, or parenthetical citation.

When the website does not number paragraphs:

> In a review of the film *Bridge to Terabithia*, Catsoulis says that the acting is "spectacular and the characters are enchanting."

When the website numbers paragraphs:

> In a review of the film *Bridge to Terabithia*, Catsoulis says that the acting is "spectacular and the characters are enchanting" (para. 8).

General Formatting Guidelines for the APA References List

If you cite any sources within a paper, be sure to include a References list at the end of the paper. Below are some general formatting guidelines to follow when setting up a References list.

1. Put the References list at the end of your paper as a separate page.
2. Use one-inch margins on all sides.
3. Include any header used for the paper on the References page.
4. Center the title References at the top of the page, using no underlining, quotation marks, or italics.
5. Place the first line of each entry flush left with the margin. Indent any additional lines of the entry one-half inch (or one tab) to form a hanging indent.
6. Double-space the entries in the References list; do not add any extra spaces between entries.
7. Alphabetize the References list. Use the first major word in each entry, not including articles such as *a, an,* or *the*, to determine the alphabetical order. If the

cited source does not have an author, alphabetize by using the first word of the source's title.

8. Put the author's last name, first initial, and middle initial, if given (e.g., Ebert, R.). If a work has more than one author, invert all the authors' names, follow each with a comma, and then continue listing all the authors, putting a comma and ampersand (, &) before the final name (e.g., Ebert, R., & Siskel, G.).

9. Arrange two or more works by the same authors in the same name order by year of publication.

10. Capitalize only the first word in a title and a subtitle unless the title or subtitle includes a proper noun, which would also be capitalized.

11. Do not use quotation marks for titles of shorter works, including articles, book chapters, episodes on television or radio, poems, and short stories.

12. Italicize the titles of longer works, including album or CD titles, art pieces, books, films, journals, magazines, newspapers, and television shows.

13. Give the edition number for works with more than one edition [e.g., Publication manual of the American Psychological Association (6th ed.)].

14. Include the DOI (digital object identifier), a unique alpha-numeric string assigned by a registration agency that helps identify content and provides a link to the source online. All DOI numbers begin with a 10 and contain a prefix and suffix separated by a slash (for example, 10.11037/0278-6133.27.3.379). The DOI is usually found in the citation detail or on the first page of an electronic journal article near the copyright notice. See example on the following page.

Formats for Print Sources

1. Books (includes brochures, pamphlets, and graphic novels)

Author's last name, Author's initial of first name. (Year of publication). *Title of book.* Place of publication: Publisher.

> Holder, Jean. (2010). *Don't burn our bridges: The case for owning airlines.* Jamaica: University of West Indies Press.

2. Books with two or more authors

A comma is used between the author names, even if there are only two authors.

First Author's Last name, First author's Initial of first name, & Second author's Last name, Second author's Initial of first name. (Year of publication). *Title of book.* Place of publication: Publisher.

> Dupre, J., & Gehry, F. (1997). *Bridges: A history of the world's most famous and important spans.* New York: Black Dog & Leventhal Publishers.

Indexing Details

Title:

An Ability Traitor at Work: A Treasonous Call to Subvert Writing From Within.

Authors:

Holbrook, Teri[1] *tholbrook@gsu.edu*

Source:

Qualitative Inquiry; Mar2010, Vol. 16 Issue 3, p171-183, 13p

Document Type:

Article

Subject Terms:

*DISABILITIES

*QUALITATIVE research

*MANAGEMENT science

*WRITING

Author-Supplied Keywords:

assemblage

disability

multimodal writing

NAICS/Industry Codes:

541930 Translation and Interpretation Services

Abstract:

In questioning conventional qualitative research methods, St. Pierre asked, "What else might *writing* do except mean?" The author answers, it oppresses. Co-opting the race traitor figurative, she calls on qualitative researchers to become "ability traitors" who interrogate how a valuable coinage of their trade—the written word—is used to rank and categorize individuals with troubling effects. In this article, she commits three betrayals: (a) multigenre *writing* that undermines the authoritative text; (b) assemblage as a method of analysis that deprivileges the written word; and (c) a gesture toward a dis/comfort text intended to take up Lather's example of challenging the "usual ways of making sense." In committing these betrayals, the author articulates her "traitorous agenda" designed to interrogate assumptions about inquiry, power, equity, and *writing* as practice-as-usual. [ABSTRACT FROM AUTHOR]

Author Affiliations:

[1]Georgia State University

ISSN:

10778004

DOI:

10.1177/1077800409351973

Accession Number:

47934623

Database:

Academic Search Premier

View Links:

Find Fulltext

3. Two books by the same author

Be sure the entries are in sequential time order with earliest date first.
McCullough, D. (1978). *The path between the seas: the creation of the Panama Canal, 1870-1914*. New York: Simon & Schuster.

McCullough, D. (1983). *The epic story of the building of the Brooklyn Bridge*. New York: Simon & Schuster.

4. Anthology or collection

Editor's Last name, Editor's Initial of first name. (Ed). (Year of publication). *Title of book*. Place of publication: Publisher.

Hummel, H. (Ed.). (2008). *Bridges: An anthology*. New York: PathBinder Publishing.

5. Article in a scholarly journal without DOI (digital object identifier)

Include the issue number if the journal is paginated by issue. If there is no DOI available and the article was found online, give the URL of the journal home page.
Author's Last name, Author's Initial of first name. (Year of publication). Title of the article. *Journal Title, volume number* (issue number), pages. URL (if retrieved online).

Adam, M.D. & Hayes, J.P. (2000). Use of bridges as night roosts by bats in the Oregon coast range. *Journal of Mammalogy*, 81(2), 402-407. Retrieved from E-Journals database.

6. Article in a scholarly journal with DOI (digital object identifier)

Author's Last name, Author's Initial of first name. (Year of publication). Title of the article. *Journal Title, volume number* (issue number), pages. DOI:

Clark, R. (2008). A tale of two bridges: dangerous and still standing. *Leadership and Management in Engineering*, 4, 186-190. DOI: 10.1061/(ASCE)1532-6748(2008)8:4(186)

7. Article in a newspaper

Use p. or pp. before the page numbers in references of newspapers.
Author's Last name, Author's Initial of first name. (Year of publication, Month and Date of publication). Title of article. *Newspaper Title*, pp. page numbers.

Maeder, J. (2011, February 18). In the naming of a bridge, a lesson in democracy foiled. *The New York Times*, p. 18.

Note: If the newspaper article appears on discontinuous pages, be sure to give all the page numbers, separating them with a comma (e.g., pp. A4, A10, A13–14).

8. Article in a magazine

Author's Last name, Author's Initial of first name. (Year of publication, Month of publication). Title of article. *Magazine Title, volume number* (issue number), pages.

Bukota, George. (2004, May). Big bridges; local spans expanding and receiving facelifts. *Northwest Construction, 13*(11), 25.

Note: Use the day only if the magazine is published on a weekly or bi-weekly basis.

9. Review

Be sure to identify the type of work being reviewed by noting if it is a book, film, television program, painting, song, or other creative work. If the work is a book, include the author name(s) after the book title, separated by a comma. If the work is a film, song, or other media, be sure to include the year of release after the title of the work, separated by a comma.

Reviewer's Last name, Reviewer's Initial of first name. (Year of publication, Month and Date of Publication). Title of review [Review of the *Title of work*, by Author's Name]. *Magazine or Journal Title, volume number* (issue number), pp. page numbers. DOI number (if available).

Holden, S. (2006, Oct. 27). That beautiful but deadly San Francisco span. [Review of the film *The Bridge*, 2006]. *The New York Times*, pp. E11.

11. Article in a reference book

Author's Last name, Author's Initial of first name. (Year of publication). Title of chapter or entry. In A. Editor (Ed). *Title of book* (pp. xx-xx). Location: Publisher.

Jones, A. (2006). Bridge. In P. Morehead (Ed.). *New American Webster Handy College Dictionary* (pp. 99). New York: Signet.

Formats for Online Sources

1. Website

The documentation form for a website can also be used for online message, blog, or video posts.

Author's Last name, Author's Initial of first name (if author given). (Year, Month Day). *Title of page* [Description of form]. Retrieved from http://www.xxxx

United States Post Office (2010). United States Post Office Services Locator [search engine]. Retrieved from http://usps.whitepages.com/post_office

2. Article from a website, online newspaper, blog, or wiki (with author given)

Author's Last name, Author's Initial of first name. (Year, Month Day of publication). Title of article. *Name of webpage/Journal/Newspaper.* Retrieved from http://www.xxxxxxx

Catsoulis, J. (2007, February 16). Bridge to Terabithia: Transcending pain, a friendship fed on imagination. *The New York Times.* Retrieved from http://movies.nytimes.com/2007/02/16/movies/

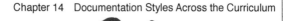

3. Article from a website, online newspaper, blog, or wiki (with no author given)

Title of article. (Year, Month Day of publication). *Name of webpage/Journal/Newspaper*. Retrieved from http://www.xxxxxxx

> Building Big: Bridge Basics. (2001, October). PBS. Retrieved from http://www.pbs.org/wgbh/buildingbig/bridge/basics.html

4. Online journal article

The reference for an online journal article is set up the same way as for a print one, including the DOI.
Author's Last name, Author's Initial of first name. (Year of publication). Title of the article. *Journal Title, volume number* (issue number), pages. doi:xxxxxxxxxxx

> Clark, R. (2008). A tale of two bridges: dangerous and still standing. *Leadership and Management in Engineering*, 4, 186-190. DOI: 10.1061/(ASCE)1532-6748(2008)8:4(186)

If a DOI is not assigned to content you have retrieved online, use the home page URL for the journal or magazine in the reference (e.g., Retrieved from http://www.xxxxxx).

> Adam, M.D., Hayes, J.P. (2000). Use of bridges as night roosts by bats in the Oregon coast range. *Journal of Mammalogy 81*(2), 402-407. Retrieved from http://www.asmjournals.org/

5. Article from an online service, such as General One- File, LexisNexis, JSTOR, ERIC

When using APA, it is not necessary to include database information as long as you can include the publishing information required in a normal citation. Note: this is quite different from using MLA documentation, which requires full information about the database.

6. Article in an online reference work

Author's Last name, Author's Initial of first name. (Year of publication). Title of chapter or entry. In A. Editor (Ed) *Title of book*. Retrieved from http://xxxxxxxxxx

> Alder, P. & Morehead, A. (2012). Bridge. *Encyclopedia Britannica*. Retrieved from http://www.britannica.com/EBchecked/topic/79272/bridge

Formats for Other Commonly Used Sources

1. Television or radio program (single episode)

Writer's Last name, Writer's Initial of first name. (Writer), & Director's Last name, Director's Initial of first name. (Director). (Year). Title of episode [Television/Radio series episode]. In Executive Producer's name (Executive Producer), *Title of show*. Place: Network.

> Cruse, C. (Writer), Cruse, C. (Creator), & Nimoy, A (Director). (1997). Lost and found [Television series episode]. In C. Carter (Executive Producer), *Nash Bridges*. San Francisco, CA: CBS.

2. Sound recording

Writer's Last name, Writer's Initial of first name. (Copyright year). Title of song. [Recorded by Artist's name if different from writer]. On *Title of album* [Medium of recording]. Location: Label. (Date of recording if different from song copyright date).

> Simon, P. (1969). Bridge over troubled water. [Recorded by Paul Simon and Art Garfunkel]. On *Bridge over troubled water* [LP]. Location: Columbia Records.

3. Film

Producer's Last name, Producer's Initial of first name. (Producer), & Director's Last name, Director's Initial of first name. (Director). (Year). *Title of film* [Motion picture]. Country of Origin: Studio.

> Weiss, M. (Producer), & Weiss, D. (Director). (2006). *Quake proof: building the perfect bridge* [film]. USA: Cry Havoc Productions.

4. Painting, sculpture, or photograph

Artist's Last name, Artist's Initial of first name. (Year, Month Day). *Title of material*. [Description of material]. Name of collection (if available). Name of Repository, Location.

> Gainsborough, T. (1745). *Conversation in a park*. [Oil painting on canvas]. Louvre, Paris, France.

5. Personal interview

Unlike MLA documentation, personal interviews and other types of personal communication are not included in APA References lists. Be sure to cite personal communications in the text only.

6. Lecture, speech, address, or reading

Speaker's Last name, Speaker's Initial of first name. (Year, Month). Title of speech. *Event name*. Lecture conducted from Sponsor, Location.

> Gibson, D. (1999, March). Building bridges: professional development advising teams. *Annual meeting of the Association of American Medical Colleges*. Address conducted from Kansas City, MO.

Sample References List Using APA

Following is an example of how a completed References list would look at the end of your paper.

References

Jackson, T., & Chen, H. (2011). Risk factors for disordered eating during early and

middle adolescence: Prospective evidence from mainland Chinese boys and

girls [Electronic version]. *Journal of Abnormal Psychology, 120*(2), 454-464.

Klump, K. L., Suisman, J. L., Burt, S. A., McGue, M., & Iacono, W. G. (2009).

Genetic and environmental influences on disordered eating: An adoption

study [Electronic version]. *Journal of Abnormal Psychology, 118*(4), 797-805.

Mash, E. J. & Wolfe, D. A. (2010). Eating disorders and related conditions. In

Abnormal child psychology (4th ed., chap. 13). Belmont, CA: Wadsworth

Publishing.

McVey, G. L., Pepler, D., Davis, R., Flett, G. L., & Abdolell, M. (2002). Risk

and protective factors associated with disordered eating during early

adolescence [Electronic version]. *The Journal of Early Adolescence, 22*(1),

75-95.

Stice, E., Shaw, H., Burton, E., & Wade, E. (2006). Dissonance and healthy weight

eating disorder prevention programs: A randomized efficacy trial [Electronic

version]. *Journal of Consulting and Clinical Psychology, 74*(2), 263-275.

Striegel-Moore, R. H., & Bulik, C. M. (2007). Risk factors for eating disorders

[Electronic version]. *American Psychologist, 62*(3), 181-198.

Wilksch, S. M., & Wade, T. D. (2010). Risk factors for clinically significant

importance of shape and weight in adolescent girls [Electronic version].

Journal of Abnormal Psychology, 119 (1), 206-215.

CMS

Instructors in a wide variety of disciplines may require you to use documentation guidelines created by the University of Chicago Press. *The Chicago Manual of Style* (CMS), in its 16th edition, provides a full description of the conventions used by this particular community of writers. Updates to the Chicago manual can be found at www.chicagomanuelofstyle.org.

Chicago documentation style uses two different systems: the notes-bibliography system (NB) is usually used by those in literature, history, and the arts; the author-date system, which is similar in content but different in form, is often used by the social sciences, particularly history.

When using NB, each time a source is used you must have a note (endnote or footnote). Footnotes are listed at the bottom of each page and endnotes come at the end of the document. The first time a source is used, a full citation must be included in the note (author's full name, title of document, relevant publication information). The next time that source is used in the document, a shorter version of the citation is needed. If a source is cited with the same page numbers more than twice in a row, each consecutive citation should read "Ibid." If the source is the same but the page number is different, use: "Ibid., new page numbers".

When using the author-date system, each time a source is used you must have an in-text citation. The author's last name (or the title of the work, if no author is listed) and the date of publication must appear in the body text of your paper. The author's name can appear either in the sentence itself or in parentheses following the quotation or paraphrase. The date of publication can appear either in the sentence itself, surrounded by parentheses, or in the parentheses that follow the quotation or paraphrase. The page number(s) always appears in the parentheses following a quotation or close paraphrase.

Your parenthetical citation should give enough information to identify the source that was used for the research material as the same source that is listed in your References list. Where this in-text information is placed depends on how you want to phrase the sentence that is summarized, paraphrased, or quoted. Be sure that the in-text citation guides the reader clearly to the source in the References list, where complete information about the source is given.

The following are some of the most common examples of Note and Bibliography entries.

Formats for Print Sources

1. Books (includes brochures, pamphlets, and graphic novels)
Footnote or Endnote (N):

> 1. Firstname Lastname, *Title of Book* (Place of publication: Publisher, Year of publication), page number.

> 1. Jean Holder, *Don't Burn our Bridges: The Case for Owning Airlines* (Jamaica: University of West Indies Press, 2010), 43.

Bibliography entry (B):

> Lastname, Firstname. *Title of Book*. Place of publication: Publisher, Year of publication.

> Holder, Jean. *Don't Burn our Bridges: The Case for Owning Airlines*. Jamaica: University of West Indies Press, 2010.

2. Books with two or more authors

N:

> 1. Judith Dupre and Frank O. Gehry, *Bridges: A History of the World's Most Famous and Important Spans*. (New York: Black Dog & Leventhal Publishers, 1997), 122.

B:

> Dupre, Judith, and Frank O. Gehry. *Bridges: A History of the World's Most Famous and Important Spans*. New York: Black Dog & Leventhal Publishers, 1997.

3. Translated work with one author

N:

> 1. Tadaki Kawada, *History of the Modern Suspension Bridge*, trans. Richard Scott (Virginia: American Society of Engineers, 2010), 156.

B:

> Kawada, Tadaki. *History of the Modern Suspension Bridge*. Translated by Richard Scott. Reston, Virgina: American Society of Engineers, 2010.

4. Article in a scholarly journal

Citations for journal articles should include author's name, title of document, journal title, and issue information (volume, issue number, month, year, page numbers). Retrieval information and date of access are required for online documents.

N:

> 1. Robert Clark, "A Tale of Two Bridges: Dangerous and Still Standing," *Leadership and Management in Engineering* 4, no. 3 (2008): 186.

B:

> Clark, Robert. "A Tale of Two Bridges: Dangerous and Still Standing." *Leadership and Management in Engineering* 4, no. 3 (2008): 186–194.

5. Article in a scholarly journal online

Online journal articles are cited the same as printed articles with one addition: online articles need to include either a DOI or URL.

N:

> 1. M. D. Adam and J.P. Hayes, "Use of Bridges as Night Roosts by Bats in the Oregon Coast Range," *Journal of Mammology* 81, no. 2 (2000): 402–407.

B:

> Adam, M.D., and Hayes, J.P. "Use of Bridges as Night Roosts by Bats in the Oregon Coast Range." *Journal of Mammalogy* 81, no. 2 (2000): 402-407. Accessed January 7, 2012. http://www.asmjournals.org/.

6. Article in a newspaper

In the names of newspapers, the word the is left out of the citation. Include the city of publication for less well-known newspapers. Headlines can be written either with all the major words capitalized or with just the first word and proper nouns capitalized (the first option is recommended).

N:

> 1. Jay Maeder, "In the Naming of a Bridge, a Lesson in Democracy Foiled," *New York Times,* (NY), Feb. 18, 2011.

B:

> Maeder, Jay. "In the Naming of a Bridge, a Lesson in Democracy Foiled." *New York Times*, (NY), Feb. 18, 2011.

7. Article in a magazine

Include author, article title, magazine name, date, page number.

N:

> 1. George Bukota, "Big Bridges; Local Spans Expanding and Receiving Facelifts," *Northwest Construction,* May 2004, 25.

B:

> Bukota, George. "Big Bridges; Local Spans Expanding and Receiving Facelifts." *Northwest Construction,* May 2004.

Formats for Online Sources

1. Web Sources

N:

> 1. Firstname Lastname, "Title of Web Page," *Publishing Organization or Name of Website,* publication date and/or access date, URL.

B:

> Lastname, Firstname. "Title of Web Page." *Publishing Organization or Name of Website*, publication date and/or access date, URL.

2. Article from a website with author and date

N:

> 1. Jeannette Catsoulis, "Bridge to Terabithia: Transcending Pain, a Friendship Fed on Imagination," *New York Times,* last modified February 16, 2007, http://movies.nytimes.com/2007/02/16/movies/.

B:

> Catsoulis, Jeannette. "Bridge to Terabithia: Transcending Pain, a Friendship Fed on Imagination," *New York Times,* last modified February 16, 2007. http://movies.nytimes.com/2007/02/16/movies/.

3. Article from a website with no author or date given

N:

>   1. "Building Big: Bridge Basics," PBS, accessed February 2, 2012, http://www.pbs.org/wgbh/buildingbig/bridge/basics.html.

B:

>   "Building Big: Bridge Basics." PBS. Accessed February 2, 2012. http://www.pbs.org/wgbh/buildingbig/bridge/basics.html.

Formats for Other Commonly Used Sources

1. Television, Film, or Radio Program

N:

>   1. Group, Composer, or Performer, *Title*, Medium, Recording Company or Publisher, Catalog Number, Year of Release.

B:

>   Group, Composer, or Performer. Title. Medium. Recording Company or Publisher, Catalog Number. Year of Release.

N:

>   1. "Lost and Found," *Nash Bridges*, CBS, San Francisco, CA: CBS, September 19, 1997.

B:

>   "Lost and Found." *Nash Bridges*. CBS. San Francisco, CA: CBS, September 19, 1997.

2. Lecture, speech, address, or reading

These citations usually include information including location and date of the meeting, and the sponsoring organization.

N:

>   1. Denise Gibson, "Building Bridges: Professional Development Advising Teams," (presentation, Annual Meeting of the Association of American Medical Colleges, Kansas City, MO, March 1999).

B:

>   Gibson, Denise. "Building Bridges: Professional Development Advising Teams." Presentation at the Annual Meeting of the Association of American Medical Colleges, Kansas City, MO, March 1999.

Sample References List Using CMS

Following is an example of how a completed References list would look at the end of your paper.

Bibliography

Boquet, Elizabeth. "Disciplinary Action: Writing Center Work and the Making of a Researcher." In *Writing Center Research: Extending the Conversation*, edited by Paula Gillespie, Alice Gillam, Lady Falls Brown, and Byron Stay, 23-38. Mahwah, NJ: Lawrence Erlbaum, 2002.

Carino, Peter. "Writing Centers and Writing Programs: Local and Communal Politics." In *The Politics of Writing Centers*, edited by Jane Nelson and Kathy Evertz, 1-14.   Portsmouth, HN: Heinemann, 2001.

Geller, Anne Ellen, Michele Eodice, Frankie Condon, Meg Carroll, and Elizabeth H. Boquet. *The Everyday Writing Center: A Community of Practice*. Logan: Utah State UP, 2007.

Grimm, Nancy. *Good Intentions: Writing Center Work in Postmodern Times*. Portsmouth, NH: Boynton/Cook, 1999.

Nicolas, Melissa. "Why There is No 'Happily Ever After': A Look at the Stories and Images That Sustain Us." In *Marginal Words, Marginal Work?: Tutoring the Academy in the Work of Writing Centers*, edited by William J. Macauley, Jr. and Nicholas Mauriello, 1-17. Cresskill, NJ: Hampton Press, 2007.

Singh-Corcoran, Nathalie. "You're Either a Scholar or an Administrator, Make Your Choice: Preparing Graduate Students for Writing Center Administration." In *(E)Merging Identities: Graduate Students in the Writing Center*, edited by Melissa Nicolas, 27-18. Southlake, TX: Fountainhead Press, 2008.

Welch, Nancy. "Playing with Reality: Writing Centers After the Mirror Stage." *College Composition and Communication* 51 no. 1 (1999): 51-69.

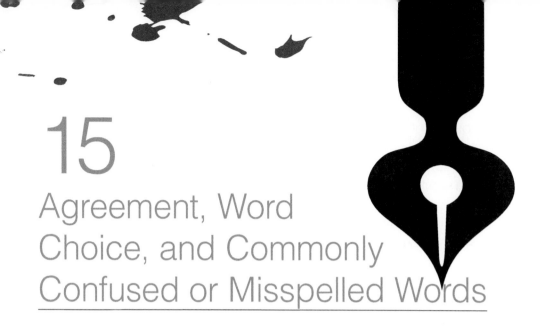

15

Agreement, Word Choice, and Commonly Confused or Misspelled Words

Agreement

Pronoun/Antecedent Agreement

When using pronouns to replace or refer to nouns, be sure that a pronoun agrees with its antecedent noun (the noun it replaces or refers to) in number, person, case, and gender. The following are some of the most common pronoun agreement problems that student writers have.

15a Check if a noun is singular or plural

Use singular pronouns to refer to singular nouns, and use plural pronouns to refer to plural nouns.

→ The pilot of Air Force One is on-call; her phone could ring at any time.

→ Pilots of Air Force One are on-call; their phones could ring at any time.

15b Check if a noun is definite or indefinite

Use a singular pronoun with an indefinite pronoun.

Okay→ Each has his own special call number.

Okay→ Each has her own special call number.

Okay→ Each has his or her own special call number.

Not okay→ Each has their own special call number.

If you are unsure of which pronoun to use in this situation, it is always possible to rephrase the sentence to avoid the situation.

Okay➜ Each pilot has a special call number.

Okay➜ All pilots have their own special call number.

15c Check if a noun is generic

Use a singular pronoun with a generic noun, a noun that is general or unidentified by name.

➜ Each pilot has his own special call number.

➜ A pilot of Air Force One must have her plane ready at all times.

15d Check for compound antecedents

Use a plural pronoun to refer to antecedents that are joined with an *and*.

➜ The pilots of Air Force One and Navy One work at the request of their president.

15e Check for pronouns with correlative conjunctions

Use a singular pronoun to refer to antecedents that are joined with *either...or/neither... nor*.

➜ Either the pilot of Air Force One or the pilot of Navy One will take his plane to the disaster area.

➜ Neither the pilot of Air Force One nor the pilot of Navy One has his plane ready.

Use a plural pronoun to refer to antecedents that are joined with *both...and*.

➜ Both the pilot of Air Force One and the pilot of Navy One will take their planes to the disaster area.

Exercise 1: Directions: Change any ungrammatical pronoun to a more appropriate one.

Tim, my boss, told the advertising staff today that she would be promoting one lucky person due to the success of the latest billboard design. This individual would be recognized at the end of the week for their hard work and dedication to their job, and they would also get their own private office. I thought it might be Sue, who had spent many of his nights and weekends diligently working overtime on the project. The employees were excited that one of its own would soon be working in administration, but it couldn't figure out who the lucky person might be. Since everybody had spent so much of his personal time on the ad campaign, everyone on staff felt he had a chance at the big promotion—and his own office. Unfortunately, the company had a policy of only promoting one of their staff members per year. Tim had a tough decision to make.

Subject/Verb Agreement

Subjects and verbs need to agree grammatically. This section highlights some of the most common problems writers have in making subjects and verbs agree.

15f Check for simple subjects or head nouns

Knowing which word is the simple subject or the head noun can help you with subject-verb agreement, especially when there are post-modifiers that come between the head noun and the verb. In the following sentences, the complete subject is in blue, and the simple subject or head noun is underlined.

→ The pilot is ready to take off.

→ The call sign for the president's plane changes with different planes; Air Force One is maintained by the Air Force, Navy One by the Navy, and Coast Guard One by the Coast Guard.

15g Check for prepositional phrases

A prepositional phrase can come between a subject and its verb and cause confusion.

→ Each of the pilots is ready to fly Air Force One.

In the sentence above, *each* is the simple subject or head noun, and it is this simple subject that needs to agree with the verb *is*. Except with a few indefinite pronouns (see 15i), you can ignore prepositional phrases when trying to determine what the simple subject is.

→ To fly in the clouds is a great way to escape everyday problems.

15h Check for parenthetical statements or interjections

Parenthetical statements or interjections that interrupt the sentence should not be considered when determining subject-verb agreement. These types of interrupters are easy to spot if punctuated correctly with commas.

→ The pilot, in addition to the co-pilot, was unable to fly the plane.

→ Scott Johnson, though, was able to take control in the cockpit.

15i Check for indefinite pronouns as subjects

Most indefinite pronouns when used as subjects take singular verbs.

→ Something is wrong with the cockpit door today. Is that a sign of trouble?

Some indefinite pronouns when used as subjects take plural verbs. These include *both, few, many, others,* and *several*.

→ Both Sally and John are pilots.

→ Both are pilots.

Some indefinite pronouns when used as subjects can take either singular or plural verbs. These include *all, any, enough, more, most, none,* and *some*. The noun that the indefinite pronoun refers to determines whether the subject is considered singular or plural.

→ Some of the pilots are unhappy about the coming tests.

→ Some of the ice is melting.

15j Check for compound subjects

In compound subjects, there will be more than one head or simple subject.

When the compound subject is joined by *and,* use a plural verb form.

→ She and he are able to fly the plane.

→ Sally and John always leave when the situation gets uncomfortable.

→ The pilot and the co-pilot always leave the controls unattended.

When the compound subject is joined by *or,* use a singular verb form.

→ She or he is able to fly the plane.

→ Sally or John leaves when the situation gets uncomfortable.

→ When the pilot or co-pilot leaves the controls unattended, a buzzer sounds in the cockpit.

When the indefinite pronouns *every* and *each* are used before compound subjects, look only at the indefinite pronoun and use a singular verb for subject-verb agreement.

→ Every pilot and co-pilot learns how to land in dangerous situations.

When the correlative conjunctions *either...or/neither...nor* are used to join compound subjects, the verb should agree with the subject that is closest to the verb.

Singular→ Neither John nor Sally is here today to fly the plane.

Plural→ Neither John nor the other pilots are here today to fly the plane.

> ♟ Exercise : Directions: Change thirteen verbs in the following paragraph that do not agree with their subjects.
>
> Evil omens and signs of bad luck is known throughout the world. Western cultures believes walking under a ladder or having a black cat crosses your path will ensure a disaster of some kind. Spilling salt are also bad luck; the only remedy is to throw some salt over your right shoulder. Breaking a mirror cause seven years of bad luck, and you might as well stay in bed on Friday the 13th, because nothing good happen on this day. In fact, the number 13 should just be avoided altogether. In Russian culture, people who whistle indoors will loses all their money. Also, two people is never supposed to shake hands or talk across a threshold, and, if you forgets an item at home, don't go back for it: bad luck come to anyone who return home for a forgotten item. Never forgets that superstitious signs is around every corner.

Word Choice

15k Check for exactness and clarity

1. Be precise

Make every word and phrase count by making your point in the fewest possible words.

Wordy:

➜   In point of fact, in language, a code is a sign or rule that allows you to change a piece of information into another sign, form, or representation, and this new sign, form, or representation does not necessarily have to be of the same system.

Concise:

➜   A code is a sign that changes information into another sign, sometimes not in the same system.

2. Use specific, concrete words

Student writers often are asked to give their opinions about literature, films, or music. Using vague descriptors such as *good, bad, great, best, greatest,* and *worst* weakens writing. Make descriptions stronger by using specific, concrete words.

Vague:

➜   *The Old Man and the Sea* is the best novel.

Specific:

➜   In *The Old Man and the Sea*, Ernest Hemingway depicts the accurate and heart-wrenching life of a fisherman.

In addition, be sure to use concrete words, instead of vague or abstract ones, to make a description the strongest it can be. This would be a good time to check a thesaurus.

Using specific, concrete words	
Instead of this...	**Try this...**
blue	azure, cobalt, navy, sea blue, turquoise
car	Ford Escort, Toyota Camry, Volkswagen Beetle
friend	school acquaintance, close friend, movie pal
house	home, abode, igloo, apartment, student dormitories
hungry	famished, ravenous, starving
piece of literature	short story, poem, novel, play
river	Danube, Mississippi, Nile
the city	Austin, Los Angeles, Nashville, New York

When searching for a more specific or concrete word, be careful not to just let your computer thesaurus make an automatic replacement. For instance, if you just automatically substitute a more specific word for *blue*, you might end up with a problematic sentence, as shown below.

➜   I wanted to buy the blue car.

Automatic substitute from thesaurus➜ I wanted to buy the depressed car.

Effective substitute from thesaurus➜ I wanted to buy the navy car.

3. Delete empty words and phrase

It is not the number of words you use, but the exactness of the words that demonstrates writing maturity. Using empty phrases or expletives, such as *there/it + be*, may be grammatically correct, but you can be more concise by just dropping them.

Wordy:

→ There were only three sailors on *The Enterprise* who knew semaphore signs.

Concise:

→ Only three sailors on *The Enterprise* knew semaphore signs.

If your instructor assigns a first-person essay, be sure that you do not overuse the empty phrases that can sometimes go along with this type of writing. Some instructors call these empty phrases "weasel words" because they can make your writing sound non-authoritative. By dropping these empty phrases or weasel words, you can present your views with more authority.

Wordy:

→ In my opinion, I think that learning Morse code is difficult.

Concise:

→ Learning Morse code is difficult.

Weasel Words	
I am sure (that)	In my opinion
I believe (that)	It is my opinion (that)
I know (that)	It is true (that)
I think (that)	To my knowledge
I think the facts reveal (that)	

4. Replace wordy prepositional phrases with more concise adverbs

Wordy descriptions sometimes fill up a lot of space but do not say anything important or necessary. This type of wordiness usually includes unnecessary prepositional phrases that can be deleted without changing any real meaning.

Wordy:

→ In this day and age in the event that a boat has trouble in the water, sema-phores or Morse code can be used to signal for help.

Concise:

→ When in trouble, boaters can use semaphores or Morse code to signal for help.

Using adverbs for conciseness	
Replace these prepositional phrases	with these adverbs
at all times	always
at that point in time	then
at the present time	now, today
at this moment	now, today
beyond a shadow of a doubt	certainly, surely
due to the fact that	because
for the purpose of	for
in order to	to
in point of fact	undoubtedly, clearly
in spite of the fact that	although
in the event that	if, when
in the final analysis	finally
in this day and age	today
in view of the fact that	because
it is clear that	clearly
it is obvious that	obviously
it is my opinion that	(drop completely)
there is no question that	unquestionably, certainly
without a doubt	undoubtedly

5. Describe exactly who, what, when, where, why, and how

Vague descriptions or empty words contribute nothing to the meaning of the sentence or the description you are trying to give. Rephrase these vague descriptions into specific words. Once you have identified the specifics (who, what, when, where, why, how), do not repeat the same information.

Wordy:

→ When on the water and not in close contact with other boats, boaters can use Morse code, but when on the water and in eye view of another boat, boaters can use semaphores.

Concise:

→ Boaters can use semaphores when close to another boat and Morse code when farther than eye view.

6. Use figurative language when appropriate

Using words in an imaginative or creative way, rather than in the literal sense, is figurative language. The most common figures of speech are metaphors (a comparison of dissimilar things) and similes (a comparison of dissimilar things using *like* or *as*).

Simile→ The boat glided on the water like a pelican in flight.

Metaphor→ Morse code is the Model T of communication.

However, be careful about being too flowery with descriptions. Flowery language is writing that often contains too many adjectives, adverbs, or words that you have looked up in a thesaurus and used incorrectly.

Flowery:

→ The old faded scarlet dinghy sashayed on the cool, fresh, and blue water like a storm-tossed pelican in dangerous flight.

Concise:

→ The old red dinghy bounced on the water.

Exercise 1: *Directions: In the following sentences, revise any word choice problems.*

Example: In my opinion, the signs posted in my city should have reflective letters. The traffic signs in Murfreesboro should have reflective letters.

1. There has been an accident at a corner near campus every day beyond a shadow of a doubt.
2. Fraught with tension, the room where the recent city manager's meeting was held felt like it was swimming with the sweat of all the attendees in the room.
3. I think the facts reveal that better signs are needed.
4. It is quite surprising that in this day and age more people do not protest the number of accidents that have occurred in our city each and every day.
5. We all hope that the city manager will come out of the apparent comatose state he is in and work on changing how the signs are made and posted.

15f Check for completeness

The words we use in conversations often have clear references in the environment or context around us. However, in academic and professional writing, some conversational words need to be replaced for full clarity and transparency.

Deictic or pointing words, such as *here, there, this,* and *that*, that are frequently used in spoken language need clear antecedents or full descriptions in writing.

Unclear reference:

→ When traveling by sea, be sure to take that manual.

Clear reference:

→ When traveling by sea, be sure to take the semaphore manual.

Intensifiers, such as *so, such*, and *too*, that are used in speech to mean "very" or "exceptionally" usually need an extra phrase or clause to describe **why** something is being intensified.

Unclear reference:

→ Morse code is so out of date.

Clear reference:

➔ Morse code, which was created in the early 1840s, is so out of date that it is rarely used anymore.

When comparing two or more things in academic writing, be sure to provide both parts of the comparison.

Unclear reference:

➔ Semaphore codes are even older.

Clear and full reference:

➔ Semaphore codes, created in the early 1800s, are even older than Morse code, which was first used in the 1840s.

15g Check for tired, stale, or unnatural language

Descriptive language that is innovative can quickly capture the reader's attention and interest. Note the difference between the following two sentences.

Simple➔ The boat floated out to sea.

Descriptive➔ The rowboat drifted two miles off shore.

However, as writers, we need to be careful not to get so caught up in our description that we borrow the overused expressions of others. As a rule, it is best to stay away from clichés and idioms that have lost their original innovativeness.

Some clichés to avoid	
after all is said and done	easier said than done
beat around the bush	face the music
believe it or not	fish out of water
best foot forward	flat as a pancake
better late than never	food for thought
calm before the storm	grin and bear it
cart before the horse	in a nutshell
chalk up a victory	in one ear and out the other
come through with flying colors	in the nick of time
crying shame	last but not least
don't rock the boat	more than meets the eye
drop in the bucket	raining cats and dogs

Overused idiom/cliché:

➔ I felt like I was *out to sea* as I learned Morse code.

Straightforward description:

➔ Morse code was difficult to learn.

If you are asked as a writer to be creative and innovative in your expressions, such as when you write a narrative or descriptive essay, stay away from clichés, and use some creativity of your own.

Innovative/creative description:

→ Morse code was as difficult to learn as snowboarding on a mountain of Jell-O.

Jargon, the language used by a particular profession or a group of people, is usually too technical to be natural for an academic essay. Reword techno-speak into more straightforward descriptions.

Jargon:

→ Morse code is a type of character encoding that uses rhythmic language and telegraphic information to transmit a given communication.

Straightforward description:

→ Morse code uses dots and dashes to send out messages.

> **Did You know?** William Shakespeare is credited with the first usage of around 2,000 words in the English language. He is also responsible for some of the most well-known idioms, some of which are now clichés: *neither rhyme nor reason, in my mind's eye, I must be cruel only to be kind, dead as a door-nail, it was Greek to me, love is blind, pomp and circumstance, a good riddance,* and *I have been in such a pickle.*

15h Check for appropriate levels of formality

What is Academic English? For some instructors, this term refers to good grammar and formal style. For others, it refers to having students be constructive critics and clear writers. Whatever it means, most instructors will expect you to use a style that is more formal than your conversational English but not to the point where your writing sounds stilted and pretentious. Remember that formality depends on the audience and purpose of the writing assignment; if you are unsure about what is expected of you, ask your instructor.

Informal language, in the form of slang or colloquial language, is usually not part of your academic writing, unless you are writing a narrative that uses dialogue. Even though some slang words (such as *jazz* or *mob*) can become part of the broader standard language, most slang is considered too localized and too informal for academic writing.

Slang description:

→ That boat was too cool.

→ That boat was wicked.

→ That boat was tight.

→ That boat was dope.

Academic description:

→ *The Enterprise,* a new addition to the fleet, has innovative engines that are less harmful to the environment.

Colloquial language, relaxed or casual speech used across many speakers, is also not usually part of academic writing. Words or expressions such as *a lot, gonna,* and *wanna* are too informal for essay writing.

Colloquial description:

→ The boaters wanna learn how to use semaphores in case of emergency.

Academic description:

→ The boaters want to learn how to use semaphores in case of emergency.

Doublespeak or doubletalk are words or expressions that are used to hide or distort the truth, such as using *protective custody* instead of *imprisonment* or *pre-hostility* instead of *peace*. In argumentative essays, using doublespeak can sound cagey or shifty.

Doublespeak description:

→ State employees now have job flexibility.

Academic description:

→ State employees now have a lack of job security because they are only employed week to week.

Be careful that when you are more formal in your writing, you do not go too far and sound pretentious, sometimes referred to as writing *gobbledygook*. This can happen if you use a thesaurus without considering the context or formality of the essay or letter you are writing. Also, be sure to use American English spelling, rather than British English.

Pretentious:

→ When I finalized my perusal of the optimal methodology to acquire the semaphore signals, I ascertained that it was more effortless to gain knowledge of Morse code.

Academic:

→ Learning Morse code was easier than learning semaphore signs.

Pretentious words	
Instead of...	Try...
aficionado	fan
ascertain	find out
commence	begin
conviviality	friendliness
desist	stop
imbroglio	mess
instantiate	support
finalize	finish, complete
impact	affect

Pretentious words	
Instead of...	Try...
jejune	boring, childish
lugubrious	gloomy
methodology	method
nadir	lowest point
optimal	best
peruse	look at, read
potentiate	improve effectiveness
utilize	use

Did You Know? British and American English, though mutually intelligible, have a number of distinct differences. Aside from pronunciation and vocabulary, spelling is often very different. We can thank Noah Webster (writer of the eponymous dictionary) for standardizing many American spellings, such as dropping the *u* from words like *colour* and *labour*, ending words with *–er* instead of *–re* (*center/centre*), and replacing *–ce* endings with *–se* (*offense, suspense*) to name a few examples. Not all of Webster's spelling reforms were accepted, though—*medicin, soop,* and *tung* never caught on.

15i Check for sexist and offensive language

Use language that gives equal value and respect for all people and places.

1. Use appropriate words for gender

Give equal treatment to each gender; do not privilege either. Also, be sure not to use the generic *he* for all writing occasions. Try rephrasing singular subjects to plural ones; this allows you to switch from the singular pronoun (she or he) to a plural one (they).

Possible sexist language:

→ The sailor learned Morse Code in his training.

Inclusive language:

→ Sailors learn Morse Code in training.

Do not assume that one gender cannot do a particular type of work or gender role, as in *the male nurse, the female astronaut, faculty wives,* and *both men and their wives.*

Sexist language:

→ The stewardess learned Morse code in training.

Inclusive language:

→ The flight attendant learned Morse code in training.

Sexist language:

→ The sailors brought their wives and kids to the dock party.

Inclusive language:

→ The sailors brought their families to the dock party.

Here are some substitutions that you might consider when writing about job titles.

Recommended terms for job titles	
Instead of...	Try...
barman, barmaid	bartender
businessman	businessperson, executive, manager, staff person
chairman	chair, presiding officer, moderator
congressman	member of Congress, representative, senator
comedienne	comedian
fireman	firefighter
mailman	letter carrier, mail carrier, postal worker
salesman	salesperson, sales representative
sculptress	sculptor
steward, stewardess	flight attendant
usherette	usher
waiter, waitress	server

2. Use appropriate words for age

In academic writing, use non-offensive terms when referring to the age of a person.

Recommended terms for age	
Instead of...	Try...
kids (to age 18)	children
kids (college students)	students, young adults, adults, men, women
elderly, old man, old woman	senior citizens, older adults

3. Use appropriate words for ethnicity or race

Be sure to use terms that are non-discriminatory and non-offensive when referring to the ethnic backgrounds or races of people. If unsure, you can check for acceptable general or specific terms in a current dictionary.

Acceptable terms for ethnicity or race	
General Terms for People in the United States	Specific Terms for People in the United States
African American, Black	
American Indian, Native American	Alaska Native, Cherokee, Hopi, Navajo
Anglo-American, White American, White	French American, Irish American, Polish American
Arab American	Egyptian American, Lebanese American
Asian American	Chinese American, Japanese American, Korean American, Thai American
Hispanic, Hispanic American, Latino/a	Mexican American, Puerto Rican
Pacific Islander American, Native Hawaiian	

4. Use appropriate words for disability or illness

The current preference in referring to people with disabilities or illnesses is to put the *person* first. For example, refer to *a person with disabilities* or *a person who is differently abled* rather than *a disabled person*.

Recommended terms for disability or illness	
Instead of this...	Try this...
AIDS victim	a person with AIDS
blind person, visually impaired person	a person with a visual impairment
deaf person	a person with a hearing impairment
dumb person	a person with speech impairment
handicapped person, disabled person	a person with disabilities
neurotic person	a person with a psychological disability
quadriplegics	a person who is quadriplegic

5. Use appropriate words for geographical areas

Because social and political boundaries may change, you can use *a person from (place name)* when referring to someone and her place of origin or residence and rarely be wrong. Definitely, stay away from any derogatory terms for a person's origin. The terms that are most frequently seen as problematic include the following.

Recommended terms for geographical areas	
Instead of...	Try this...
American	person from the United States, U.S. citizen
Arab	Egyptian, Iraqi, Saudi Arabian, Yemeni
English, Irish (from Northern Ireland), Welsh	British, person from the United Kingdom, U.K. citizen
Oriental	Asian, Asian American, Japanese, Korean, Chinese
Polish	Pole, person from Poland

EXERCISE 2: *Directions: The following summary of a news event contains 12 words that are not appropriate for the more standardized language used for summarizing. Change these words to more appropriately reflect the summary writing you might do in a writing course.*

Two kids have been taken into custody by the cops in connection with a recent string of vandalism in the area. The kids are accused of vandalizing stop signs in commemoration of the latest volume of the Harry Potter film franchise, *Harry Potter and the Half-Blood Prince*, by writing the name of evil wizard Voldemort on dozens of stop signs. Fanatics of the series might appreciate the vandals' urging to "STOP Voldemort," but the authorities were less entertained by the trick, which will cost the county $50 per devastated sign. The cops gave a statement warning would-be vandals that vandalism will not be tolerated, no matter how harmless or humorous vandalism may seem.

http://www.wisn.com/news/20061083/detail.html

Commonly Confused or Mispelled Words

We can trace why words become commonly confused back to one thing—spelling. English spelling comes from a set of conventions or rules that have been agreed upon by dictionary editors. Since English has been a language for around 1600 years, how some words are spelled has changed many times. Regardless of these historic changes and how they often make it difficult to figure out a standardized alphabetic form for many sounds, most English words now have fixed spellings that can be looked up in dictionaries at any time.

Since using good spelling is usually considered a sign that a writer is educated, it is a good idea to work on improving your spelling, no matter how good you are at it. One way to improve your spelling is to read more, keeping a spelling list or journal in which you write down and practice new words. Another way is to own your own college dictionary, using it to look up the spellings and definitions of words you have trouble spelling. Since computerized dictionaries often lead you to use words you may not understand, be sure not only to use the dictionary provided with your word processor, but to use print dictionaries as well.

> **Did You Know?** Ever wonder why English spelling is so unpredictable? English has a long history of foreign influence, which not only accounts for many of the unusual spellings, but also often indicates the origin of the word. For example, the words *doubt* and *debt* originally entered English from French influence, but misguided linguists added the silent *b* hundreds of years ago to both words to reflect the words' Latin origins (*dubitare* and *debitum*, respectively). While these alterations might make spelling and pronunciation frustrating (especially for non-native speakers), they reveal the rich history of English.

15j Check for words that are always separate

A common spelling error is to run together words that should be written as two. The following phrases should always be written as separate words.

→   a lot, all right, even if, even though, going to, in fact, just as, no one, of course

15k Check for words that can be written together or apart

The spelling of some words depends on the meaning you intend. For example, *already* means "previously" and *all ready* means "to be prepared." First, decide upon the meaning, and then choose the correct form by consulting your dictionary.

Different spacing, different meaning	
One word	**Two words**
already	all ready
altogether	all together
always	all ways
anybody	any body
anyone	any one
anyway	any way
awhile	a while
everybody	every body
everyday	every day
everyone	every one
however	how ever
into	in to
maybe	may be
nobody	no body
somebody	some body
someone	some one
whatever	what ever
whoever	who ever

15l Check for words that are pronounced the same or similarly

In English, we have many homophones—words that are pronounced the same but have different meanings. Homophones use different spellings, and since this is what distinguishes the meaning, you need to use your dictionary to find the correct word. Here is a list of the most commonly misspelled homophones.

Most commonly misspelled homophones	
it's (it is or it has)	its (possessive)
you're (you are)	your (possessive)
they're (they are)	their (possessive), there (place)
who's (who is or who has)	whose (possessive)

sweet???

try one of these
cookies or rice
crispy treats!!!

Their delicious

What's the problem with this sign
at a bake sale?

Here are some other commonly confused or misspelled words. Learning these will
help you become a proficient speller and editor.

| Other commonly confused words | |
A	A
a	an
*alot (ungrammatical)	a lot
accept	except
access	excess
adapt	adopt
adverse	averse
advice	advise
affect	effect
agree to	agree with
aisle	isle
allude	elude
allusion	illusion
already	all ready
alright	all right
altar	alter
altogether	all together
among	amongst between
amoral	immoral
amount	number
and/or	and or
angry at	angry with

annual	biannual
	semiannual
	biennial
	perennial
ant	aunt
ante-	anti-
anybody	any body
anyone	any one
anymore	any more
anyway	anyways
assistance	assistants
assure	ensure
	insure
ate	eight
awhile	a while
B	**B**
backup	back up
bad	badly
	poorly
bare	bear
base	bass
be	bee
beach	beech
because of	due to
being as	being that
berry	bury
berth	birth
beside	besides
between	among
	amongst
blew	blue
board	bored
brake	break
bring	take
breadth	breath
breath	breathe
business	busyness
by	bye
	buy

C	C
can	may
canvas	canvass
capital	capitol
cell	sell
censor	censure
cent	sent scent
cereal	serial
chord	cord
chose	choose
climactic	climatic
coarse	course
compare to	compare with
complement	compliment
conscience	conscious
consequently	subsequently
continual	continuous
could have	could of
counsel	council
criteria	criterion
D	**D**
dairy	diary
data	datum
dear	deer
decent	descent
desert	dessert
device	devise
dew	due
die	dye
different from	different than
disinterred	uninterested
discreet	discrete
do not	don't
dual	duel
due to	because of
dying	dyeing

E	E
effect	affect
elicit	illicit
elude	allude
emigrate from	immigrate to
eminent	imminent
ensure	insure
everyone	every one
except	accept
explicit	implicit

F	F
faint	feint
fair	fare
farther	further
fewer	less
firstly	first
flour	flower
for	fore four
former	latter
formally	formerly
further	farther

G	G
good	well
gorilla	guerilla
grate	great

H	H
hair	hare
hanged	hung
he/she	he or she
heal	heel
healthful	healthy
hear	here
heard	herd
higher	hire
his/her	her or her
hole	whole
hostel	hostile
hung	hanged

I	I
idle	idol
if	whether
illusion	allusion
immigrate	emigrate
immoral	amoral
implicit	explicit
imply	infer
in	into
ingenious	ingenuous
insure	assure ensure
in regard to	in regards to
*irregardless (ungrammatical)	regardless
it's	its
K	**K**
knew	new
know	no
L	**L**
later	latter
lay	lie
lead	led
learn	teach
leave	let
led	lead
lend	borrow loan
less	fewer
lie	lay
like	as as if
literally	figuratively
loose	lose loss
lots	lots of
M	**M**
made	maid
mail	male
main	mane
may	can
maybe	may be

maze	maize
meat	meet
medal	metal, meddle
media	medium
miner	minor
moral	morale
N	**N**
number	amount
O	**O**
oar	ore
of	off
OK	O.K. okay
off	off of
one	won
P	**P**
pain	pane
pair	pear, pare
passed	past
patients	patience
peace	piece
peak	peek, pique
peer	pier
percent	per cent percentage
personal	personnel
phenomena	phenomenon
plain	plane
pore	pour poor
precede	proceed
pretty	rather quite
principal	principle
proceed	precede
Q	**Q**
quiet	quite
quote	quotation
R	**R**
rain	reign, rein
raise	rays

real	very really
respectfully	respectively
right	write wright rite
rise	raise
role	roll
S	**S**
sail	sale
scene	seen
scent	sent, cent
seed	cede
seem	seam
set	sit
shall	will
should of	should have
sight	cite site
should have	should of
sit	set
site	cite sight
sole	soul
some	sum
somebody	some body
someone	some one
sometime	some time sometimes
so	very
stationary	stationery
steal	steel
suppose to	supposed to
sure	surely
T	**T**
take	bring
taught	taut
team	teem
than	then
that	which

their	there
	they're
*theirselves (ungrammatical)	themselves
there	their
	they're
thorough	through
threw	through
tide	tied
to	too
	two
toward	towards
U	**U**
*most unique (ungrammatical)	unique
*use to (ungrammatical)	used to
V	**V**
vain	vane
	vein
W	**W**
waist	waste
wait	weight
wait for	wait on
wander	wonder
ware	wear
	where
way	weigh
way	ways
weather	whether
well	good
were	where, wear
which	that
	who
while	whereas
who	which
	that
who	whom
who's	whose
wood	would
would have	would of
Y	**Y**
your	you're

EXERCISE 1 *Directions: Correct any problems with commonly confused or misspelled words.*

Who would of thought that a simple hike threw the woods would result in a classic emblem of Americana? Beginning in the mid 19ᵗʰ century, people from all over started coming too Lookout Mountain near Chattanooga, Tennessee too see "Rock City" and experience it's natural rock formations. In the 1920s, a businessman named Garnet Carter began developing Lookout Mountain into a residential neighborhood called Fairyland, but his wife had other plans. Freida Carter began exploring Rock City—now her property—and turning it into an elaborate rock garden. Recognizing the potential profit of his wife's ornate garden, Garnet opened Rock City to the public in 1932. Business was slow, however, so Garnet had to find a way to entice visitors to there garden with more advertising then they currently had. Garnet hired Clark Byers to paint farmers' barns for free as long as the phrase "See Rock City" was added. Farmers from Michigan to Texas excepted the offer, and the iconic black and white signs on red barns became part of are American landscape. The advertisements had—and continue to have—a significant effect on the Carters' business; every year, over half a million people see the sites of Rock City, likely having past many of the famous signs on there way to Lookout Mountain.

16
Punctuation and Mechanics

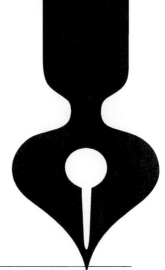

Basic punctuation principles exist in written English and other languages to provide general guidelines on how to present different types of phrases and clauses. Learning these basic rules can help you present your writing in a way that is consistent across the papers you write for your college courses and other types of writing you may do in the future.

Punctuation is a set of rules generally agreed upon by editors and academics although some variety in the application of rules may occur across different types of college disciplines or businesses. The punctuation and mechanics you use can do more than just highlight sentence beginnings and endings; it can also carry or change meaning. For example, consider how punctuation changes the meaning in the following sentences.

The rock is over Fred.

It is over Fred.

It is over, Fred.

It is over, Fred!

In the first sentence, someone is describing a falling rock over Fred's head. In the second sentence, someone is describing where the rock is. However, in the third sentence, with the addition of the comma, the meaning changes to someone telling Fred that his life is over, possibly due to the falling rock over his head. The period indicates that this is a declaration and not an exclamation and that there is probably no way out of the situation. However, add an exclamation mark, and the sentence turns into an exclamation—a warning to Fred to watch out for the rock.

The basic principles presented in this section can guide you when you have questions about how to use appropriate punctuation and mechanics at the word or sentence level. This way, you can understand and use the conventions of written English or even change the meanings of sentences as you present them to your reader.

The Comma

Commas are one of the most frequently used punctuation marks. Unfortunately, commas are also the most frequently misused punctuation mark. Having a reference tool available is always a good idea when you are not sure about how a comma rule applies to your sentence, but the abundance of comma rules can sometimes be frustrating. In this chapter, you will find a few ways to help you use comma rules more effectively.

In this section, comma rules are presented in the order of frequently used sentence-level comma rules followed by less frequently used rules. In addition to this useful set-up, you will also find a laminated one-page QUICK EDITING ROADMAP inside your copy of this handbook. Using up-to-date research on college writing, I have developed this guide as a quick reference to the sentence-level rules that confuse writers the most. Half of the rules included on the QUICK EDITING ROADMAP are comma rules.

16a Set off introductory words, phrases, and clauses

1. Set off introductory words and phrases

→ Commas are often used to set off introductory words and phrases. If the word or phrase includes a verb, a comma should always be used to separate the word or phrase from the main sentence.

→ Shocked, Alex put out his cigarette when he saw the new No Smoking sign.

→ Frustrated by the new sign, Alex put out his cigarette.

If the introductory word is a single preposition or adverb, you may omit the comma.

→ Yesterday the guests grumbled about the new sign.

If the introductory prepositional phrase is short (usually viewed as being five words or fewer), you may also omit the comma.

→ Below the stage the guests grumbled about the new sign.

> **Helpful hint:** If you are unsure about punctuating an introductory word, phrase, or clause, use a comma. The presence of a comma, rather than its absence, is always a good choice.
>
> → Yesterday, the guests grumbled about the new sign.
>
> → Below the stage, the guests grumbled about the new sign.

2. Set off introductory clauses

Always use a comma after an introductory clause. The use of a verb in any kind of introductory word, phrase, or clause is the clue to always using a comma.

→ Since he had recently quit smoking, Alex was happy to see the new No Smoking sign.

→ Although Chris was unhappy about the new sign, Alex was quite content.

16b Combine independent clauses in compound sentences

A comma is used between two independent clauses that are joined by a coordinating conjunction, such as any of the FANBOYS—*for, and, nor, but, or, yet, so.*

> Independent clause/simple sentence→Chris was unhappy about the new sign.

> Independent clause/simple sentence→Alex was quite content about the new sign.

> Compound sentence→ Chris was unhappy about the new sign, but Alex was quite content.

Be sure that the clauses on each side of the comma + conjunction are independent. A comma is never used between conjoined noun phrases or conjoined verb phrases.

> Misused comma→ Chris, and Alex had a terrible argument outside the building.

> OK→ Chris and Alex had a terrible argument outside the building.

> Misused comma→Chris was unhappy about the sign, and left campus early.

> OK→ Chris was unhappy about the sign and left campus early.

You can sometimes omit the comma when the two clauses are short—this is not always acceptable to all instructors or editors, though. You will always be correct if you include it.

> → Chris was unhappy and he left.

> → Chris was unhappy, and he left.

EXERCISE 2: *Directions: Add commas in the following sentences when and where needed. Some sentences may not need commas. Be able to explain why you chose to add a comma.*

1. An asterisk is a typographical symbol or it can also be classified as a glyph.

2. The asterisk symbol resembles a star and the word *asterisk* comes from the Greek for "little star."

3. Some printers and computer programmers refer to the asterisk as a *splat*.

4. Three asterisks together can be used to represent a change of thought or scene but an asterisk on its own can also represent zero.

5. A great defensive play in baseball can be noted on a baseball trading card with an asterisk.

16c Separate items in a series

Commas are used to separate words, phrases, or clauses in a series. A series contains at least three items that are parallel with each other (e.g., three nouns or three phrases).

→ Chris, Alex, and Max spent three hours arguing about the new signs around campus.

→ I saw the three musketeers—Chris, Alex, and Max—outside the building.

→ Chris talked, cajoled, and yelled as he tried to convince the administrators.

→ As I left the building, Max was taking down the sign, yelling at some strangers, and jumping up and down.

If the items in a series that you are connecting already have commas, use semi-colons to separate them.

→ When the campus police arrived, they wanted to ticket Chris, who began the argument; Alex, who escalated the argument; and Max, who threw the first punch.

16d Set off non-essential elements

Commas can be used to enclose non-essential information that is included in a sentence. To be non-essential, the information needs to be unnecessary for a reader to understand the central meaning of the sentence.

1. Relative clauses

Relative clauses can be essential or non-essential when it comes to understanding the main meaning of the full sentence. Relative clauses that are not necessary are non-restrictive and need to be set off by commas.

→ Chris and Alex, who were in my English class, were arguing violently.

In the above sentence, the information about which class Chris and Alex were in is non-essential to the meaning of the independent clause.

If a relative clause is essential to the full meaning of the sentence, it is restrictive and should not have any commas around it.

→   The audience that was closest to Chris and Alex was getting violent as well.

In the sentence above, the relative clause ("that was closest to Chris and Alex") is essential information. It was just the audience closest to Chris and Alex who were getting violent, not those in the audience farther away.

Using *that* for non-essential relative clauses and a comma plus a relative pronoun, such as *which* or *who*, for essential relative clauses is a way that some editors and writers help distinguish between non-essential and essential sentence elements. If you are required to follow MLA (Modern Language Association) or APA (American Psychological Association) guidelines, follow this convention. However, even MLA acknowledges that some writers do not follow this convention, so it's a good idea to check with your instructor about this grammar rule that is in flux.

Remember, though, that punctuation works together with meaning. Two sentences that look almost the same can use different punctuation due to the meaning the writer has in mind.

Non-restrictive relative clause→ Tennessee, which is a beautiful state, has all the signs of a bad economy.

Restrictive relative clause→ I like the Tennessee that is a beautiful state and not the one that has signs of a bad economy.

In the first sentence above, the main idea of the sentence can be understood without the relative clause *which is a beautiful state.* This makes the relative clause non-essential, requiring commas. In the second sentence, the main idea of the sentence can only be understood with the two relative clauses *that is a beautiful state* and *that has signs of a bad economy* included. This makes the two relative clauses essential, thus requiring no commas.

2. Participial phrases

Participial phrases are verb phrases that describe nouns. They take commas wherever they occur—at the beginning of the sentence, in the middle of the sentence, or at the end of the sentence.

Sentence with participial phrase→   The Hollywood sign, first built in 1923, was re-stored in 1978 with money from Gene Autry, Alice Cooper, and others.

Sentence with participial phrase→ The Hollywood sign, located in Griffith Park and not Hollywood, was restored in 1978 with money from Gene Autry, Alice Cooper, and others.

3. Appositives

Appositives are nouns, noun phrases, and noun clauses that rename nouns. The same restrictive/non-restrictive comma rule that applies to relative clauses applies to appositives (see 16d for more information on restrictive and non-restrictive elements).

Sentence with non-restrictive appositive➔ The Hollywood sign, a national monument, was restored in 1978 with money from Gene Autry, Alice Cooper, and others.

Sentence with restrictive appositive➔ The musician Alice Cooper helped fund the restoration of the Hollywood sign.

> **EXERCISE 3:** *Directions: Add commas where needed, setting off non-essential clauses, phrases, and appositives. Not all sentences will need a comma.*
>
> 1. The ampersand is a symbol that represents the word *and*.
> 2. The ampersand is rarely used in academic writing which is more formal than personal writing.
> 3. However, if an ampersand is part of the name of a business such as in Jacoby & Meyers, then a writer should use the ampersand.
> 4. In APA documentation style, the ampersand representing the word *and* is used.
> 5. Stephen Fry now a prolific author and Hugh Laurie now television's Dr. House performed a skit about ampersands on their television show.

16e Separate coordinate adjectives

A comma is used to separate coordinate adjectives. Adjectives are considered coordinate when they directly and equally modify a noun phrase. One test to see whether you are using coordinate adjectives is to reverse their order—if the original modification relationship exists, you have coordinate adjectives. Another test to see whether you are using coordinate adjectives is to place an *and* between the two adjectives—once again, if the original meaning exists, you have coordinate adjectives.

➔ Sam and Alex saw the dull, unappealing billboard for the movie and changed their minds about seeing it.

➔ Sam and Alex saw the unappealing, dull billboard for the movie and changed their minds about seeing it.

> **Did You Know?** Put a comma where you pause." Have you ever been told to punctuate based upon how a sentence is spoken? While you'll get in trouble if you follow this advice too much, it's not entirely misguided. Punctuation marks were originally intended to aid orators when reading a text aloud, and only in the past 100 or so years has punctuation become standardized. The comma can be traced back to the 3rd century BCE when Aristophanes of Byzantium invented a system of dots to separate verse; different groupings of dots represented different types of breaths needed to complete the reading of part of a text. Although the word comma comes from the Greek *komma* ("something cut off"), the shape of today's comma was standardized in the 16th century when the original comma—the diagonal slash (/)—dropped to the bottom of the line and curved.

16f Set off interrupters

1. Transitions

When an adverbial conjunction (also called a conjunctive adverb) appears in the middle of a sentence, it is separated off from the main sentence with commas.

→ The Hollywood sign, moreover, does not include any of the original letters.

→ Alice Cooper, however, donated money for the renovation in honor of Groucho Marx.

Adverbial conjunctions can also be used to connect two independent clauses when the adverbial conjunction is enclosed by a semi-colon and a comma. Since adverbial conjunctions function as both transitions and as compound sentence connectors, it is wise to always double check the punctuation that you use with an adverbial conjunction.

Adverbial conjunctions
Addition → moreover, furthermore, likewise, finally, additionally, also, incidentally
Contrast → however, nevertheless, in contrast, on the contrary, nonetheless, otherwise, on the other hand, in comparison, conversely, instead
Comparison → similarly, likewise
Exemplification → for example, for instance
Intensification → indeed, in fact, moreover, still, certainly
Result → therefore, thus, consequently, as a result, finally, then, accordingly, hence, subsequently, undoubtedly
Time → meanwhile, then, next, finally, still, now

2. Interjections

A comma is used to mark or enclose a weak exclamation or interjection, separating it from the rest of the sentence. An interjection can come at the beginning, in the middle, or at the end of a sentence.

→ For goodness sake, the instruction book about traffic signs is over 20 pages long.

→ The instruction book about traffic signs is over 20 pages long, for goodness sake.

→ I do not understand, for goodness sake, why that book about traffic signs is so long.

3. Direct address

A comma is used to mark or enclose a noun phrase that is used as a direct address. When you use a noun phrase that names the person or persons being spoken to, you are using the form of a direct address.

→ "Sam, did you see the billboard for *Terminator: Salvation*?"

→ "Did you see the billboard for *Terminator: Salvation*, Sam?"

→ "I thought the billboard for *Jumper* was good, Sam, but did you see the one for *Terminator: Salvation*?"

EXERCISE 4: *Directions: Add commas where needed for transitions, interjections, direct address, or tag questions.*

1. The writer uses many bulleted lists on the first page of his essay doesn't he?
2. A bullet granted is a typographical symbol that writers use to highlight a list of items.
3. A writer can however overuse bulleted lists; they should only be used sparingly and when absolutely necessary to organize information that may be difficult to process.
4. Bullets come in many shapes and sizes and are common in academic writing.
5. Chris do you use a lot of bullets in your essay writing?

---

4. Tag questions

Commas are also used to mark tags, which are added to the end of a sentence to question whether the statement that precedes the tag is accurate or not.

→ The poster for *Sherlock Holmes* made the main character look somewhat dastardly, didn't it?

→ It has been a long time since we have had a modern Sherlock Holmes, hasn't it?

16g Set off quotations or dialogue

Commas are used to set off a speaker's words from the rest of the sentence.

→ Chris complained, "That book is over 20 pages long."

→ "That book is over 20 pages long," Chris complained.

→ "That book," Chris complained, "is over 20 pages long."

Commas are not used with indirect quotations or speech.

→ Chris complained that the book was too long.

Commas are not used after an exclamation point or question mark.

→ "That book is too long!" complained Chris.

→ "How long is that book on traffic signs?" asked Chris with a frown on his face.

16h Set off geographic locations

Commas are used to set off items in an address or in the name of a place.

→ Please send any comments about the new sign to Department of Signage, Box 50, Fairbanks, Alaska 99701.

→ Murfreesboro, Tennessee, is near Nashville.

→ Be sure to check out the new sign at The Stone's River Mall, Murfreesboro, Tennessee.

A comma is never used between the name of a state and a Zip Code.

→ You should send your card and return postage to the Department of Signage, Box 50, Fairbanks, AK 99701.

16i Set off dates

Commas are used to set off items in a date. Use commas between the day and month, the date and year, and the year and the rest of the sentence.

→ The smoking signs were changed on Monday, January 1, 2010, when the new law took effect.

A comma is never used between the date and month or the month and year when the date is written in inverted order.

→ The smoking signs were changed on Monday, 1 January 2010, when the new law took effect.

A comma is never used when only the month and year are given.

→ The smoking signs were changed in January 2010.

16j Set off titles

A comma is used to set off a person's title or degree.

→ Dr. Watson had a sign outside his front door that said John H. Watson, M.D.

→ Juliet Freestone, PhD, noted expert on Sherlock Holmes, will speak at the library today.

> **Helpful hint:** Commas are not always used for Jr., Sr., II, or III, which are considered part of someone's name. This rule is in flux; check with your instructor about his or her preference.
>
> → Robert Downey, Jr. played Sherlock Holmes in the film by the same name.
>
> → Robert Downey Jr. played Sherlock Holmes in the film by the same name.

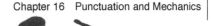

16k Set off numbers

When numbers are longer than four digits, use commas to separate them, placing a comma every three numbers starting from the right.

→ 1,000

→ 1,000,000

→ 1,000,000,000

Do not use commas in the above way when writing years, telephone numbers, street addresses, or zip codes.

16l Prevent confusion

Most grammar handbooks will tell you to use commas to prevent confusion or for clarity. These might be the kinds of examples shared with you.

→ What Chris did, did affect all of us.

→ It was the sign she had waited for, for years.

However, if you find yourself needing to use a comma to avoid confusion, you probably need to revise the entire sentence.

→ What Chris did that day affected all of us.

→ She had waited for years for the sign.

The Semi-colon

A semi-colon connects phrases or clauses that are closely linked in meaning. Using a semi-colon is limited to three situations.

16m Connect independent clauses

Semi-colons can connect two independent clauses (or simple sentences) to form a compound sentence.

Simple sentence/independent clause→ The Chinese zodiac uses twelve animals to represent human qualities.

Simple sentence/independent clause→ The Chinese zodiac runs on a twelve-year cycle.

Compound sentence→ The Chinese zodiac uses twelve animals to represent human qualities; it also runs on a twelve-year cycle.

16n Use with adverbial conjunctions or transitional phrases to connect clauses

Two simple sentences can be connected with an adverbial conjunction (also known as a conjunctive adverb) when a semi-colon is used to the left of the adverbial conjunction and a comma to the right of it. See 16f for a list of adverbial conjunctions.

→ The Chinese zodiac uses twelve animals to represent human qualities; furthermore, it runs on a twelve-year cycle.

→ The Chinese zodiac uses twelve animals to represent human qualities; in fact, it runs on a twelve-year cycle.

Transitional phrases	
after all	in contrast
as a matter of fact	in fact
as a result	in like manner
at any rate	in other words
at the same time	in the meantime
equally important	on one hand
even so	on the contrary
for example	on the other hand
for instance	to illustrate
in addition	while this may be true
in conclusion	

16o Separate groups that contain commas

If the items in a series that you are connecting already have commas, use semi-colons to separate them.

→ The Chinese zodiac uses twelve animals, such as the boar and the snake, to represent human qualities; runs on a twelve-year cycle; and is widely used throughout Asia, not just in China.

> **EXERCISE 1:** *Directions: Revise these sentences, adding semi-colons where needed. Not all sentences will need semi-colons.*
>
> 1. Bob Berner first introduced the backslash to computer programming in the 1960s it is sometimes called a slosh.
> 2. The backslash is a typographical mark furthermore it is an ASCII character.
> 3. The backslash is also used to separate the directory and file parts of a Web site address.
> 4. The backslash, a typographical mark, is used in computing to indicate that whatever follows should be treated differently or specially it is used in mathematics to indicate a set difference and it is used with the forward slash in linguistics to indicate phonemes.
> 5. Asian programmers can use other characters that are treated exactly as the backslash consequently this can cause some confusion.

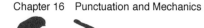

The Colon

A colon has a variety of uses, but its overall function is to connect elements while still keeping them slightly separated from each other.

MLA guidelines suggest using one space after a colon; however, the MLA also allows for two spaces if this strategy is used consistently. APA guidelines require one space after a colon.

According to the MLA, the first letter of the word that follows a colon should be in lower case, unless that word is one that is normally capitalized or is part of a rule, principle, or quotation. However, according to the APA, the first letter of the sentence following a colon should be in upper case if the sentence is an independent clause. Since the rule for using capitalization with a colon can change across documentation styles, it is a good idea to ask your instructor for clarification about which style she or he prefers.

16p Connect independent clauses

A colon is used to connect two independent clauses (or simple sentences) when the clause to the left of the colon is of a general or abstract nature and the clause to the right gives more specific information.

→ The Chinese zodiac uses twelve animals and runs on a twelve-year cycle: the animals represent different qualities of human nature, such as calmness or righteousness.

16q Add emphasis

Colons can be used to emphasize words, phrases, or clauses.

→ When I first studied the Chinese zodiac, I could not believe my sign: the pig.

16r Introduce a series or list

A colon is used to introduce a list or a series of words or phrases. As you can see in the sentence below, on the left side of the colon is an independent clause.

→ The Chinese zodiac also describes its animal signs with four elements: fire, metal, water, and wood.

Colons should not follow phrases like *such as, for example, includes,* or *including.* In fact, no punctuation should be used after these phrases when giving a list.

Okay→The Chinese zodiac has signs such as roosters, snakes, and boars.

16s Introduce a quotation or saying

A colon should be used to introduce a quotation or saying when it is a complete sentence.

→ I have a Chinese proverb by which I live: "When you only have two pennies left in the world, buy a loaf of bread with one and a lily with the other."

16t Use for salutations in formal letters

In a formal business letter, the colon is commonly used in the salutation. A comma can be used for personal letters.

→ Dear Judge Smith:

16u Connect numbers

Colons are used for connecting numbers in a variety of ways.

1. Connect ratios

→ The ratio of sunny days to snow days is 45:1.

2. Connect chapters and verses of holy texts

→ Ezra 6:18

→ Job 29:4

→ Qur'an 3:3

→ Vedanta-sutra 4:1:12

3. Connect hours, minutes, and seconds

→ 11:05:01

→ 3:13 a.m.

→ 7:03 p.m.

16v Connect titles and subtitles

→ *The Chinese Zodiac: Twelve Personalities Represented by Animals*

16w Separate geographical location and publisher name in bibliographic entries

→ Southlake, TX: Fountainhead, 2010.

EXERCISE 1: *Directions: Add colons where needed in the following sentences. Not all sentences may need a colon.*

1. The English word *colon* came to English through two languages that influenced many English words Greek and Latin.

2. The colon was introduced to English in the 1600s early British printers, such as William Caxton, embraced its use.

3. Be sure to use a colon when writing any of these types of elements a ratio, a scriptural verse, or a subtitle.

4. How colons are used in different ways is discussed in *Girl Talk Complete Guide to IM Lingo, Emoticons, and More!*

5. While trying to use commas accurately, the author was upset by the variations in MLA and APA rules "Why is it that so many different styles exist?"

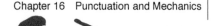

The Period, Exclamation Point, and Question Mark

Choosing end punctuation is easy if you know the type and function of the sentence you are writing. Writers use declarative sentences to give information, imperative sentences to give instructions or commands, interrogative sentences to obtain information, and exclamatory sentences to express emotion.

Declarative sentence or statement➜ The Chinese zodiac has four elements.

Imperative sentence or command➜Tell me which zodiac sign I am.

Interrogative sentence or question➜How many Chinese zodiac signs are there?

Exclamatory sentence or exclamation➜ You're a Boar! Really!

16x Use a period to end a sentence or separate initials or abbreviations

> No iron can pierce the heart with such force as a period put just at the right place.
>
> —Isaac Babel

1. End a sentence

A period ends a declarative sentence that gives information, makes a statement, or gives a mild command.

Gives information➜ In the Chinese zodiac, different animals not only rule each year, different ones rule each day.

Makes a statement➜ The Chinese zodiac is fascinating, especially when it is compared to our Western zodiac.

Gives a mild command➜Learn the animals and elements of the Chinese zodiac for the quiz tomorrow.

2. Separate initials or abbreviations

Periods are placed after an initial or an abbreviation.

➜ Ms. Smith, Mr. Smith, Mrs. Smith, Dr. Allison D. Smith, Adam D. Smith, Jr., Sen. Thomas P. Smith, Prof. Adam Smith, Rev. Smith

Using periods for the above list is always correct. Some other initials or abbreviations can take a period or not. This is something you will need to check with your instructor or with the specific style guidelines you are using, such as Modern Language Association (MLA) or American Psychological Association (APA). For instance, both MLA and APA suggest not using periods or spaces in abbreviations composed only of capital letters, but some instructors prefer that students use periods.

The following abbreviations can appear with or without periods.

→ BA, BS, MA, PhD

→ GP, LPN, MBA, MD, RN

→ BC, BCE, AD, CE, AM, PM

States can often be abbreviated in a variety of ways, including some forms that take periods. For instance, *PA* or *Penn.* can be used for the state of Pennsylvania. However, in formal writing, it is not commonly accepted that states be abbreviated in any way except in complete addresses.

16y Emphasize with an exclamation point

An exclamation mark is used at the end of an exclamatory sentence to express a strong feeling or to give emphasis.

→ This is the last time I will comment. Stop asking me!

→ Imagine! The foundation of astrology goes back thousands of years.

Cut out all those exclamation marks. An exclamation mark is like laughing at your own jokes.

−F. Scott Fitzgerald

16z End a direct question, show uncertainty, or embed a short question with a question mark

1. End a direct question

A question mark is used at the end of a direct question or interrogative.

→ Are there any similarities between the Chinese zodiac and Western astrology?

> **Helpful hint:** A question mark is never used for an indirect question.
> → Molly asked why I used Chinese zodiac examples.

2. Show uncertainty

A question mark can also be used to show uncertainty about a fact or piece of information. When used this way, the question mark should be placed within parentheses.

→ Western astrology began in the 2nd century AD (?).

3. Embed a short question within the middle of a sentence

A short question can be embedded within a longer sentence in three ways: within parentheses, enclosed by dashes, or just within the sentence itself.

→ Western astrology began in the 2nd century AD (is this similar to Chinese astrology?) and has twelve signs.

→ Western astrology began in the 2nd century AD—is this similar to Chinese astrology?—and has twelve signs.

→ When she asked the question, why are Western and Chinese zodiacs so similar? at the lecture, the speaker gave her a point-by-point answer.

> **Helpful hint** Although embedding questions within longer sentences is grammatical, it is rarely done and often questioned. A writer might want to revise these types of sentences into something that is more common.

> **EXERCISE 1:** Directions: Fill in the blanks with the correct punctuation mark: period (.), exclamation point (!), or question mark (?).
>
> 1. Have you ever gotten lost reading something that is poorly written___
> 2. Punctuation marks are like tiny road signs for the reader___
> 3. Also referred to as a full stop, the period tells the reader that a complete thought, or sentence, has come to an end___
> 4. Although periods are the most common way to end a sentence, did you know that there are two other ways to do this___
> 5. The exclamation point is sometimes overused by excited students___ Be careful___

The Apostrophe

The apostrophe is used in a variety of situations and is one of the most complicated punctuation marks to use. Unless you know for sure that the way you use it is always correct, it is a good idea to double check its use during your editing sessions or revise your sentence to avoid it.

16aa Mark omissions when parts of words are removed

An apostrophe is used to show that one or more letters have been omitted. For instance, use an apostrophe to show in *I'm* that the *a* has been deleted.

1. Mark contractions when parts of words are removed

→ I'm, you're, he's, she's, it's, they're, we're

→ I hadn't, you haven't

→ I can't, I couldn't, you won't, you wouldn't, they'll, they shouldn't

2. Mark numbers when parts of numbers are removed

→ in the year '95

3. Mark words used to represent oral language

When using unusual or informal spellings to represent oral language, you can use apostrophes to mark contractions.

→ a-walkin', trekin', y'all

> **Did You Know?:** You ain't ever gonna believe this! *Ain't* is, in fact, a word. This "improper" word is a contraction of *am* (from the verb *to be*) and *not*—similar in construction to *isn't* and *aren't*. Grammatically, it should follow a first person pronoun (*I*), but it is often used in informal speech following any noun. But watch out! *Ain't* ain't acceptable in formal English.

16ab Form plurals

The MLA recommends that an apostrophe along with an *–s* be used to create the plural of abbreviations that include lowercase letters, uppercase letters, or both.

→ A's, B's, C's, D's, E's

→ PhD's, Mind your P's and Q's!

However, many instructors prefer that no apostrophe be used at all.

→ As, Bs, Cs, Ds, Es

→ PhDs, Mind your Ps and Qs

Some instructors may prefer that you italicize the letter and use regular font style for the *–s* ending.

→ *A*s, *B*s, *C*s, *D*s, *E*s

It is best to check with your instructor on how he or she wants you to format letters.

> **Helpful hint:** Apostrophes, in general, should not be used to form the plurals of numbers, abbreviations or acronyms that include all uppercase letters, and phrases that refer to words.
>
> → 1980s, the 60s
>
> → TAs, CEOs, IOUs
>
> → She uses many *ands* but not enough other conjunctions in her writing.

How would you edit this sign?

16ac Form possessives

An apostrophe is used in various ways to form possessives. Knowing the difference between singular nouns, indefinite pronouns, and plural nouns will help you use the apostrophe correctly.

1. Form singular possessives

A. Singular nouns

An apostrophe and –s can be added to most singular nouns and acronyms to form the possessive.

→ Sam's book, the student's pen, the new sign's message

→ the CEO's email, MLA's style guide

> **Helpful hint** In the past, several apostrophe rules were dependent on what letter ended the singular noun. However, *The MLA Handbook for Writers of Research Papers* now recommends always using an apostrophe and –s at the end of any singular noun. If your instructor wants you to use another style guide for your research and writing, you will need to check how this rule is handled in that system.
>
> → Giles's plan, the boss's idea, Ms. Jones's books

B. Personal pronouns

Personal pronouns do not take an apostrophe since they already show possession.

→ my, your, yours, his, her, hers, its, our, ours, their, theirs

C. Indefinite pronouns

An apostrophe and an –s is used at the end of an indefinite pronoun to show possession.

→ anyone's, anybody's, everyone's, everybody's, someone's, somebody's

2. Mark plural possessives

Plural nouns that do not end in –s take an apostrophe plus an –s to form the possessive. Plural nouns that end in –s only take the apostrophe.

→ the children's song, the geese's honk, the data's collection

→ the cats' meows, the judges' decision, the zodiacs' signs, the Smiths' house , the Joneses' cat

3. Form possessive compound nouns

When a sentence includes conjoined nouns, the type of ownership or possession determines how to use the apostrophe. If each noun has separate ownership, each noun is marked by the possessive. If the nouns have ownership together, only the last noun is made possessive by using the apostrophe.

Separate ownership→Sam's and Alex's zodiac signs are not compatible.

Joint ownership →Jack and Jill's pail fell down the hill.

16ad Form compounds

An apostrophe and –s is placed at the end of a compound word when signaling possession.

→ my mother-in-law's sign, mother-of-pearl's color

An apostrophe and –s can be placed at the end of a plural compound word, or the possession can be signaled with an *of* phrase.

→ my brothers-in-law's zodiac signs

→ the zodiac signs of my brothers-in-law

http://jeffreyhill.typepad.com/english/2008/11/apostrophe-catastrophes.html

What is wrong with the sign in this picture?

Quotation Marks

Quotation marks are used in a variety of situations as described below. Generally, when a quotation mark falls at the end of a clause or sentence, place periods and commas inside the quotation mark.

→ My instructor assigned us a new story entitled "Signs and Symbols."

→ When I read "Signs and Symbols," I was reminded of a story from my child-hood.

When you use MLA style for in-text citations, the period follows the citation in parentheses.

→ Margaret Jones, in her essay on sign language, says that "anyone who really wants to learn sign language can do so relatively easily" (101).

16ae Signal titles of short works

Quotation marks are used to enclose the titles of short works, including poems, short stories, lectures, book chapters, song titles, magazine articles, newspaper articles, encyclopedia entries, and television/radio episodes.

→ "Pedestrians Not Permitted on this Highway" – a poem by Jackson H. Day

→ "Signs and Symbols" – a short story by Vladimir Nabokov

→ "The Signs of Life" – a lecture by Augustus D. Waller, MD

→ "Signs Inconjunct" – a book chapter by Ptolemy

→ "Signs" – a song by Five Man Electrical Band

→ "Swine Flu Myth: The Symptoms Are Like Regular Flu" – a magazine article

→ "CDC: Swine Flu Outbreak Signs Encouraging" – a newspaper article

→ "Sign Language (Communications)" – an encyclopedia entry

→ "Born Under a Bad Sign" – episode from television's *Supernatural*

16af Set off a direct quotation

Quotation marks are also used to set off direct quotations.

→ "The thunderstorm last night was the first sign of spring," said the ABC weatherman.

→ Albert Einstein said, "The true sign of intelligence is not knowledge but imagination."

16ag Set off dialogue in prose

Quotation marks are used to set off dialogue. Be sure to use a separate paragraph for each speaker, and use quotation marks around everything each person says.

→ from *Signs* (2002 film):
"What kind of a machine bends a stalk of corn without breaking it?" asked Officer Caroline.
Graham responded, "It can't be by hand; it's too perfect."

16ah Share a few lines of poetry

Quotation marks are used when quoting four or fewer lines of poetry. Be sure to enclose all material from the poem in quotation marks, and use a slash—with a space on each side of the slash—to show where the original line was divided. When quoting material from a source, be sure to give the documentation information.

→ I cannot help but compare my visit to the lines of one of my favorite poems by Jackson H. Day called "Wesley Theological Seminary: No Thoroughfare": "O you who see this sign, pray it may go/And all it represents; and later, lo/ This path can be the broadest thoroughfare" (ll.4-6).

16ai Share personal thoughts

→ During the visit, I could not help but compare my reception to the metaphor of a favorite poem: "I wish these people would think about how they could create the broadest of thoroughfares."

16aj Signal something being discussed, defined, or used in an unusual or ironic manner

→ I never thought there were so many sentences with the word "sign" in them.

→ Joe has been "signing off" to his girlfriend lately, meaning that he has been showing off.

→ At the bar, when Joe said his "sign" meant he was open for business, I had to laugh.

> **Helpful hint:** When you want to place a quotation within a quotation, use single quotation marks within double quotation marks.
>
> "What would you suggest I do when I'm feeling frustrated at being left out of things?" Mark asked his friend, the 60s fan.
>
> His friend replied, "I'd go and listen to 'Signs' by the Five Man Electrical Band."

What's wrong with this sign?

> **EXERCISE 1:** *Directions: Add quotation marks and capital letters where needed.*
>
> 1. What does a red sky mean? asked my friend John.
> 2. I asked when did you see the red sky? The time of day can influence the meaning of red sky.
> 3. Shakespeare has a quotation in his play *Venus and Adonis* about a red morn.
> 4. An old adage about sailing during a red sky says red sky at night, sailor's delight. red sky in morning, sailor's warning.
> 5. Malcolm Coleman even wrote a poem entitled red sky.

The Hyphen

16ak Join words to make compound adjectives

A hyphen is used to join two adjectives into a compound adjective before a noun. Do not use a hyphen between the two adjectives when they follow a verb and are not in front of a noun to describe it.

→ freeze-dried coffee, red-light district, well-lighted sign, carry-on luggage

→ She can't tolerate coffee that is freeze dried.

16al Connect prefixes and suffixes to root words

1. Join certain prefixes (*all-*, *ex-*, *half-*, and *self-*) to a root word

→ all-inclusive, ex-husband, half-back, self-starter

2. Link a single letter to a noun or participle

A hyphen can also be used to join single letters to a noun or participle.

→ X-ray, y-axis, U-turn, G-rated

16am Join words to make compound numbers

A hyphen is used to join compound numbers from *twenty-one* to *ninety-nine*.

→ twenty-one, thirty-two, forty-three, forty-four

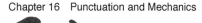

What's wrong with this sign?

16an Join numbers

Hyphens are used to join the numerator and denominator in a fraction. They are also used to give a person's life span or a score.

→   one-fourth, two-thirds, four-fifths

→   Edward Minor Gallaudet (1837-1917) was the founder and first president of a university for the deaf.

→   In last night's bowling championship, Smith beat Jones 222-219.

16ao Prevent confusion

A hyphen should be used to avoid awkward spelling or confusion when using a prefix or suffix.

→   pre-eminent, re-educate, anti-infective

→   The football player will re-sign. vs. The football player will resign.

EXERCISE 1: *Directions: Add a hyphen where necessary.*

1. My motherinlaw's Xray was the first sign of her health crisis.

2. The recreation or remodeling of a piece of art can cause controversy.

3. *Signs* is a hairraising film from beginning to end, even though the audience does not know what is truly happening until halfway through.

4. Although M. Night Shyamalan is best known for *The Sixth Sense*, *Signs* is also a well known film.

5. Both *The Sixth Sense* and *Signs* are truly all American films.

Photo from: crackdmuskegonnewz.blogspot.com: "Hyphen-Nation."

The Dash

A dash is two strokes of the hyphen key without spacing before or after. Dashes are used in a variety of ways as seen below. Be sure, though, that you need to use a dash and not a hyphen.

16ap Highlight introductory material

A dash can be used to highlight introductory material. Usually, the clause that follows the dash will give further explanation about the introductory material.

➔ A pig or a boar—those are the two names for my Chinese zodiac sign.

16aq Set off parenthetical, explanatory, or contrasted material

➔ I cannot accept either name—a pig or boar—for my Chinese zodiac sign.

➔ Chinese zodiac signs—based on animals and natural elements—describe general qualities of a person's nature.

➔ I'd much rather be a dragon—not a pig—for my Chinese zodiac sign.

16ar Add emphasis

Dashes can be used instead of commas when you want to add emphasis to something.

➔ I still can't believe what my Chinese zodiac sign is—a pig or boar!

EXERCISE 1: *Directions: Add a dash where needed.*

1. Latin and Old French these are languages that had the word "sign" before English.
2. Signs usually flat and clearly visible help us navigate the world around us.
3. Astrology, however, can also have signs, and these signs whether Native American, Indian, or Chinese often share some common descriptions.
4. Omens a different kind of sign entirely can be taken quite seriously.
5. A sign such as a thumbs-up can often be understood across language or cultural boundaries.

Parenthses

A parenthesis (the singular form of "parentheses") is a type of bracket. A dash is more commonly used nowadays in formal writing although parentheses and dashes basically have the same function.

16as Enclose explanatory, minor, or secondary information

Parentheses are used to add material that might interrupt the flow of the sentence. The added information is considered secondary or minor to the main idea of the sentence.

→ In the Chinese zodiac, a person with the boar (a pig) sign is honest, sociable, and hard-working.

16at Enclose in-text citations

Parentheses are also used to enclose in-text citations when you need to document your source(s).

MLA in-text citation→ Williams theorizes that the overlap in different systems of astrology is due to "the inherent relationship between travel and storytelling" (234).

APA in-text citation→ Although astrology systems around the world may differ, some overlap is possible due to how stories and travel go together (Williams, 234).

Helpful hint: You can embed parenthetical elements within other elements; however, this is not common in formal writing. Use different types of brackets to set off both elements in this case.

→ Astrology (whether it is Indian [from India] or Chinese) usually is based in some way on nature.

16au Enclose numbers or letters in outlines

Parentheses can be used at different levels of outlines to enclose numbers or letters.

→ I.

   A.

   B.

      1.

         a.

         b.

            (1)

            (2)

         c.

            (1)

               (a)

               (b)

            (2)

Brackets

16av Use square brackets to signal corrections or errors

1. Signal editorial correction

Square brackets are usually used to signal that an editorial correction or clarification has been made within a quotation.

→ "The inherent relationship between [the Chinese and Western] systems of astrology is due to exploration and storytelling" (Williams 234).

2. Signal editorial error

Square brackets that are placed around the word *sic* ("as such" in Latin) signal that an editorial error was made by the original writer or speaker.

→ "The inherent relationship between [*sic*] the three systems of astrology is due to exploration and storytelling" (Williams 234).

16aw Use angle brackets to signal Web addresses

Angle brackets (< >) are used to signal Web addresses and separate them unmistakably from the rest of the sentence.

Angle brackets also allow for the end punctuation to fall outside the brackets, thus not creating any confusion about whether the end punctuation is part of the Web address.

→ To learn more about Chinese astrology, visit <http://chinesezodiac.com>.

The Slash

The slash (/) is often called the forward slash to distinguish it from the backslash (\) used in Web addresses. It is also sometimes called the diagonal or the oblique.

16ax Quote lines of poetry

When quoting more than one line of poetry, the slash (or diagonal) is used to show where each line of poetry ends. Be sure to place a space on each side of the slash.

→ I cannot help but compare my visit to the lines of a favorite poem by Jackson H. Day called "Wesley Theological Seminary: No Thoroughfare": "O you who see this sign, pray it may go / And all it represents; and later, lo / This path can be the broadest thoroughfare" (ll.4-6).

16ay Show a choice

A slash can also be used between two words to show that either choice is available or acceptable.

→ the in/out door, the up/down button

Ellipses

16az Signal omissions

Ellipses (or ellipsis points) consist of three periods that are spaced equally apart. They are used in quotations to indicate that words have been omitted. If the omission occurs at the end of a sentence, put the ellipses after the period that is at the end of the sentence.

> Original➔ "My attitude towards punctuation is that it ought to be as conventional as possible. The game of golf would lose a good deal if croquet mallets and billiard cues were allowed on the putting green. You ought to be able to show that you can do it a good deal better than anyone else with the regular tools before you have a license to bring in your own improvements."
>
> —Ernest Hemingway

> Quotation➔"My attitude towards punctuation is that it ought to be as conventional as possible. . . . You ought to be able to show that you can do it a good deal better than anyone else . . . before you have a license to bring in your own improvements."

When quoting poetry, use a line of ellipsis points to signal that you have dropped a line or more of the poem.

Give Me a Sign

By Linda R. O'Connell
2008

Give me a sign
of any kind
at all.

That tells me we share
the same soul.

. . . .

And walk with me
forever.

Until the moonlight is not required.

For this love
within our hearts,

Would light the world
on fire.

16ba Signal a pause or hesitation

Ellipses can also be used to signal a pause or hesitation.

> ➔   I wish . . . that punctuation was as conventional as possible, just as Hemingway describes it.

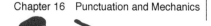

Capitalization

16bb Indicate the first word

1. Indicate the first word in a sentence

Capitalization is used for the first word in every sentence.

→ Traffic signs are sometimes difficult to understand.

2. Indicate the first word in a quotation

Capitalization is also used to indicate the first word in a quotation.

→ My brother told the police officer, "But the sign was covered by a tree branch."

3. Indicate the first word inside parentheses

Capitalization is used when a full sentence is placed within parentheses. If the parenthetical statement is inserted into another sentence, do not capitalize.

→ My brother told the officer that the sign was covered by a tree branch. (However, it wasn't.)

→ My brother told the officer (from our father's precinct) that the sign was covered by a tree branch.

→ My brother told the officer (the officer was from our father's precinct) that the sign was covered by a tree branch.

4. Indicate the first word in a sentence following a colon

Capitalization after a colon is optional; however, capitalize the first word after a colon if you want to emphasize the sentence.

→ My brother has had several tickets: he has been caught driving with a broken headlight, driving too fast in a school zone, and not stopping for a pedestrian in the crosswalk.

→ The police officer voided the ticket: He was from our father's precinct.

16bc Indicate proper nouns and proper adjectives

Capitalization is used to indicate proper nouns and proper adjectives.

1. Indicate proper nouns

Proper nouns name specific people, places, things, or ideas. For more information on proper nouns.

People➜Abigail Breslin, Joaquin Phoenix, Aunt Joan, Uncle Ralph, Senator Jones, Reverend Smith, Dr. Black, Chief Johnson, Professor White

Places➜ Europe, Australia, Alaska, Washington, D.C., the South, the Northeast, the Mississippi River, the Grand Canyon, New York City, United States

Organizations, governmental institutions, and academic institutions➜Federal Bureau of Investigation, Department of Labor, the United Nations, Long Beach City College, Harvard University

Abbreviations of titles and organizations➜ AAA, FBI, MD, MLA, PhD, UN, UCLA

Monuments and buildings➜ the Washington Monument, the Willis Tower, the Taj Mahal, the Eiffel Tower

Languages➜ Chinese, English, Arabic, Swahili, Spanish, French, Japanese, Russian, Mandarin, American Sign Language

Races➜ American Indian, Alaskan Native, Pacific Islander, African American, Black, White, Asian

Nationalities➜Spanish, Ethiopian, Arabic, Chinese, South African, Greek, American

Religions and religious terms➜ Buddhism, Islam, Christianity, Judaism, Shinto, Protestant, Catholic, Baptist, Buddha, Mohammed, God, Jesus, Moses, Talmud, Bible, Koran, Allah, Jehovah, Genesis

Course titles➜ English 101, Biology 1001, French 300, English Composition 101, Modern War Ethics, An Introduction to Computer History

Days and months➜ January, March, May, Sunday, Tuesday, Thursday

2. Indicate proper adjectives

Capitalization is also used for proper adjectives, which are usually derived from proper nouns and can be found inside a proper noun phrase.

➜   Chinese food, English language, Spanish eyes

16bd Indicate titles and subtitles

Capitalization is used for titles of books, stories, plays, poems, songs, articles, films, newspapers, magazines, works of art, musical compositions, and photographs. Always capitalize the first word in the title, no matter the type of word. Also, if using MLA (Modern Language Association) style, capitalize all other words in the title or subtitle except for articles (*a, an, the*), conjunctions (*for, and, nor, but, or, yet, so*), and short prepositions (*in, on, for, to*). If using another style, such as from the APA (American Psychological Association), be sure to check specific guidelines.

Books➜ *The World According to Garp*

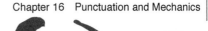

Books with subtitles➜ *Chinese Astrology: Exploring the Eastern Zodiac*

Short stories➜ "Everyday Use"

Plays➜ *Hamlet*

Poems➜ *"Casey at Bat"*

Songs➜ "Rudolph, the Red-Nosed Reindeer"

Articles➜ "Fifty Ways to Avoid the Flu"

Films➜ *Moulin Rouge*

Newspapers➜ *The New York Times*

Magazines and journals➜ *Vogue, English Journal*

Works of art➜ *Starry Night*

Musical compositions➜ *Romeo et Juliette*

Photographs➜ *The Kiss*

Vessels➜ *Spruce Goose, Queen Mary*

16be Indicate acronyms

Acronyms are made up of the first letter of each word in a phrase. For instance, *FBI* is the acronym for "Federal Bureau of Investigation." Acronyms are usually capitalized except for those that have become regular words such as *scuba*, *laser*, and *radar*.

Acronyms ➜CBS, CEO, CIA, FAQ, SAT, USA, WGN

Did You Know? The official name for the Roman Empire, long before the Christian era, was SPQR, an acronym that means *enatus opulus ue omanus* or "the Senate and the People of Rome."

EXERCISE 1: *Directions: Capitalize where needed.*

1. when I visited china and the great wall, I had two books in my backpack: *the signs of life in the universe* and *life after school*.
2. i learned quite quickly that I should have been carrying a chinese-english dictionary.
3. people often asked me on my asian trip whether i was canadian, australian, or american.
4. while visiting monasteries, my brother alex and i learned about buddha and buddhism (and also lao tse and taoism).
5. we also learned that the people's republic of china (the prc) and the republic of china (roc) are considered two different countries (china and taiwan, respectively) by all countries except for the prc.

Italics

Italics are used to emphasize special words, phrases, or clauses. If you are writing by hand or are unable to use italics, you can underline the items that should be in italics.

16bf Highlight titles

1. Highlight titles of longer works

To highlight the title of a larger or longer work, use italics. Thus, you should italicize the titles of poetry or short story collections, anthologies, books, albums/CDs, magazines, newspapers, encyclopedias, television series, and radio series.

→ *Signs of Life: A Book of Visual Poetry* by John Ecko

→ *Vital Signs: International Short Stories on Aging* by Dorothy Sennett and Anne Czarniecki

→ *The Signs of Language Revisited: An Anthology in Honor of Ursula Bellugi and Edward Klima* – edited by Karen Emmorey and Harlan L. Lane

→ *Lonely Planet Signspotting* – a book by Doug Lansky

→ *The Sign* – a CD by Ace of Base

→ *Vital Signs* – a magazine

→ *Encyclopedia Britannica* – an encyclopedia

→ *Sign of the Times* – a television series

→ *The Bob and Tom Radio Show* – a radio series

> **Helpful hint:** Quotation marks are used to enclose the titles of short works, including poems, short stories, lectures, book chapters, song titles, magazine articles, newspaper articles, encyclopedia entries, and television/radio episodes.
>
> → "Signs and Wonder" is episode 7.9 of *The X-Files*.

2. Highlight legal cases

Italics are used to highlight the titles of legal cases.

→ *Roe v. Wade, Brown v. Board of Education of Topeka, State v. Scopes*

3. Identify naval and air ships

Italics are used to identify naval crafts, aircraft, and spacecraft.

→ *Nimitz, Titanic, Queen Mary*

→ *Spruce Goose, Spirit of St. Louis, Lockheed Vega, Air Force One*

→ *Challenger, Atlantis, Enterprise, Sputnik, Explorer*

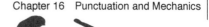

16bg Highlight special letters, words, phrases, or clauses

Italics are used to highlight special letters, words, phrases, and clauses.

1. Highlight non-English words

Italics are used when you write a non-English word or phrase. If the word or phrase is used multiple times, use italics only the first time it is used.

> French phrase for "joy of living"➔ Every time I see Karen, I drink in her *joie de vivre*.

> Japanese word for "special singing and dancing"➔ My favorite part of Japanese night was the *kabuki* theater.

> Arabic phrase for "have a safe journey"➔ As he left me on the trail, the guide wished me, "*Bissalama*."

The English language has borrowed heavily from other languages for centuries, and some of these words are now considered part of English. For these types of everyday words, you do not use italics.

> ➔ soy (Japanese), glasnost (Russian), banana (Wolof), Kwanzaa (Swahili), cider (Hebrew)

> **Did You Know?** In 1973, a survey (by Thomas Finkenstaedt and Dieter Wolff) of about 80,000 words found in the *Shorter Oxford Dictionary* (3rd edition) showed that 28.3% of the English words were borrowed from French, 28.24% from Latin, 25% from Germanic languages (including Old and Middle English), and 5.32% from Greek. All other languages contributed less than 1% of the borrowed words (with 3.28% deriving from proper names and 4.03% of the word origins being unknown).

2. Highlight referenced or discussed letters, words, phrases, and clauses

You also use italics to highlight words that you are discussing, defining, or using in a special way.

> ➔ Words with the letters *SK* at the beginning are usually of Scandinavian origin.

> ➔ I had no idea that the word *banana* came from the African language Wolof.

> ➔ *Leviathan* had the original meaning of "sea monster" but now refers to anything of an unusual size.

1. On The Bruce and Janet Show on satellite radio, they often end the show by saying au revoir or adios.

2. Once, on the Queen Mary, Bruce ended the show by saying adios.

3. Some of the show's best conversations have been collected on Talk the Talk with Bruce and Janet, a limited-edition CD.

4. The Dictionary of American Radio Dialects also has three entries that describe some of the funny expressions that Bruce uses.

5. My favorite Bruce expression is quack like a duck but roar like a lion.

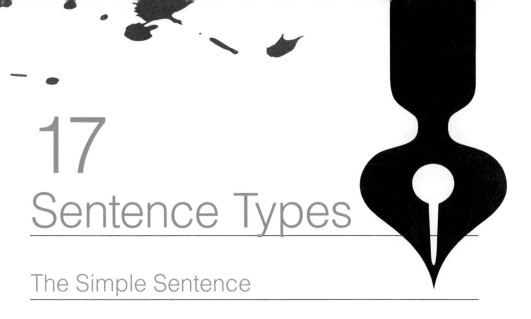

17

Sentence Types

The Simple Sentence

17a The simple sentence

A simple sentence contains a subject and main verb combination, either or both of which may be conjoined. There are two kinds of clauses: independent and dependent. An independent clause, sometimes called a main clause, can stand alone as a simple, but complete, sentence. A dependent clause—with its own subject and verb—can never stand alone and is never part of a simple sentence.

Independent clause/simple sentence➜ Sam saw the stop sign.

Conjoined noun phrase➜ Sam and Chris saw the stop sign.

Conjoined verb phrase➜ Sam saw the stop sign and braked the car at the same time.

An independent clause can be modified in a variety of ways and still be a simple sentence. Most often, simple sentences are modified with either participial verb phrases, which are verb phrases that do not include an auxiliary, or prepositional phrases.

➜ **Driving down Elm Street,**
　　　　　Participial VP
Sam saw the stop sign.
　　Independent Clause

➜ **Stopped at the corner, Sam saw the stop sign.**
　　Participial VP　　　　　　Independent Clause

➜ **Sam saw the stop sign at the corner.**
　　Independent Clause　　Prep Phrase

Simple sentences can be modified by participial phrases and prepositional phrases at the same time.

→   **Driving down Elm Street,**
        Participial VP

→   **Sam saw the stop sign at the corner.**
        Independent Clause   Prep Phrase

Multiple prepositional phrases can also be used in the same simple sentence.

→   **Sam saw the stop sign** at the corner of Elm and Sixth.
        Independent Clause   Prep Phrase   Prep Phrase

As you may have already noticed, participial phrases that appear at the beginning of the sentence always have a comma that separates the phrase from the independent clause. In fact, all phrases or clauses that contain a verb and occur at the beginning of a sentence should be separated from the main clause by a comma.

When you write a sentence that has a prepositional phrase at the beginning, you have the option of including a comma or not; however, if the introductory prepositional phrase is five words or longer, it usually takes a comma.

OK→ In spring the stop sign at Elm and Sixth is covered with a tree branch.

OK→ In spring, the stop sign at Elm and Sixth is covered with a tree branch.

OK→ At the corner of Elm and Sixth, the stop sign is covered with a tree branch.

17b Check for common errors with the simple sentence

1. Check for overuse of simple sentences

Simple sentences are often used for effect or emphasis and should be used sparingly. Be sure that you do not overuse simple sentences, so when you are ready to use them for emphasis, they can stand out from the more complex sentences around them. See how the addition of a simple sentence in the combination below stands out against the more complex sentence that precedes it.

→   Our city manager says that there are no funds available to cut the overgrown tree branch on Elm and Sixth; however, there were enough funds for her recent junket to Las Vegas. She needs to stop irrelevant spending now.

2. Check for fragments

Be sure that simple sentences have both a subject and predicate. If one or the other is missing, you have created a common sentence error—the fragment.

Fragment (missing a subject)→ Leaving the party with his friends in the blue car.

OK→ Sam left the party with his friends in the blue car.

OK➔ Leaving the party early, Sam went with his friends in the blue car.

Fragment (missing a predicate)➔ My neighbor Sam and his friends, along with many of the people at the party.

OK➔ My neighbor Sam and his friends, along with many of the people at the party, were in the backyard.

Sentences that give directions or a command have an understood subject (*you*), so even though a subject may not appear explicitly in the sentence, the implied subject makes the sentence an independent clause and not a fragment.

➔ (You should) Go east on Elm, and then turn on Sixth.

3. Check for parallelism

When conjoining multiple instances of the same type of word class or phrase, be sure that they are in parallel form.

Not parallel➔ Sam ran quickly to the sign at the corner, returned just as quickly, and singing all the while.

OK➔ Sam ran quickly to the sign at the corner, returned just as quickly, and sang all the while.

> **EXERCISE 1:** *Directions: Revise any fragments below into full sentences.*
>
> *Example: Many people have had accidents at the tree-covered stop sign. For instance, my neighbor John. ➔ Many people, including my neighbor John, have had accidents at the tree-covered stop sign.*
>
> 1. Nothing has been done to fix the problem. No tree work. No sign moving.
> 2. I like to visit my friends on Elm Street. Who have a pool and a hot tub.
> 3. My friends' daughter had an accident at the stop sign at Sixth and Elm. Not seeing the sign.
> 4. The city manager needs to take the accidents seriously. Along with other city officials losing more funds due to court cases.
> 5. Running for office to fix the small problems of our city, including the overgrown trees that are blocking traffic signs.

The Compound Sentence

17c The compound sentence

One way to add variety to your writing is to use coordination to join some of your simple sentences together. When you coordinate or combine together two simple sentences (also known as two independent clauses), you create a compound sentence.

→ **The signs for American Sign Language were originally based**
                     Independent Clause
on French, and the signs for Signed English were originally
                     Independent Clause
based on English.

You can choose from four options to create compound sentences, and the option you choose determines the punctuation you will use.

> **Helpful hint:** The compound sentence includes the combination of two full sentences, not two subjects, two verbs, or two verb phrases. For instance, the following sentences are not compound sentences, just simple sentences.
>
> Compound subjects➤ Mary and the new professor left the classroom early.
>
> Compound verbs➤ Mary laughed and cried at the same time.
>
> Compound verb phrases➤ Mary laughed at the joke and cried at the picture at the same time.

17d Use appropriate punctuation for the compound sentence

1. Punctuating a compound sentence—Option 1: Using a comma + conjunction

Notice that the two independent clauses on the previous page are joined together with a comma and a conjunction (*and*). Independent clauses can be joined in a variety of acceptable ways, and using a comma plus a coordinating conjunction is one of the most popular.

The conjunctions that you can use to join together two independent clauses can be remembered by using the mnemonic device **FANBOYS**, in which each letter represents one conjunction.

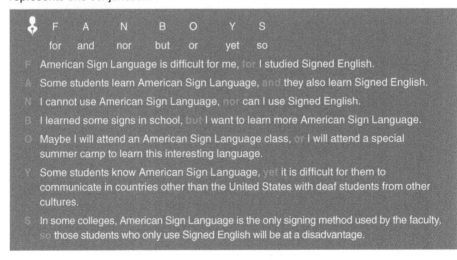

> F   A   N   B   O   Y   S
> for   and   nor   but   or   yet   so
>
> F American Sign Language is difficult for me, for I studied Signed English.
>
> A Some students learn American Sign Language, and they also learn Signed English.
>
> N I cannot use American Sign Language, nor can I use Signed English.
>
> B I learned some signs in school, but I want to learn more American Sign Language.
>
> O Maybe I will attend an American Sign Language class, or I will attend a special summer camp to learn this interesting language.
>
> Y Some students know American Sign Language, yet it is difficult for them to communicate in countries other than the United States with deaf students from other cultures.
>
> S In some colleges, American Sign Language is the only signing method used by the faculty, so those students who only use Signed English will be at a disadvantage.

2. Punctuating a compound sentence—Option 2: Using a semi-colon

A semi-colon can be used to connect two independent clauses. When you use a semi-colon in this way, you suggest to the reader that the two connected clauses are related in some way.

➜ Some students learn American Sign Language; **they can also**
Independent Clause
learn Signed English.
Independent Clause

3. Punctuating a compound sentence—Option 3:

Using a semi-colon + adverbial conjunction

Another way to connect two independent clauses is with a semi-colon plus an adverbial conjunction (sometimes called a conjunctive adverb). Note that a comma follows the adverbial conjunction.

➜ Some students attend a school that requires American Sign
Independent Clause
Language; therefore, **knowing Signed English is not enough.**
Independent Clause

You can use the acronym THIN TIC to help you remember some common adverbial conjunctions.

T	therefore
H	however
I	in fact
N	nevertheless
T	thus
I	indeed
C	consequently

Adverbial conjunctions signify relationships such as result, cause, contrast, or condition. Be sure to signal the appropriate relationship with the adverbial conjunction you use.

Result/cause ➜ I learned Signed English in elementary school; therefore, I had problems understanding some American Sign Language signs later on.

Contrast ➜ American Sign Language is popular at Gallaudet University; however, English is used alongside ASL.

Condition/intensification ➜ American Sign Language and English are popular at Gallaudet University; indeed, many students use both.

Other than the common THIN TIC adverbial conjunctions, there are other adverbial conjunctions that can be used to connect two independent clauses and signify particular relationships. Here is a list to help you make appropriate choices.

Addition → moreover, furthermore, likewise, finally, additionally, also, incidentally, further, similarly, in addition

Contrast → however, nevertheless, in contrast, on the contrary, nonetheless, otherwise, on the other hand, in comparison, conversely, instead

Comparison → similarly, likewise, at the same time, comparatively

Exemplification → for example, for instance, namely, that is

Intensification → indeed, in fact, moreover, still, certainly, notably, undoubtedly

Result →therefore, thus, consequently, as a result, finally, hence, then, accordingly, henceforth, subsequently, undoubtedly, in fact

Time → meanwhile, then, next, finally, still, now, thereafter

This image of a note placed on an information desk shows a compound sentence that is missing the appropriate punctuation. How could you fix the punctuation problem?

4. Punctuating a compound sentence—Option 4: Using a colon

Although not as common as the first three methods of joining two independent clauses together, you can also use a colon if the clause following the colon defines or elaborates the clause before the colon.

→ American Sign Language and Signed English are different in
　　　　　　　Independent Clause
one important way: many linguists consider American Sign
　　　　　　　Independent Clause
Language a full and complete language and Signed English not.

Since both independent clauses are connected in meaning and since the second independent clause elaborates on the first, giving more information about why, a colon can be used.

The above sign is missing the appropriate punctuation—how ironic!
How would you edit this sign to make it grammatically correct?

17e Common sentence errors with the compound sentence

1. Use a variety of punctuation, conjunctions, and adverbial conjunctions

Be careful when you decide how to join compound sentences. Combining sentences in the same way each time or in a way that creates an obviously consistent pattern will negatively impact your writing. It is best to use a variety of punctuation, conjunctions, and adverbial conjunctions.

2. Check for comma splices

Mistakenly joining two independent clauses together with only a comma creates one of the most frequent sentence errors that writers make. You can fix a comma splice by using one of the four options given above.

Comma splice➜ Some American students learn Signed English as children, they learn American Sign Language as adults.

OK➜ Some American students learn Signed English as children, and they learn American Sign Language as adults.

OK➜ Some American students learn Signed English as children; they then learn American Sign Language as adults.

OK➜ Some American students learn Signed English as children; then, they learn American Sign Language as adults.

3. Check for run-on or fused sentences

If you fail to join two independent clauses together with the appropriate punctuation, you can create another common sentence problem—the run-on or fused sentence.

Run-on/fused sentence➜ My third-grade teacher taught us some (signs they) were Signed English.

OK➜ My third-grade teacher taught us some signs, yet I don't know many now.

OK➜ My third-grade teacher taught us some signs; they were Signed English.

EXERCISE 1: *Directions: The following paragraph contains five comma splices. Correct the errors by turning the comma splices into compound sentences.*

I've never been one for believing in astrological signs, I couldn't really even tell you what my sign, Scorpio, actually means. But every now and then, I'll run across a daily horoscope chart, curiosity gets the better of me. One day in particular, my horoscope said to be careful in business dealings and avoid conflict. I had been having a disagreement with one of my clients, who was threatening to give her business to our biggest competitor, immediately that situation came to mind as I read the horoscope over my morning breakfast. I walked into the office later that morning, my secretary informed me that the client was waiting on me—and not happy. I quickly made up an excuse and left the office, remembering what was in store for Scorpios that day. Come to find out, the client's anger was not directed at me, but because she wasted her time coming to the office that morning, she decided to take her business elsewhere. My decision to avoid the conflict altogether resulted in my losing this client and significant income for my company, needless to say, I try to avoid horoscopes now.

Citation = http://news.bbc.co.uk/2/hi/uk_news/magazine/7292252.stm

---

EXERCISE 2: *Directions: The following paragraph contains five run-on sentences. Correct them by adding the appropriate punctuation.*

Who would have guessed that a simple piece of fruit would become synonymous with innovative technology well this is exactly what has happened with the symbol for Apple, Inc. With the increasing international popularity of the iPhone, Apple's logo is becoming one of the most recognizable symbols in business and technology today. The trademark silhouette of an apple missing a bite has been around practically since the company's inception although the company's earliest logo features a sketch of Isaac Newton sitting under the apple tree. Apple co-founder Steve Jobs hired Rob Janoff in 1976 to redesign the company's logo and the iconic rainbow apple design was born this version of Apple's apple remained in use until a redesign of the Macintosh operating system and computer hardware in 1998 warranted a monochrome makeover. Two more versions of the symbol would follow: an aqua theme in 2001 and the current glass theme unveiled in 2003, both of which gave the trademark a three dimensional, textured appearance though it's already an internationally recognized symbol, the Apple logo will only become even more common as the company continues to expand.

The Complex Sentence

17f The complex sentence

Another way to add variety to your writing is to use subordination and modification to create complex sentences. A complex sentence consists of a simple sentence (also known as an independent clause) plus one or more dependent clauses.

Dependent clauses, like independent clauses, contain a subject and predicate; however, whereas independent clauses can stand alone, dependent clauses are dependent or subordinate to an independent clause and must be attached to that independent clause to form a complete sentence. You can track most dependent clauses back to their independent counterparts, as in the set of sentences below.

Independent clause➔ Each letter in our alphabet is a sign.

Independent clause➔ Each letter in our alphabet gives us information about our language's history and sound system.

Complex sentence➔ Because each letter in our alphabet is a
                                           Dependent Clause
sign, it gives us information about our language's history and sound system.
                   Independent Clause

Note that the dependent clause above includes the subordinator "because" at the beginning of the clause. A dependent clause usually begins with a subordinator—also called a subordinating conjunction—or a relative pronoun. A subordinator or relative pronoun gives information about the relationship between the independent and dependent clause.

Common subordinators	Relative pronouns
Cause ➔ because, since, as if, why	that
Concession ➔ although, even though, certainly, though	what
	whatever
Condition ➔ if, unless, how, rather than, where, whether	which
	whichever
Effect ➔ so that, in order that	who
Place ➔ where	whoever
Sequence ➔ after, before, while, until	whom
Time ➔ when, as, until, once	whomever
	whose

17g Dependent clauses

Dependent clauses can be nominal (used like nouns), adjectival (used like adjectives), or adverbial (used like adverbs). This means that dependent clauses can be used as subjects, objects, or modifiers. Although it is sometimes difficult to distinguish which type of dependent clause is being used, it is a good idea to learn the different clause types because your choice of punctuation depends on how a clause is being used.

17h Noun (or nominal) clauses

Dependent noun clauses can function as subjects, direct objects, subject complements, objects of prepositions, or appositives. Since these types of clauses are dependent or subordinate, they are always attached to an independent clause or a critical part of an independent clause. Noun clauses usually begin with a relative pronoun or with one of these subordinators: when, where, how, why or whether. There are two types of noun clauses: nominal relative clauses and appositive clauses.

1. Nominal relative clauses

Nominal relative clauses take the place of a subject, direct object, or an object of a preposition. A good way to see whether you are using a nominal relative clause is to see if you can substitute a pronoun (*it, she, he*) for the clause in question.

In place of a subject ➜ What sound a letter makes is complicated.
                    Dependent Clause/Nominal Relative Clause

In place of a direct object ➜ For new language learners, it is sometimes difficult to know which letter represents a particular sound.
        Dependent Clause/Nominal Relative Clause

In place of a subject complement ➜ This alphabet disconnection is why many linguists suggest changing our alphabet.
Dependent Clause/Nominal Relative Clause

In place of an object of the preposition ➜ Many linguists theorize about when the alphabet will become more transparent.
Dependent Clause/Nominal Relative Clause

2. Appositive clauses

Appositive clauses follow nouns that are general or abstract in nature, such as a theory, reason, fact, or story. The appositive clause begins with a "that" and provides more information about the abstract noun.

The alphabet disconnection theory that letters do not clearly
                    Dependent Clause/
match sounds is widely known by linguists.
Appositive Clause

It is important to be able to distinguish these dependent clauses as noun clauses because neither one of these dependent noun clauses requires a comma. Putting a comma around these clauses to highlight them or separate them in some way from the independent clause is a comma error.

EXERCISE 1: *Directions: Underline the noun clauses in the following sentences, and then label the types of noun clauses.*

Example: This section contradicted my belief <u>that you should use a comma with all noun clauses.</u> (appositive clause)

1. The assumption that English is the most difficult language to learn has not been proven.

2. What we know about learning English is only a small piece of the language puzzle.

3. Linguists know that many languages are learned in similar ways.

4. Some people seem to like the idea that English is difficult for others to learn.

5. However, this so-called reason is why some non-English speakers give up on learning English.

17i Adjective (or adjectival) clauses

Adjective clauses, another type of dependent or subordinate clause, modify noun phrases, which can be made up of either nouns or pronouns. There are two types of adjective clauses: the comparative clause and the relative clause.

1. Comparative clauses

Comparative clauses compare two noun phrases and use the phrase *as XXX as* to make the comparison, where *XXX* is filled in with an adjective. The clause to the left of the *as XXX as* phrase is the beginning of the independent clause, and the clause to the right of the *as XXX as* phrase is the dependent clause.

→ That sign is as uninformative as the one I saw at the zoo last week.
      Dependent Clause

→ She is as tall as the sign is.
        Dependent Clause

2. Relative clauses

Relative clauses, the most common type of dependent clause, are used to modify or give more information about the noun phrase to the clause's left. These clauses usually begin with a relative pronoun, such as that, which, who, whom, or whose.

→ Highway signs that are funny often defeat the purpose of their warning.
        Relative Clause

→ The student who is signing for the deaf audience is obviously
        Relative Clause
still learning American Sign Language.

→ The highway workers whose job it was to paint the new sign forgot the paint.
        Relative Clause

Relative pronouns can sometimes be dropped if they can be understood to be part of the relative clause.

→ The signs [that] the highway workers need to paint are the
              Relative Clause
   ones [that] taggers have covered with graffiti.

                    Relative Clause

Relative clauses can be essential or necessary for the full meaning of the sentence to be understood, or they can be non-essential. An essential relative clause is described as a restrictive relative clause. Restrictive relative clauses never take commas around the clause.

→ Highway signs that are covered in mud
              Restrictive Relative Clause
   can cause accidents.

In the sentence above, **ALL** highway signs do not cause accidents; only highway signs that are covered in mud can cause them. Thus, the relative clause is essential to understand the meaning of the full sentence.

→ The architect who designed the building has a plaque with his
              Restrictive Relative Clause
   name on it near the front.

Likewise, in the sentence above, it is only the architect who designed the building who has a plaque, not just any architect. Therefore, this relative clause is also essential to the sentence.

A relative clause that is not essential to understand the full meaning of the sentence is described as a non-restrictive relative clause. Non-restrictive relative clauses always take commas around the clause.

→ The signs along Route 66, which are often stolen, classify
              Non-Restrictive Relative Clause
   it as a national monument.

In the sentence above, the relative clause is not essential for us to understand the meaning of the main sentence. In the relative clause, we get extra or non-essential information. With or without the relative clause, we still understand that the signs along Route 66 label it as a national monument.

→ The architect, who wore a seersucker suit to the ceremony, was
              Non-Restrictive Relative Clause
   awarded a plaque.

Likewise, in the above sentence, the relative clause is not essential. Whether he wore a seersucker or wool suit is not important; the architect would still have been awarded the plaque either way.

> **Example:** *Language learners <u>who study their new language in school</u> usually do not speak any better than those <u>who learn their new language through immersion</u>.*

1. When living in a language's culture, you can learn more than just the vocabulary that is introduced in a textbook.

2. Many language learners who live outside their native country find themselves learning new vocabulary from another language quickly.

3. The younger that a language learner is, the more chance she has of learning a new language.

4. Language textbooks, which are often published by a variety of publishers, can only get you so far into your new language.

5. It is a good idea to stay as long as you can in the country of the language that you are learning.

Common subordinators
Cause→ because, since, as if, why
Concession → although, even though, certainly, though
Condition → if, unless, how, rather than, where, whether
Effect → so that, in order that
Place → where
Sequence → after, before, while, until
Time → when, as, until, once

17j Adverb (or adverbial) clauses

Adverbial clauses begin with a subordinator (sometimes called a subordinating conjunction) and usually give information about cause/reason, concession, condition, effect, place, sequence, and time. The clauses do this by answering the questions *when? where? why? how? how frequently?* and *in what manner?* Adverbial clauses are always dependent or subordinate to the main or independent clause.

→ **Because she was caught with the freeway sign in her car**, she
        Adverbial (Dependent) Clause
    was arrested for theft.

Notice that the adverbial clause above gives the reason why the woman was arrested, thus giving information about cause.

Adverbial clauses can function like adverbs, moving to various points in a sentence. When an adverbial clause is at the beginning of the sentence, use a comma to separate it off from the main or independent clause.

→ **Because the highway trooper watched him**
        Adverbial Clause
    closely, the driver followed the detour sign.

When an adverbial clause appears in the middle of a sentence, you should also set it off by placing commas around the adverbial clause.

→ The driver, because the highway trooper
    Adverbial Clause
watched him closely, followed the detour sign.

However, when an adverbial clause appears at the end of a sentence, it usually does not take a comma.

→ The driver followed the detour sign because the highway
    Adverbial Clause
trooper watched him closely.

EXERCISE 3: *Directions: Underline the adverbial clauses in the following sentences, and circle the subordinator.*

Example: You usually do not need a travel guide <u>when you travel in your own neighborhood.</u>

1. When you travel to a foreign country, it is a good idea to bring a travel guide.
2. Although travel guides can be helpful, they cannot get you out of complicated situations.
3. If you do find yourself with a serious problem in a foreign country, you should check if there is an embassy located near you.
4. Finding an embassy is a good idea, so that you feel more secure when dealing with the problem.
5. While embassy employees can usually help you with serious problems, they cannot provide a translator for you for everyday use.

17k Common sentence errors with the complex sentence

1. Check for fragments

Dependent clauses do not express a complete thought, and they need to be attached to an independent clause to be grammatically complete. Because dependent clauses are clauses, they contain a subject and a full verb, a fact that sometimes leads a writer to use a dependent clause as a complete sentence. When dependent clauses are presented as a full sentence, they are fragments.

Fragment→ Because the highway trooper watched him closely.
    Dependent Clause

OK→ The driver took the detour because the highway trooper watched him closely.
    Dependent Clause

Fragment→ When she saw the tornado.
    Dependent Clause

OK→ When she saw the tornado, she took it as a sign to take cover.
    Dependent Clause

Our office was chosen to design the latest advertising campaign. For an internationally known sporting goods company. They've specifically requested a series of promotional billboards. Which will be displayed along highways in major cities. Because of the company's high profile. Our focus and dedication to the project is of the utmost importance, and we've also been told to keep the details of the project a secret. This advertising campaign will bring a significant amount of revenue to our relatively small company, so my boss has told me. That he will be creating a new administrative position. Will be filled by an internal promotion. The promotion, however, will be contingent upon the success of this latest campaign. With this information, the office is dedicated to not only satisfying our client, but also excelling in this project. To ensure our boss promotes one of the many qualified, hard-working employees in the office.

Source= http://news.bbc.co.uk/2/hi/uk_news/magazine/7292252.stm

2. Check for unnecessary commas

A noun clause can replace a subject, direct object, subject complement, or object of a preposition. When using a noun clause to replace these items, avoid placing an unnecessary comma between the noun clause and the rest of the sentence.

Extra comma➜ What I like about Saturdays, is seeing all the
                        Dependent Noun Clause
yard sale signs in my neighborhood.

OK➜ What I like about Saturdays is seeing all the yard sale
        Dependent Noun Clause
signs in my neighborhood.

3. Check for restrictive or non-restrictive punctuation

Be sure to use the correct punctuation for relative clauses. When they provide essential information, they are restrictive and should not have commas. When relative clauses provide non-essential or extra information, they are non-restrictive and should always be separated from the rest of the sentence with commas.

Extra commas➜ The protester, who had the derogatory sign, was removed from
the lecture.   Restrictive Relative Clause

OK➜ The protester who had the derogatory sign was removed from the lecture.
                Restrictive Relative Clause

In the above example, the relative clause gives necessary information—the reason the protester was removed from the lecture. Therefore, the relative clause is restrictive and does not take commas.

Missing commas➜ M. Night Shyamalan who directed *Sixth*
                                Non-Restrictive
Sense and *Signs* has not won an Academy Award.
Relative Clause

OK→ M. Night Shyamalan, who directed *Sixth Sense* and
Non-Restrictive Relative Clause
Signs, has not won an Academy Award.

In the example above, the information that Shyamalan directed the movies *Sixth Sense* and *Signs* is not essential to the main point that he has not won an Academy Award. Thus, the relative clause is non-restrictive and needs to have commas surrounding it.

4. Check for adverbial clause punctuation

When including an adverbial clause in your writing, be sure to use the appropriate punctuation. If the clause appears at the beginning of the sentence, use a comma between it and the independent clause. If the adverbial clause appears in the middle of the sentence, surround the clause with commas. And, finally, if the adverbial clause appears at the end of the sentence, do not separate the dependent adverbial clause and the independent clause.

Missing comma→ As I left the movie I saw a sign advertising
Dependent Clause
next week's feature.

OK→As I left the movie, I saw a sign advertising next week's
Dependent Clause
feature.

Extra comma→ I saw a sign advertising next week's feature, as I left the movie.
Dependent Clause

OK→ I saw a sign advertising next week's feature as I left the movie.
Dependent
Clause

The Compound-Complex Sentence

17| The compound-complex sentence

A compound-complex sentence is made up of two or more simple sentences or independent clauses (this is the compound part) and one or more subordinate or dependent clauses (this is the complex part).

→ While she waited for a sign from the employees, other shop-
Dependent Clause
pers sneaked into the toy store, and they were the ones fortu-
Independent Clause
nate enough to find the most popular toy for Christmas.
Independent Clause

When you punctuate a compound-complex sentence, you use the rules for both compound and complex sentences. For instance, in the above sentence, the dependent adverbial clause appears at the beginning of the sentence; thus, it needs a comma between it and the independent clause. In addition, the combination of a comma and coordinating conjunction is used to join together the two independent clauses.

17m Common sentence errors with the compound-complex sentence

Pay attention to the common sentence errors for both compound and complex sentences, and you will be successful in punctuating a compound-complex sentence.

1. Check for run-on or fused sentences

Run-on/fused sentence→ Students who use both American Sign Language and Signed English understand that some of the signs are the same and this makes it easier for them to learn both.

OK→ Students who use both American Sign Language and Signed English understand that some of the signs are the same, and this makes it easier for them to learn both.

2. Check for comma splices

Comma splice→ Students who use both American Sign Language and Signed English understand that some of the signs are the same, this makes it easier for them to learn both.

OK→ Students who use both American Sign Language and Signed English understand that some of the signs are the same, and this makes it easier for them to learn both.

3. Check for fragments

Fragment→ Students who use both American Sign Language and Signed English understand that some of the signs.

OK→Students who use both American Sign Language and Signed English understand that some of the signs are the same, and this makes it easier for them to learn both.

18

Style

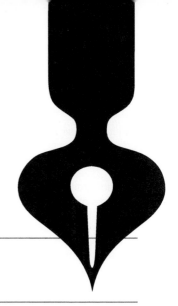

Sentence Focus

Be sure that all your sentences are focused on the main idea of your paragraph, essay, or document. In addition, check that the sentence style you use helps each idea flow from sentence to sentence.

18a Use transitions

You can use transitions to connect from one sentence to the next, creating a flow of ideas that all support the main idea. Transitions can also help clarify meanings by highlighting relationships between words, phrases, or sentences. Writing without transitions often sounds disjointed and rambling, but be sure that the transitions you use fit the relationship you are trying to describe.

→   The Chinese zodiac has twelve signs; similarly, so does Western astrology.

→   As previously mentioned, I am frustrated that my Chinese zodiac sign is the boar.

Transitions	
Addition→moreover, furthermore, besides, likewise, also, too, finally, second, third, last, additionally	Intensification→ indeed, in fact
	Place→ where, here, near, beyond
	Purpose→ (in order) to, to this end
Cause→ since, because	Repetition→ in other words, as I have said, as previously mentioned, as stated above
Comparison→ similarly, likewise	
Concession→ although, though, despite	
Condition→ unless, provided that, if	Result→therefore, thus, consequently, as a result, hence
Contrast→ but, yet, however, nevertheless, in contrast, on the contrary, nonetheless, whereas, even though, although, otherwise, on the other hand	Summary→ in conclusion, in short, all in all, overall, finally
	Time→ when, after, before, until, as long as, meanwhile, while, immediately, soon, afterward, then, henceforth
Exception→ except	
Exemplification→ for example, for instance	

18b Emphasize key ideas

1. Use sentence order for emphasis

When you use a sentence that includes a list or series, be sure to use an order that is consistent. Listing items from most important to least important, or vice versa, will help you emphasize key ideas.

> Poor order ➔ Before completing the sign project, we will need to check with these levels of government: city, national, regional, and county.

> OK➔ Before completing the sign project, we will need to check with these levels of government: city, county, regional, and national.

2. Use end-focus for emphasis

In English, it is normal to arrange sentences so that the most important information comes at the end of the sentence. This type of end-focus allows you to organize general knowledge—information that is obvious or already known to the reader—at the beginning of a sentence and lead up to the most important or emphasized information at the end.

> End-focus➔ Before the sign project can be completed, we will need to get approval from the governor's office.

3. Use front-focus for emphasis

You can also place a sentence element in an abnormal position—usually at the front of the sentence—to make the element more emphatic. This type of front-focus is used effectively if you know the regular patterns of English sentences (see Chapter 35).

> Front-focus➔ Red paint they used rarely for the signs, so using it at the governor's mansion allowed the signs to stand out.

4. Reorder negative adverbials for emphasis

Placing a negative adverbial at the beginning of a sentence places an emphasis on that part of the sentence.

> Fronting a negative adverbial➔ Never have I seen such a paint color on a government sign!

5. Use parenthetic expressions

Parenthetic expressions, which are enclosed by punctuation, place an emphasis on the previous sentence element.

> Parenthetic expression➔ At the governor's mansion, for example, they used red paint.

> Parenthetic expression➔ Red paint, of course, will grab pedestrian attention.

18c Be clear

1. Avoid tangents

To keep your sentence on topic, avoid tangents or irrelevant information.

Lack of focus➔ I am frustrated that my Chinese zodiac sign is the boar, which by the way is also the sign for Arnold Schwarzenegger and Ronald Reagan, because I see myself more of a dragon.

OK➔ I am frustrated that my Chinese zodiac sign is the boar because I see myself more as a dragon.

2. Rephrase ambiguous expressions

Watch out for misplaced expressions that cause ambiguity. Place modifiers effectively in sentences, so the meaning you want to give is clear. Check out how the following ambiguous sentence can be rewritten to show its two different meanings.

Ambiguous sentence➔ Writing clearly is important.

Meaning #1➔ It is important to write clearly.

Meaning #2➔ It is clear that writing is important.

Ambiguity can occur with conjoined noun phrases that have adjectives placed in an ambiguous position.

Ambiguous sentence➔ The gray foyer and hallway were being painted next.

Meaning #1➔ The gray foyer and gray hallway were being painted next.

Meaning #2➔ The hallway (not gray) and the gray foyer were being painted next.

Be sure that any adjective that is used to describe the first noun in a conjoined noun phrase is placed in a position that allows for clear understanding.

3. Make sentence elements parallel

Make sure that your sentence meanings are clear by using parallel sentence elements. Combined or coordinated sentence elements should be similar in type. Notice the lack

of parallelism in the sentence below. The *and* is used to join a full clause and a noun phrase. To fix the problem, you need to use either two full clauses or two noun phrases. The second sentence below is parallel and uses two full clauses.

Lack of parallelism➔ They discontinued the painting because the results did not satisfy the governor and a lack of funding.
          Independent Clause   NP

Parallel➔ They discontinued the painting because the results did not satisfy the governor and there was a lack of funding.
Independent Clause   Independent Clause

18d Show confidence

When you write, show that you know the topic well by using authority in your phrasing. Stay away from what some teachers and editors call *weasel words*, such as *I think, I believe, I know, I think I know*. See 15k for more information on how not to "weasel."

Non-authoritative sentence➔ I think that I know why the Chinese zodiac has twelve signs and four elements.

OK➔ The Chinese zodiac has twelve signs, based on the months, and four elements, based on the seasons.

> **EXERCISE 2:** *Directions: Each of the following sentences has a clarity problem; rewrite them so their meanings are clear.*
>
> 1. A letter requesting that the governor stop the painting of the mansion and choose another paint color was sent.
> 2. Although the governor only saw three letters, he knew there was a problem.
> 3. The color of the atrium, the color of the foyer, and the driveway concrete color did not match.
> 4. The angry governor and secretary both called the painters' office.
> 5. The governor wanted the painters, groundskeepers, and the painting supervisors to all be on the same page

Sentence Functions

In English, there are four sentence functions that serve different purposes. Writers use declarative sentences to give information, imperative sentences to give instructions or commands, interrogative sentences to obtain information, and exclamatory sentences to express emotion. In academic writing, you will probably use more declarative sentences than any other. However, if you are writing a narrative or descriptive essay or a piece of creative writing, you will want to use sentences with a variety of functions since that will most closely replicate real life.

18e Use declarative sentences to give information

Use declarative sentences that end with a period for statements that give information. Declarative sentences are the most common type of sentence function in English.

Declarative sentence→ The Chinese zodiac has five elements.

18f Use imperative sentences to give commands

Imperative sentences usually do not have a subject; they are used to give instructions or commands.

Imperative sentence→ Tell me what zodiac sign I am.

Imperative sentence→ Do not tell me that you forgot the answer.

Imperatives can also take the form of *let* plus a subject.

Imperative sentence→ Let's talk about the Chinese zodiac.

The imperative sentence can include *you* or a third person subject, but these types of subjects are not used very often.

Imperative sentence→ You should tell me the answer now.

Imperative sentence→ The guilty party should stand up now.

Imperative sentences can also add a noun phrase that directly addresses the subject of the sentence.

→ You, tell me the answer now.

→ Those students at the back, tell me the answer now.

18g Use interrogative sentences to ask questions

To ask questions, use one of the six types of interrogative sentences, including yes/no questions, wh-questions, declarative questions, alternative questions, tag questions, and rhetorical questions.

A yes/no question begins with a verb and can be answered with a *yes* or *no* but can also be answered with other information as well.

Yes/No question→ Should we mention that the Chinese zodiac is different from other zodiacs?

A wh-question starts with an interrogative word or phrase, usually *who, what, where, when, why,* or *how.*

Wh-question→ How many Chinese zodiac signs are there?

A declarative question is in the form of a declarative sentence but asks a question. These types of questions take the declarative form but usually end with a question mark.

Declarative question→ The Chinese zodiac has five elements?

Alternative questions give a choice or choices.

Alternative question→ Do you prefer to be called a boar or a pig?

Tag questions can attach to declarative or interrogative sentences, making the sentences into questions. If the sentence part is negative, the tag will be positive, and vice versa.

Tag question→ You're a boar, aren't you?

Tag question→ Tell me your sign, won't you?

Rhetorical questions are basically equal to forceful declarative statements. You do not reply to a rhetorical question.

Rhetorical question→ Who could be happy being called a *pig*?

18h Use exclamatory sentences to show surprise

Exclamatory sentences (sometimes called exclamatives) show surprise and end with an exclamation mark. They can begin with *what* or *how*.

Exclamatory sentence→ What a strange name that is!

Exclamatory sentence→ How strange that is!

These types of sentences can also look like a forceful declarative statement.

Exclamatory sentence→ You're a Boar! Really!

EXERCISE 1: *Directions: Take the declarative sentence given, and revise it into the type of sentence given in the parentheses.*

Example: In medicine, signs are different than symptoms. (yes/no question) Did you know that in medicine signs are different than symptoms?

1. A symptom is reported by a patient, and a sign is found by a doctor. (alternative question)

2. Fatigue is considered a symptom. (exclamatory sentence)

3. In an examination, a doctor looks for clinical signs. (declarative question)

4. Doctors make hypotheses, and they use signs to support their hypotheses. (Wh-question)

5. Reddening of the hands is considered a sign. (imperative sentence)

Sentence Order

18i Vary basic sentence order

In English, there are seven basic sentence orders for declarative sentences, influenced by different types of verbs and the elements that work with those verbs. Becoming familiar with these basic sentence orders will help you revise your writing if you find yourself frequently writing the same pattern or order. For more in-depth discussion of the word classes that form these patterns, see Section I.

1. Subject + intransitive verb

A sentence that includes an intransitive verb does not need anything to follow the verb for the sentence to be complete. However, the intransitive verb **can** be followed by an adverb or other optional elements, such as a prepositional phrase, and other optional elements can occur in other places in the sentence.

→ Money talks.

→   S   V

→ Money talks loudly.

→ Sometimes, money talks loudly.

→ Sometimes, money talks loudly in a bad economy.

→ Sometimes, in a bad economy, money talks loudly.

Notice that all of the sentences above have the same basic sentence order with the subject and intransitive verb at the center of the sentence. Even though these sentences might appear different to you, they have the same underlying pattern, and as such, if you write most of your sentences using this same pattern, your prose style will take on a monotonous rhythm.

2. Subject + transitive verb + direct object

A sentence that has a subject, transitive verb, and direct object is the most frequently used English sentence order. The transitive verb requires a noun or noun phrase as its direct object. A noun that comes after a direct object answers one of these questions: What? Whom? (What did the highway workers clean? Whom did John see?) Just like any other sentence pattern, this one can take optional elements, such as adverbs or prepositional phrases.

→ The highway workers cleaned the sign.
      S   V   DO

→ Yesterday, the highway workers cleaned the sign.

→ Yesterday, the highway workers cleaned the sign vigorously.

3. Subject + transitive verb + indirect object + direct object

Some transitive verbs require both a direct object and an indirect object. There is a simple way to tell the difference between an indirect object and a direct object. Direct objects answer one of these questions: What? or Whom? Indirect objects answer one of these questions: To what? To whom? For what? For whom?

→ The foreman **gave Chris** the work order.
    S   V   IO   DO

Gave what? the work order

To whom? Chris

You can also add optional elements to this type of sentence order.

→ At the beginning of the shift, the foreman gave Chris the lost work order.

4. Subject + transitive verb + direct object + object complement

A small number of transitive verbs—such as *declare, call, name*—require a direct object and object complement. The object complement is a necessary element in this type of sentence; it describes the direct object. Remember that a direct object answers one of these questions: Whom? What? An object complement can be either a noun phrase or an adjective phrase.

→ Sarah **called me a novice**.
    S   V   DO   NP

Whom did Sarah call a novice? me

→ Sarah **called me lazy**.
    S   V   DO Adj

Whom did Sarah call lazy? me

Just like with any other sentence pattern, you can add other optional elements, but you still have the same sentence pattern.

→ When I could not do the ASL sign for *water,* Sarah called me a novice.

5. Subject + transitive verb + direct object + adverbial complement

Some transitive verbs—such as *place, put*—require both a direct object and an adverbial complement. An adverbial complement is the name for a prepositional phrase that gives information about when, where, why, and how.

→ Alex **put the sign on the door**.
    S   V   DO   Adv

You can also lengthen this type of sentence pattern with optional elements.

→ Yesterday morning, Alex put the sign on the door with the red stripes.

6. Subject + linking verb + subject complement

A common sentence pattern includes a subject, linking verb, and subject complement. Linking verbs are verbs that describe a state of being: *be, appear, seem, taste, sound*. The linking verb, if you think in terms of math, functions as an equal sign, and the subject complement renames (noun phrase) or describes (adjective phrase).

→ A changing traffic signal is a sign.
     S   V NP

→ A changing traffic signal is frustrating.
     S   V Adj

Optional elements can also be added to this type of sentence.

→ In the spring, a sound like a train engine is a sign.

→ A sound like a train engine is scary, especially in the spring.

→ A sound like a train engine is scary, especially when a tornado warning has sounded.

7. Subject + linking verb + adverbial complement

A linking verb can also take an adverbial complement. The adverbial complement—usually a prepositional phrase—is required for this type of sentence to be complete.

→ The warning signs are on the back wall.
     S   V   Prep Ph

Did You Know? You might think that sentences in all languages are structured the same as many English sentences: begin with a subject, add a verb, and end with an object (e.g., *Sam drank the water*). But not all languages are subject-verb-object (SVO) languages. Many are SOV (e.g., *Sam the water drank*), including Japanese and Persian. There are even a few languages with VOS, OVS, and OSV word orders; Fijian, for example, has a VOS word order: *Drank the water Sam.*

18j Vary sentence openings

You can vary sentence openings to help your writing not take on a dull or boring sentence rhythm.

1. Add introductory words, phrases, and clauses

Adding in optional introductory words, phrases, or clauses can also lengthen your sentences, a sign of a more sophisticated and complex writing style.

> Sample of dull or boring sentence rhythm➔ The Hollywood sign is a national monument. The Hollywood sign is in Griffith Park in Los Angeles. The sign is 45 feet tall, and it has white letters. It was created as an advertisement in 1923.

> Add a transitional/introductory word➔ The Hollywood sign is a national monument. However, it is located in Griffith Park and not Hollywood.

> Add an introductory verb phrase➔ Located in Griffith Park, the Hollywood sign is a national monument.

> Add an introductory prepositional phrase➔ In Griffith Park, the Hollywood sign is a national monument.

> Add an introductory clause➔ Although the Hollywood sign was first created as an advertisement in 1923, it is now a national monument.

EXERCISE 2: *Directions: Join the pairs of sentences together by using introductory words, phrases, or clauses.*

Example: The Hollywood sign was created in 1923. The Hollywood sign is a national monument. ➔ Created in 1923, the Hollywood sign is a national monument.

1. The Welcome to Las Vegas sign is a historic landmark. The Welcome to Las Vegas sign is on the U.S. National Register of Historic Places.
2. The Welcome to Las Vegas sign is a historic landmark. It was funded and erected in May 1959.
3. The sign is in the town of Paradise. The sign is roughly four miles away from the city limits of Las Vegas.
4. In March 2009, Clark County council members nominated the sign to be placed on the U.S. National Register of Historic Places. On May 1, 2009, the sign was placed on the U.S. National Register of Historic Places.
5. The sign is 25 feet tall. The sign is a classic roadside pole design.

---

2. Avoid subject-itis

When you use the same sentence pattern or order, your sentences can start to look like they all have the same beginning. Some teachers and editors call this *subject-itis*, labeling it as a sentence disease. Check out this group of sentences that all begin with a subject.

> The Hollywood sign is a national monument. The Hollywood sign is in Griffith Park in Los Angeles. The sign is 45 feet tall, and it has white letters. It was created as an advertisement in 1923.

One of the ways you can cure *subject-itis* is by using introductory words, phrases, or clauses. Another way is to do some sentence combining, joining some of the sentences together to form compound or complex sentences.

Add an introductory verb phrase➔ Standing 45 feet tall with white letters, the Hollywood sign is a national monument located in Griffith Park in Los Angeles.

Join sentences together➔ The Hollywood sign is a national monument located in Griffith Park in Los Angeles; its white letters stand 45 feet tall.

Add an introductory verb phrase➔ Created as an advertisement in 1923, the Hollywood sign is a national monument located in Griffith Park; its white letters stand 45 feet tall.

> **Helpful hint:** *Subject-itis* can quickly turn into *I-itis* (with every sentence beginning with an *I*) when you write a first-person narrative. Be especially careful of this type of repetition when using the first-person for narratives or other types of academic writing.

18k Fix misplaced modifiers

Modifiers can be used to add information to sentences, but they can sometimes cause problems as well if not placed in the correct position in the sentence.

1. Check for misleading or misplaced modifiers

If a modifier is misplaced, it can cause confusion or even give an unwanted meaning to a sentence. There are three main types of misleading or misplaced modifiers: squinting, limiting, and disruptive.

Squinting modifiers are words or phrases that can refer to more than one word or phrase in the sentence. Revise the sentence so the modifier is placed directly where it refers to only a single word or phrase.

Squinting modifier➔ The girl in my English class is in the corner with the protest sign.

Is the girl in the corner? Is the protest sign in the corner? Are they both in the corner? Place the modifier where its meaning cannot be misleading.

OK➔ The girl with the protest sign is in the corner; I know her from English class.

Limiting modifiers, such as *almost, even, just, merely,* and *only*, usually give information about how many or how often. Be careful where you place these modifiers since poor placement can cause ambiguity.

Limiting modifier poorly placed ➔ We almost had 30 signs painted by the end of the day.

How can you *almost have* something? The *almost* is modifying how many signs were done by the end of the day, so this limiting modifier needs to be next to the phrase it modifies.

> OK➔ We had almost 30 signs painted by the end of the day.

Disruptive modifiers are any type of modifiers that come in the middle of a phrase or sentence, **and** their position allows them to disrupt that same phrase or sentence. Some disruptive modifiers can be grammatically correct and still be disruptive. Be sure that modifying phrases or clauses do not become long and winding paths that lead the reader off the main point.

> Disruptive modifier ➔ We had 30 signs—ten blue ones, five yellow ones, five red ones, three green ones, three purple ones, three orange ones, and one black one—that needed to be painted by the end of the day.

> OK➔ We had to paint 30 signs by the end of the day; they included ten blue ones, five yellow ones, five red ones, three green ones, three purple ones, three orange ones, and one black one.

Splitting a verb infinitive (*to + verb*) with a modifier is also disruptive. Although some instructors and editors accept split infinitives, many do not; it will always be fine to rework a split infinite.

> Split infinitive➔ The foreman warned us to carefully place the signs in the truck.

> OK➔ The foreman warned us to place the signs carefully in the truck.

> **Helpful hint:** Some split infinitives are part of our culture; fixing them might cause confusion and comment.
>
> ➔ On *Star Trek*, the captain and crew want to boldly go where no one has gone before.

2. Check for dangling modifiers

Dangling modifiers are verbals (to + verb, verb + *–ing*, or verb + *–en/ –ed*) placed either at the beginning or end of the sentence and has the verbal modifying the wrong word.

> Dangling modifier ➔ Having been painted, we put the signs into the delivery truck.

The dangling modifier (*having been painted*) appears to modify *we*, but it should modify *the signs*. You can fix a dangling modifier in a variety of ways, including moving the word being modified into the correct position or rewording the entire sentence.

> OK➔ Having been painted, the signs were put into the delivery truck.

> OK➔ The painted signs were put into the truck.

> OK➔ We put the painted signs into the truck.

Participial verb phrases (with –*ing* or –*ed*) endings are often at the beginning of a dangling modifier.

> Dangling modifier ➜ Left on their own, the signs were put into the truck by the kids.

> OK➜ The kids, left on their own, put the signs into the truck.

EXERCISE 3: *Directions: Rewrite each sentence to avoid the misplaced or misused elements.*

1. He says sometimes that he worries about the job his painters are doing.
2. The painters, who he had hired only one month ago and who had previously worked for the city of Las Vegas where one had been fired, were doing an acceptable job overall.
3. Calling the painters each morning, the painters then went to the job the manager assigned.
4. The painters sometimes left their equipment at the job site which sometimes included brushes and paint.
5. The manager wants his painting crew to only do good work.

18l Check direct v. indirect speech

Direct speech is highlighted with quotation marks. Indirect quotations or speech do not take quotation marks. When you use an indirect quotation or indirect speech, be sure to change the order of the sentence, if necessary, and use the correct punctuation.

> Direct quotation➜ The manager said, "Put the signs in the truck."

> Indirect quotation➜ The manager said to put the signs in the truck.

> Direct question➜ Did you put the signs in the truck?

> Indirect question➜ He asked if the signs had been put in the truck.

18m Check for empty phrases and clauses

Even though sentences that begin with *it* or *there* + *be* are grammatically correct, they use extra words or empty phrases that sometimes can be easily removed if the sentence is rephrased.

1. Check for empty *it*

> Empty phrase ➜ It had taken three hours for the students to paint the signs.

> OK➜ The students took three hours to paint the signs.

2. Check for empty *there*

Empty phrase ➔ There were three signs that the students forgot to paint.

OK➔ The students forgot to paint three signs.

Sentence Length

A variety of sentences with a mixture of sentence lengths is a sign of a mature, sophisticated writing style. Becoming familiar with how to shorten or lengthen sentences will help you revise when your sentences are too choppy, too repetitive, or too underdeveloped.

18n Check for choppy sentences

Nothing is wrong with a short simple sentence every once in a while; however, many short simple sentences in a row can create a dull and repetitive rhythm that is uncomfortable for the reader. Consider the following sentences.

➔ The Hollywood sign is a national monument. The Hollywood sign is in Griffith Park in Los Angeles. The sign is 45 feet tall. It has white letters. It was created as an advertisement in 1923.

What can you do to rephrase these short and choppy sentences that have the same simple-subject-predicate rhythm? You can join some of the sentences together by using coordinating conjunctions (*for, and, nor, but, or, yet, so*) and creating some compound sentences.

Compound sentences➔ The Hollywood sign is a national monument, and it is located in Griffith Park in Los Angeles. The sign is 45 feet tall, and it has white letters. It was created as an advertisement in 1923.

What do you notice about the above sentences? Does compounding make that dull and repetitive rhythm disappear? Probably not enough. Plus, it was difficult to join the last sentence to the rest of the description. To improve even more, you can try combining more of the sentences by using complex sentences.

Complex sentences➔ The Hollywood sign, which is located in Griffith Park in Los Angeles, is 45 feet tall with white letters. It was created as an advertisement in 1923.

Combining sentences by creating complex sentences helped cut out words and made the first sentence flow much better. However, we are still left with the last simple sentence that was difficult to combine. To improve even more, you can combine all the sentences using both complex and compound strategies.

Compound and complex➔ The Hollywood sign, which is located in Griffith Park in Los Angeles, is 45 feet tall with white letters; it was created as an advertisement in 1923.

For more information on using sentence combining to create compound, complex, and compound-complex sentences, see Chapter 17.

> **Helpful hint:** You can check the grade level of your writing by looking at the Flesch-Kincaid index. You can pull this up in Microsoft Word under the grammar checker and spell checker menu.

18o Check for excessive coordination

When you use compound sentences to bring some variety to your writing, you are using a combining strategy that we use quite often in oral language. Be careful, though, that you do not overuse it in your writing since doing so will make your writing sound too conversational for academic writing.

Too conversational → The Hollywood sign is located in Griffith Park in Los Angeles, and it is 45 feet tall and has white letters, and it was created as an advertisement in 1923.

Use compound sentences sparingly, and mix them with complex sentences or compound-complex sentences to bring more intricacy to your writing.

OK→ The Hollywood sign, which is located in Griffith Park in Los Angeles, is 45 feet tall with white letters; it was created as an advertisement in 1923.

> **EXERCISE 1:** *Directions: Revise these sentences that have excessive coordination, subordination, or modification.*
>
> 1. The McDonald's sign that is in Pine Bluff, Arkansas, is the only surviving example of a single arch McDonald's sign in Arkansas; the sign was erected in 1962, and it remained in its original location until 2007, and it was added to the U.S. Register of Historic Places in 2006.
>
> 2. In 2007, the sign, which is in Pine Bluff, Arkansas, was moved to a new location, which was also in Pine Bluff, Arkansas.
>
> 3. The Pine Bluff sign has many of the typical features of an early single arch McDonald's sign; it is back-lit; it has plastic panels in a metal frame; it has red advertising midway down the arch.
>
> 4. No one knows how many single arch McDonald's signs still exist, but there is one in Biloxi, Mississippi, and there is one in Lancaster, Pennsylvania, and there is one in Green Bay, Wisconsin, and there is one in Huntsville, Alabama.
>
> 5. The sign that is in Pine Bluff is the only single arch McDonald's sign that is on the U.S. Register of Historic Places, which is the United State's official list of buildings that are deemed worthy of preservation.

18p Check for excessive subordination and modification

Creating complex sentences is done by using subordination and modification, and adding this complexity to your writing gives a more sophisticated style. However, be careful that you do not overuse subordination and modification to the point where it is difficult for the reader to understand what you are joining or describing.

> Too complex→The Hollywood sign, which was created as an advertisement in 1923 and which is located in Griffith Park, which is in Los Angeles, is 45 feet tall with white letters.

> OK→ The Hollywood sign, which is located in the Griffith Park of Los Angeles, is 45 feet tall with white letters; it was created as an advertisement in 1923.

18q Add descriptive words and phrases

You can enhance the descriptiveness of your sentences by adding modifiers in different places in the sentence.

1. Add descriptive nouns and noun phrases

Develop more descriptive noun phrases by adding pre-modifiers, such as adjectives, and post-modifiers, such as appositives, prepositional phrases, or relative clauses. Doing so will lengthen your sentences and show off your vocabulary.

> Noun Phrase→ the house

> With pre-modifier→ the big blue house
>   Adj Adj

> With pre-modifier and post-modifier→ the big blue house,
>   Adj Adj

> a Colonial, which is sitting on the corner of Sixth and Elm.
> Appositive   Relative Clause

You can also lengthen your sentences and show off your vocabulary by replacing simple nouns with words that carry more than a simple description.

> Simple noun→ house

> Possible variations→ abode, adobe, Colonial, domicile, dwelling, habitat, igloo

2. Add descriptive verbs

Your sentences can become more descriptive by changing out simple verbs for ones that fit the scene you are trying to set or describe. Remember, though, that your vocabulary should match the type of academic writing you are doing.

> Simple verb→ go

Possible variations→ depart, exit, hit the road, make tracks, take leave

3. Add descriptive adjectives

Adjectives can be used in three different ways to add more description to a sentence. Showing that you have the facility to use all three types demonstrates a more sophisticated writing style.

A. Adjectives as pre-modifiers

An adjective or adjective phrase can be used to modify the noun that follows it.

Adjective→ the wet sign

Conjoined adjective phrase→ the wet and moldy sign

Adjective phrase with modifying adverb→ the extremely wet and moldy sign

B. Adjectives as post-modifiers

An adjective or adjective phrase can modify the noun it follows.

Adjective→ That problem, undoable, was the only one I did not complete.

Conjoined adjective phrase→ The sign, wet and moldy, needs to be replaced.

Adjective phrase with modifying adverb→ The sign, quite wet and moldy, needs to be replaced.

C. Adjectives as complements

An adjective or adjective phrase can modify a subject as a subject complement, or it can modify a direct object as an object complement.

Subject complement/adjective→ That problem is frustrating.

Subject complement/adjective phrase→ That problem is quite frustrating.

Object complement/adjective→ All the students called the problem undoable.

Object complement/adjective phrase→ All the students called the problem frustratingly undoable.

4. Add descriptive adverbs

Adverbs or adverb phrases can be used to bring more description to your sentences by modifying verbs, adjectives, other adverbs, or even full sentences.

Modifying a verb→ The Hollywood sign was created originally as an advertisement.

Modifying an adjective→ The extremely tall Hollywood sign was created as an advertisement.

Modifying another adverb➜ The answer to the problem was quite frustratingly obvious after the teacher revealed it.

Modifying a sentence➜ The answer to the problem was frustrating; consequently, the students failed the test.

5. Add descriptive prepositional phrases

Prepositional phrases can be used to modify a variety of elements in a sentence. They can give optional adverbial-type information about time or place; they can give more detail to a noun phrase, adjective phrase, or adverbial phrase; or they can function as an adverbial complement.

Optional adverbial➜ In the spring, the Hollywood sign is cleaned.

Post-modifier to a noun➜ The Hollywood sign, in Griffith Park, is cleaned each spring.

Post-modifier to an adjective➜ Climbing to the Hollywood sign is supposed to be difficult for most people.

Post-modifier to an adverbial➜ The park ranger looked angrily at us when we started up the path to the Hollywood sign.

EXERCISE 2: *Directions: Revise the following simple sentences by using the modifier type given in parentheses.*

1. The Skipping Girl Vinegar sign is located on Victoria Street in Melbourne, Australia. (add descriptive adjective)

2. The sign is a painted metal structure. (add descriptive prepositional phrase)

3. The sign is also known as Little Audrey. (add descriptive noun phrase)

4. The sign was manufactured in 1936 to advertise vinegar. (add descriptive verb phrase)

5. The sign replicates the skipping girl on the original vinegar bottle. (add descriptive adjective)

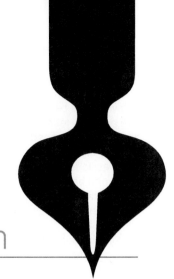

Appendix:
Essays for Discussion

Honesty

John F. Ahearne

Ultimately, ethics in scientific publishing, as in life, comes down to one word.

During my 20-year career in the United States capital advising several levels of government on matters of energy and defense, I witnessed many instances of honesty, as well as some of dishonesty, and the consequences of each. Those experiences reinforced my commitment—one held throughout my adult life—to practice the virtue of honesty and to instill it in my colleagues. But even though truthfulness is essential to progress, it is clearly not so easy to uphold. As the Roman poet Juvenal wrote in the first century a.d., "Honesty is praised and then left to freeze." Touted but not applied. This frailty of human nature, lamented for millennia, clearly has ongoing implications for the progress of both science and society.

What Is Honesty?

A dictionary definition of honesty belies the rigor and complexity of its practice. According to the Random House description, honesty is: 1. The quality or fact of being honest; uprightness and fairness. 2. Truthfulness, sincerity or frankness. 3. Freedom from deceit or fraud. The commitment required to realize these simple terms is more clearly implied in a second definition, drawn from *Funk & Wagnalls Standard Handbook of Synonyms, Antonyms and Prepositions:* "One who is honest in the highest and fullest sense is scrupulously careful to adhere to all known truth and right even in thought."

Few would contest the desirability of honesty, and good intentions are nearly universal. As Tina Gunsalus, director of the National Center for Professional and Research Ethics, observes: "Almost everybody wakes up every day and wants to do the right thing." Later in the day, the goal may be thwarted; the potential pitfalls are many.

One might ask, for example, what long-term damage could come from seemingly insignificant transgressions. This reasoning seems to be a common justification among students who cheat on exams, papers and even theses. If such students don't understand who is harmed, it is hard to convince them that the detriments of deceit outweigh the benefits. Ethicist Sissela Bok, however, warns that "trust and integrity are precious resources, easily squandered, hard to regain. They can thrive only on a foundation of respect for veracity." Thus small transgressions, if discovered, can easily destroy one's credibility on a larger scale. And, even if undiscovered, missteps set up the classic "slippery slope" on which small transgressions lead to larger ones. Habits form, and harm is done first to one's self and then to others.

Dishonesty may also take the form of omission, as opposed to overt deception. To address the entire truth without exception can demand extraordinary courage, as United Nations Secretary General Ban Ki-moon has demonstrated. In early November 2010, Ban met with President Hu Jintao of China in Beijing. He discussed climate change, tensions on the Korean peninsula and peacekeeping. However, as the editors of *The New York Times* pointed out, "He was shamefully silent on one critical issue: China's poor human rights record and its unjustified imprisonment of Liu Xiaobo, the country's leading democracy activist and … winner of the [2010] Nobel Peace Prize." Ban has many responsibilities, but speaking truth to power is one of them, and in Beijing he was unable to deliver.

This is not to say that it is impossible to elevate ethical commitments above the immediate obstacles. In his 1955 book *Profiles in Courage*, then-Senator John Kennedy emphasized that individuals can rise above their desire for personal advantage and advocate positions that they know are right—even when doing so may damage their careers. Among the courageous figures featured in the book are John Quincy Adams, Daniel Webster, Sam Houston and Robert Taft. Although these men held positions that were often right, they suffered politically for doing so. Robert Taft, for example, was a leading figure in the Republican Party when he gave a speech attacking the Nuremberg Trials of Nazi war criminals. Although he did not support any of the Nazi actions, he concluded that the injustices in the trials were too great to ignore. He was harshly criticized by his party.

In today's political environment of bitter attack ads and communications at the speed of the Internet, such courageous positions can have immediate negative consequences. Perhaps because of that, in recent years principled stands taken by political leaders seldom seem to be positions that could harm their careers.

A House of Cards

The value of honesty to science is not essentially different from its value to society as a whole, but the progress and application of science do depend fundamentally on the truthful reporting of research. As Nobel Laureate Michael Bishop explained to a group of high-school students, "Each of us builds our discoveries on the work of others; if that work is false, our constructions fall like a house of cards and we must start all over again." This dependency is widely recognized and acknowledged in science and engineering. Consider, for example, the National Academies' instruction manual for new interns, which states that the "responsible and ethical conduct of research is critical for excellence, as well as public trust, in social science, science and engineering, and is considered essential to the preparation of future scientists and engineers."

In the later decades of the 20th century, examples of scientific misconduct led scientific establishments to formalize ethical guidelines. One such code was published by the National Academies in *On Being a Scientist: A Guide to Responsible Conduct in Research*. First printed in 1988 and now in its third edition, the booklet clearly addresses the role of honesty and trust in research:

> Over many centuries, researchers have developed professional standards designed to enhance the progress of science and to avoid or minimize the difficulties of research.... Researchers have three sets of obligations that motivate their adherence to professional standards. First, researchers have an obligation to honor the trust that their colleagues place in them.... Second, researchers have an obligation to themselves. Irresponsible conduct in research can make it impossible to achieve a goal.... Third, because scientific results greatly influence society, researchers have an obligation to act in ways that serve the public.

A failure to meet these obligations is corrosive to science. As the authors of *On Being a Scientist* explain:

> The scientific enterprise is built on a foundation of trust.... When this trust is misplaced and the professional standards of science are violated, researchers are not just professionally affronted—they feel that the base of their profession has been undermined. This would impact the relationship between science and society.

Thus a failure to be honest can directly damage the scientific enterprise and can also erode the public's faith in science.

Publication and Temptation

Of course, each discipline of science and engineering faces unique ethical challenges, including the humane treatment of research animals and the environmental consequences of engineering designs. But one nearly universal ambition among scientists and engineers at all stages of their careers is publication. In the words of biologist and former editor-in-chief of *Science* Donald Kennedy, "in the world of scholarship, we are what we write. Publication is the fundamental currency ... research quality is judged by the printed word." And as stated in *On Being a Scientist:*

> The rewards of science are not easily achieved. At the frontiers of research, new knowledge is elusive and hard won. Researchers often are subject to great personal and professional pressures.

Authorship is therefore essential for scientists who seek career advancement in academia, industry and government. But the high-pressure obligation to publish may drive some researchers to ethical violations. Triggered by ethical lapses in two prominent physics cases, the American Physical Society (APS) formed a Task Force on Ethics. The team, led by Frances Houle, surveyed all APS members who had completed a Ph.D. within the past three years. The results, published in 2004, were disturbing: 39 percent of respondents said they had personal knowledge of ethical transgressions, the two most common of which were inclusion of inappropriate authors on a publication and exclusion of appropriate authors. One respondent wrote that "many breaches of ethics arise from the pressure to publish.... The recent sad events [show] that it is for many people more important to publish spectacular results than to publish true results."

Physicists are not alone in their difficulties with authorship, the fair assignment of which presents a major and ongoing challenge in all fields of science and engineering that have been surveyed. Abuse of power may lead to the exclusion of deserving authors, and "guest" authorship may be offered to individuals who did not participate substantially in the research. Temptations to cut corners can be great.

Among the ethical transgressions involving authorship, perhaps the most egregious are fabrication, falsification and plagiarism. According to *Responsible Science*, "fabrication is making up data or results," and "falsification is changing data or results." These usually involve experimental results. Plagiarism does not: It is "the appropriation of another person's ideas, processes, results or words without giving appropriate credit," says the Federal Policy on Research Misconduct. Under pressure, some authors maintain honesty and follow the guidelines of science. Some do not.

The other side of the publication coin is peer review, a necessary form of quality control that helps ensure the value of a publication. But controversy continues about the fairness and adequacy of the process, and serving as a reviewer can be both an honor and a burden.

W. Robert Connor, the former director of the National Humanities Center, summed up the ethical complexity of a reviewer's task in *The Responsible Researcher*, a Sigma Xi handbook that I wrote:

> [For] investigators who may find themselves asked to participate in peer review decisions at a relatively early stage in their careers ... there are a host of issues that need to be thought through—how one deals with friends or rivals whose applications may be in the pile, how one deals with approaches and methodologies that may be legitimate but with which one is not sympathetic, how much one can legitimately "borrow" from research proposals one reviews, etc.

Clearly, the issues surrounding authorship and peer review are many. Their nuances have been and will be discussed further in these pages throughout the year. At the root of any publication decision, however, should be the basic quality of honesty. Without it, the system of credit, responsibility and quality control in the scientific record is undermined—and the house of cards will fall.

Not So Fast

The virtue of honesty seems to be under great challenge in the world of blogs, Twitter and television "news" programs. Mark Twain identified the fundamental problem: "A lie can travel halfway around the world while the truth is putting on its shoes." If only these media were used as often to expose lies and herald truths.

Honesty is necessary for science to advance. Unfortunately, it does not seem to be necessary for society's leaders, the individuals who largely hold the purse strings for science, to practice honesty. Recently, *The New York Times* columnist Thomas Friedman wrote about this problem:

> When widely followed public figures feel free to say anything, without any fact-checking, we have a problem. It becomes impossible for a democracy to think intelligently about big issues—deficit reduction, health care, taxes, energy/climate—let alone act on them. Facts, opinions and fabrications just blend together.

For the long-term health of the research community and of the individual, honesty *is* the best policy.

Bibliography

Ahearne, J. 1999. *The Responsible Researcher: Paths and Pitfalls.* Research Triangle Park, NC: Sigma Xi.

Bok, S. 1978. *Lying: Moral Choice in Public and Private Life.* New York: Pantheon Books.

Committee on Science, Engineering, and Public Policy, National Academy of Sciences, National Academy of Engineering and Institute of Medicine. 2009. *On Being a Scientist: A Guide to Responsible Conduct in Research,* third edition. Washington: National Academies Press.

Friedman, T. L. 2010. Too good to check. *The New York Times* (November 16).

Gudeman, K. 2010. University of Illinois to develop national center for ethics in science, mathematics and engineering. Coordinated Science Laboratory News. http://csl.illinois.edu/news/university-illinois-develop-national-center-ethics-science-mathematics-and-engineering (Accessed January 19, 2011)

Hamilton, J., et al. 2003. Report of Ethics Task Force to APS Council. http://www.phys.utk.edu/colloquium_blume_spring2004_ethics.pdf (Accessed January 19, 2011)

Kennedy, D. 1997. *Academic Duty.* Cambridge: Harvard University Press.

Kirby, K., and F. A. Houle. 2004. Ethics and the welfare of the physics profession. *Physics Today* 57:42–46.

The New York Times editors. 2010. Mr. Ban pulls his punches. *The New York Times* (November 2).

Panel on Scientific Responsibility and the Conduct of Research, National Academy of Sciences, National Academy of Engineering, Institute of Medicine. 1992. *Responsible Science, Volume I: Ensuring the Integrity of the Research Process.* Washington, D.C.: National Academies Press.

University of Notre Dame. 2010. Responsible Conduct of Research Statement. http://or.nd.edu/compliance/responsible-conduct-of-research-rcr/responsible-conduct-of-research-statement/ (Accessed January 19, 2011)

"Handed My Own Life"

By Annie Dillard

After I read *The Field Book of Ponds and Streams* several times, I longed for a microscope. Everybody needed a microscope. Detectives used microscopes, both for the FBI and at Scotland Yard. Although I usually had to save my tiny allowance for things I wanted, that year for Christmas my parents gave me a microscope kit.

In a dark basement corner, on a white enamel table, I set up the microscope kit. I supplied a chair, a lamp, a batch of jars, a candle, and a pile of library books. The microscope kit supplied a blunt black three-speed microscope, a booklet, a scalpel, a dropper, an ingenious device for cutting thin segments of fragile tissue, a pile of clean slides and cover slips, and a dandy array of corked test tubes.

One of the test tubes contained "hay infusion." Hay infusion was a wee brown chip of grass blade. You added water to it, and after a week it became a jungle in a drop, full of one-celled animals. This did not work for me. All I saw in the microscope after a week was a wet chip of dried grass, much enlarged.

Another test tube contained "diatomaceous earth." This was, I believed, an actual pinch of the white cliffs of Dover. On my palm it was an airy, friable chalk. The booklet said it was composed of the silicaceous bodies of diatoms—one-celled creatures that lived in, as it were, small glass jewelry boxes with fitted lids. Diatoms, I read, come in a variety of transparent geometrical shapes. Broken and dead and dug out of geological deposits, they made chalk and a fine abrasive used in silver polish and toothpaste. What I saw in the microscope must have been the fine abrasive—grit enlarged. It was years before I saw a recognizable, whole diatom. The kit's diatomaceous earth was a bust.

All that winter I played with the microscope. I prepared slides from things at hand, as the books suggested. I looked at the transparent membrane inside an onion's skin and saw the cells. I looked at a section of cork and saw the cells, and at scrapings from the inside of my cheek, ditto. I looked at my blood and saw not much; I looked at my urine and saw long iridescent crystals, for the drop had dried.

All this was very well, but I wanted to see the wildlife I had read about. I wanted especially to see the famous amoeba, who had eluded me. He was supposed to live in the hay infusion, but I hadn't found him there. He lived outside in warm ponds and streams, too, but I lived in Pittsburgh, and it had been a cold winter.

Finally late that spring I saw an amoeba. The week before, I had gathered puddle water from Frick Park; it had been festering in a jar in the basement. This June night after dinner I figured I had waited long enough. In the basement at my microscope table I spread a scummy drop of Frick Park puddle water on a slide, peeked in, and lo, there was the famous amoeba. He was as blobby and grainy as his picture; I would have known him anywhere.

Before I had watched him at all, I ran upstairs. My parents were still at table, drinking coffee. They, too, could see the famous amoeba. I told them, bursting, that he was all set up, that they should hurry before his water dried. It was the chance of a lifetime.

Father had stretched out his long legs and was tilting back in his chair. Mother sat with her knees crossed, in blue slacks, smoking a Chesterfield. The dessert dishes were still on the table. My sisters were nowhere in evidence. It was a warm evening; the big dining-room windows gave onto blooming rhododendrons.

Mother regarded me warmly. She gave me to understand that she was glad I had found what I had been looking for, but that she and Father were happy to sit with their coffee, and would not be coming down. She did not say, but I understood at once, that they had their pursuits (coffee) and I had mine. She did not say, but I began to understand then, that you do what you do out of your private passion for the thing itself.

I had essentially been handed my own life, in subsequent years my parents would praise my drawings and poems, and supply me with books, art supplies, and sports equipment, and listen to my troubles and enthusiasm, and supervise my hours, and discuss and inform, but they would not get involved with my detective work, nor hear about my reading, nor inquire about my homework or term papers or exams, nor visit the salamanders I caught, nor listen to me play piano, nor attend my field hockey games, nor fuss over my insect collection. My days and nights were my own to plan and fill.

* * *

When I left the dining room that evening and started down the dark basement stairs, I had a life, I sat to my wonderful amoeba, and there he was, rolling his grains more slowly now, extending an arc of his edge for a foot and drawing himself along by that foot, and absorbing it again and rolling on. I gave him some more pond water.

I had hit pay dirt. For all I knew, there was paramecia, too, in that pond water, or daphniae, or stentors, or any of the many other creatures I had read about and never seen: volvox, the spherical algal colony; euglena with its one red eye; the elusive, glassy diatom; hydra, rotifers, water bears, worms. Anything was possible. The sky was the limit.

An American Childhood. Copyright © 1987 by Annie Dillard. Used with permission.

Black Men in Public Space

By Brent Staples

My first victim was a woman—white, well dressed, probably in her early twenties. I came upon her late one evening on a deserted street in Hyde Park, a relatively affluent neighborhood in an otherwise mean, impoverished section of Chicago. As I swung onto the avenue behind her, there seemed to be a discreet, uninflammatory distance between us. Not so. She cast back a worried glance. To her, the youngish black man—a broad six feet two inches with a beard and billowing hair, both hands shoved into the pockets of a bulky military jacket— seemed menacingly close. After a few more quick glimpses, she picked up her pace and was soon running in earnest. Within seconds she disappeared into a cross street.

That was more than a decade ago. I was twenty-two years old, a graduate student newly arrived at the University of Chicago. It was in the echo of that terrified woman's footfalls that I first began to know the unwieldy inheritance I'd come into—the ability to alter public space in ugly ways. It was clear that she thought herself the quarry of a mugger, a rapist, or worse. Suffering a bout of insomnia, however, I was stalking sleep, not defenseless wayfarers. As a softy who is scarcely able to take a knife to a raw chicken—let alone hold it to a person's throat—I was surprised, embarrassed, and dismayed all at once. Her flight made me feel like an accomplice in tyranny. It also made it clear that I was indistinguishable from the muggers who occasionally seeped into the area from the surrounding ghetto. That first encounter, and those that followed, signified that a vast, unnerving gulf lay between nighttime pedestrians— particularly women—and me. And I soon gathered that being perceived as dangerous is a hazard in itself. I only needed to turn a corner into a dicey situation, or crowd some frightened, armed person in a foyer somewhere, or make an errant move after being pulled over by a policeman.

Where fear and weapons meet—and they often do in urban America—there is always the possibility of death.

In that first year, my first away from my hometown, I was to become thoroughly familiar with the language of fear. At dark, shadowy intersections in Chicago, I could cross in front of a car stopped at a traffic light and elicit the thunk, thunk, thunk, thunk of the driver—black, white, male, or female hammering down the door locks. On less traveled streets after dark, I grew accustomed to but never comfortable with people who crossed to the other side of the street rather than pass me. Then there were the standard unpleasantries with police, doormen, bouncers, cabdrivers, and others whose business is to screen out troublesome individuals before there is any nastiness.

I moved to New York nearly two years ago and I have remained an avid night walker. In central Manhattan, the near-constant crowd cover minimizes tense one-on- one street encounters. Elsewhere—visiting friends in SoHo, where sidewalks are narrow and tightly spaced buildings shut out the sky—things can get very taut indeed.

Black men have a firm place in New York mugging literature. Norman Podhoretz in his famed (or infamous) 1963 essay, "My Negro Problem—And Ours," recalls growing up in terror of black males; they "were tougher than we were, more ruthless," he writes—and as an adult on the Upper West Side of Manhattan, he continues, he cannot constrain his nervousness when he meets black men on certain streets. Similarly, a decade later, the essayist and novelist Edward Hoagland extols a New

York where once "Negro bitterness bore down mainly on other Negroes." Where some see mere panhandlers, Hoagland sees "a mugger who is clearly screwing up his nerve to do more than just ask for money." But Hoagland has "the New Yorker's quick-hunch posture for broken-field maneuvering," and the bad guy swerves away.

I often witness that "hunch posture," from women after dark on the warrenlike streets of Brooklyn where I live. They seem to set their faces on neutral and, with their purse straps strung across their chests bandolier style, they forge ahead as though bracing themselves against being tackled. I understand, of course, that the danger they perceive is not a hallucination. Women are particularly vulnerable to street violence, and young black males are dramatically overrepresented among the perpetrators of that violence. Yet these truths are no solace against the kind of alienation that comes of being ever the suspect, against being set apart, a fearsome entity with whom pedestrians avoid making eye contact.

It is not altogether clear to me how I reached the ripe old age of twenty-two without being conscious of the lethality nighttime pedestrians attributed to me. Perhaps it was because in Chester, Pennsylvania, the small, angry industrial town where I came of age in the 1960s, I was scarcely noticeable against a backdrop of gang warfare, street knifings, and murders. I grew up one of the good boys, had perhaps a half-dozen fistfights. In retrospect, my shyness of combat has clear sources.

Many things go into the making of a young thug. One of those things is the consummation of the male romance with the power to intimidate. An infant discovers that random flailings send the baby bottle flying out of the crib and crashing to the floor. Delighted, the joyful babe repeats those motions again and again, seeking to duplicate the feat. Just so, I recall the points at which some of my boyhood friends were finally seduced by the perception of themselves as tough guys. When a mark cowered and surrendered his money without resistance, myth and reality merged— and paid off. It is, after all, only manly to embrace the power to frighten and intimidate. We, as men, are not supposed to give an inch of our lane on the highway; we are to seize the fighter's edge in work and in play and even in love; we are to be valiant in the face of hostile forces. Unfortunately, poor and powerless young men seem to take all this nonsense literally.

As a boy, I saw countless tough buys locked away; I have since buried several, too. They were babies, really—a teenage cousin, a brother of twenty-two, a childhood friend in his mid-twenties—all gone down in episodes of bravado played out in the streets. I came to doubt the virtues of intimidation early on. I chose, perhaps even unconsciously, to remain a shadow—timid, but a survivor.

The fearsomeness mistakenly attributed to me in public places often has a perilous flavor. The most frightening of these confusions occurred in the late 1970s and early 1980s when I worked as a journalist in Chicago. One day, rushing into the office of a magazine I was writing for with a deadline story in hand, I was mistaken for a burglar. The office manager called security and, with an ad hoc posse, pursued me through the labyrinthine halls, nearly to my editor's door. I had no way of proving who I was. I could only move briskly toward the company of someone who knew me.

Another time I was on assignment for a local paper and killing time before an interview. I entered a jewelry store on the city's affluent Near North Side. The proprietor excused herself and returned with an enormous red Doberman pinscher straining at the end of a leash. She stood, the dog extended toward me, silent to my questions, her eyes bulging nearly out of her head. I took a cursory look around, nodded, and bade her good night.

Relatively speaking, however, I never fared as badly as another black male journalist. He went to nearby Waukegan, Illinois, a couple of summers ago to work on a story about a murderer who was born there. Mistaking the reporter for the killer, police hauled him from his car at gunpoint and but for his press credentials would probably have tried to book him. Such episodes are not uncommon. Black men trade tales like this all the time.

In "My Negro Problem—And Ours," Podhoretz writes that the hatred he feels for blacks makes itself known to him through a variety of avenues—one being his discomfort with that "special brand of paranoid touchiness" to which he says blacks are prone. No doubt he is speaking here of black men. In time, I learned to smother the rage I felt at so often being taken for a criminal. Not to do so would surely have led to madness—via that special "paranoid touchiness" that so annoyed Podhoretz at the time he wrote the essay.

I began to take precautions to make myself less threatening. I move about with care, particularly late in the evening. I give a wide berth to nervous people on subway platforms during the wee hours, particularly when I have exchanged business clothes for jeans. If I happen to be entering a building behind some people who appear skittish, I may walk by, letting them clear the lobby before I return, so as not to seem to be following them. I have been calm and extremely congenial on those rare occasions when I've been pulled over by the police.

And on late-evening constitutionals along streets less traveled by, I employ what has proved to be an excellent tension-reducing measure: I whistle melodies from Beethoven and Vivaldi and the more popular classical composers. Even steely New Yorkers hunching toward nighttime destinations seem to relax, and occasionally then even join in the tune. Virtually everybody seems to sense that a mugger wouldn't be warbling bright, sunny selections from Vivalid's Four Seasons. It is my equivalent of the cowbell that hikers wear when they know they are in bear country.

Vivaldi

Doing Nothing Is Something

By Ann Quindlen

Summer is coming soon. I can feel it in the softening of the air, but I can see it, too, in the textbooks on my children's desks. The number of uncut pages at the back grows smaller and smaller. The loose-leaf is ragged at the edges, the binder plastic ripped at the corners. An old remembered glee rises inside me. Summer is coming. Uniform skirts in mothballs. Pencils with their points left broken. Open windows. Day trips to the beach. Pickup games. Hanging out.

How boring it was.

Of course, it was the making of me, as a human being and a writer. Downtime is where we become ourselves, looking into the middle distance, kicking at the curb, lying on the grass or sitting on the stoop and staring at the tedious blue of the summer sky. I don't believe you can write poetry, or compose music, or become an actor without downtime, and plenty of it, a hiatus that passes for boredom but is really the quiet moving of the wheels inside that fuel creativity.

And that, to me, is one of the saddest things about the lives of American children today. Soccer leagues, acting classes, tutors—the calendar of the average middle-class kid is so over the top that soon Palm handhelds will be sold in Toys "R" Us. Our children are as overscheduled as we are, and that is saying something.

This has become so bad that parents have arranged to schedule times for unscheduled time. Earlier this year the privileged suburb of Ridgewood, N.J., announced a Family Night, when there would be no homework, no athletic practices and no after-school events. This was terribly exciting until I realized that this was not one night a week, but one single night. There is even a free-time movement, and Web site: familylife1st.org. Among the frequently asked questions provided online: "What would families do with family time if they took it back?"

Let me make a suggestion for the kids involved: how about nothing? It is not simply that it is pathetic to consider the lives of children who don't have a moment between piano and dance and homework to talk about their day or just search for split ends, an enormously satisfying leisure-time activity of my youth. There is also ample psychological research suggesting that what we might call "doing nothing" is when human beings actually do their best thinking, and when creativity comes to call. Perhaps we are creating an entire generation of people whose ability to think outside the box, as the current parlance of business has it, is being systematically stunted by scheduling.

A study by the University of Michigan quantified the downtime deficit; in the last 20 years American kids have lost about four unstructured hours a week. There has even arisen a global Right to Play movement: in the Third World it is often about child labor, but in the United States it is about the sheer labor of being a perpetually busy child. In Omaha, Neb., a group of parents recently lobbied for additional recess. Hooray, and yikes.

How did this happen? Adults did it. There is a culture of adult distrust that suggests that a kid who is not playing softball or attending science-enrichment programs—or both—is huffing or boosting cars: if kids are left alone, they will not stare into the middle distance and consider the meaning of life and how come your nose in pictures never looks the way you think it should, but instead will get into trouble. There is also the culture of cutthroat and unquestioning competition that leads even the parents of preschoolers to gab about prestigious colleges without a trace of irony: this suggests that any class in which you do not enroll your first grader will put him at a disadvantage in, say, law school.

Finally, there is a culture of workplace presence (as opposed to productivity). Try as we might to suggest that all these enrichment activities are for the good of the kid, there is ample evidence that they are really for the convenience of parents with way too little leisure time of their own. Stories about the resignation of presidential aide Karen Hughes unfailingly reported her dedication to family time by noting that she arranged to get home at 5:30 one night a week to have dinner with her son. If one weekday dinner out of five is considered laudable, what does that say about what's become commonplace?

Summer is coming. It used to be a time apart for kids, a respite from the clock and the copybook, the organized day. Every once in a while, either guilty or overwhelmed or tired of listening to me keen about my monumental boredom, my mother would send me to some rinky-dink park program that consisted almost entirely of three-legged races and making things out of Popsicle sticks. Now, instead, there are music camps, sports camps, fat camps, probably thin camps. I mourn hanging out in the backyard. I mourn playing Wiffle ball in the street without a sponsor and matching shirts. I mourn drawing in the dirt with a stick.

Maybe that kind of summer is gone for good. Maybe this is the leading edge of a new way of living that not only has no room for contemplation but is contemptuous of it. But if downtime cannot be squeezed during the school year into the life of frantic and often joyless activity with which our children are saddled while their parents pursue frantic and often joyless activity of their own, what about summer? Do most adults really want to stand in line for Space Mountain or sit in traffic to get to a shore house that doesn't have enough saucepans? Might it be even more enriching for their children to stay at home and do nothing? For those who say they will only watch TV or play on the computer, a piece of technical advice: the cable box can be unhooked, the modem removed. Perhaps it is not too late for American kids to be given the gift of enforced boredom for at least a week or two, staring into space, bored out of their gourds, exploring the inside of their own heads. "To contemplate is to toil, to think is to do," said Victor Hugo. "Go outside and play," said Prudence Quindlen. Both of them were right.

Why We Crave Horror Movies

Stephen King

I think that we're all mentally ill; those of us outside the asylums only hide it a little better—and maybe not all that much better, after all. We've all known people who talk to themselves, people who sometimes squinch their faces into horrible grimaces when they believe no one is watching, people who have some hysterical fear—of snakes, the dark, the tight place, the long drop . . . and, of course, those final worms and grubs that are waiting so patiently underground.

When we pay our four or five bucks and seat ourselves at tenth-row center in a theater showing a horror movie, we are daring the nightmare.

Why? Some of the reasons are simple and obvious. To show that we can, that we are not afraid, that we can ride this roller coaster. Which is not to say that a really good horror movie may not surprise a scream out of us at some point, the way we may scream when the roller coaster twists through a complete 360 or plows through a lake at the bottom of the drop. And horror movies, like roller coasters, have always been the special province of the young; by the time one turns 40 or 50, one's appetite for double twists or 360-degree loops may be considerably depleted.

We also go to re-establish our feelings of essential normality; the horror movie is innately conservative, even reactionary. Freda Jackson as the horrible melting woman in Die, Monster, Die! confirms for us that no matter how far we may be removed from the beauty of a Robert Redford or a Diana Ross, we are still light-years from true ugliness.

And we go to have fun.

Ah, but this is where the ground starts to slope away, isn't it? Because this is a very peculiar sort of fun, indeed. The fun comes from seeing others menaced—sometimes killed. One critic has suggested that if pro football has become the voyeur's version of combat, then the horror film has become the modern version of the public lynching.

It is true that the mythic "fairy-tale" horror film intends to take away the shades of grey . . . . It urges us to put away our more civilized and adult penchant for analysis and to become children again, seeing things in pure blacks and whites. It may be that horror movies provide psychic relief on this level because this invitation to lapse into simplicity, irrationality and even outright madness is extended so rarely. We are told we may allow our emotions a free rein . . . or no rein at all.

If we are all insane, then sanity becomes a matter of degree. If your insanity leads you to carve up women like Jack the Ripper or the Cleveland Torso Murderer, we clap you away in the funny farm (but neither of those two amateur-night surgeons was ever caught, heh-heh-heh); if, on the other hand, your insanity leads you only to talk to yourself when you're under stress or to pick your nose on your morning bus, then you are left alone to go about your business . . . though it is doubtful that you will ever be invited to the best parties.

The potential lyncher is in almost all of us (excluding saints, past and present; but then, most saints have been crazy in their own ways), and every now and then, he has to be let loose to scream and roll around in the grass. Our emotions and our fears form their own body, and we recognize that it demands its own exercise to maintain proper muscle tone. Certain of these emotional muscles are accepted—even exalted—in civilized society; they are, of course, the emotions that tend to maintain the status quo

of civilization itself. Love, friendship, loyalty, kindness—these are all the emotions that we applaud, emotions that have been immortalized in the couplets of Hallmark cards and in the verses (I don't dare call it poetry) of Leonard Nimoy.

When we exhibit these emotions, society showers us with positive reinforcement; we learn this even before we get out of diapers. When, as children, we hug our rotten little puke of a sister and give her a kiss, all the aunts and uncles smile and twit and cry, "Isn't he the sweetest little thing?" Such coveted treats as chocolate-covered graham crackers often follow. But if we deliberately slam the rotten little puke of a sister's fingers in the door, sanctions follow—angry remonstrance from parents, aunts and uncles; instead of a chocolate-covered graham cracker, a spanking.

But anticivilization emotions don't go away, and they demand periodic exercise. We have such "sick" jokes as, "What's the difference between a truckload of bowling balls and a truckload of dead babies?" (You can't unload a truckload of bowling balls with a pitchfork . . . a joke, by the way, that I heard originally from a ten-year-old.) Such a joke may surprise a laugh or a grin out of us even as we recoil, a possibility that confirms the thesis: If we share a brotherhood of man, then we also share an insanity of man. None of which is intended as a defense of either the sick joke or insanity but merely as an explanation of why the best horror films, like the best fairy tales, manage to be reactionary, anarchistic, and revolutionary all at the same time.

The mythic horror movie, like the sick joke, has a dirty job to do. It deliberately appeals to all that is worst in us. It is morbidity unchained, our most base instincts let free, our nastiest fantasies realized . . . and it all happens, fittingly enough, in the dark. For those reasons, good liberals often shy away from horror films. For myself, I like to see the most aggressive of them—*Dawn of the Dead*, for instance—as lifting a trap door in the civilized forebrain and throwing a basket of raw meat to the hungry alligators swimming around in that subterranean river beneath.

Why bother? Because it keeps them from getting out, man. It keeps them down there and me up here. It was Lennon and McCartney who said that all you need is love, and I would agree with that.

As long as you keep the gators fed.

Works Cited

"20 Years Later, San Ysidro McDonald's Massacre Remembered." Web log post. *North County Times*. Lee Enterprises Inc., 2004. Web. 17 July 2004.

"A $300 Idea that Is Priceless." *The Economist* 28 Apr. 2011. Print.

Adler, Mortimer. "How to Mark a Book." *The Saturday Review of Literature* 6 July 1941. Print.

Ahearn, John F. "Honesty." *American Scientist* 99.2 (2011): 120-22. Print.

Aimes, Alexander. "Bringing History to Life with Primary Sources." Student essay. Used by permission.

Dillard, Annie. "Handed My Own Life." *An American Childhood*. New York: Harper and Row, 1987. Print.

Duggan, Paul. "In Sex-Crime Cases, Credibility a Thorny Issue." *The Washington Post* 1 July 2011. Print.

Echanove, Matias, and Rahul Srivastava. "Hands Off Our Houses." The New York Times 1 June 2011: A27. Print.

Fogarty, Mignon. *Grammar Girl: Quick and Dirty Tips for Better Writing*. New York: St. Martin's Press, 2008. Print

Gleiberman, Owen. "Film Review: The Hangover." Rev. of *The Hangover*, by Dir. Todd Phillips. *EW.com* 2 June 2009. Web. 15 Nov. 2010.

Govindarajan, Vijay. "The $300 House: A Hands-On Approach to a Wicked Problem."
Web log post. *HBR Blog Network*, Harvard Business School Publishing, 7 June
2011. Web. 22 Oct. 2011.

Greene, Andy. "All Star Rockers Salute Buddy Holly." *Rolling Stone*. Straight Arrow
Publishers, 7 July 2011. Print.

Jayawardhana, Ray. "Alien Life, Coming Slowly into View." *The New York Times* 27
March 2011: WK10. Print.

Johnson, Judith. "The Truth about Writer's Block." *The Huffington Post*. HuffPost
News, 25 July 2011. Web. 11 Nov. 2011.

King, Jr., Martin Luther. "I Have a Dream." Speech. March on Washington for Jobs and
Freedom. Lincoln Memorial, Washington, D.C. 28 Aug. 1963. *Americanrhetoric.
com*. Michael E. Eidenmuller. n.d. Web. 12 Nov. 2011.

King, Stephen. "Why We Crave Horror Stories." *Playboy Magazine* Dec. 1981. Print.

Lincoln, Abraham. "Gettysburg Address." Speech. Dedication of the Soldiers' National
Cemetary. Gettysburg, Pennsylvania 19 Nov. 1863. *Ourdocuments.gov*. n.d.
Web. 15 Nov. 2011.

McArdle, Megan. "Anatomy of a Fake Quotation." *The Atlantic* 2 May 2011. Print.

McGrath, Charles. "The Lexicon." *NYTimes.com* 8 Sept. 2011. Web. 9 Sept. 2011.

Meyers, Justin. "How to Make a Kindle Cover from a Hollowed Out Hardback Book."
Wonder How To. n.p., March 2011. Web. 12 Nov. 2011.

Neil, Dan. "BMW 1M: Miniature, Mighty and Miles of Fun." *The Wall Street Journal* 3
Sept. 2011. Print.

Obama, Barack. "Remarks by the President on Osama bin Laden." Speech. Address
to the Nation that Osama bin Laden is dead. The White House, Washington,
D.C. 1 May 2011. *The White House Blog*. Macon Phillips. 2 May 2011. Web. 29
Sept. 2011.

Quindlen, Anna. "Doing Nothing is Something." *Newsweek* May 2002. Print.

Rosen, Jeffrey. "The Web Means the End of Forgetting." *The New York Times* 25 July 2010: MM30. Print.

Schalet, Amy. "The Sleepover Question." *The New York Times* 23 July 2011: SR9. Print.

Scham, Sam. "Top Ten Distractions for Writers, or Any Job Really." *Yahoo.com* 12 Aug. 2008. Web. 12 Nov. 2011.

Shemtob, Zachary, and David Lat. "Executions Should Be Televised." The New York Times 31 July 2011: SR4. Print.

Skinner, E. Benjamin. "People for Sale." *Foreign Policy*. March–April 2008. Print.

Staples, Brent. "Just Walk on By: Black Men in Public Space." *Ms Magazine* 1986. Print.

Thornburgh, Nathan. "Violent Rhetoric and Arizona Politics." Editorial. *Time* 9 Jan. 2011. Print.

Wynn, Craig. "Take a Leap Into Writing." Student essay. Used by permission.

Young, Neil. "Let's Roll." *Are You Passionate?* Reprise Records, 2002. CD.

Zuniga, Janine. "San Ysidro Shooting Survivor Lives His Dream of Being a Cop." *San Diego Union-Tribune* 18 July 2004. Print.

Index

A

ACS: American Chemical Society 261
action research 256
action verbs 153
ad hominem 90, 93
ad populum 91
ad verecundium 91
aesthetic reading 60
American Psychological Association (APA) 283
analysis paralysis 217
annotated bibliography 186
APA in-text citations 283
apostrophe, 342–345
appeals 86
argument 25, 26, 27, 28, 29, 30, 31, 34, 35, 37, 39, 40, 42, 44, 45, 46, 47, 50, 52, 53, 54, 58, 60, 61, 66, 67, 69, 71, 72, 73, 75, 77, 79, 80, 81, 86, 87, 89, 90, 91, 92, 97, 98, 100, 102, 133
Aristotle 26, 30, 31, 34, 86, 87, 89, 90, 94, 97, 100
arrangement 107
artistic proofs 106
ASME: American Society of Mechanical Engineers 261

B

begging the question 91, 92, 93
BMES: Biomedical Engineering Society 261
brackets 353
business 251

C

capitalization 356–358
Chicago Manual of Style (CMS) 295
cliché 152
closed questions 173
colon, 338–339
comma, 328–333
conclusion 89
confusing cause and effect 91
Cook, Tim 101
Council of Science Editors (CSE) 268
creative writing 201
critical thinking 49, 50, 60
critique 204

D

dash, 351
deductive fallacy 90
deductive reasoning 89, 257
delayed construction 152
delivery 107
digital presentation 207
documentation APA 283
documentation CMS 295
documentation MLA 273

E

editing policy for student writers 19
efferent readers 60
either/or 91
ellipses 355
essay 209